Accept Me As I Am

SERVING SPECIAL NEEDS SERIES

Accept Me As I Am

Best Books of Juvenile Nonfiction on Impairments and Disabilities

Accept me as I am. Only then will we discover each other.
—Federico Fellini

Joan Brest Friedberg
June B. Mullins
Adelaide Weir Sukiennik

R. R. Bowker Company
New York and London, 1985

Published by R. R. Bowker Company,
  a division of Reed Publishing USA
245 West 17th Street, New York, NY 10011
Copyright © 1985 by Reed Publishing USA,
  a division of Reed Holdings, Inc.
All rights reserved
Printed and bound in the United States of America

Reprinted with corrections, 1986

Library of Congress Cataloging in Publication Data

Friedberg, Joan Brest, 1927-
    Accept me as I am.

    (Serving special needs series)
    Bibliography: p.
    Includes indexes.
    1. Children's literature—Bibliography. 2. Bibliography
—Best books—Children's literature. 3. Physically
handicapped—Juvenile literature—Bibliography.
4. Mentally handicapped—Juvenile literature—
Bibliography. 5. Mentally ill—Juvenile literature—
Bibliography. I. Mullins, June B., 1927-   .
II. Sukiennik, Adelaide Weir, 1938-   . III. Title.
IV. Series.
Z1037.9.F73   1985   [PN1009.A1]   011'.62'0880826   85-3778
ISBN 0-8352-1974-7

P. 44: Courtesy Cutter Laboratories, Emeryville, Calif.

P. 152: Photograph by Sally DiMartini from Patricia Dendtler Frevert,
Patrick, Yes You Can (Mankato, Minn.: Creative Education, 1983),
p. 10. Reprinted with permission.

P. 232: Photograph by Patricia Agre from Harriet Langsam Sobol,
My Brother Steven Is Retarded (New York: Macmillan, 1977), p. 22.
Copyright © 1977 by Patricia Agre. Reprinted with permission.

P. 290: Photograph by George Ancona from *My Friend Leslie*
by Maxine B. Rosenberg. Copyright © 1983 by George Ancona.
By permission of Lothrop, Lee & Shepard Books (A Division
of William Morrow & Co.).

Cover design: Lundgren Graphics, Ltd.

To all those who have so courageously lived
the lives described here.

Contents

viii   Contents

Preface

At least ten percent of all school-age children in the United States have what may be regarded as a significant disability. Many of them spend some part of their school days mainstreamed and interacting with other classmates and with teachers who generally have had limited experience with disabled people and who may initially react with varying degrees of discomfort.

Literature has proven a powerful agent for providing information and influencing attitudes and development. Many adults looking back on childhood can remember a book or story that indelibly moved, delighted, or frightened them, sometimes for reasons only dimly remembered or understood. The passion of censors and book-banners, so disturbing to those who cherish free access to the printed word, attests to literature's power. Every literary genre has the potential to affect readers and that power is not necessarily tied to quality; works judged mediocre by accepted critical standards may move readers to a surprising degree.

Nonfiction carries the unique power of verifiable authenticity, giving special effect to biography, autobiography, concept, and information books about people who are disabled. Children are born without prejudice toward disabilities, but as they meet those who differ from themselves in significant ways, they are affected by societal attitudes as well as by their own individual reactions. Books that sensitively and honestly depict persons with disabilities expand limited experience and can mitigate the unease that stems from ignorance, misconception, and anxiety. Young readers can profit from material that helps them deal with anxieties and suggests ways that problems can be solved and the good life lived, even in the face of imperfection and adversity.

This guide to juvenile nonfiction about individuals with impairments and disabilities is selective rather than inclusive; the assumptions and criteria that influenced our choices are discussed more fully in the chapters that follow. The concentration is on nonfiction books that encourage all readers, disabled or not, to develop open, tolerant attitudes and on books that enrich understanding and show how, against odds, disabled people have led constructive lives. Because all life is precious, differences, including disabling ones, have value and significance in the scheme of things. Exposure to fair and realistic representation of disabilities—our own, those of others, and those that may befall us—leads to greater understanding and tolerance of ourselves and others and to the possibility of ameliorating the human condition.

Like Barbara Baskin and Karen Harris, authors of *Notes from a Different Drummer* and *More Notes from a Different Drummer* (Bowker, 1977; 1984), we adhere to the principles of mainstreaming and normalization and hope that this book facilitates these principles. We acknowledge that children and adults, disabled or able-bodied, are more alike than they are different. The books described here should prove of common interest and value to disabled and able-bodied readers, although people who face particular disabilities—their own or those of family members, classmates, or friends—may be interested in a specific condition. The manner in which the protagonists in these books meet adversity, grasp opportunities, and develop character is often more important than the precise description of individual disabilities.

This guide will be of use to librarians, teachers, counselors, health professionals, and parents. In school libraries it will be a resource for students and teachers, particularly those in classes that mainstream children with disabilities. School personnel will find it useful for parents who want to locate books for their children that foster understanding of disabled classmates, family, or friends. Parents, both disabled and able-bodied, who are working to help their children with disabilities to achieve the maximum possible independence and satisfaction will find support in this literature. Books are included that are appropriate for age levels from preschool through high school, but many of the titles will also appeal to junior college and college students as well as to teachers-in-training and education department faculty.

Notes from a Different Drummer and *More Notes from a Different Drummer* survey juvenile fiction portraying disabled people published between 1940 and 1981. *Accept Me As I Am* is a companion volume and includes nonfiction books to 1984. Not all the books annotated here are still in print, but all are available in library collections. (The library of the Rehabilitation Institute of Pittsburgh, Pennsylvania, is assembling these titles, to be called the Deborah Bisdee Collection.)

In Chapters 5 through 8, the annotations are arranged in broad categories of problem, disability, or impairment. In each category books are listed alphabetically by author. The following reading-level designations are used: Preschool (ages 2 to 5), Grades K–3 (ages 5 to 8), Grades 4–6 (ages 9 to 11), Grades 7–9 (ages 12 to 14), and Grades 10–12 (ages 15 to 17, with many titles in this category of interest to adult readers). These divisions are necessarily arbitrary and many young readers can enjoy books from more than one grade category. Some books span more than one grade level designation. Author, title, and subject indexes follow the annotations.

The lengths of annotations vary and are not necessarily an indication of the size of the book, its complexity, or its merit. In general, however, books designed for Grades 10–12 tend to be longer and more complex and, therefore, the entry may reflect this.

This book is dedicated to the vision of an ideal society that values all its members, each with a unique potential and a special contribution to make. The more we break down the barriers of fear, distrust, and ignorance that often separate one group of human beings from another—whether these groups are categorized by gender, race, religion, class, age, or disability—the closer we come to achieving that ideal. In sharing experiences and insights, the writers of the books selected for this work, and their subjects, make it possible for us to grow in wisdom and understanding about living with disabilities and impairments.

We owe all of our children the opportunity to develop their gifts, to grow beyond ignorance and anxiety, to accept and sometimes to cherish their differences. Reading in the literature annotated here can help everyone in this direction, at the same time supporting both disabled and able-bodied persons in the pursuit of their dreams—whatever they be.

Acknowledgments

Many people have helped us in the preparation of this book. We should like to especially thank:

Patricia Colbert, Suzanne Cooke, and Ingrid Glasco of the Interlibrary Loan Staff, Hillman Library, University of Pittsburgh, for cheerfully processing our orders and helping us gather our books;

Margaret L. Kartanas and Edith A. Smith in the Office of the Dean of Education, University of Pittsburgh, for typing hundreds of manuscript pages on the word processor;

Amy Kellman and the staff of the Children's Room, Carnegie Library of Pittsburgh, and Marilyn Hollinshead and Penelope Greene of Pinocchio Bookstore for Children, Pittsburgh, for helping us locate books and for bringing titles to our attention;

Hillman Library, for granting a sabbatical to Adelaide Sukiennik and thus making our task easier;

Ann Rayne for her painstaking copy editing;

numerous secretaries who typed numerous drafts, including Phyllis Belles and Mary Fitzwater;

Julia Moore, acquisitions editor, at R. R. Bowker for her wise suggestions and calm, steady support—we could not have asked for a better editor;

Iris Topel, editing supervisor, at R. R. Bowker, for her attention to the details in the manuscript;

our spouses and children for their patience and willingness to listen.

Accept Me As I Am

- (Family)
\# - Qunch - Christmas DAY

→ <u>Eve Night</u>
- Kinnie's
(5:00)

1

The Power of Nonfiction to Portray People with Disabilities

We know the truth, not only by the reason, but by the heart.
—Pascal, *Pensees*

All literature, whatever the genre, has the potential to reflect human experience, expand knowledge, enlarge understanding, and heighten sensitivity. Whatever "reality" may mean, however one may define it, poetry or drama or fictional narrative can mirror the real world as powerfully and truthfully as biography or exposition. Yet, in the field of books written about people with disabilities, nonfiction carries a special power. Information about disabled people is often scanty or inaccurate; attitudes held by the able-bodied may be tinged with condescension, pity, or sentimentality. Nondisabled persons may have fears about their own physical, mental, and emotional health that might impede their relationships with those who deviate from the expected norm. The message implicit in nonfiction is that the situations portrayed actually do exist and the people in those pages actually have lived or are now living. Therefore, nonfiction has the power to say to its audience: "This is what really *is* out there."

All authors, of course, write from their particular subjective viewpoints. All authors, of nonfiction as well as fiction, can alter so-called objective reality. Yet readers have the right to expect authors of nonfiction to give them a particular kind of truth-telling. When it is done well, truth-telling about people with disabilities can affect the perceptions and expectations of readers, counteracting ignorance, anxiety, and misinformation.

What Is Nonfiction?

Nonfiction literature for children consists of biography, autobiography, informational books, and concept books. In this survey, we look at titles in all these categories.

In *Children's Literature in the Elementary School*, Huck distinguishes between authentic biography, fictionalized biography, and biographical fiction.

> Authentic biography corresponds to that written for adults. It is a well-documented and researched account of a person's life. Only those statements that are actually known to have been made by the subject are included in the conversation. . . . Fictionalized biography is grounded in thorough research, but allows the author more freedom to dramatize certain events and personalize the subject than does the straight reporting of authentic biography. . . . When the biography consists entirely of imaginary conversation and reconstructed action, it becomes biographical fiction.[1]

Biographies of all three types are included in these annotations. Occasionally, as in *Lovey* by MacCracken,[2] the subject of a biography is a composite persona based on several real people. Sometimes authors have changed names of places and persons to protect privacy.

Autobiography is, of course, written by the subject and may, like fictionalized biography, include reconstructed dialogue. Some of the autobiographies in this collection cover the author's entire life; others begin with the onset of disability and concentrate on the experience of changed expectations and rehabilitation, for example, *"Keep Your Head Up, Mr. Putnam!"*[3]

Informational books convey material through expository narrative, sometimes using interviews, brief sketches, case studies, and dialogue as illustration. Berger's *Learning Disabilities and Handicaps* is such a book.[4]

Concept books deal with abstract ideas, such as color, spatial relations, or numbers. An ABC is a concept book and so is a book about manual signs, for example, *The Joy of Signing* by Riekehof.[5]

The difference between fiction and nonfiction may seem obvious: Nonfiction deals with a verifiable body of material; fiction tells a story that springs from the mind and imagination of its author and need not be based in reality. Although, as Huck suggests, biographies for children sometimes invent incidents, and more often invent dialogue, they do not invent characters.

Very young children do not readily distinguish between fact and fantasy; indeed, the difference is generally unimportant to them, and much of their later understanding of so-called real life and reality grows out of their early pretend play and imaginings. By the age of four or five, most children recognize a distinction between what is "real" and what is, as they would say, "make-believe." Yet there is often a blurring of these two, and many of us carry fantasies into adulthood: for example, romantic notions about achieving a perfect love relationship or a perfect friendship.

Misconceptions might be regarded as a kind of fiction also, warped though they may be. Many adults and children, disabled or not, lack adequate information about disabilities, their causes, effects, and treatment. In looking at the person who differs from the norm, some see only the distortion. Even adults often fear what they fail to understand and may shudder at this shattering of the ideal of perfection. Nonfiction books about people with impairments can offer information to counter such lack of understanding. If successful, such books enable the reader to see that the most important thing about any person is his or her individual, unique quality and selfhood, not just the limitations.

An examination of fictional and nonfictional treatments of the same subject may sharpen critical perception of the particular qualities inherent in each approach. *I Have a Sister—My Sister Is Deaf* by Jeanne Whitehouse Peterson, illustrated by Deborah Ray, and *Anna's Silent World*, with text and photographs by Bernard Wolf, are both picture books directed toward the five- to eight-year-old reader.[6] Both focus on small deaf girls. In the Peterson book, which is fiction, the narrator is the older sister, who is probably six or seven. Using repetition and poetic phrases, she describes the worlds of one who hears and one who does not: "I am the one who listens for small sounds. She is the one who watches for quick movements in the grass." Wolf, in his nonfiction book, chooses telling, poignant details to picture the world of the hearing-impaired child: "Most mornings when Anna wakes up the first thing she sees is Tycho. When Anna touches him she can feel his rumbling purr" (p. 5). At the end, after a description of Anna's Christmas, Wolf concludes, "And Anna's favorite present is a recorder. Now she can add her own music to the sounds of her silent world" (p. 48). The third-person narration, a choice open, of course, to the writer of fiction and nonfiction alike, creates more distance between speaker and subject. Wolf concentrates on conveying a considerable body of information as well as on giving the flavor of Anna's life. Peterson gives information as well, but also touches on many feelings. The biggest difference between the two books, and the one that most sharply reflects the difference between the two modes of writing, is in the illustrations. Ray's drawings for *I Have a Sister . . .* , with their soft lines and tones, are realistic but with selected detail. For example, in a double-page spread showing the two children in the bathroom with their mother, the floor and walls are not indicated. In contrast, the black-and-white photographs of *Anna's Silent World* are rich in pattern, texture, and explicit detail; in the pictures showing Anna's ballet class, for example, Anna's body aids (about which, the text reveals, she was self-conscious at first) show clearly through her leotard on the front of her body.

Another fiction/nonfiction pair to examine are *My Friend Jacob* by Lucille Clifton, illustrated by Thomas DiGrazia, and *My Brother Steven Is Retarded* by Harriet Langsam Sobol, with photographs by Patricia Agre.[7] Here both books are written in the first person. In Clifton's fiction work, the narrator is eight-year-old Sam, who talks about his friendship with Jacob, nine years older. In the Sobol nonfiction book, eleven-year-old Beth talks about her older brother. Could the reader, without being told, identify which is fiction and which nonfiction? Probably not. Both narratives sound authentic. Sobol, however, includes honest if perhaps less attractive feelings that give the text a particular ring of reality—as, for example, when Beth says, "If someone in our family has to be retarded, I'd rather it were Steven than me. Maybe that's not very nice, but it's true anyway" (p. 11). And with these books too, the illustrations are dramatically different. DiGrazia, in *My Friend Jacob,* uses soft tones moving from charcoal black to light gray and soft outlines; Agre's black-and-white photographs focus on the children and emphasize repeatedly the distinct difference between Beth and Steven. Both Steven's features and gait mark him as a retarded person. Jacob, on the other hand, does not look so very different from Sam, except in size (Jacob is very tall) and color (he is white, Sam is black), nor does Jacob appear to differ significantly from the norm, despite the description of his limited mental abilities.

For another comparison, note the Newbery Award book *The Summer of the Swans,* a novel by Betsy Byars for 10-to-14-year-old readers.[8] The principal character, adolescent Sara, has a 10-year-old brother, Charlie, who has been retarded since the age of 3 when he experienced a critical illness. Byars, with an uncanny ear for dialogue and a sure touch in choosing scenes and details, has drawn a sensitive, believable picture of a family, and particularly of a sibling relationship. This book is utterly realistic, utterly credible. Fictionalized Charlie is as real in his way as nonfictionalized Steven is in his.

What are the differences, then, between the fiction and nonfiction modes? Are we straining to find and describe them? And if differences do exist, do they have any effect on young readers? Clearly, this is not a question of quality. All five of the books noted here are outstanding; all are sensitive to the implications of impairment and difference; all respond to feeling as well as to fact; all recognize and even emphasize the various ways in which the characters contribute to their worlds. If there is a difference, then, it is probably to be found in the statement at the beginning of this chapter—that nonfiction tells us about people who actually lived or still live, and thus mirrors reality with a sharpness, a poignance, and an authenticity that are not necessarily better than the quality of fiction, but are undeniably different.

Criteria for Selection

As already noted, this bibliography is a selective guide. We have tried to choose books that will be most worth reading for children and young people, whether they are disabled or able-bodied. No special distinction is made between books addressed to readers with impairments and those directed to readers without them. There are not many books in the first category anyway, but the most important reason for the decision is philosophical. People with disabilities want to live as all people wish to live, as fully and equally as possible in the larger world; they do not wish to be what Robert Russell has called "white crows." To offer them a separate body of reading materials accentuates their differences to no good purpose and denies to so-called normal readers the opportunity, and indeed the obligation, to participate as fully as possible, even if vicariously, in the lives of disabled people.

Some of the books included here may be seriously flawed and yet have a redeeming quality or ingredient. The judgments for inclusion were subjective, as all critical judgments must be, but certain criteria were always kept in mind: (1) adherence to known facts as they were available at the time the books were written; (2) avoidance of stereotypes, clichéd attitudes, and condescension toward people with disabilities, and an absence of sentimental misconceptions (such as the idea that impairments automatically ennoble); (3) assurance that the dialogue, although often invented as it is in children's nonfiction, is consistent with the subject, period, and environment portrayed, and that it is natural and believable; (4) appropriateness of the material for the book's intended audience, keeping in mind the age and experience of the readers; and (5) an honest recognition displayed by the writers of the limitations imposed by the disability described and of the possible discouragement, bitterness, and frustration felt by the person with that condition. To be recommended, a book should convey a realistic assessment of the disability and of the achievements possible for persons in such a situation. At the same time, one must allow for individuals who transcend the expected and the realistic. All of us, disabled or able-bodied, need to believe in the power of spirit to take wing. The best of the books described in this guide reflect such a belief.

Notes

A short form of reference is used for works cited fully in Chapters 5–8.

1. Charlotte Huck, *Children's Literature in the Elementary School*, 3rd ed. (New York: Holt, 1976), p. 557.
2. MacCracken, *Lovey*.
3. Putnam, *"Keep Your Head Up, Mr. Putnam!"*
4. Berger, *Learning Disabilities and Handicaps*.
5. Riekehof, *The Joy of Signing*.
6. Jeanne Whitehouse Peterson, *I Have a Sister—My Sister Is Deaf* (New York: Harper & Row, 1977); Wolf, *Anna's Silent World*.
7. Lucille Clifton, *My Friend Jacob* (New York: Dutton, 1980); Sobol, *My Brother Steven Is Retarded*.
8. Betsy Byars, *The Summer of the Swans* (New York: Viking, 1970).

2

Evolution of Attitudes, Practice, and Terminology

Tell him to be different from other people if it comes natural
and easy being different.
—Carl Sandburg, "A Father Sees a Son Nearing Manhood"

The literature about people with disabilities exhibits an easily discernible evolution in terms of society's attitudes toward those judged to be different, in the policies that have governed the lives of disabled people, and in the terminology used to speak to and about them.

Attitudes

Exceptional—that is, different or unusual—individuals have been set aside by other human beings probably since the beginning of the species, certainly for as long as history has been recorded. There are many examples of "differences" in ancient art. A stone carving in an Egyptian tomb shows an achondroplastic dwarf who was Keeper of the Royal Wardrobe, and wall drawings in another tomb depict blind harpists and singers; in Aztec society the royal zoo included a display of dwarfs, bearded women, and deformed humans who lived on scraps tossed into their cages. Throughout European history, the careers of court pet, entertainer, jester, circus performer, and sideshow exhibition have been assigned to exceptional persons. People with physical and behavioral differences have been subject to a whole range of treatment, including being revered as beloved mascots, found fascinating as freaks, treated with ridicule, and marked for extermination.

What is evident in historical perspective is the ambivalence that all

7

societies have shown toward disabled and different people. This is certainly true in society today, where most people truly want to make just and humanitarian gestures, but are still at the very least apprehensive of the consequences. Most adults have been segregated from disabled persons for a lifetime, so that added to concerns about disability and difference is the fear of the unknown.

Fiedler, whose book is annotated in Chapter 5, suggests that the "myths and images of the secret self," the remnants of childlike archaic thinking, shape our subliminal perceptions of those with physical disfigurements or disabilities. Hence, he feels that confrontations with those who are different evoke our basic and primal insecurities: about scale, sexuality, our status as more than beasts, and our tenuous individuality.[1]

Young people, even little children, share the ambivalence of their elders. There is ample evidence that youngsters adjust easily to disabled classmates and are very interested in the crutches, braille books, sign language, and such that they use. It is also true that children have deep fears of mutilation, of transmission of illness by association, and may also have a propensity to bully those who are different.

In his book on the value of fairy tales for children, *The Uses of Enchantment,* Bettelheim discusses the confusion that children experience between what is real and what is fantasy.[2] Experience in the real world may not help to resolve inner conflicts, but it can help to distinguish what is outer reality.

Literature about disabled people provides various experiences on which to build respect and understanding. Intimacies and emotions that would be too painful or embarrassing to show face to face can be explicated in books. Details about the exact nature of special problems can be objectively explained. Able-bodied children often will find easy identification with disabled subjects of those stories, as will disabled children themselves.

Practice

> The idea of "one world" for mankind is not merely sentimental, or even "religious" in any sectarian sense. It is an idea whose time simply has not come yet, because not enough of us have to walk far enough in someone else's shoes.
> —Sidney Harris

In Western culture, attitudes and policies toward disabled persons have been very much a function of the social milieu of the time.

Negative Trends

In the latter part of the nineteenth century, a misunderstanding of Darwin's explication of evolution led to preoccupation with the hereditary nature of defects. A eugenics movement led to segregation of so-called defective children and adults in socially isolated communities. By the turn of the century, "warehousing" of such persons became the practice. At the same time, legislation requiring sterilization for mentally retarded persons and those with epilepsy, among others, became widespread in the United States and England.

Positive Trends

Despite the early negative attitudes, some constructive work with disabled people went forward in Europe and in the United States. Persons with specific disabilities were usually grouped for treatment in institutions such as the Perkins School for the Blind in Massachusetts, the American School for the Deaf opened by Thomas Gallaudet in Hartford, Connecticut, in 1817, and Gallaudet College in Washington, D.C.

By 1918, all states had legally effective public education, but it frequently excluded disabled children as well as other minority groups such as rural blacks and migrant workers. In 1922, the Council for Exceptional Children was organized, with emphasis on the education of children with disabilities and the establishment of professional standards for special-education teachers.

During the nineteenth century, literature began to emerge about persons with disabilities, and by the middle of the twentieth century, a considerable body of work, fiction and nonfiction, about disabled people had been published. Parents wrote about raising a child who was disabled, and disabled people chronicled their experiences in dealing with various conditions.

The civil rights movement of the 1950s ushered in a trend toward legal protection of minority groups. People with disabilities formed self-help organizations, such as Little People of America. The efforts of many individuals and organizations, including the Council for Exceptional Children, culminated in the passage of Public Law 94-142, The Education of All Handicapped Children Act, signed into law by President Gerald Ford in 1975. This law derives its strength from substantial financial incentives for compliance, and by the inclusion of due-process procedures that parents may undertake if they object to placement or lack of it for their disabled children, all of whom are assured a free and appropriate public education by the law.

The stipulation in the law of the "least restrictive environment" has had broad social implications. Those responsible for the wording made the assumption that the most desirable educational environment is a student's community public school, and a regular classroom setting whenever possible, and that the least desirable is a segregated and institutional setting. Although this basic assumption is challenged by some, the concept of least restrictive environment has been generally accepted. It has led to a "normalizing" of the lives of many disabled children and adults, placing them in the mainstream of school and society to the fullest extent possible. Public Law 94-142 became effective in 1978, assuring all disabled children a full public education and a variety of accompanying rights.

In tracing the history of policy and practice in the United States, we find that education for disabled persons, and indeed any treatment for them, began as a private, charitable enterprise. In time the government intervened to assist in the voluntary efforts and to increase services. Finally, in the twentieth century, a national framework was created, and the equal rights of disabled persons have been asserted in the courts and in legislation.

Terminology

> Who is the more seriously handicapped—the child trying to lead a
> normal life despite his defects or the physically healthy person who is
> unable to accept him? In a world whose moral disabilities are far
> greater than its physical imperfections, the question deserves thought.
> —Robert Massie and Suzanne Massie, *Journey*

Those who work with or are otherwise involved with disabled persons, and disabled people themselves, are understandably concerned and often troubled by the labels used socially and professionally to apply to one or another group or person. So, too, are those who work with literature, since they are particularly aware of the power of language. Indeed, professionals keep changing labels as each becomes devalued. Consider the evolution of terminology from "handicapped" to "exceptional" to "special needs"; from "moron" to "mentally retarded" to "developmentally delayed"; from "learned disabled" to "mildly handicapped"; from "crippled" to "disabled." These labels need to be put into perspective.

It is useful to identify and label unusual characteristics of disabled children so that their special needs are recognized and met. With disabled and impaired schoolchildren returned to or remaining in regular classes, everyone needs to understand their situations. The person who cannot hear, who lacks mobility, or who has specific health problems may need the help of rehabilitation and education specialists. Labels have allowed society to channel funds and efforts to serve those with special needs. Furthermore, denial of a person's reality can be demeaning. When others gloss over someone's disorders or differences, they are distancing themselves from a reality that may be unpleasant and frightening to them, but they also preclude the possibility of authentic human contact with the impaired child or adult.

Explanation of Terminology in This Book

In this book, three general terms are used as consistently and precisely as possible to conceptualize the problems of disabled persons and to make labels serve rather than demean. The terms are *impairment*, *disability*, and *handicap.*

Impairment. An impairment is a physical deviation from what could be considered physically normal in structure, function, physical organization, or development. It is clearly objective and measurable. Examples are cleft lip or palate, sickle cells (found in persons with sickle cell anemia), spina bifida, and detached retina (which will limit a person's visual capacity).

Many of the headings in this book are structured on the basis of impairment. For example, under *Health Problems*, the reader can look for cystic fibrosis. Under *Orthopedic/Neurological Disabilities* are listed the impairments epilepsy and scoliosis.

Disability. A disability is a functional limitation experienced by the individual *because of an impairment.* It refers to what the individual cannot do—in the expected or usual way—because of an impairment. A disability is to some extent measurable and objective, but its severity is related to subjective factors such as age, vocation, grit, and intelligence. (Obviously, not all impairments cause disabilities; an extensive birthmark may result in a cosmetic difference but not a functional limitation.)

Examples of disabilities are the inability to walk without crutches (caused by a number of impairments), the inability to hear consonant sounds (caused by impairments in the auditory system), and the inability to digest sugar (usually a result of impairment in the pancreas).

Some headings in this book are classified on the basis of disabilities. Examples are the disabilities of deafness and blindness caused by sensory impairments. The term *disabled* is generally used to describe persons whose functional disabilities are more important to their life situations than are the specific impairments causing the disabilities. For example, the fact that a person cannot hear speech is more relevant to his or her adjustment than whether the impairment causing the deafness is in the middle ear, inner ear, auditory nerve, or brain.

Handicap. A handicap is the disadvantage imposed by the impairment or disability, which the person *experiences* in his or her particular environment. It depends on the physical and psychological characteristics of the person, on the culture, and on specific circumstances in place and time in which the handicapped person finds him- or herself.

A handicap is not objective and measurable. It is an experience. The action and reaction of the handicapped person's mind and body to the impairment are part of that experience. The action and reaction of others in the environment are also part of the experience.[3] Notice that in this book the concept of handicap is linked to impairment and disability.

Classification Terminology in This Book

The classification scheme is shown in the Contents and is as follows. Chapters 5 through 8 organize the literature in four basic types of problems or disabilities: physical (Chapter 5), sensory (Chapter 6), cognitive and behavior (Chapter 7), and multiple/severe (Chapter 8).

Within each chapter are major categories. For example, Chapter 7, "Books Dealing with Cognitive and Behavior Problems," has four categories: Emotional Disturbances, Learning Disabilities, Mental Retardation, and Speech and Language Impairments. Annotations appear alphabetically by author's last name within these categories. The specific disability or impairment (for example, autism under Emotional Disturbances in Chapter 7) is signaled in the citation.

To find a book on a specific impairment or disability when the author is not known, the user should consult the Subject Index.

Physical Problems

These are classified under either Health Problems or Orthopedic/ Neurological Disabilities. A great number of different problems are found under these two classifications in Chapter 5.

People are born with or develop physical differences or anomalies, such as very short or very tall stature, great or little weight, baldness or hirsutism, resemblance to animals, ambiguous sexuality, and birthmarks.

Extreme physical problems can be caused by faulty development, disease, trauma, or an unnurturing environment, as in the case of malnutrition or child abuse. These physical impairments can be as minor as a skin blemish or so major that they result in total paralysis. Various types of impairments may be present at birth, caused congenitally or by inheritance, or they may be acquired at any time throughout life.

Physical deviations are objective and measurable, and can therefore be labeled with relative precision. In this book, labels regarding health and physical impairments—whether they are anomalies, defective functions (as in the pancreas of a person with diabetes), defective genetic makeup (as in Down's syndrome), defective development (as in dwarfism), or defective structure (such as cleft lip)—are applied as precisely and objectively as possible.

While physical impairments are measurable and objective, the disabilities (such as immobility, fatigue, faulty speech production, or incoordination) that may result from them are more relative and subjective. What might be considered a mild inconvenience by one person might be an enormous burden for another, depending on occupation, culture, age, and personality.

Sensory Problems

Books dealing with sensory problems are grouped in Chapter 6 under Deaf-blind, Hearing Impairments, or Visual Impairments. When the impairments involve various parts of the visual or auditory systems, they are separately listed as Visual Impairments or Hearing Impairments, which may be congenital or acquired at any time during life. Persons with both problems are called Deaf-blind.

Those with visual impairments may be labeled blind or partially sighted. Definitions of blind vary because of differences in legal, medical, and educational interpretations. The educational definition is a practical one: A person is considered blind who cannot use the visual avenue for academic learning even with the use of corrective aids. A blind person usually has some residual vision, which may be helpful for travel, for locating light sources, and for distinguishing the presence of objects. For academic learning, blind people will use other senses: tactile, to read and write braille; auditory, to hear tape recordings. The general thrust of education of blind children today is to teach them to utilize their remaining vision to the greatest extent possible. Persons are considered partially sighted when they have reduced visual acuity after correction, but can use the visual avenue for learning.

Such people may need large-print books, strong light, or special visual aids to read and write.

As with the label *blind*, the educational definition of *deaf* is a practical one. A person is considered deaf who cannot use the auditory channel for academic learning. More specifically, the deaf person cannot hear or learn from the spoken word. Deaf people usually have some residual hearing and are aware of the presence of sound. They may use hearing aids to enhance those sounds—to detect direction of sound, for example. The deaf person will substitute other sensory channels in academic learning—the visual avenue for speech reading, finger spelling, and signs, or tactile vibration for a car. Some deaf persons can speak very intelligibly, although they cannot hear themselves.

Hard-of-hearing persons have some hearing loss or distortion, but they can understand and use speech. They may need hearing aids to be able to decipher speech, and they may need other modifications, such as a learning environment without extraneous noise.

A few people have both sensory impairments and are deaf-blind. The age at which these deprivations occur is important. In the case of author Robert Smithdas, for example, he was blind as a very young child, but he had mastered his native language before his progressive deafness, which began in later childhood. Babies who are impaired visually and auditorily by rubella (measles) before birth have a more difficult time learning language than those adventitiously deafened.

Cognitive and Behavior Problems

Cognitive and behavior problems are covered in Chapter 7 under Emotional Disturbances, Learning Disabilities, Mental Retardation, and Speech and Language Impairments.

Some persons who appear to be physically normal fall into the category of disabled because of unusual or different emotional or social behavior. The fact that behavior is considered "exemplary" or "acceptable" or "eccentric" or "unacceptable" is a social judgment very much tied to the culture in which the person actually lives, as well as the age, sex, social status, and vocation of the person. All judgments made in this book are from the viewpoint of an "ordinary" and, it is hoped, enlightened modern-day American. The heading Emotional Disturbances covers various serious problems subsumed under such expressions as "socially and emotionally maladjusted," "autistic," "schizophrenic."

Children are considered for special education by school systems when they are diagnosed as having learning problems that will preclude their being maintained in a regular classroom without special help. The labels frequently employed to classify these students, and used here, are Learning Disabilities and Mental Retardation.

The impairments leading to cognitive disorder are many. Their causes may be genetic or developmental, or due to physical or psychological trauma. Whatever the cause, the impact is on the cognitive functioning of the person. The disruption may be rather general, or very specific as in the case of dyslexia.

A few books have been written for children and youth about speech and language problems. These are listed separately as Speech and Language Impairments. They may be disorders of articulation, voice, rhythm, or cognition, and they may be due to specific physical problems or of unknown cause.

Multiple/Severe and Various Disabilities

Some people have very severe impairments and disabilities, resulting in a number of the problems discussed above. For example, when cognitive deficits are severe, they are often accompanied by sensory and physical problems. Such persons are classified under the heading Multiple/Severe (Chapter 8). For their protection and safety, such individuals may be targeted for a lifetime sheltered environment at home, in the community, or in an institution. In general, persons who are severely or multiply handicapped fare better in our society today than they did during earlier years of segregation and neglect.

When books deal with persons who have many different impairments and/or disabilities, they are listed under Various Disabilities.

Some books are cross-referenced because a primary diagnosis is unclear or is disputed.

To summarize, the classification in this book is as follows:

> Physical problems (Chapter 5)
>   Health problems
>   Orthopedic/neurological disabilities
> Sensory problems (Chapter 6)
>   Deaf-blind
>   Hearing impairments
>   Visual impairments
> Cognitive and behavior problems (Chapter 7)
>   Emotional disturbances
>   Learning disabilities
>   Mental retardation
>   Speech and language impairments

Multiple/severe and various disabilities (Chapter 8)
Multiple/severe disabilities
Various disabilities

Notes

A short form of reference is used for works cited fully in Chapters 5–8.

1. Fiedler, *Freaks: Myths and Images of the Secret Self.*
2. Bruno Bettelheim, *The Uses of Enchantment* (New York: Random House, 1976).
3. June B. Mullins, *A Teacher's Guide to Management of Physically Handicapped Students* (Springfield, Ill.: Charles C. Thomas, 1979), p.24.

3

Treatment of Disabilities
in Printed Sources

Being deaf is an accident of nature. Being indifferent is very often a
deliberate choice of mankind. Of these two wounds in our society,
one is at least curable.
—Nanette Fabray

B ooks about disabled or different people have been a part of children's and young adults' literature for a long time, but only recently have reference works begun to include them as a specific category. Moreover, more titles are being published. For these reasons, it is important for teachers, librarians, and other professionals to be aware of stereotypic images that mar the portrayal of persons with disabilities or differences. Part of the propagation of these stereotypes lies in the kind of language used in books and, particularly, in the subject headings and indexing terms in card catalogs, bibliographies, indexes, and other reference sources.

One of the earlier reference works to include a category for books about persons with disabilities was a 1973 publication by Lonsdale and Mackintosh, which had an index entry "Handicapped children, stories about."[1] In 1975, Mullins and Wolfe surveyed all the major organizations serving disabled or different persons and consulted many unpublished bibliographies to compile *Special People behind the Eight Ball: An Annotated Bibliography of Literature Classified by Handicapping Conditions.*[2] The work included trade books for adults and children, with both fictional and nonfictional listings.

In 1976, Rudman, in *Children's Literature: An Issues Approach*, included brief synopses of books dealing with people who have disabilities.[3] The following year, the topic "disability" appeared in the index of the fourth edition of Arbuthnot and Sutherland's *Children and Books*.[4] Also in that year, Huck added it to her third edition of *Children's Literature in the Elementary School*.[5] But, as Schwartz pointed out at the time, none of these attempts evaluated the books, nor was an awareness of stereotypes apparent.[6] Now, with attention at long last focused on the "literature of deviancy," concern has developed regarding the implicit and explicit messages contained in the portrayals of disabled people.

In 1977, Baskin and Harris published *Notes from a Different Drummer: A Guide to Juvenile Fiction Portraying the Handicapped*, which offers a comprehensive guide to juvenile fiction written between 1940 and 1975 and depicting disabled or different characters, followed in 1984 by *More Notes from a Different Drummer: A Guide to Juvenile Fiction Portraying the Disabled* (note the difference in terminology in the subtitle between 1977 and 1984), which covers titles published between 1976 and 1981.[7] The annotations of approximately a page each are of more than 650 identified books (in the two volumes) that reveal attitudes or convey information about impairments. In addition, the literary merit of each work is addressed.

Fassler reviewed contemporary children's literature to find books and stories that would help children grow, reduce fears and anxieties, and initiate open, honest communication between youngsters and adults.[8] The sections dealing with death, separation, hospitalization, and illness are pertinent for disabled or different children and their siblings. Lass and Bromfield identified factors to be considered in selecting a book about disabilities or differences.[9] In addition, they provided an up-to-date selection of good books to be used with children.

Dreyer developed *The Bookfinder: A Guide to Children's Literature about the Needs and Problems of Youth Aged 2–15*, a reference work that describes and categorizes 1,031 current children's books according to more than 450 psychological, behavioral, and developmental topics of concern to children and adolescents from ages 2 through 15. Dreyer says of the book: "It is written primarily for parents, teachers, librarians, counselors, psychologists, psychiatrists and other adults who want to identify books that may help children cope with the challenges of life. In short, the *Bookfinder* was created to fill the need for a way to match children and books."[10]

Reading Ladders for Human Relations, now a joint publication of the American Council on Education and the National Council of Teachers of English, has, since its first edition in 1947, always listed a few outstanding books on people with disabilities or differences, although these titles appeared in themes such as "adjusting to change." The sixth edition, published in 1981,[11] has a 19-page section, "Understanding the Handicapped," which contains useful, pertinent titles and annotations.

Stereotypes in Literature

Weinberg and Rossini decry the stereotypic images of disabled or different persons, particularly in comic books.[12] They have found comic-book characters to be highly stereotypic with generally negative depictions of impairments. Biklen and Bogdan discuss the stereotypes in media portrayals of those with disabilities.[13] They found "handicapism" pervading society and prevalent in literature, the mass media, and in the language itself. A common thread appears in the stereotype, that two diametrically opposed concepts or extremes are embraced. These are evident among the ten common handicapist stereotypes that Biklen and Bogdan list:

1. "The disabled person as pitiful and pathetic." An example is the characterization of the lame Laura Wingfield in Tennessee Williams's *The Glass Menagerie*.
2. "The disabled person as object of violence." An example is the film *Wait until Dark*, in which the beautiful young heroine, who is blind, is terrorized by thugs searching for a drug cache in her home.
3. "The disabled person as sinister and/or evil." Consider Stevenson's villainous and treacherous characters in *Treasure Island*. Black Dog is a "tallow-faced man, wanting two fingers," and Per is described as a "hunched and eyeless creature."
4. "The disabled person as 'atmosphere.' " The authors say "blind musicians, news dealers and the 'blind men with a cup' are frequently thrown in for seasoning in movies and TV stories, a practice which dilutes the humanity of disabled people by reducing them to the status of colorful or curious objects."
5. "The disabled person as 'Super Crip.' " Human interest stories in newspapers and magazines often feature the extraordinary achievements of disabled persons who "overcame" their handicaps.
6. "The disabled person as laughable." The nearsighted Mr. Magoo is an example, and is actually one of the kinder genre, in which blindness, deafness, speech handicap, or cerebral palsy becomes the butt of jokes.
7. "The disabled person as his/her own worst- and only-enemy." Biklen and Bogdan point out that children's authors seem particularly prone to this kind of stereotyping, showing characters who learn to make it in society after getting over self-pity about their fates and rising to the challenge.
8. "The disabled person as burden." The example, in Steinbeck's *Of Mice and Men*, is Lenny, who is retarded and usually considered

utterly helpless and dependent on the hero, George. (On a deeper, more subtle level, however, Lenny's physical strength provides the economic basis of George's livelihood.)

9. "The disabled person as nonsexual." The television show "Iron-sides" features a detective (played by Raymond Burr) who apparently had a love life before he was shot in the spine and "confined" to a wheelchair. His old flames turn up now and again, but even though the episodes feature Detective Ironsides as a perfectly capable and functioning adult in most all ways, it seems to be assumed that romance is out. Curiously, certain mild disabilities, perhaps sustained in a war, are considered "sexy" in a man. Real-life Israeli hero Moshe Dayan was copied by models with an eye patch in Hathaway shirt advertisements.

10. "The disabled person as incapable of fully participating in every-day life."[14]

This stereotype is mainly one of omission in that disabled people are rarely shown as integral and productive members of society—as part of the work force, as functioning members of families, as students or teachers, etc. The absence of such portrayals feeds the concept that disabled people are inferior human beings who should be segregated (a concept that fortunately seems to be on the way out). Movies like "Charley" and "Larry," about mentally retarded people, reinforce this concept. Charley is presumed to be incapable of doing anything except sitting on a park swing. Larry is reintegrated into society *only* when it's discovered that he isn't retarded—the implication being that retarded people are hopeless dependents who require lifelong institutionalization. Regular inclusion of disabled people as participants in society would lend emphasis to the extremely wide range of things they *can* do, rather than to what they cannot do.[15]

The Center on Human Policy, the Center for Independent Living in Berkeley, Disabled in Action of Metropolitan New York, and the Council on Interracial Books for Children compiled guidelines to assist authors, reviewers, and readers in counteracting common stereotypes about disabled or different people. Authored by Biklen and Bogdan in *The Bulletin: Interracial Books for Children*, they are reprinted here in their entirety.

Shun one-dimensional characterizations of disabled persons. Portray people with disabilities as having individual and complex personalities and capable of a full range of emotions.

Avoid depicting disabled persons only in the role of receiving; show disabled people *inter*acting as equals and giving as well as receiving. Too often the person with a disability is presented solely as the recipient of pity.

Avoid presenting physical characteristics of any kind as determining factors of personality. Be especially cautious about implying a correlation between disability and evil.

Refrain from depicting persons with disabilities as objects of curiosity. It is entirely appropriate to show disabled people as members of an average population or cast of characters. Most disabled people are able to participate in all facets of life and should be depicted in a wide variety of situations.

A person's disability should not be ridiculed or made the butt of a joke. (Blind people do not mistake fire hydrants for people or bump into every object in their path, despite the myth-making of Mr. Magoo.)

Avoid the sensational in depicting disabled people. Be wary of the stereotype of disabled persons as either the victims or perpetrators of violence.

Refrain from endowing disabled characters with superhuman attributes. To do so is to imply that a disabled person must overcompensate and become superhuman to win acceptance.

Avoid a Pollyanna-ish plot that implies a disabled person need only have "the will" and the "right attitude" to succeed. Young readers need insights into the societal barriers that keep disabled people from living full lives—systematic discrimination in employment, education and housing; inaccessible transportation and buildings; and exorbitant expense for necessities.

Avoid showing disabled people as nonsexual. Show disabled people in loving relationships and expressing the same sexual needs and desires as nondisabled people.[16]

Schwartz studied contemporary children's books, analyzing them to apply Biklen's and Bogdan's guidelines.[17] Selections for the study were made from two book lists: the Physical Disabilities Section of the *Early Childhood Bibliography* and the Physically Handicapped section of *Children's Books in Print*.[18] Other books were chosen by selected librarians. Schwartz found that even the most popular literature contained ageist, sexist, and handicapist deceptions. For example, a limp old crone has supernatural powers in *Dwarf Long-Nose* by Wilhelm Hauff; a blind adult is "rescued" from loneliness by two young boys in *Apt. 3* by Keats; in *Shadow in the Sun* by Grohskopf, a girl in a wheelchair is portrayed as mean, self-centered, and spoiled (her own worst enemy) and likened in the title to Shakespeare's bitter, deformed Richard III.[19] Schwartz describes the practice of naming characters according to their disability; Captain Hook in *Peter Pan*, *Crazylegs Merrill* by Carol, and *Limpy the Lion* by Whitney and Graboff, a book for the very young.[20]

Children's authors, says Schwartz, tend to glamorize well-known public figures (the "George Washington never told a lie" syndrome). He writes: "However, the serious questions disabled rights activists have raised about these biographies lead one to conclude that they should be used with caution. How helpful is it, really, to give children, as role models, persons with extraordinary talents—that is, super achievers?"[21]

Language Guidelines

Mullins in *Education Unlimited* discusses language that is stereotypic and alternatives that work to eliminate handicapism.[22] She includes guidelines for judging a literary work, the outcome of a consortium including handicapped people, parents, publishers, and special educators. *Guidelines for the Representation of Exceptional Persons in Educational Material* were written to aid publishers in producing and selecting educational materials that would fairly and positively portray exceptional (disabled or different) persons.[23]

1. "In print and nonprint educational materials, ten percent of the contents should include or represent children or adults with an exceptionality." The work should predominately feature someone with whom the reader can identify in a positive way.
2. "Representation of persons with exceptionalities should be included in materials at all levels (early childhood through adult) and in all areas of study" such as career education, guidance, health studies, language arts, vocational education, mathematics, physical education, science, and social studies.
3. "The representation of persons with exceptionalities should be accurate and free from stereotypes." The evaluator will be sensitive to literature that either unrealistically elevates or demeans the handicapped person, putting him or her out of the pale of ordinary existence.
4. "Persons with exceptionalities should be shown in the least restrictive environment. They should be shown participating in activities in a manner that will include them as part of society." Some litera-

ture of a few decades ago espoused the then prevailing belief in segregation and institutionalization as opposed to normalization and mainstreaming of handicapped persons. Such literature would not be considered appropriate today.

5. "In describing persons with exceptionalities, the language used should be nondiscriminatory and free from value judgments." Evaluators should be sensitive to patronizing, pitying, or overcheerful tones in books. Such may not be avoidable, but positive and negative aspects of a work should be weighed carefully.

6. "Persons with exceptionalities and persons without exceptionalities should be shown interacting in ways that are mutually beneficial." Literature should be selected that emphasizes mutual interaction and respect—not doing *for* or *to* persons confronted with handicaps.

7. "Materials should provide a variety of appropriate role models of persons with exceptionalities." The success of Helen Keller or Charles Steinmetz might give to some normal children false expectations for disabled peers, and to some of the latter, an unattainable role model.

8. "Emphasis should be on uniqueness and worth of all persons, rather than on the differences between persons with and without exceptionalities." The tone of the work should foster an attitude of "one of us" rather than "one of them." The language should imply that disabilities and differences are a part of, not apart from, our society and our common human condition.

9. "Tokenism should be avoided in the representation of persons with exceptionalities." Some ingenuity may be required to find literature not limited to deaf, blind, physically disabled, or mentally retarded persons. With diligence, materials can be found portraying all types and levels of physical and behavioral variation.

Handicapist Language in Library Work

Guidelines such as those above represent the ideal. Reality is another matter. Even in the best literature, the occurrence of the word *handicapped* rather than *disabled* is overwhelming. The tendency to create superheroes—or to write only about them—still exists, side by side with the Pollyanna syndrome. Subject headings and indexing terms show a wide disparity. Persons who write book reviews and annotations for the library press and for publications issued by libraries often use terms and express ideas that conflict with the letter and intent of these guidelines.

As an illustrative parallel, let us review the battle against sexist language. Those who have fought and continue to fight for nonsexist language have learned that even when beliefs and concepts change, change in language usage lags far behind. This resistance springs from a variety of sources, a major one being the commonly accepted notion that language use is primarily a matter of custom, tradition, and "correctness" rather than a representation of thought and meaning, and that, therefore, changes in ways of thinking do not require changes in language. A parallel but sometimes intersecting source is resistance to or rejection of the changing roles of men and women in society. Many people are unwilling to verbalize this rejection, and some are unable to admit their resistance to it, even to themselves. Some people rapidly adopt nonsexist language, but its use does not reflect new or different beliefs and concepts on their part. In their social circles, it has become "trendy" to adopt a feminist viewpoint, and they mean to be trendy people. The real point is whether the change in language will eventually influence their beliefs and thought patterns.

As even a brief analysis of the current status of sexism in language reveals, the issue is complex and will not easily be resolved. Resistance to change, especially change that is threatening, is an axiom of human existence. The problems of handicapism in language are very similar. Yet, one important difference must be noted. Public consciousness of handicapist language has not yet reached the same level as that of sexist language. Awareness is still limited largely to people who have contact, in some way, with persons who are disabled or with organizations that are concerned with disabilities or differences. Few of the trendy have yet adopted this awareness.

Sensitivity to Labels

Librarians and reviewers for library publications need to develop greater sensitivity to the type of language they use when referring to disabilities or differences. Phrases such as "how blind people lead near-normal lives," "a blind 12-year-old," and "a blind child with his normal fifth-grade class" can be rephrased in many ways; for example, "how people function without sight" (or, even better, omit this illusion entirely and describe their daily lives and the adaptations they make to vision loss); "a 12-year-old child who is blind," "a blind child (or a child who is blind) with her or his class of sighted fifth-graders (or fifth-graders who are sighted)." These sample phrases, which were noted in reviews and annotations of books for children and teenagers, are not highly offensive, except for the use of the word *normal*. The phrase "a blind child" is not unacceptable, but "a child who is blind" is better. The former should be used only if awkwardness or repetition results from use of the latter.

"The blind" and "the deaf" are used frequently as labels, often by persons who themselves are blind or deaf. The problem here is that such usage involves potential depersonalization and stereotyping; "deaf persons," "people who are blind," "members of the deaf community," and the like are alternatives. "The mentally handicapped," another term that appears frequently in reviews, can be replaced by "mentally disabled" or "mentally retarded," and these terms should be used as adjectives, not as nouns. The person is not the disability; the person *has* the disability. A disability is one of the many facts about a person's life, not the totality of that life. Some alternatives are "Mary, who is mentally retarded," "mentally disabled adults," "adults who are mentally disabled," "mentally retarded children," "children who are mentally retarded," and so on.

One frequently recurring phrase that is totally unacceptable is "deaf-mute." Deafness and muteness are not one and the same condition; deaf people cannot hear and, therefore, may have to receive instruction in speech.

Terms referring to persons with physical disabilities should also be used with care. Typical phrases include "physically handicapped" or "crippled" when referring to people with orthopedic/neurological impairments. These phrases often appear as nouns, which should be avoided. "The physically handicapped" can be changed to "persons with physical disabilities" and "crippled John" or "John, who is confined to a wheelchair" can be rephrased as "John, who uses a wheelchair," *if* that fact is relevant to the discussion. Disabled persons should not be referred to as "confined" to home or to a wheelchair, nor should their disabilities be brought up unless that information is needed within the context of the book review or discussion.

Descriptions of a book such as "Can crippled Jennie enter the marathon?" or "A cerebral palsy victim as photographer" should also be avoided. Both of these actually were used in an effort to be brief, succinct, and pithy, to create a gripping, accurate description in a few words. Librarians and others often find themselves in such a predicament, an unavoidable one for persons trying to create a bibliography or book talk with brief descriptions designed to appeal to children and teenagers. Even greater care must be taken with actual meanings in such short phrases that are meant as a summary of an entire book.

Both of the above descriptions sound melodramatic. In "Can crippled Jennie enter the marathon?" the emphasis falls too strongly on "crippled" and not enough on "Jennie." The word *crippled* is troublesome; it should never be used as a noun (a *cripple*) but it does describe certain disabilities that result from impairments. If possible, it is better to use the term for the impairment, or a description of the disability or difference. A possibility here might be "Could Jennie, who walked with a limp, enter the marathon?"

The phrase "a cerebral palsy victim as photographer" has multiple problems. "Cerebral palsy" receives primary attention; "victim" is in second place; the most important fact comes last: "photographer." This phrase could be rewritten as "a photographer, who has cerebral palsy." The word *victim* should not appear at all. People who have disabilities or differences should not be portrayed as victims, nor referred to by that term.

Terminology from the Authorities

Book reviews and annotations are not the only places in the library where problems arise with handicapist language. When users wish access to materials about disabilities or differences, they meet a bewildering array of terminology that at various times, according to the source in use, is confusing, overlapping, extremely precise, vague, inconsistent, anachronistic, pejorative, and/or compatible or incompatible with current thinking about disabilities or differences.

People are slow to change, and so is spoken language. Authority lists for subject headings and indexing terminology create a controlled vocabulary frozen in the time period when the list was created. All these lists are periodically updated, but the slow processes of change, along with the cumbersome process of updating a controlled vocabulary list and the problems that result in cross-referencing between old and new terms, have left the impression that changing subject terminology in catalogs and indexes is on the same level as changing words engraved in granite. This problem may well be alleviated by the age of electronic marvels, but until total on-line access is available, librarians and users of libraries must struggle on. Part of that struggle should be an effort to bring terminology into a reasonable, consistent, logical pattern that reflects today's realities about disabilities or differences rather than yesterday's prejudices and stereotypes about handicaps.

An examination of *Library of Congress Subject Headings, Thesaurus of ERIC Descriptors, British Education Index,* and *Thesaurus of Psychological Indexing Terms* reveals some interesting contrasts as well as similarities in an overview of terms relating to deafness and blindness.

Library of Congress Subject Headings, ninth edition,[24] uses Blind as a noun when referring to persons who are blind, and the term Blindness when referring to the disability (p. 254), as with Deaf and Deafness (p. 621). Under Deafness is this scope note: "Here are entered works on the lack of sense of hearing, including the lack combined with the inability to speak; i.e., deaf-mutism" (p. 621). A subject heading "Deaf Services" is cross-referenced as a "see also" from "Handicapped Service" (p. 621). The term used for persons who are deaf-blind is "Blind-deaf," with appropriate cross-references (pp. 257 and 621).

The *Thesaurus of ERIC Descriptors*,[25] which in 1977 underwent a total revision of all terms established since 1966 when it began, and since then has an ongoing vocabulary review group and a vocabulary coordinator in each ERIC clearinghouse, uses Blindness (p. 29), Deafness (p. 65), and Deaf-Blind (p. 65). Until 1980, terms differentiating between disabilities and persons, similar to those currently in *Library of Congress Subject Headings*, had been used, along with Deafness and Blindness.

British Education Index,[26] for the one year examined, uses Blind, Blind Children, Visually Handicapped, Visually Handicapped Pupils, Deaf Children, Deaf Persons, Deaf Pupils, and Schools for Deaf Pupils. The *Thesaurus of Psychological Indexing Terms*, third edition,[27] uses Deaf, which is defined as "profoundly or severely hearing impaired" (p. 45). Aurally Handicapped, defined as "persons with varying degrees of hearing loss" (p. 18), is listed as a broader term for Deaf along with a second broader term, Handicapped. Related terms include Hearing Disorders, Lipreading, and Partially Hearing Impaired.

These examples of the treatment of two terms and related ones show that only ERIC is really current. *British Education Index* is not far behind, which is interesting considering the disparity that has always existed between the state of special-education terminology in Great Britain and the United States.

An examination of terms relating to persons who are mentally retarded, emotionally disturbed, or physically disabled shows a similar trend. With the exception of Handicap Identification (p. 115), which was formerly Handicap Detection, ERIC has purged all use of the word *handicap* and has gone to the total use of *disability*. Emphasis is entirely on the condition, not on the person. Also, it has gone from Mentally Handicapped to Mental Retardation (p. 162), with narrower terms for Mild . . . , Moderate . . . , and Severe Mental Retardation, and for Down's Syndrome. It has also gone from Mental Illness to Mental Disorders (p. 162), with the instruction that a more specific term, such as Emotional Disturbances, Neurosis, or Psychosis, is preferable. Many related terms are listed under Emotional Disturbances, including Anorexia Nervosa, Anxiety, Attention Deficit Disorders, Autism, Behavior

Disorders, and Depression. Emotional Problems is used for less severe difficulties.

Library of Congress uses Handicapped, with numerous subdivisions, and Handicapped Children, Handicapped Youth, and Handicapped Services (p. 1024). Developmentally Disabled and Disability Evaluation are given as "see also" references under Handicapped, along with Physically Handicapped and Mentally Handicapped. These are the only instances of the use of *disability*, except for a cross-reference from Disability to Handicapped. In keeping with this more traditional approach, Library of Congress also uses Mental Deficiency and Mentally Handicapped instead of Mental Retardation. Ironically, Mental Retardation was a valid subject heading many years ago, but was replaced by Mentally Handicapped, apparently considered a more appropriate term at the time.

British Education Index is also somewhat more traditional, using Mentally Disordered, Mentally Handicapped, and Mentally Retarded (but not Mental Retardation), sometimes followed by other terms specifying groups of persons, such as Mentally Retarded Adolescents, Mentally Disordered School Leavers. Instead of Emotionally Disturbed, the heading is Maladjusted, usually followed by other terms, as Maladjusted Children. Mental Illness is a separate term. Physically Handicapped, with various terms following, is used instead of Disabled or Disabilities.

The *Thesaurus of Psychological Indexing Terms* also employs traditional terminology when indexing physical disabilities, mental retardation, and emotional disturbances. The terms used include Handicapped, Physically Handicapped, Mentally Retarded, and Mental Retardation. Because of the highly specialized nature of this index, numerous specific terms refer to emotional disturbances. Some obsolete words are still used as cross-references (but not as active indexing terms), such as "Imbecility, Feeblemindedness, and Idiocy. Use Mental Retardation," and "Crippled. Use Physically Handicapped."

The state of subject heading/indexing terminology is less than ideal, as can be seen from these brief examples. ERIC provides the model for others to follow. In the meantime, however, information about disabilities or differences and about individuals who have disabilities or differences must be retrieved, both manually and by computer, by employing a wide variety of terminology, much of which is inconsistent, overlapping, and far behind current facts and philosophies about disabilities. As outdated terms appear less and less, and finally not at all, in book reviews, annotations, and articles in the library press, subject heading and indexing terminology will eventually follow suit.

Notes

A short form of reference is used for works cited fully in Chapters 5–8.

1. Bernard J. Lonsdale and Helen K. Mackintosh, *Children Experience Literature* (New York: Random House, 1973).
2. June B. Mullins and Suzanne Wolfe, *Special People behind the Eight Ball: An Annotated Bibliography of Literature Classified by Handicapping Conditions* (Johnstown, Pa.: Mafex Associates, Inc., 1975).
3. Masha Kabakow Rudman, *Children's Literature: An Issues Approach* (Lexington, Mass.: Heath, 1976).
4. May Hill Arbuthnot and Zena Sutherland, *Children and Books,* 4th ed. (Glenview, Ill.: Scott, Foresman, 1972).
5. Charlotte Huck, *Children's Literature in the Elementary School,* 3rd ed. (New York: Holt, 1976).
6. Albert V. Schwartz, "Disability in Children's Books: Is Visibility Enough?" *The Bulletin: Interracial Books for Children* 8 (1977): 10–15.
7. Barbara H. Baskin and Karen H. Harris, *Notes from a Different Drummer* and *More Notes from a Different Drummer* (New York: Bowker, 1977, 1984).
8. Joan Fassler, *Helping Children Cope: Mastering Stress through Books and Stories* (New York: Free Press, 1978).
9. Bonnie Lass and Marcia Bromfield, "Books about Children with Special Needs: An Annotated Bibliography," *Reading Teacher* 34 (February 1981): 530–533.
10. Sharon S. Dreyer, *The Bookfinder: A Guide to Children's Literature about the Needs and Problems of Youth Aged 2–15.* (Circle Pines, Minn.: American Guidance Service, 1980), p. ix.
11. Eileen Tway, ed., *Reading Ladders for Human Relations,* 6th ed. (Urbana, Ill.: National Council of Teachers of English, 1981).
12. Nancy Weinberg and Santana Rossini, "Comic Books: Champions of the Disabled Stereotype," *Rehabilitation Literature* 39 (November–December 1978): 327–331.
13. Douglas Biklen and Robert Bogdan, "Media Portrayals of Disabled People: A Study in Stereotypes." *The Bulletin: Interracial Books for Children* 8 (1977): 4–9.
14. Ibid., pp. 6–9.
15. Ibid., p. 9.
16. Ibid.
17. Schwartz, "Disability in Children's Books."
18. Barbara Wolfson, *Early Childhood Bibliography; Children's Books in Print* (New York: Bowker, 1976).
19. Wilhelm Hauff, *Dwarf Long-Nose* (New York: Random House, 1969); Ezra Jack Keats, *Apt. 3* (New York: Macmillan, 1971); Bernice Grohskopf, *Shadow in the Sun* (New York: Atheneum, 1975).
20. James Barrie, *Peter Pan;* Bill J. Carol, *Crazylegs Merrill* (Austin, Tex.: Steck-Vaughn, 1969); David C. Whitney and Abner Graboff, *Limpy the Lion* (New York: Franklin Watts, 1969).
21. Schwartz, "Disability in Children's Books," p. 15.
22. June B. Mullins, "Making Language Work to Eliminate Handicapism," *Education Unlimited* 1 (June 1979): 20–24.
23. *Guidelines for the Representation of Exceptional Persons in Educational Material* (Reston, Va.: National Center on Educational Media and Materials, n.d.).

24. Library of Congress, Subject Cataloging Division, *Library of Congress Subject Headings,* 9th ed. (Washington, D.C.: Library of Congress, 1980).
25. *Thesaurus of ERIC Descriptors,* 10th ed. (Phoenix, Ariz.: Oryx, 1984).
26. *British Education Index,* Vol. 17 (London: The British Library, Bibliographic Services Division, 1981).
27. *Thesaurus of Psychological Indexing Terms,* 3rd ed. (Washington, D.C.: American Psychological Assn., 1982).

4

Patterns and Trends

> My question is not "Why me?" but "What next?"
> Susan Daniels, *Comeback*

Progressing from Chapter 1, which looks at the power of nonfiction to reflect and describe experience in a realistic way, to Chapter 2, a brief summarization of the changes in societal attitudes toward people who are different by reason of disabilities, to Chapter 3, covering the treatment given disabilities in printed sources, Chapter 4 examines the patterns and trends that became evident in reading this growing body of literature as the basis for this book. As a summary of what was observed, five questions are answered in this chapter. In illustrating the answers, examples are always taken from titles that are fully cited in the annotations in Chapters 5–8 (see both the Author Index and Title Index).

Who Are the Authors of This Literature?

Included is a varied group of writers. Disabled people representing a broad span of ages write about themselves—for example, the young contributors to *What It's Like to Be Me*, the youthful Helen Keller in *The Story of My Life*, and Ved Mehta in *Face to Face*. Some are mature or elderly people like Carlson (*Born That Way*) or Miers (*The Trouble Bush*) who are contemplating an entire lifetime and who both give an interesting glimpse into earlier times.

Parents and foster parents describe the effects on their families and themselves of recognizing that a child has disabilities. They show us how they dealt with the impairment itself and recount the child's response to disability. They talk about interaction with doctors, nurses, and teachers. There are many books in this category, such as *This Is the Child* by Terry Pringle, *Alex* by Frank DeFord, and *19 Steps Up the Mountain* by Joseph Blank. Both mothers and fathers have written books and occasionally they are coauthors, as in the Massies' *Journey*.

Siblings sometimes write of brothers and sisters, as in *Like Normal People* by Robert Meyers and *Mary Fran and Mo* by Maureen Lynch. There are books written from the perspective of a sibling, although not actually penned by the child, as in Sobol's *My Brother Steven Is Retarded*. Occasionally, a nondisabled child of a disabled parent has written a book, such as Henry Edwards's *What Happened to My Mother?*

There are many books by counselors and teachers. Torey Hayden has written several narratives about treating and teaching children with disabilities, and Mira Rothenberg relates her work with emotionally disturbed youngsters in *Children with Emerald Eyes*.

Professional photographers like Bernard Wolf and professional writers like Milton Meltzer have turned their attention to disabled people; Wolf has contributed both text and photographs for a number of books (*Anna's Silent World*, *Don't Feel Sorry for Paul*, and others), and Meltzer has written about Samuel Gridley Howe's experimental work with deaf-blind Laura Bridgman. Candid snapshots are used extensively in such works as *Parents Speak Out*. (The four illustrations used in *Accept Me As I Am* are reproduced from works annotated in this bibliography.)

Religious leaders from or members of the major religions are represented among the authors, for example, Rabbi Hyman Agress ("*Why Me?*"). Religious publishing houses, such as Zondervan and Westminster, have brought out books included in this list.

Professional writers and some professionals in specific disability areas have written rather didactic books targeted at young children. The Silversteins have written a series, including books on allergies and diabetes. Several dictionaries of sign language are included.

Some of the books annotated here have been written in other languages: Truss deVries-Kruyt's book about her son, who had Down's syndrome, was translated from the Dutch and Palle Petersen's *Sally Can't See* from the Danish. Segal's *The Man Who Walked in His Head* was a prize-winning French book.

A number of authors give a glimpse into totally different cultures, such as *Life* magazine writer Parks's book *Flavio*, about the Brazilian barrios, *Sadako and the Thousand Paper Cranes*, about Japan at the end of World War II, or Lucy Ching's *One of the Lucky Ones*, about life in China.

Some books are written by and about minorities, such as Patterson's *No Time for Tears*, in which a close black family faces their first son's hydrocephalus with sensitivity and intelligence; Wilma Rudolph's orthopedic problems in *Wilma*, about the great Olympic champion; Mathis's *Ray Charles,* about the black musician who is blind; or Darryl Stingley's *Happy to Be Alive,* the biography of a black former professional football player who has paraplegia as the result of an injury received during a game. Several children's books about Stevie Wonder are particularly recommended because his race is a positive but only incidental part of his upbeat story, and even his blindness is secondary to his considerable musical success and ebullient personality. In these books, he is a fine role model for all young children.

Several authors explicitly state a motivation for their selection of subjects; it is a deep fascination. This same motivation may propel many who write or read about people who are different because of extreme human variations. Roth and Crome (*Little People*) and Fiedler (*Freaks*) seem to have found, through their concentration on the unusual, a deeper self-awareness and some resolution to the question "What is reality and what is illusion?" Bosworth (*Diane Arbus*) reports that this was also the quest of the great photographer, who found her identification through the stories and images of the weird, contorted subjects of her most famous photographs. These people have been criticized for expressing themselves so openly in this regard, and for exhibiting their subjects as freaks, but they have all felt a reverence for and closeness with these persons, whom they have accepted as totally like them.

People who write nonfiction, about themselves or others, are inclined to be educated and middle class. In the case of authors writing about others, their subjects also tend to be from an educated, middle-class background. They are apt to be relatively affluent, to have the means to search out the best medical care, and to possess the talent for expressing themselves well on paper, not to mention getting a publisher and following through on a book. Many examples can be cited, including Helms's *Against All Odds,* Valens's *A Long Way Up: The Story of Jill Kinmont,* Frevert's *It's Okay to Look at Jamie* and *Patrick, Yes You Can.* While this fact in no way devalues these and similar titles (in fact, most of those mentioned are among the best reviewed), care should be taken to balance the selection so that young readers can identify with the lives of the characters in books recommended to them by classroom teachers, parents, librarians, and other adults.

Who Is the Audience for This Literature?

The books surveyed include titles that can be read by or to an audience that ranges in age from preschool years through young adulthood. Overrepresented in terms of numbers are books in the young-adult category and others that are classified as adult books but seem to have relevance to younger good readers and high school level youth. The publication of good books on disabilities and about disabled people aimed at preschoolers and elementary-level children is a relatively new but growing phenomenon. Three excellent examples are *My Friend Leslie* by Maxine Rosenberg, *Someone Special, Just Like You* by Tricia Brown, and Stein's *About Handicaps* with dual texts. Parents can read aloud or suggest many of these books to their children, whether or not the youngsters have yet had direct experience with disability. Such books are particularly appropriate for helping all children to understand differences and disabilities, and for allaying fears.

Able-bodied children can extend specific situations found in these books to their own lives, since all human beings inevitably face challenges. The families and friends of disabled people can similarly expand their understanding of the thoughts and experiences of siblings, children, or classmates who have impairments. All parents might find books here that will add to their knowledge about human development in a helpful way. Jablow's book about her daughter with Down's syndrome contains a wealth of material on child development and includes information on the reaction of her four older children to a disabled sibling. Certainly young readers who themselves have disabilities can find information and inspiration as they learn about the lives, thoughts, and satisfactions of others with analogous problems.

Because some of these books concentrate on life at school, they have the potential to increase understanding and acceptance of disabled schoolmates and create a classroom atmosphere where mainstreaming can benefit all participants. *Janet at School* is a most appealing book for little children, as are the two titles by Frevert noted earlier. Some, like Jones's *Kids Called Crazy*, would be valuable for discussion at the high school level. One, the Turnbulls' *Parents Speak Out*, includes provocative questions for discussion.

Although this literature was reviewed specifically with an eye to how young readers might respond, many of the books could be valuable to teachers, teachers-in-training, and those choosing or already active in professional work with disabled people, such as medical students and social workers. Such books vary from personal essays by youngsters, like those found in *Like It Is: Facts and Feelings about Handicaps from Kids Who Know*, to books by parents and teachers, such as Torey Hayden's *Murphy's Boy* and Elaine Ipswitch's *Scott Was Here*. Books like Gary Kleiman's on growing up with diabetes (*No Time to Lose*) and Margaret Sullivan's *Living with Epilepsy* could also help professionals. Moreover, physicians and others who might need to understand the emotional and psychological problems of the people in their care could benefit from many of the titles annotated here, for their own knowledge and to be able to introduce the books to their patients and clients.

What Are the Subjects?

Ultimately, the subject is people, but under the general topic of disability, subjects vary widely. Some books explain specific disabilities, using an approach and language appropriate to the age of the intended readers. *Being Blind* by Rebecca Marcus is such a book. Other titles, a large category, are accounts about famous people with disabilities. Some are autobiographical, for example, Susan Hampshire's *Susan's Story: An Autobiographical Account of My Struggle with Dyslexia*, Roy Campanella's *It's Good to Be Alive*, and Elizabeth Quinn's *Listen to Me*. Others are biographies. The notable biographees include athletes, actors, statespersons, artists, teachers, doctors, scientists and inventors, musicians, and writers. While some well-known people have been much written about—Helen Keller, for instance—others seem due for more attention. For example, this guide includes only one biography of Steinmetz, the electrical genius, and one of Thomas Edison. Books about "ordinary" children and adults with disabilities are also numerous, many by the parents of such children or by the disabled adults themselves.

Some of the books give a picture of the experience of disabled people in other cultures. *Take My Hands! The Remarkable Story of Dr. Mary Verghese* is about a physician in India.

All through the period examined, there are authors who have written from a strong religious orientation and who have resolved their struggle with disability and death within their own religious frameworks. This theme is evident in *If I Die at Thirty*, written by Meg Woodson, whose children have cystic fibrosis. *Joni* and its sequel well illustrate a disabled person transcending tragedy through belief in God's love and will. These books might attract readers with similar views or even—for purposes of argument—those with quite different attitudes.

The number of books on a subject does not always keep pace with the prevalence of the disability. Spina bifida is a fairly common birth defect, but very few books have been written by parents with children in this category (one is Pieper's *Sticks and Stones*). We might expect to see more in the future, and even autobiographies, since some with this condition have entered adulthood.

A glance through the Subject Index gives an idea of the range of disabilities found in this literature. Two of the largest categories are Visual Impairments and Orthopedic/Neurological Disabilities. There are a few books on speech impairment and learning disabilities, many more on hearing and health impairments, a handful on mental retardation and emotional disturbances.

The literature has always to a great extent reflected the medical progress of the time in which a book is written. Many blind writers, such as Harold Krentz (*To Race the Wind*), experienced a congenital degeneration of the retina due to overadministration of oxygen at birth. After the cause was understood and more precisely monitored incubators were developed, blindness from this condition was much diminished. Therefore, we can expect fewer books about blindness due to retrolental fibroplasia in the future. On the other hand, with a new era of organ transplants, more stories can be expected such as Poole's *Thursday's Child* about a teenager with a heart transplant or Seidick's book about her young son who has a kidney transplant (*Or You Can Let Him Go*).

Medical advances have increased the life span of children with potentially fatal diseases. Hence, families may endure a protracted cycle of hopes, fears, renewed hope, and finally resignation. Perhaps writing is a catharsis for parents under such stress. There is an extremely large number of books by parents of children with leukemia, and some by writers whose children had other cancers and cystic fibrosis. These books may be heart-wrenching, but in most of them, the description of a final acceptance of the family's fate and the appreciation for the child's brief life are sublime.

Some conditions may have existed for a long time but may have been widely diagnosed and treated only recently. This is true of eating disorders and learning disabilities. Books for children and adolescents about eating disorders have just begun to be published, and many more may be anticipated.

Medical science has had little impact on some human conditions— notably infantile autism. Autistic children have intrigued and baffled people since Itard's account of the Wild Boy of Aveyron, first published in 1801 and written before the malady had even been named (see Harlan Lane's book in Chapter 7). A number of contemporary accounts are included, such as those by Pinney, Kaufman, and Park. Perhaps such books have particular usefulness because families and classmates can see that they are not alone in their confusion and frustration with regard to an autistic child. A measure of hope is offered also in the limited but definite progress some of the children have made.

What Are the Types of Books?

There are picture books for readers of all ages, from *Someone Special, Just Like You* and *My Friend Leslie* (both for grades K–3) to *Little People*, published as an adult book. Full-length biographies and autobiographies are numerous, as well as accounts that focus on a particular period in the life of an individual or family, such as *This Is the Child* by Terry Pringle or *Silent Dancer* by Bruce Hlibok. Also included are a number of books with collected vignettes, profiles, and mini-biographies, such as *Champions by Setback: Athletes Who Overcame Physical Handicaps*. Some titles fall into the category of informational books, for example, *The Epilepsy Fact Book* by Sands and Minters, and there is one book of poetry, *The Poems of Gitanjali*.

All of the books annotated here can be read by both disabled and able-bodied people. Some, however, are specifically directed to readers with impairments—see, for example, *Sports for the Handicapped* by Allen, *Your Future: A Guide for the Handicapped Teenager* by Feingold and Miller, and *You and Leukemia* by Baker.

What Are the Themes?
Living and Coping with Disability

Not surprisingly, this is a primary theme—living and coping with a disability, one's own or another person's. Into this category fall the many personal accounts, and biographies, autobiographies, and profiles. Stories about the ingenious ways in which people have been taught new skills, as in accounts about The Seeing Eye, Inc., or have invented ways to do what they wanted to, as in Paul Brickhill's description of how he resumed work as a pilot in the Royal Air Force after a double amputation (Chapter 5), make interesting reading.

Parents and teachers have coped with the problems of disabled youngsters in creative and inventive ways, as described in books by Park, Plummer, MacCracken, Cameron, and many others. Most say that they are better people because of their struggle and that they have been given more than they gave.

Finding a Meaning to Life

Often, the person writing on the topic of disability finds or affirms a religious faith growing out of adversity or searches for a philosophy that makes life with a disability positive and meaningful. Many of the authors and their subjects testify to the belief that the disability was in some ways an enriching and strengthening experience.

Acknowledging Reality and the Negative Aspects of the Disability

Older books written for young adults, even by professional writers, are usually more descriptive and optimistic in tone, as Miers' *The Trouble Bush* illustrates. Modern writers are inclined to reveal more of their inner thoughts, and they are more self-analytic and introspective about the effects of the disability on their lives. In Segal's *The Man Who Walked in His Head*, the story of the author's life has become an allegory with inner reality more real than actual events. In *No Time to Lose*, Gary Kleiman, while positive about his life, appears to be realistically apprehensive about what his diabetes is doing to him.

To a great extent, nonfictional works have to be truthful and realistic since they are recounting real events experienced by real people, themselves or others, in the world. Books written in recent years tend to become more explicit in describing the disability, and some writers are frankly angry and resentful. On the other side, authors of nonfiction are, of course, human, and they may give accounts that, to some, may be too optimistic, oversentimental, or overzealously religious.

Some parents, like Josh Greenfeld in *A Place for Noah* and Fern Kupfer in *Before and after Zachariah*, acknowledge that life would have been much better if their children had not had disabilities. The person living with disease and disability must frequently reckon with imminent death, either her or his own or that of someone close, so these books often deal with trying to come to terms with mortality.

A decided change can be noted in the way disabled people are portrayed in photographs and drawings. Whereas once the disability might not have been pictured at all, or might have been presented so that anomalies appeared insignificant, illustrations are now often graphic and realistic. The boy in *Don't Feel Sorry for Paul* by Bernard Wolf is shown putting on his protheses, and his attenuated limbs are plainly visible; Ginny in *Feeling Free* by Mary Beth Sullivan et al. is clearly a dwarf; there is no mistaking the fact that Steven in *My Brother Steven Is Retarded* by Harriet Langsam Sobol is different physically and mentally from most teenagers. Such illustrations graphically dramatize narratives that realistically portray the negative impact of disabilities.

Such nonfictional works that are very explicit about actual disabled persons should be particularly helpful to youngsters in separating fact from fancy and inner from outer reality. Sapon-Shevin discusses the attitude in society that staring is "not polite, particularly at people who look different or who do things differently." She advocates books about differences because "it is perfectly permissible and inoffensive to study books intently; a child may want to look at a photograph of a boy wearing an artificial arm until he/she has examined every detail of the photo to his/her satisfaction."[1]

Feeling of Alienation on the Part of Disabled People and Their Families

Sometimes authors describe and exhibit alienation resulting from the disability itself and society's reaction to it. One can see Bill Kiser struggling with this in *New Light of Hope*, about his cerebral palsy. Harold Krentz, who is blind, describes himself sitting in the midst of the crowded high school cafeteria, but absolutely alone. Seidick feels that her whole family was forced into alienation by the experience of her boy's kidney dialysis and transplant. Christy Brown, who has cerebral palsy, describes his ineffable sorrow when he, as a boy looking in the mirror, found that he was not like other people.

Conflicting Attitudes toward the Medical Establishment and Other Helping Organizations

A frequent theme is the professional treatment experienced by disabled people and their families, ranging from the positive and supportive to the coldly negative. The amount of negativism still found in accounts of recent experience is surprising, although we must always be aware that what is published can never accurately reflect the experience of the entire disabled population and their families, nor the attitudes of all professionals.

Frequently parents and patients express frustration over the inability of professionals to diagnose and/or treat the problems about which they are supposed to be expert. When this is compounded by the experts' refusal to admit their powerlessness in the situation, the experience becomes truly frustrating. On the other hand, people seem particularly prone in dealing initially with a disability to seek out an expert to fix it up. Hence, the professional is often put in the untenable situation of being expected to perform the impossible, and subsequently becomes the target of great anger and hostility.

The appreciation of honesty on the part of professionals is expressed repeatedly in these books, even when the diagnosis is not reassuring—as in *This Is the Child* or in the case of Walter Thornton, who was grateful to be told immediately that he had lost his eyes in a bomb explosion.

On the other hand, a prognosis based on a diagnosis that is overly pessimistic is also reported over and over again in books written by parents of children with congenital disabilities or by disabled people themselves. For example, in *Bittersweet Triumph*, Betty Heymanns describes a doctor who examined her in early childhood and told her parents, "She'll never amount to much." Others, such as Robert Meyers's parents (*Like Normal People*) and Nicola Schaefer (*Does She Know She's There?*), were strongly advised to institutionalize their children since the youngsters were seen as hopeless cases who had no viable futures. These parents understandably lost faith in professionals who made such heartless and sometimes mistaken pronouncements, often in a cold, abrupt manner. Institutionalization is sometimes the best answer for a family, but can never be a healthy decision if roughly imposed (see Fern Kupfer's *Before and after Zachariah* for a moving account of processes of decision making).

Advances in medical research, diagnosis, and treatment have produced a different disabled population. For example, although there may be isolated cases of polio, it is no longer a health threat or a subject of current writing, but many new conditions are described. There are annotated books on kidney and heart transplants, on learning disabilities, on people who have survived leukemia and bone cancer, on life-threatening eating disorders. Some disabilities, such as cerebral palsy, have existed for centuries, but the treatment has changed dramatically over the years, as can be seen by looking at old books such as *My Left Foot*. Other disorders, such as learning disabilities, have existed but have not been recognized or have been differently understood. At the same time, conditions have persisted but often with different causes, for example, blindness, as noted earlier, that resulted from the faulty administration of oxygen to premature babies.

An old and recurrent theme is the reluctance on the part of organizations and institutions designed to serve persons with disabilities to allow them the fullest opportunity for growth and independence. In the disability area of blindness, problems have been particularly acute. This is nowhere more clearly revealed than in the several biographies of Louis Braille (by Margaret Davidson, Etta DeGering, and J. Alvin Kugelmass). The school for blind students in which Braille lived fought his ideas, even to the point of burning the books he translated into his new notation system, so that blind people could not use them. Tomi

Keitlen (*Farewell to Fear*) discusses how rehabilitation institute staff tried to discourage her from living and working in the community after she became blind. Robert Russell in *To Catch an Angel* describes the rather stifling situation in his residential school for blind children. David Hartman (*White Coat, White Cane*) was rejected by many medical schools due to his blindness before he was finally accepted by Temple University.

In the area of hearing impairment, there is, of course, a controversy that has raged for years regarding the relative value of the oral and manual approaches to communication. Professionals who have looked first at their philosophies rather than at the needs and talents of children have been chided by writers such as the Spradleys (*Deaf Like Me*) and Arden Neisser (*The Other Side of Silence*). The Spradleys believe that deaf children who are discouraged from using sign are denied access to their native language.

Individuals who have had to undergo long hospitalization, often because of spinal cord injury, speak of the insensitivity and bureaucratic structure of medical facilities. According to Segal (*The Man Who Walked in His Head*), even when physical care is excellent (and it is not always described as such), there may be a demeaning of the patient due to a subtly patronizing attitude. Jonathan Nasaw, in *Easy Walking*, describes sharply different facilities in which he was hospitalized. Ron Kovic, author of *Born on the Fourth of July*, relates the unsanitary conditions and negligence of patient care in a veterans' hospital during the Vietnam era. (Other writers have very positive remarks, such as those whose experiences involved the Institute of Rehabilitation Medicine, founded by Dr. Howard Rusk.)

A particular insensitivity to hospitalized children is noted by parents over and over, as in Beverly Plummer's *Give Every Day a Chance*. While the quality of care has certainly improved since her child with osteogenesis imperfecta endured so many lonely and painful hours in hospital rooms, a lack of acknowledgment of the suffering of children is still reported. The insensitivity and senselessness of some medical bureaucracies is nowhere more scathingly reported than in *Kids Called Crazy* with its description of a mental hospital.

Parents write about years-long quests to get their children admitted to schools and to secure the right kind of education. Schooling for retarded children has improved since the days described by Anderson in *Don't Forget Me, Mommy*, but the present-day difficulties related by Agress ("*Why Me?*") and by Jablow (*Cara*), whose child with Down's syndrome tested too high for a special-education program, reveal that problems relating to the educational bureaucracy still exist. Even when a condition has virtually no educational significance, as with Eric's hemophilia in *Journey*, school people are often reluctant to get involved.

Disabled Persons as Full Members of Society

Many books explore interacting with and understanding the disabled person in school, in the family, and in a therapeutic setting. A number of works for young readers fall into this category, such as *The New Boy Is Blind* by William E. Thomas.

A pervasive motif is the belief that people are more alike than different, that all people have flaws and disabilities to some degree, and that even the person with the most severe disability can contribute to those around her or him and to society at large. This motif can be found whether writers are angry or accepting, whether they are actively critical of attitudes expressed by society and professionals or have had positive experiences, and whether the disabling condition has improved or has even led to death.

Reflections of Social Change

In surveying the literature of the past 40 and more years, it is fascinating to see the way in which it reflects fundamental changes in the diagnosis, management, and incidence of disabilities, as well as in personal and societal attitudes toward them. The emphasis on mainstreaming children in public schools and the trend toward caring for disabled children at home where possible have created a more general interest in the subject of disabilities; this is reflected in the increasing number of books on the topic. The effect of such changes can also be seen in the expanded audience and new approaches. Some 20 years ago, one would have looked in vain for books that introduced young children to disabled youngsters, as do *My Friend Leslie* by Rosenberg, *What If You Couldn't* by Kamien, *Janet at School* by White, and others. Most of the writing in this area approaches the subject with sensitivity and honesty. The best books recognize the natural anxiety of children when confronted with anomalies; in conveying information clearly, calmly, and honestly, they foster understanding. At the same time, heightened consciousness on the part of disabled people and their friends has led to more emphasis on the rights of this segment of the population. One can see this in public life, in the gradual increase of facilities and access for people with disabilities (although much still needs to be done in this area), and in literature, in books such as *We Are People First* by Jean Parker Edwards.

Terminology Changes

As noted in Chapter 2, the use of terminology to describe people with differences is more than a matter of taste. Professionals in special education and rehabilitation feel strongly that a pejorative label can have a very negative effect on a disabled person and on social attitudes and practices generally.[2] Terminology related to the field is still a problem. In this book, we prefer to talk about "people with disabilities" rather than "people with handicaps or exceptionalities," but these words do appear in titles and texts of the books reviewed. Similarly, we prefer "disability" and "impairment" to "handicap," and try never to use such words as nouns, but some books do refer to "the blind, the deaf, or the disabled." Mention of some of these linguistic shortcomings, including sexist expressions, is noted in the annotations.

Notes

1. Mara Sapon-Shevin, "Teaching Children about Differences: Resources for Teaching," *Young Children* 38 (January 1983): 24–31.
2. James J. Gallagher, "The Sacred and Profane Uses of Labeling," *Mental Retardation* 14 (December 1976): 3–7; Nicholas C. Hobbs, ed., *Issues in the Classification of Children*, 2 vols. (San Francisco: Jossey-Bass, 1976); Norman C. Hooge, "Labeling in the Counseling Process," *Journal of Applied Rehabilitation Counseling* 8 (Summer 1977): 84–88; Gerald I. Manus, "Is Your Language Disabling?" *Journal of Rehabilitation* 41 (September–October 1975): 35; J. R. Mercer, "Institutionalized Anglocentrism: Labeling Mental Retardates in the Public Schools," in *Race, Change, and Urban Society*, ed. by P. Orleans and W. R. Eliss (Los Angeles: Sage, 1971); Laurence Severence and L. L. Gasstrom, "Effects of the Label 'Mentally Retarded' on Causal Explanations for Success and Failure Outcomes," *American Journal of Mental Deficiency* 81 (May 1977): 547–555.

5

Books Dealing with Physical Problems

This chapter classifies titles in two sections: Health Problems and Orthopedic/Neurological Disabilities.

■ Citations are alphabetical by author in each of these two main sections.

■ Among the disorders dealt with in books annotated under Health Problems are allergies, cancer, eating disorders, heart problems, hemophilia, and kidney disease.

■ Books annotated in the Orthopedic/Neurological Disabilities section focus on conditions such as cerebral palsy, epilepsy, paraplegia, and spina bifida.

■ Bear in mind that there is inherent overlapping of subjects between the two main sections. A book about a person who has had an amputation because of cancer, for instance, is usually annotated in the first section, Health Problems; a book telling of someone who had a leg amputated due to injury or perhaps birth defect is listed in the second section, Orthopedic/Neurological Disabilities.

Health Problems

Baker, Lynn S., in collaboration with Charles G. Roland and Gerald S. Gilchrist. *You and Leukemia: A Day at a Time.* Illus. by the author. Philadelphia: Saunders, 1978. 205 pp. Reading Level: Grades 4–9.
Disability: Leukemia

Baker was a third-year medical student at Mayo Medical School when she wrote this book in collaboration with Gilchrist, consultant in Pediatric Hematology and Oncology at the Mayo Clinic, and Roland, professor of the History of Medicine at McMaster University. Addressed to the young person with leukemia, the book gives clear information not only to the patient, but indirectly to parents, nurses, social workers, and teachers who work with families with leukemic members.

The author begins by describing the body, paying detailed attention to the blood. She discusses leukemia, its possible causes and different manifestations, diagnosis, treatment, and complications. The third chapter is subtitled "Living with Leukemia." The chapter on treatment describes chemotherapy, spinal taps, radiation therapy, blood transfusions, bone marrow transplants, and immunotherapy.

A bibliography suggests further reading. There is a glossary and an index. Black-and-white drawings illustrate the text. At certain points, Baker leaves blank pages, inviting the young reader to note such things as a list of clinic friends or new drugs.

Analysis. Baker approaches both subject and audience with tact, compassion, humor, and understanding. Without overestimating the ability of the young reader to understand difficult material, she presents a tremendous body of information with admirable clarity in a tone that is informal and warm, yet never condescending or sentimental. Nor does she underestimate the severity of the disease or the possibility that it may cut life short. At the same time, the variety of treatments available and the evidence that researchers are constantly at work offer reassurance and a realistic basis for optimism. Baker emphasizes that it is best to take life "a day at a time." Her line drawings are lighthearted and casual, at the same time presenting detailed information clearly. The same freckle-faced youngster appears throughout. Although work in the field has added to what is known about leukemia and its treatment since the date of publication, this is a valuable book for patients, families, and professionals.

Brady, Mari. *Please Remember Me.* New York: Doubleday, 1977. 104 pp. Reading Level: Grades 7–12.
Disability: Cancer

The author accepted as her first job a position in the recreation department of a cancer center. She and two other young women were responsible for planning activities for and boosting the morale of an entire floor of cancer patients. She first met tall, well-built Graham Banks shortly before Christmas when he entered for preliminary tests, after which he returned home to his studies and high school football team. Gradually, however, his brief visits stretched into longer stays as he began to undergo treatments during the ensuing year. As his friendship with Brady warmed, Banks confided that he had cancer in his lymph system and would undergo surgery. Chemotherapy treatments followed with subsequent nausea and loss of hair.

The course of Banks's cancer was irreversible, and he was finally faced with the loss of his battle to fight the disease and the inevitability of death. He and Brady also had to help his mother accept those realities. Brady confided to the young man that she had lost a brother to cancer. In an effort to help someone else through his death, Graham Banks wrote to a drug-addicted cousin urging him not to throw his life away. The next day he left the cancer center on a stretcher, frail and weak, but happy to be going home for Christmas. He hugged his friend and asked Brady to remember him. He died on December 23 at the age of 16.

Analysis. Brady is a careful observer who takes the reader through the stages faced by a terminally ill person. Her own reactions to the painful situations described are somewhat veiled, and the prose consequently muted.

This book might appeal to "turned-off" young people or those who have become overdependent on drugs or alcohol, because of Banks's struggle and his impassioned deathbed letter.

Bruce, Shelley. *Tomorrow Is Today.* Illus. Indianapolis: Bobbs-Merrill, 1983. 224 pp. Reading Level: Grades 7–12.
Disability: Leukemia

Child actress Shelley Bruce started her career in the role of an orphan with one line in the Broadway production of *Annie,* and eventually achieved the starring role in the play. At the height of her success, she developed leukemia. Bruce tells not only the story of her illness, but also the story of her life in the theater, particularly her work in the highly successful *Annie.* At the time of the writing of this book, she was in remission and had resumed her career.

Black-and-white pictures highlight Bruce's career and life.

Analysis. Bruce is a role model of pluck and courage. The book is full of stories about the theater and of Bruce's coping strategies, determination, courage, and zest for life.

Burns, Sheila L. *Allergies and You.* Illus. New York: Messner, 1980. Reading Level: Grades 4–6.
Disability: Allergies

Beginning with a fictional sketch about a boy who is asked by his doctor to make notes that track his coldlike symptoms, Burns defines allergy and discusses the varieties of allergens and how they can be found. She devotes a chapter each to food allergies, contact allergies, and asthma. The last chapter discusses allergy shots. The book concludes with a glossary, a list of sources of information, and an index.

Included are black-and-white photographs and drawings. Key words, such as *immune system* and *allergy*, are printed in heavier type.

Analysis. Burns's text is clear and readable. The chapters are short and the sketches of two fictional allergy patients add interest, as do the many illustrations. Without condescending to young readers, the author has written a book that should be useful to a general audience as well as to youngsters who have allergies.

Burns, Sheila L. *Cancer: Understanding and Fighting It.* Illus. New York: Messner, 1982. 62 pp. Reading Level: Grades 6–8.
Disability: Cancer

Burns begins with a child's overhearing her mother and aunt whispering about her grandmother's lab report, which has shown cancer. They are trying to keep the diagnosis from Mary Ann, but the grandmother is more forthcoming and includes the girl in her visit to the doctor so that he and his assistant can answer Mary Ann's questions. The text then moves to a discussion of cells, both normal and cancerous; causes and treatment of cancer are also described. The book ends with a list of organizations offering information and support, a glossary, and a short index.

Analysis. The story of Mary Ann and her grandmother provides a reasonable frame for the book, making the information more personalized. Scientific explanations are clear and the diagrams helpful. In a couple of places, the photos do not show exactly what is described in the text.

Center for Attitudinal Healing, Tiburon, Calif. *There Is a Rainbow behind Every Dark Cloud.* Illus. Millbrae, Calif.: Celestial Arts, 1978. 96 pp. Reading Level: Grades 4–12.
Disability: Various health impairments

Written and illustrated by eleven children, 8 to 19 years of age, this book records their experiences in a support group for young people facing life-and-death situations due to illnesses. Part I, "What We Experienced," is divided into seven chapters that cover such topics as "Before We Got Sick," "Seeing the Doctor for the First Time," "Going to the Hospital," and "Hearing the News." Part II, "Choices You Have in Helping Yourself," is divided into seven chapters also and deals with such practical therapeutic activities as "Things You Can Do about Your Feelings," "Using Your Imagination to Help Yourself," "Talking about Death Can Help," and "Praying Can Help."

Each chapter is introduced by a brief paragraph; the rest of each chapter consists of captioned drawings by the children centered around the chapter topic. These black-and-white line drawings by the children are entertaining, humorous, touching, and sad, and all very honest.

Analysis. This unique book is "the result of group meetings of children who had to face life and death situations because of their illness. . . . We think healing or 'getting well' means being happy and peaceful inside. We think healing takes place when we feel nothing but love inside and when we are no longer scared or feeling bad about anything. . . . The adult volunteers and children have been equally interested in healing themselves by finding ways of getting rid of their fears" (p. 3). The book would be useful both to children facing similar situations and to adults working with young people in a medical or therapeutic setting.

Claypool, Jane, and Cheryl Diane Nelsen. *Food Trips and Traps: Coping with Eating Disorders.* New York: Franklin Watts, 1983. 90 pp. Reading Level: Grades 7–12.
Disability: Eating disorders

Compulsive eating, bulimia, and anorexia nervosa are now major behavioral disorders among junior and senior high school students, about 90 percent of them female. The authors explain the symptoms, causes, and treatments. A section entitled "For Further Information and Reading" provides a list of research groups and institutions offering therapy, a list of support groups, and a bibliography of books, articles, pamphlets, and newsletters dealing with eating disorders. There is also a brief name-subject index.

Analysis. The authors employ a straightforward, factual approach and concentrate on giving information about eating disorders in a logical, organized, clear fashion. Value judgments are avoided; the emphasis is on the nature and treatment of the disorders and on how they are harmful to health. The subject is complex, and the treatment here is of necessity relatively superficial, but this is an excellent introduction to the topic and could be used by good readers below seventh grade.

Coerr, Eleanor. *Sadako and the Thousand Paper Cranes.* Illus. by Ronald Himler. New York: Putnam's, 1977. 63 pp. Reading Level: Grades K–6.
Disability: Leukemia

This simply written story is based on the life of a Japanese girl, Sadako Sasaki, who lived from 1943 to 1955. The nine chapters describe her last year of life. In Hiroshima when the atom bomb was dropped on that city, she died of leukemia, the "atom bomb" disease. After her death, her schoolmates from her bamboo class published Sadako's letters, which included an account of her effort to make one thousand paper cranes; she thought that might cause the gods to grant her health again. Sadako is first shown as a vigorous, healthy member of a devoted family, her cherished dream being to qualify for the relay racing team. Japanese concepts and customs are depicted, with memory of the atomic bombings and the desire for peace ever present. As Sadako's illness proceeds, she is confronted with situations common to many dying children. No one answers her explicit question, "Am I dying?" The book touches on the medical procedures, loneliness, and pain experienced by the dying child, as well as the bittersweet comfort of family, friends, and occasional remissions.

Sadako's story parallels the story of the destroyed city. Like the destruction rained by the bomb, the cancer it later caused inexorably takes the life of its young and vibrant victim. The paper cranes, like the Peace Park and Peace Day celebration, embody hope. The epilogue describes how young people throughout Japan collected money for a statue of Sadako, who is shown standing on top of a granite mountain of paradise holding a golden crane; the statue was unveiled in the Hiroshima Peace Park in 1958.

Analysis. Sadako's fears, despair, and eventual reconciliation with her fate are simply and poignantly detailed. The reader can find catharsis in her peaceful death, as she contemplates the love of her family. The epilogue moves the reader to see the beauty rather than the painfulness of Sadako's brief life. The illustrations are of high quality, although they lose much in the paperback edition; they heighten the effect of another cultural milieu, but do not distance the reader from Sadako and her plight.

Since the book deals with issues of life and death and wanton destruction, it may be best read by younger children only when an adult is present. For example, a child might need reassurance that not all sick children must anticipate an early death, that leukemia is not catching, that the destruction of her or his city is not inevitable. *Sadako* might be a helpful story for a class or family to read when they have experienced the loss of a child. It portrays forthrightly the predicament of a sick child who has had to accept the inevitability of an early death, and yet concentrates on her life until the end.

Connelly, John P., and Leonard Berlow. *You're Too Sweet: A Guide for the Young Diabetic.* Illus. New York: Astor-Honor, 1968. 61 pp. Reading Level: Grades 4–9.
Disability: Diabetes

Nine-year-old Billy Rodgers has just been told by his doctor that he has diabetes. Short chapters take the reader from Billy's initial symptoms through the doctor's detailed explanation of his disease and a description of its treatment. On his first visit to the doctor, Billy learns to give himself his insulin shot and how to take care of himself. The doctor has told him about insulin reaction, and a brief chapter describes Billy's experience with dizziness and weakness after he has eaten too little breakfast and played hard at recess.

Line drawings in black, green, and white illustrate the text; a series of ten sketches shows how to prepare and administer an insulin shot. A quiz with answers and a list suggesting additional reading conclude the book.

Analysis. Although there is a certain degree of artificiality in some of the conversations, which carry a great deal of information in a short space, the authors have done an effective job of covering the subject. At the time of writing, Connelly was pediatrician to and Chief of Children's Service at the Massachusetts General Hospital and a professor of pediatrics at Harvard Medical School; Berlow was Chief, Administrative Office, Department of Pathology, Armed Forces Institute of Pathology. The explanation of the cause, manifestations, and treatment of diabetes is careful and clear. However, although Billy's doctor tells him in detail about his medication and advises him about exercise and hygiene, the suggestions about diet are more general; the text might well have included a sample diet, such as the one the doctor gives Billy's mother in the story. The book has good information for children and adults, and it could be read aloud to young children, those with diabetes and those without. Since the book was written in 1968, some of the information might be dated.

> Covelli, Pat. *Borrowing Time: Growing Up with Juvenile Diabetes.* New York: Crowell, 1979. 160 pp. Reading Level: Grades 10–12.
> *Disability:* Diabetes

The author states in the preface that he has written this book to be of help to people who must face the physical and psychological facts of diabetes. The story begins when he was ten years old and, unknowingly, heading toward diabetic coma. His gradually deteriorating condition was characterized by weakness, constant urination, thirst, hunger, and weight loss, due to the fact that his pancreas had stopped producing the insulin needed for his body to metabolize sugar. In short, he was starving to death. He writes, "I believe I lost my boyhood forever the day we went to the doctor. I state it that way without regret or a sense of loss. On that day, one life ended and a new one began" (p. 19). Hence, he joined the ranks of one million children with juvenile diabetes in the United States.

After completing high school, Covelli went off to college, battling his disease and ignorant professionals, all the while facing the more universal struggles of youth striving toward independence and adulthood. With college completed, he set out to pursue a career in writing, always challenged by medical complications, exacerbated by his diabetes. The book ends with an account of his youthful romance with the girl who becomes his wife and the mother of his child. Armed with his hard-won philosophy of life, he states, "I have seen the possibility of great pain in the future. I have been given great joy in the present. I have found myself, and I am content" (p. 160).

Analysis. As this book well illustrates, diabetes is not a disease that affects all people in the same way. The author had more severe and earlier onset complications than most. For him, reduced life-span, progressive deterioration of vision, and possible amputations are probable medical realities. "No one seems to have bothered to write about problems like these," he says (p. 155). He emphasizes emotional concerns and fears related to diabetes. His prose is explicit with regard to medical encounters. For example, he describes in bloody detail the removal of his brittle teeth and the disastrous treatment of a plantar's wart on the bottom of his foot.

Covelli has faced his problems head on and has been able to reach an optimistic philosophy of life. His energetic style allows the reader to share in his physical and spiritual struggles, and to care about their resolution.

Cunningham, Glenn, with George X. Sand. *Never Quit.* Illus. Lincoln, Va.: Chosen Books, 1981. 143 pp. Reading Level: Grades 7–12. *Disability:* Burns

The authors begin with a chapter about a troubled, defiant boy who comes to Cunningham's ranch; Cunningham helps him to win a race. Then follows a chronological account of Cunningham's life. Most of the book is devoted to his boyhood; the final chapters take the reader quickly through the Olympics of 1932 and 1936 and Cunningham's subsequent career.

Glenn Cunningham was born in the Midwest in 1910 and grew up in Kansas. When he was seven, he and one of his older brothers were severely burned in a fire that began in the schoolhouse stove. His brother died nine days later. Glenn lay in bed for months with legs so badly burned and infected that the doctor thought they might have to be amputated. His parents, poor, hardworking, determined people, refused to give up or let their son become an invalid. His father's philosophy is expressed in the book's title: Never quit. Eventually, their care and support and Cunningham's own persistence and self-discipline got him out of bed and on his feet. He learned to walk again, and then to run.

Cunningham had shown signs of ability as a runner before the accident, although his father had always discouraged the idea of running for show. In high school, he entered his first athletic competition without his father's knowledge; he was so green he did not even know that he had to break the tape at the end of the track to win. Still in high school, he set a record for the interscholastic mile. College scholarship offers followed, and so did the Depression of 1929. Cunningham refused to accept scholarship money, and worked his way through the University of Kansas. He competed in the 1932 Olympics in Los Angeles, coming in fourth even though he was running with a bad case of tonsillitis. In the 1936 Olympics in Berlin, he won a silver medal, breaking the Olympic record for the mile, although a man from New Zealand ran faster and won the gold. Throughout his racing career, Cunningham was plagued with pain in his badly scarred legs, the result not only of his early injuries but, as it was eventually discovered, of teeth that had been abscessed for years.

After he stopped competitive running, Cunningham's search for meaningful activities led him to teaching. He and his second wife turned their Kansas ranch into a haven for homeless youngsters, and have operated it for over 30 years for the benefit of hundreds of children. The Cunninghams had ten children of their own. In 1979 Cunningham was given an award as "outstanding track performer of the century."

Black-and-white photographs show Cunningham in his athletic life and on the ranch.

Analysis. Cunningham's book is interesting not only as the story of superb athletic achievements and the conquering of physical disability and pain, but as a picture of life on the midwestern plains earlier in this century. The anecdotes are appealing and bring Cunningham's family life and other experiences to the reader in lively fashion, particularly in the sections about his childhood and young manhood. Although he does not minimize the magnitude of his challenges and accomplishments, his tone is modest and appealing. He and his wife both feel strongly the influence of religion in their lives, but this is in no way an evangelical book.

D'Ambrosio, Richard Anthony. *No Language but a Cry.* New York: Doubleday, 1970. 252 pp. Reading Level: Grades 10–12.
Disability: Burns

This is the story of Laura, who was actually fried alive in a pan at age one and a half by her mentally ill and alcoholic parents. Charred over half of her body, she was institutionalized and cared for by nuns. The author first met her when he was a young psychoanalyst called in for consultation. Laura was hunched, scarred, ugly, and fearful. She did not speak although she was 12 years old, but she always attended classes with the other children in the institution.

Hundreds of therapeutic sessions led to a gradual unfolding of Laura's personality. It was many months before she spoke her first words in play therapy, "No, I hate her" (about her mother), but it was evident that she had profited from attending school and being treated like the other children. Laura underwent operations to improve her looks and straighten her body. She finally met her parents individually and came to terms with her feelings about the suffering she had endured. After another operation (on varicose veins), she graduated from the institution's high school, ready to embark on a career of nursing. D'Ambrosio said a bittersweet goodbye to Laura and the cadre of nuns who had done so much to save her. "I likened Laura in my mind to one of those graceful palm trees that bend with the wind, but return upright when the storm is over."

Analysis. The author modestly states that this is a story about Laura and the faith of a group of maverick nuns. However, he is a vital influence in the rehabilitation of a child who had suffered so horrifically. D'Ambrosio was the first person Laura ever trusted. In a prologue he discusses the special problems of city people suffering from poverty, social deprivation, and abuse. The book is fairly long and the literary style requires good reading ability, but the account of Laura's progress is told with compassion and wry humor.

Davidson, Bill, and the Coleman Family. *Gary Coleman: Medical Miracle.* Illus. New York: Coward, 1981. 236 pp. Reading Level: Grades 7–12.
Disability: Kidney disease

Gary Coleman, a well-known television actor, was born in 1968 with obstructive disease of the ureter tubular system, a condition not discovered until he was hospitalized with pneumonia at 22 months. Surgery revealed an atrophied right kidney and a damaged left kidney in addition to the twisted tubes. The surgeon disconnected the tubes and ran them from the kidney to surgical openings in the baby's sides. A second operation closed these openings and made a new one in the lower abdomen; the surgeons extended the ureter, brought it to the opening, and arranged it to drain into a plastic pouch fixed to the skin.

From the first, the doctors and the Colemans anticipated the need for a kidney transplant, which took place successfully in 1973 when Gary was five. Since that time, aided by medication, diet, and careful monitoring, Gary Coleman has had effective kidney functioning. For reasons not yet clearly understood but that include both the disease and the steroids necessary to keep the organ, most children do not grow well after a kidney transplant; at age 12, Coleman was under 4 feet tall. Puberty is often delayed in such patients, and sometimes brings a growth spurt, so he may achieve a more normal height by maturity.

This book is the story not only of Gary Coleman's disease and its treatment but of his parents' lives and his professional career, starting as a model. Four voices—those of Davidson, Gary, and his parents, Willie and Sue Coleman—carry the narrative. Black-and-white photographs illustrate the text.

Analysis. Gary Coleman's medical history is clearly told, especially in the sections by Davidson and by Sue Coleman, a licensed practical nurse. Gary gives some of his reactions to his disease and its treatment and to his small stature, as well as to his life as a star. The book also details the Colemans' road from their beginnings in the tough and restricted world of Southern blacks to their present affluence and success. Their essential personalities and reactions are usually credible.

Deford, Frank. *Alex, the Life of a Child.* New York: Viking, 1983. 196 pp. Reading Level: Grades 10–12.
Disability: Cystic fibrosis

Alex Deford was born in 1971 and died of cystic fibrosis in 1980. This is the story of her life, her disease, her dying. It is also the story of her family and friends, the effect on them of her illness, and her extraordinary character. Frank Deford, a professional writer, kept a diary about both his children, and thus had a detailed record of Alex's brief life. Her illness was diagnosed in infancy, and, after some unsatisfactory experiences with other doctors and hospitals, she was cared for by a physician at Grace–New Haven Hospital. Treatment included hospital stays when necessary, medication, and daily pounding sessions when her parents literally had to beat on her frail body to help her expel deadly mucous. As much as possible, Alex lived the life of a healthy child, taking ballet, going to school, playing games, arraying herself in her beloved dress-up clothes, being part of a close family. As the disease attacked her system with ever-increasing ferocity, involving more of her organs, her life became more and more restricted. Like many fatally ill children, she understood the inevitable outcome without being told.

Analysis. Deford's account of his daughter's life is moving, painful, and honest. He includes his despair, his anger, and the times he wanted simply to run away. He describes both Alex's extraordinary spirit, gallant and joyous, and the times when she acted very much like a sick child. Information about the disease—its causes, symptoms, and progressive course—is given informally in the course of the narrative. However, in discussing the hereditary factor, Deford does not make clear that when a couple has had a child with cystic fibrosis, there is a one-in-four chance in each subsequent pregnancy of having another child with cystic fibrosis.

Chronology moves back and forth effectively; the book begins with Alex's death and ends with her death followed by the Defords' adoption of an infant girl from the Philippines. Deford includes scenes of almost unbearable poignancy—for example, a description of a moment when, after a romping game together, Alex turned to him and said, "Oh, Daddy, wouldn't it have been great?"

Frevert, Patricia Dendtler. *Patty Gets Well.* Illus. Mankato, Minn.: Creative Education, 1983. 47 pp. Reading Level: Grades 4–9.
Disability: Leukemia

When Patty Ness was 10 years old, she caught repeated colds. Doctors diagnosed her illness as "acute leukemia of childhood" and immediately began a program of chemotherapy to which radiation therapy was added some weeks later. She was hospitalized initially and again when she had a bacterial infection, but most of her treatment was given on an outpatient basis. Although she missed many days of school because of illness and her treatment, she kept up with her class and did well. Her successful treatments ended when she was 13, although blood tests and bone marrow biopsies would continue in order to monitor her condition. When she was in tenth grade, her doctor asked her to participate in a program sponsored by the American Cancer Society to help teachers and school nurses understand the experience of children with cancer, and she told her story to many groups. Frevert's narrative includes a description of the way Patty's illness was handled by her parents and its effect on the sister closest to her in age.

The author frames her account with pictures of Patty at 18, healthy, active, and preparing to enter college. The emphasis throughout is on leukemia as a treatable disease. Frevert does not omit reference to its life-threatening characteristics or to the difficulties associated with treatment; for example, Patty's hair fell out and for a while she wore a wig—this is pointed out in a family photograph. But her doctor and her parents believed she would get well and effectively conveyed this to Patty. Her doctor would ask her what she wanted to be when she grew up—"Patty loved that question. It meant he believed she *would* grow up" (p. 44). She always answered that she wanted to be a doctor, an ambition still held at the end of the narrative.

The book has black-and-white photographs, some illustrating technical matters, most relating to Patty and her large family.

Analysis. Despite its subject, this is a cheerful, optimistic book. Frevert emphasizes the extent to which treatment of leukemia has improved chances of survival: in 1973, about eight out of ten children with Patty's disease died within five years; ten years later, six out of ten children would "get better and stay better" (p. 26). Although many children are not as fortunate as Patty, this account is a valuable addition to the literature about leukemia and could be recommended to a general audience as well as to youngsters who are being treated for a serious illness.

Gitanjali. *The Poems of Gitanjali.* Stockfield, Northumberland, England: Oriel Press, 1982. 155 pp. Reading Level: Grades 10–12.
Disability: Cancer

Gitanjali, named after the book *Gitanjali* by the Indian poet Rabindranath Tagore, died of cancer at the age of 16 in 1977. After her death, her mother found poems that she had written and hidden in her room; she sent them to the editor of the poetry page of the *Illustrated Weekly of India.* Some time after a selection appeared in the paper, the rest of the poems were collected and published. They are the work of a young woman suffering great pain, aware that death is imminent, and unwilling to share this knowledge with her parents because she did not want to increase their anguish.

Analysis. The force of Gitanjali's work comes not so much from the poetics as from its content. Sometimes pleading for rest, sometimes sounding the note of courage, sometimes wistful, her voice speaks to the reader with powerful authenticity. Whatever her regrets, by the time she writes most of the poems, she has accepted both her pain and her death, though she still grieves not only for her own truncated life, but for the sorrow of her parents. The book might be shared in families facing or undergoing similar experiences, although its audience need not be limited to such readers. Classroom teachers could use the book as a springboard for encouraging young people to write poetry about things that matter to them.

Gunther, John. *Death Be Not Proud.* New York: Pyramid, 1963. 192 pp. Reading Level: Grades 7–12.
Disability: Cancer (malignant brain tumor)

John Gunther, Jr., son of the well-known author, was a gifted and witty boy with a zest for life. When he was 15 years old, he suddenly became ill from a brain tumor that was to take his life 15 months later. John Gunther wrote a memoir of his son "not so much . . . in the conventional sense as the story of a long, courageous struggle between a child and death" (p. 9). He wrote it, he said, for other afflicted children and their parents, to give them succor and strength.

Gunther recounts the events surrounding the initial diagnosis, the operations, the excruciating medical procedures ordered by over 30 specialists. While this is first a story of the boy's reactions, gradual deterioration, and wrestling with death, it is also the cathartic work of a father who relives the terrible, psychological roller coaster of the parent who stands by in hope, fear, and helplessness, in the face of a child's terminal illness. He asked, "Where was justice?"

As the hospitalization, remissions, and medical setbacks progress inexorably toward death, the young Gunther struggles valiantly to do what most children so easily do—keep up with school work, albeit by correspondence and tutors in his case. Literally his finest and last triumph is to return to his beloved Deerfield Academy to participate in the graduation ceremonies. His father writes: "Everything that Johnny suffered was in a sense repaid by the few heroic moments of that walk down the outer aisle of that church. Nobody who saw it will ever forget it, or be able to forget the sublime strength of will and character it took" (p. 127).

The book has an appendix of the young man's letters and diaries, and a final word from his mother.

Analysis. This is a moving story about the life struggles of a gifted boy from a privileged class. Young readers would identify with the boy himself, while older readers might feel closer to the parent's agony. The memorial John Gunther wrote must have been helpful to those young classmates from Deerfield Academy so many years ago. There is evidence in the story that young John himself did not want to discuss his illness and bring the reality of his dying painfully to the fore. Rather, he focused his limited energy toward living every moment still available to him to its fullest.

Haines, Gail Kay. *Cancer.* Illus. New York: Franklin Watts, 1980. 64 pp. Reading Level: Grades 7–9.
Disability: Cancer

In 11 short chapters, Haines examines such topics as the functioning operation of cancerous cells, the diseases that result from them, types of cancer, treatments, and research. Black-and-white photographs illustrate some of the conditions described. The book contains a glossary, a short bibliography, and an index.

Analysis. Haines writes with clarity and directness. Fictional case studies individualize the illnesses, treatment, and outcomes described;

she does not shrink from honestly confronting the high death rate despite constantly improving methods of treatment. The final chapters—"Research: Fight for the Future" and "Cancer and You"—leave young readers with a sense of hope and the knowledge that they have some control, especially if they heed the author's advice about smoking, diet, chemicals, X rays, exposure to sun, personal hygiene, and seeking expert medical care if illness strikes.

Hamilton, Marguerite. *Red Shoes for Nancy*. Philadelphia: Lippincott, 1955. 224 pp. Reading Level: Grades 7–12.
Disability: Lymphohemangioma

Hamilton writes about her daughter, Nancy, born with a rare congenital disease that affects the blood and lymphatic vessels. She had swollen and deformed legs and feet, and the disease was progressive, requiring extensive medical treatment and surgery. Both the medical expenses and the wrenching emotional trauma seemed unbearable, doubly so because Hamilton faced them as a single parent; her husband had been killed in an automobile accident three months before Nancy's birth. Hamilton found solace and comfort in the Roman Catholic Church, and both she and Nancy eventually became devout Catholics. In addition, they were helped by many people in the Santa Monica, California, area where they lived, after Nancy's condition was publicized in the newspapers. Nancy had always wanted shoes, and when she was fitted for a prothesis after surgery to remove her leg, she selected a pair of red shoes, which she was never able to wear because her condition quickly worsened, but she kept them beside her bed. Her mother sees them as a symbol of the child's hope and courage. By the age of 12, Nancy's other leg was removed in her fortieth operation since birth. Her condition, however, continued to deteriorate, and by the end of the book, the swelling and deformity have spread to her hips and abdomen.

An interesting sidelight is the friendship the Hamiltons developed with people who at one time were their closest neighbors, movie stars Roy Rogers and Dale Evans Rogers. The Rogers's third child, Robin, was described by Hamilton as "not well." Robin's death at the age of two was a great grief for Nancy and her mother. Dale Evans Rogers told Hamilton that she would be writing a book about the baby, later published as *Angel Unaware* (see Rogers, Ch. 7, p. 282). Robin was born with Down's syndrome (although Hamilton does not identify the disability) and died as a result of physical complications.

Analysis. This is a touching and tragic story. Although Nancy is alive at the end of the book, Hamilton makes it painfully clear that her daughter's death is imminent. Both mother and daughter find peace and solace through their faith and are able to accept the obvious. There are many happy moments in this story, told vividly and in detail, although paramount is the theme of the never-ending search for a cure.

Heater, Sandra H. *Am I Still Visible?* White Hall, Va.: White Hall Books, 1983. 140 pp. Reading Level: Grades 10–12.
Disability: Anorexia nervosa, Bulimia

The author developed the symptoms of anorexia nervosa, the potentially fatal disorder of willful starvation, when she was 27, a wife, a teacher, and the mother of two small daughters. She divides the book into three sections: an account of her childhood and early adulthood, with comments on the "psychological and emotional developments that led to the onset of anorexia nervosa"; a narrative of the course of the disease, its effects on her and on her family, medical and psychiatric treatment, and her recovery; and a section on research and treatment, including material that appeared in her doctoral dissertation. She concludes with a brief epilogue and an extensive bibliography.

Although Heater developed anorexia nervosa later than is typical, she exhibited earlier many of the behaviors and thought patterns characteristic of the disease. She was a top student in school, a hallmark of anorexics, who are so devoid of feelings of self-worth that only perfection makes them feel acceptable to others. She describes a small-town middle-class upbringing with the struggles and conflicts typical for a girl of the 1950s. One conflict often shared by anorexics grew from her inhibitions, fears, and ignorance in the area of sexuality; another typical characteristic was her vague dissatisfaction with her physical appearance, although she was very attractive. In college she was part of a generation of women caught on the fringe of culture change, enmeshed in the Victorian morality of their mothers and grandmothers, but swept into the new behavioral patterns of the space age. She had an illegal abortion the day after her wedding, which took place only because of her pregnancy. At 25 her apparently innocuous dieting and exercise led to what she calls her "fall" with self-starvation, compulsive physical activity, and occasional bulimia (eating binges and purges). She did not recognize or know the name of her illness until some time after it began, nor did the professionals she consulted in 1969 and 1970 identify her condition. Although she was helped to return to health and life by her family and doctors, ultimately the decision to begin to eat came, as it always must, from the patient herself. The path back was not smooth or easy, and in fact Heater suggests that a recovered anorexic is rather like a recovered alcoholic, in that the potential for relapse is always present.

Analysis. Heater's account of her life and her illness is fluent, readable, and honest. In examining the etiology of her illness, she refrains from making accusations or heaping guilt on either herself or the members of her loving, close-knit family. One area that she does not examine very closely, however, is the possible effect of guilt over her abortion on the development of her disease. She has written the book to help others understand the course of the illness and to offer the encouragement that comes from her own "hard-won triumph" (p. xi). The section on research and treatment is objective and professional.

Ipswitch, Elaine. *Scott Was Here.* Illus. New York: Delacorte, 1979. 210 pp. Reading Level: Grades 10–12.
Disability: Hodgkin's disease

The author, Scott's mother, writes this book about her son, incorporating his diaries and notes. When Scott was ten years old, he was diagnosed as having Hodgkin's disease in stage four, the most advanced. Although doctors expected him to live for only two more years, he survived until past age 15. During that time he fought his illness with humor, intelligence, and spiritual strength. Scott also had written about his life and about his disease and its treatment, sometimes for other people to read and sometimes in private words seen only after his death. What he wrote has helped doctors and other health professionals in their work with terminally ill children and adolescents. He left little messages saying "Scott was here" in unexpected places, such as the stockroom of his parents' shoestore or the column of the front porch. His mother ends the book by saying, "Scott *was* here and he left us a legacy of love and courage. This is what Scott would have wanted" (p. 196).

An appendix, "Terminal Illness and the Adolescent," includes a paper written by a young woman who worked one day a week in Children's Hospital, Los Angeles, where Scott was treated. There is a short bibliography, and black-and-white photographs show Scott and his family.

Analysis. Books about terminally ill children written by their parents are painful reading, and this lucid, unsentimental account is no exception. Scott was a youngster with great intellectual and spiritual gifts, whose energetic curiosity and sense of fun affected those who knew him. Elaine Ipswitch's book reveals a loving, close-knit family (Scott had an identical twin brother) that, while never portrayed as saintly, somewhere found the strength to meet terrible tragedy with dignity and courage. *Scott Was Here* would be of interest to young readers facing similar situations as well as to a more general audience.

Johnson, F. Leonard, and Marc Miller. *Shannon: A Book for Parents of Children with Leukemia.* Illus. New York: Hawthorn, 1975. 132 pp. Reading Level: Grades 10–12.
Disability: Leukemia

Shannon's acute lymphoblastic leukemia was diagnosed in January 1972 when she was four years old. This book, detailing her therapy, is written by a pediatric oncologist at the Children's Orthopedic Hospital and Medical Center in Seattle where Shannon was treated, and by her grandmother, a professional writer. Johnson talks about the scientific and medical aspects of leukemia and about procedures developed in combating it. Miller, who was usually with Shannon on her visits to the clinic, describes the reactions of the family and of the child herself to the course of the disease. Shannon is pictured as a bright, attractive, often funny child, tough in the way of many children experiencing serious illness.

The clinic personnel encouraged open communication about disease and treatment, and Shannon's family offered responsive, loving support. Miller concludes her last chapter with, "I feel that these three years have rearranged values. I believe her disease will be permanently arrested, but even if the day comes when we are bereft, I know that I have learned from a little girl named Shannon that one can experience in one day all that life offers, if he/she has the courage to reach out and take it" (p. 117). Both Johnson and Miller emphasize the advances that have been made in knowledge of leukemia and in successful treatment. In 1975, three years after the onset of her illness, Shannon was still in remission, a vigorous, active child.

There are family photographs of Shannon before the diagnosis, and during and after treatment. The book has an index.

Analysis. Attacking the subject from different angles and speaking in different voices, Johnson and Miller nevertheless project similar attitudes. Both believe in being realistic yet optimistic, both respond to suffering with sensitivity and yet with hope. For example, when Shannon lost her hair and was wearing a wig, an elderly woman once commented on her beautiful hair:

> Shannon grinned impishly. "Want in on a secret?" Off came the wig. The woman turned pale. "Little girl, I've got awfully weak kidneys," she said as she dashed towards the ladies' room.
>
> Shannon threw back her head and let out peals of laughter that attracted more attention. By this time the wig was back on her head, rakishly askew over one eye.
>
> I got her out of there as fast as I could (p. 48).

This book would be appropriate for young patients and for family members living through similar experiences, as well as classmates of a sick youngster.

Kipnis, Lynne, and Susan Adler. *You Can't Catch Diabetes from a Friend.* Photog. by Richard Benkof. Gainesville, Fla.: Triad, 1979. 64 pp. Reading Level: Grades 4–9.
Disability: Diabetes

In separate sections, text and photographs tell the stories of four children who have diabetes. Each section focuses on a different aspect of the disease. Ten-year-old Karen is shown giving herself an insulin injection and checking off her shot on a chart. Eleven-year-old Danny explains to his friends why he cannot trade lunches with them and chooses an apple for a snack because he has already eaten cookies earlier in the day. Seven-year-old Colleen tests her urine and has a checkup at the doctor's office. Robert, who is 14, has a lawn-mowing business with a friend and works too hard at sweeping up the grass; he has an insulin reaction, but his friend helps him eat the sugar he always carries in his pocket. The youngsters are also shown at activities unrelated to their illness.

In addition to giving facts about the disease, the book emphasizes that diabetes affects everyone in a family; each section has the refrain, "Her/his whole family felt the effects of the disease; everyone was changed a bit." Karen's sister says that she sometimes feels Karen gets too much attention and special treatment; Robert's aunt and uncle know that he must have his meals on time. The text and the black-and-white photographs describe their families.

Analysis. In the preface, the authors point to the need for clear, substantive books to help children with diabetes understand their disease so that they can participate responsibly in its management. They also wish to enable others to understand it so that they can treat people with diabetes normally. *You Can't Catch Diabetes from a Friend* presents its material informally and clearly. For the most part, the dialogue is natural, as are the attractive photographs. The book should be helpful to both diabetics and nondiabetics.

Kleiman, Gary, and Sanford Dody. *No Time to Lose.* Illus. New York: Morrow, 1983. 284 pp. Reading Level: Grades 10–12.
Disability: Diabetes

Gary Kleiman has had diabetes since the age of six. As a child he was not told how serious the illness was, nor were his parents; nor, he says, did the doctor know. The consensus of medical opinion seemed to be that with insulin he could lead a normal life. According to Kleiman's first-person account, he was an irrepressible child. As a rebellious adolescent, although he always took his insulin, he neglected other aspects of self-care, and later he wondered whether this might have hastened complications. Despite the battles of adolescence that marked his relationship with his mother, Kleiman describes a warm, close family always supportive of his efforts to live as fully as possible and to fight his disease.

After some time in college, Kleiman had eye problems so severe that eventually he had to leave school. In addition to these complications, which left him with only residual sight in one eye, he had high blood pressure and threatened kidney failure. He began writing this book while waiting for a kidney transplant from his mother.

Kleiman is a sculptor who has sold a number of pieces, and in addition works as a counselor at the Diabetic Unit of the University of Miami Hospital. In describing his counseling work with young diabetics, Kleiman discusses the importance of giving children control in the management of their disease: "Because they are forced to diet and take medicine daily, they have lost their most precious possession— freedom. Since they must comply with the rules of the game of war against diabetes, the counselor, doctor, parent or guardian must repay the child in the best coin possible. If the diabetic child can no longer have his freedom, then he must be allowed and encouraged to be his own keeper. It sounds unrealistic. It is not. I know. A child must and can be made to be in charge of himself and do *more* than what a doctor has ordered. He must be respected and trusted as the doctor's partner and then eventually be trained to be his own savior" (pp. 157–158). Later in the book, in describing a camp for diabetic children at which he was a counselor, he lists some of the procedures the children must follow every day. "These are children who must, every single day, conduct themselves with the discipline and dedication of adults in order that they may someday become them. If I belabor the point somewhat, it is because to this day, I am astonished at the amount of time I spend just staying alive. I'm used to it. It's a challenge and I've got it licked" (p. 226).

Kleiman holds no bitterness for mistakes made by others and by himself, but his professional work is devoted to helping young diabetics learn earlier the lessons he recognized in young adulthood. At the end of the book, the kidney transplant from his mother has been successful and Kleiman's valiant, hopeful, but always realistic battle continues.

Sanford Dody, listed as coauthor, is a professional writer. There are black-and-white photographs.

Analysis. In a colloquial, rather high-pitched style, which probably accurately reflects his impetuous, sometimes outrageous personality, Kleiman analyzes himself, his family, his relationships, and especially his disease and its effect on his life. While the self-analysis is sometimes repetitive and the humor overdone, Kleiman's remarks on chronic, incurable, potentially debilitating disease are well worth reading. Young diabetics may profit greatly from reading this work by one who experienced many medical complications of diabetes at a young age and yet has achieved a helpful philosophic outlook and professional fulfillment.

> Kruckeberg, Carol. *What Was Good about Today.* Illus. with drawings by Sara Beth Kruckeberg. Seattle, Wash.: Madrona, 1984. 273 pp. Reading Level: Grades 7–12.
> *Disability:* Leukemia

Sara Beth Kruckeberg was a lively, intelligent, creative eight-year-old, who in the spring of 1980 was diagnosed as having acute myeloblastic leukemia, the most severe form of this illness. After three rounds of chemotherapy, which caused side effects, including loss of her thick, curly hair, she went into remission and received an apparently successful bone marrow transplant from her father. Within a few weeks, however, graft-versus-host disease (GVH) developed and she died.

This book is her mother's account of Sara's five-month bout with this acute fatal illness. It chronicles the trips to and from doctors and hospitals; the many weeks that both mother and daughter spent in the Children's Orthopedic Hospital in Seattle; the patients and parents, the nurses, doctors, and other medical personnel who came into the Kruckeberg family's life; and the host of friends, acquaintances, and strangers who offered both help and emotional support. Kruckeberg is grateful to these people, especially the extraordinary hospital staff; she speaks less sympathetically of the faith healer, proponents of unorthodox cures, and the "soul saver" who also appeared on the scene. Sara's cancer therapist was Patti Trull, whose own struggle is documented in *On with My Life* (see this chapter under Orthopedic/Neurological Disabilities).

The emotional swings of everyone in the story are a special area of emphasis, particularly Sara's reactions, which her mother describes in detail. Both Sara and her parents experience alternating periods of hope and depression, happiness and anger, that finally culminate in the acceptance of the inevitability of death.

Sara's own artwork illustrates the text; one of the highlights is her humorous "bald is beautiful" (p. 134).

Analysis. This is a fast-paced, vividly descriptive story replete with natural dialogue. The recreation of the dialogue is a positive addition that provides immediacy and emphasizes the stark reality of the events of this five-month period. Kruckeberg relates Sara's humor, jokes, and good times, as well as her pain, misery, and cranky bad times, to portray a delightful, sensitive little girl facing impending death with surprising insightfulness and maturity. The deathbed scene and the chapter that deals with the events and emotions of the family during the year after Sara's death are gripping, poignant, and frank, but never overly sentimental or maudlin. The description of the way the minister discusses Sara's death with her friends and classmates during her memorial service might be particularly useful to others facing a similar situation.

Landau, Elaine. *Why Are They Starving Themselves? Understanding Anorexia Nervosa and Bulimia.* New York: Messner, 1983. 110 pp.
Reading Level: Grades 7–12.
Disability: Anorexia nervosa, Bulimia

Elaine Landau has been an editor and a librarian and is now Group Work Specialist for Adult Services of the New York Public Library. Here she examines the course and causes of two baffling eating disorders, anorexia nervosa (self-induced starvation) and bulimia (literally, abnormal hunger) with its binge-purge syndrome. One chapter is subtitled "What It Feels Like to Starve"; another is the account tape-recorded by a 17-year-old anorectic in which she describes the development of her illness. Brief profiles of women suffering from these disorders are scattered throughout the text. Landau discusses hospitalization and medical intervention, procedures that are often used to save the anorectic from death but may not solve the underlying psychological problems.

The last chapter is devoted to help such as that available from the National Association for Anorexia Nervosa and Associated Disorders (ANAD); from the Center for the Study of Anorexia, a division of the Institute for Contemporary Psychotherapy in New York City; and from Associates for Bulimia and Related Eating Disorders, also in New York City. The introduction is written by Ellen Schor, codirector of the Associates for Bulimia and herself a former bulimic. There is a short bibliography and an index.

Analysis. This book is well organized and clearly written. Landau expresses sympathy and insight, preserving a nonjudgmental attitude while not losing sight of the extreme seriousness of these disorders and the necessity to confront them and seek help. Such a supportive attitude is particularly important since one of the causes of anorexia and bulimia is poor self-image. While the frequency of personal accounts may lead to some reader confusion about who did what and why, the stories serve as good illustrations of the situations described; such accounts can help individuals and families in similar situations feel less isolated and more able to see themselves clearly.

Lee, Laurel. *Signs of Spring*. Illus. with drawings by the author. New York: Dutton, 1980. 118 pp. Reading Level: Grades 10–12.
Disability: Hodgkin's disease

Laurel Lee continues her story, begun in *Walking through the Fire* (see following annotation). She describes her divorce and subsequent life as a single parent after her husband leaves her while she is receiving chemotherapy, as well as the changes made in her world by the success of her first book. Her disease reappears, and again she must go through a period of aggressive treatment with chemicals and radiation. A love affair ends when the man decides that he could cope either with her disease or with her children, but not with both. Her last entry, July 1979, records that doctors have found no sign of recurrence—"Once again I am immersed in the cares and wonders of daily life" (p. 118).

A third volume, *Mourning into Dancing* (Dutton, 1984), describes a second disastrous marriage. At the time of the writing, she was still in remission.

Analysis. Using the journal form and writing mostly in simple declarative sentences, Lee records emotions and events. She captures the small moments of life, both those that attend significant occurrences and those that coalesce to form the pattern of ordinary days, for example, the responses and remarks of children. Her reaction to her disease seems courageous, honest, and realistic.

Lee, Laurel. *Walking through the Fire*. Illus. with drawings by the author. New York: Dutton, 1977. 113 pp. Reading Level: Grades 10–12.
Disability: Hodgkin's disease

When the author was pregnant with her third child, she developed troubling symptoms soon diagnosed as arising from Hodgkin's disease. She refused to consider abortion and, despite the risks, was able to carry her pregnancy to term and to deliver a healthy daughter. This book is a journal kept during the course of her treatment. Because she had to spend weeks in the hospital, she sent her newborn to California with her mother. Her husband filed for divorce, but she endured and survived. Finally, she has "completed all the medical course possible unless the disease recurred" (p. 10). She says her children's dolls no longer suffer from Hodgkin's disease but only have colds. The book ends at the time her doctor sent her journal to an editor in New York.

Lee has decorated her book with black-and-white drawings.

Analysis. Written in a style at times poetic and moving, at times fey and seemingly self-conscious, Lee's journal is the record of a woman who refuses to be crushed by her illness, her prospects, or the medical hierarchy.

Levenkron, Steven. *Treating and Overcoming Anorexia Nervosa.* New York: Scribner's, 1982. 205 pp. Reading Level: Grades 10–12.
Disability: Anorexia nervosa

Levenkron is a psychotherapist who has worked extensively with anorectic people; his novel *The Best Little Girl in the World* was made into a television movie that focused attention on this eating and behavior disorder. Here he discusses the incidence and forms of the illness, its evolution, and the treatment based on the nurturant-authoritative psychotherapy that he has developed. He uses six profiles to describe different aspects of the condition and includes material on the training of nurturant-authoritative therapists, the role of the family in the cause and treatment of anorexia, hospitalization for patients, and support groups for patients and family. There is a preface by Preston Zucker, M.D., Associate Clinical Professor of Pediatrics at Montefiore Hospital and Medical Center, Albert Einstein College of Medicine, and an index.

Analysis. This is a serious, nonsensational study that is accessible to the lay reader. Levenkron's description of the theory and practice of nurturant-authoritative therapy is persuasive. Although he does not minimize the difficulties of treating and overcoming the disease, his beliefs and experience offer the hope that with this type of treatment and with much hard work, anorexics can be successful in giving up their self-destructive behavior and adopting healthier patterns of meeting challenges and of living.

Lund, Doris. *Eric.* Philadelphia: Lippincott, 1974. 345 pp. Reading Level: Grades 10–12.
Disability: Leukemia

Eric's story is told by his mother. She first describes him as a freshman on his way to the University of Connecticut on a soccer scholarship. When he goes to the beach, his mother notices two large sores on his legs, the precursor to a diagnosis of leukemia. Two story lines are evident. One is Eric's always valiant struggle to live normally for the four and a half years after the onset of his disease. The other is his fight for independence that any adolescent would face, complete with run-ins with his mother.

Despite the demands of a chemotherapy regime, Eric did enter college, and he became captain of the varsity soccer team. He also held a job to help finance his education, and he experienced a joyous love affair with one of his nurses. At his death, Eric's last word was "Westpoint," the field where he and his soccer companions had become county champions.

Analysis. Although this book is slightly marred by the grieving mother's overidealization of Eric, it is still a deeply moving and inspirational story. It should appeal to adolescents who are having their own struggle to enter adulthood.

McCullough, David. *Mornings on Horseback.* Illus. New York: Simon & Schuster, 1981. 445 pp. Reading Level: Grades 10–12.
Disability: Asthma

The title of this book refers to young Teddy Roosevelt's quest for health through exercise. McCullough says that his intention in studying Roosevelt was not to write a biography but to examine how Roosevelt came to be. He follows the future president from his birth in 1858 to the eve of his second marriage in 1886. Although McCullough concentrates on his principal subject, he devotes much attention and detail to T.R.'s forebears, parents, siblings, other relatives, and the world in which he grew up. Roosevelt became asthmatic when he was about three years old, and all through his childhood and adolescence his attacks caused great concern in the family and precipitated sudden trips out of town in an effort to find different, more salutary air. A yearlong tour of Europe by the whole family in 1869 was undertaken at least partly in search of improved health for the child. He also suffered from attacks of an intestinal disorder. He was a spindly boy who wore glasses, and his father encouraged him to build himself up through physical activity, which he did with energy and enthusiasm.

When young Roosevelt went away to college at 17, he stood 5 feet 8 inches and weighed 125 pounds; later, after his outdoor life and work in the West, he became considerably more robust and as president weighed 200 pounds. McCullough describes asthma, discussing its symptoms and effects, the treatment available in Roosevelt's day, and current medical thinking on the illness. At college, Roosevelt experienced much better health than ever before. "The picture that emerges," McCullough writes, ". . . is of an almost miraculous transformation, an improvement of the kind often seen among present day asthmatic children who are treated by removing them temporarily from their home lives and environments. . . . There was to be a misconception in later years that he conquered his childhood infirmities mainly through will power and body building, that he rid himself of asthma by making himself a strong man. But that is not quite the way it happened. First of all, he never would be rid of asthma entirely, and if there was a point at which he clearly found reprieve from suffering of the kind he had known, it came well before he attained anything like rugged manhood. It came when he went to Harvard, when he left home and was on his own in ways he had never been" (p. 167).

An afterword gives brief sketches of the lives of Roosevelt and his brother and sisters in the years following 1886. Reference notes, an extensive bibliography, and an index complete the book.

Analysis. McCullough's book is a fascinating study of a family, a milieu, and an individual, all of whom would have been interesting even if Roosevelt had not become president. The discussion of T.R.'s asthma as well as of the illnesses and disabilities of other family members (for example, his older sister Anna had Pott's disease, tuberculosis of the bone) is informed and clear, and McCullough makes thoughtful comments about the effect of ill health both on the individual and on family relationships. Since this is a very long book, it is probably best recommended to able readers.

MacLeod, Sheila. *The Art of Starvation: A Story of Anorexia and Survival.* New York: Schocken, 1982. 181 pp. Reading Level: Grades 10–12. *Disability:* Anorexia nervosa

MacLeod, a professional writer, examines the general phenomenon of anorexia, its history and manifestations, and her own experience with the disorder. She was born on an island of the Outer Hebrides, but her family moved to England when she was five. As an adolescent, she won a scholarship to boarding school and from that time on felt increasingly separate and even alienated from her family and cultural background. She began to starve herself while at school and continued to do so for some time, eventually weighing as little as 78 pounds.

She never received any treatment and her recovery was largely self-generated. MacLeod speaks of recovery rather than cure; she has had two minor relapses and says that "certain patterns in eating, thinking and feeling remain, which can only be described as anorexic" (p. 133). She movingly describes a scene where her mother offers her a ripe plum and she is able to accept and eat it.

The two final chapters are called "Prognosis" and "Conclusions"; in the latter she discusses predisposition toward the disease and offers what she calls a recipe for conditions likely to foster it. The book includes footnotes.

Analysis. MacLeod discusses the theories and findings of many professionals, such as Hilde Bruch, Erik Erikson, and Thomas Szasz, in her efforts to reach an understanding of this disease and of her own experience. Her dispassionate examination of her background, her illness, and her life is interwoven with the material derived from these professional sources. This is a sophisticated and complex book, but one that is within the reach of mature young adults; parents, teachers, librarians, social workers, and students could find it helpful in understanding the complicated condition of anorexia and in exploring ways to deal with this puzzling disorder.

Massie, Robert K., and Suzanne Massie. *Journey.* Illus. New York: Knopf, 1975. 417 pp. Reading Level: Grades 10–12.
Disability: Hemophilia

This is the parents' story of the first 18 years with their only son, born with the hereditary and chronic "bleeder's" disease, hemophilia. Each chapter is attributed to one or other of the parents, who write from a personal perspective.

Bobbie's hemophilia was discovered when he was five months old. The family was to endure the pain and crippling that the disease wrought in their child, stupid and inhuman treatment from medical institutions, and constant financial strain. Toward the end of the book, Robert Massie makes a serious indictment against medical and government neglect of the chronically ill. Each of the family members grew in strength and character through their ordeal. Bobbie, off to college at Princeton, has taken charge of his own care. In the book he states that through 18 years of pain and troubles, he has added to his appreciation of life and its meaning.

An appendix diagrams the hereditary transmission of hemophilia. Black-and-white photographs show Bobbie with family and friends at different stages of his life.

Analysis. Both Massies are published authors and their book is well written. Robert Massie wrote *Nicholas and Alexandra,* in which hemophilia also figures prominently. Although the family has had severe financial problems, they are very cultured, with famous friends and exciting opportunities in the United States and abroad. It is evident that hemophilia is no respecter of class. The book recounts many bitter experiences and emotions, but strength, courage, and a positive viewpoint prevail. Although this is a long book, its vibrant and youthful hero should make it appealing to teenagers.

Monahan, James, ed. *Before I Sleep: The Last Days of Dr. Tom Dooley.* New York: Farrar, 1961. 275 pp. Reading Level: Grades 10–12.
Disability: Cancer

As a young Navy doctor, Tom Dooley had worked in Vietnam. Later, he organized an independent medical unit called Medico, to supply treatment to people in Southeast Asia. At 32, he developed malignant melanoma. This book, compiled from the reports and descriptions of many people—reporters, fellow health professionals, friends, supporters—describes the last months of his life, from August 1959 to January 1961. Recognizing the gravity of his disease and its probable outcome, Dooley pushed on to accomplish as much as possible before he died. He treated patients and in addition traveled widely, speaking for his organization and gathering support for it. In his last days, the cancer had spread to his bones and organs and he was in great pain, but he persisted in his efforts until the end.

Analysis. The use of many voices and observers gives a detailed and multidimensional picture of Dooley. Although most of the voices are admiring, some describe attributes that the speakers found less attractive; their inclusion makes Dooley seem more human. The book could interest readers looking back at U.S. involvement in Southeast Asia as well as those intrigued by the story of personal bravery and medical accomplishment.

Morris, Jeanne. *Brian Piccolo: A Short Season.* New York: Dell, 1971. 182 pp. Reading Level: Grades 7–12.
Disability: Cancer

This book was begun by Piccolo during his hospitalization in order to relieve boredom. It was finished after his death by the credited author. Many people in the football world and others in his life are acknowledged for contributions to the book, which is the story of the life and death of a young professional football player who inspired the television film *Brian's Song.* The book covers the events of Piccolo's life beginning with his birth to an American mother and an Italian immigrant father. The climax of his life comes when he plays professional football with the Chicago Bears. He develops a close friendship with fellow player and black athlete, Gale Sayers.

Piccolo's supportive wife and three children become an integral part of his successful career. Then his world falls apart when he is told he has incurable cancer and will never play football again. Gradually the story turns from one of battling illness to preparation for death. Brian Piccolo died in 1970 at the age of 26.

A few well-chosen photographs enhance the narrative.

Analysis. In simple, readable prose, insights are given into the lives of a number of men who make up professional football. The writer presupposes some knowledge of the game and its vernacular. The section Piccolo wrote himself lends a special authenticity to the story.

The book is full of humorous anecdotes relating to football, Piccolo's friendships, and even to the medical experiences of his last days.

Nakamoto, Hiroko, and Mildred Mastin Pace. *My Japan, 1930–1951*. New York: McGraw-Hill, 1970. 157 pp. Reading Level: Grades 7–12.
Disability: Radiation burns

Now an interior designer in Tokyo, Hiroko Nakamoto was 15 years old when Hiroshima was devastated by the atomic bomb. She was badly burned and very ill for some time afterward. Many of her family members and friends were killed. In this biography, she describes 21 years of her life, from birth through elementary and high school, to college in the United States, where she received a Methodist Church scholarship to study at Bowling Green State University in Ohio.

Each chapter and/or section of the book is decorated with greyish-black Japanese characters on a large white background, a unique and effective device.

Analysis. Nakomoto's description of her daily life as a child from a troubled family (her parents were divorced when she was very young) and as a schoolgirl is vivid. Her discussion of the war years is sobering and her chronicle of the day of the bombing and life as it was afterward is stark, horrifying, and unforgettable.

The burns are always "there"—a part of her postbomb existence, although she does not make a great issue of them within the fabric of her life, at least insofar as she portrays herself in this book. They are a part of her life's pattern, and she copes as she must. Her condition does not stop her from pursuing an education that ultimately leads her to the West and a career.

Neimark, Anne E. *Damien the Leper Priest*. New York: Morrow, 1980. 158 pp. Reading Level: Grades 4–9.
Disability: Hansen's disease (leprosy)

In 1840, a boy, the seventh of eight children, was born to a couple living in a small hamlet in Flanders. Although his family were devout Catholics, his father had destined him for a business career, so he was sent away to learn French, which, with his native Flemish, was the language of Belgium. However, at age 19 he felt compelled to enter a monastery. His progress was impressive, and finally he replaced his brother on a mission to Hawaii, then known as the Sandwich Islands. The long ship ride is described, as well as the rivalry between Protestant and Catholic missionaries on the eight islands. In Honolulu, Damien was confirmed and then sent to Puna on the island of Hawaii to establish churches and schools. There he was to fight the idolatry and witchcraft found among some cults.

As commerce with the islands increased, travelers brought many diseases to the natives, the worst of which was leprosy, a degenerative illness that causes rotting flesh, loss of nerve sensation, and disfiguration. In 1865, a year after Damien had landed, the reigning king of Puna ordered all lepers isolated on a small northern promontory on the island of Molokai to protect the rest of the population. The leper community, actually an isolated, neglected prison, existed in a horrible anarchy of diseased people.

When Damien was 33 years old, he volunteered for what was to be his life's work and the eventual cause of his death—ministry to the lepers of Molokai. He overcame his revulsion of rotting bodies and lived closely with his people, ministering to them, building for them, and comforting them. Damien made the plight of his colony known and he received money from all over the world. This infuriated the government because they did not want the public to know how remiss they had been.

Of course, Damien contracted leprosy in the colony and battled increasing ill health. Finally, other priests and nuns were sent to the island to carry on his work. In 1888, the British artist Edward Clifford came to the colony and sketched Damien, who died in 1889 in the colony that housed 1,200 lepers. By 1940 only 300 lepers were left on Molokai. The last chapter discusses a feud between writer R. L. Stevenson and Dr. Hyde of Honolulu when the latter tried to discredit Damien, as well as a discussion of the cure now available for leprosy.

The book is indexed and contains a bibliography.

Analysis. The author has drawn on Damien's correspondence and diaries to produce this portrait of an extraordinary man for young readers. The context is religious. Although this is a recent book, there is an old-fashioned feeling in the prose, as if Neimark is writing in the style of Damien's time. The descriptions of the ravages of leprosy are plentiful and vivid.

O'Neill, Cherry Boone. *Starving for Attention.* Illus. New York: Continuum, 1982. 187 pp. Reading Level: Grades 10–12.
Disability: Anorexia nervosa, Bulimia

The author, oldest daughter of recording star Pat Boone, suffered from anorexia nervosa and bulimia during her adolescence and into her twenties. The book details the course of her illness, with its swings of mood and weight. O'Neill discusses the attempts of her parents to combat her condition even before any of them knew what to call it, family tensions and interactions, her self-deceptions and distorted self-image, and her relationship with her husband as it was affected by her disorder. Eventually, O'Neill was helped back to health by psychotherapy that both she and her husband participated in with Dr. Ray Vath of Seattle.

The Boones are a devout Protestant family; the O'Neills eventually became Roman Catholics. Religion has always played a large part in Cherry O'Neill's life, and her recovery was aided by two years that she and her husband spent in a religious community in Hawaii. At the time of the writing of this book, Cherry O'Neill had given birth to a healthy daughter and was once again leading an active life, with successful musical work and speaking appearances on the problems of anorexia. The book concludes with letters by Shirley and Pat Boone, Dan O'Neill (the author's husband), and Ray Vath, and with a directory of sources of help.

Black-and-white family photographs illustrate the text.

Analysis. O'Neill looks honestly and without guilt at her illness and her recovery. While understanding the part played in the development of the disease by family dynamics, she has progressed from dependence to rebellion (expressed in her self-starvation) to mature acceptance. The reader is always aware of the role of religion in her life, but O'Neill does not push a particular affiliation or approach, choosing to emphasize her individual response during the years she describes. She stresses the role of developmental process in growth, recovery, and reconciliation. Although at times marred by heavy reliance on clichés, the writing is adequate and the insights invaluable, both for those who suffer from this disease and for their baffled families and friends.

Palmer, R. L. *Anorexia Nervosa: A Guide for Sufferers and Their Families.* London: Penguin, 1980. 156 pp. Reading Level: Grades 10–12. *Disability:* Anorexia nervosa

Palmer is a British psychiatrist who has done research into anorexia nervosa. He describes the characteristics of this self-starvation disorder and examines ideas and theories about its nature. Palmer offers his "psychobiological regression hypothesis" to explain the causes. Then he discusses physical, psychological, and emotional aspects of the problem and approaches to treatment. Brief patient histories, based largely on true situations, appear at intervals. The last chapter is called "Living with Anorexia Nervosa." It is followed by a weight chart, suggestions for further references to sources drawn on for the text, and an index.

Analysis. The author directs his book toward a nonspecialist readership. His tone is serious, the material demanding but not inaccessible.

Palmer takes the position that anorexia nervosa is complicated, difficult for professionals, for the patient, and for the family, but not intractable; his attitude is neither judgmental nor accusatory. The text is British in the use of stones as a measure of weight and in references to the British health system, but nearly all the material can readily be grasped by Americans. Palmer is not a popularizer or a sensationalist; this is a book for the serious reader and would probably be most helpful to young adults and adolescents who might have this problem, as well as to their families.

Parks, Gordon. *Flavio*. Illus. New York: Norton, 1978. 198 pp. Reading Level: Grades 10–12.
Disability: Asthma, Malnutrition

Parks, the first black photo journalist hired by *Life* magazine, was on assignment to find a typical Brazilian family in the slums near Rio de Janeiro in 1961. By chance he happened on a small frail boy who won his heart with a smile on his starving, sunken face. Flavio, at 12, was diagnosed as having severe asthma and malnutrition with the prospect of death within two years. Nevertheless, the boy labored cheerfully to carry wood and water, cook for his large family, and care for numerous brothers and sisters as his parents drudged for a meager living. He was literally killing himself to keep his family going. Parks, himself familiar with the American black ghetto, describes in lurid detail the relentless poverty, violence, and hopelessness among the teeming thousands in the *favela*.

After publication of the article on Flavio in *Life* magazine, enough money was donated by readers to enable Flavio to receive treatment at the Asthma Institute in Denver and to help his family to a new home. Since the child's condition had worsened by that time, it was a race for his life.

The second half of the book begins with Flavio's new, often stormy rehabilitation and education in the United States, as his family began their new life outside the ghetto. The citizens of the *favela* also embarked on an improvement campaign of their own. After two years, Flavio's asthma was brought under control and his physical condition was much improved; he returned to Brazil, where he experienced another cultural adjustment with his reentry to his own country. Finally, he finished school and married, a man on his own.

The last chapter recounts the reunion of Parks and Flavio 15 years later. Although Flavio had a fair job, handsome sons, and a happy home, he dreamed of returning to America. His mother, a broken woman after 15 children, lived almost as pathetically as she had when Parks first met her. In a bittersweet ending, the author decides that the future has been won for Flavio's children, if not for him.

The black-and-white photos are plentiful and dramatic. Several pages of pictures contrast Flavio's siblings when they were babies in the hovel in 1961 and as beautiful young adults at the time of Parks's last visit, after they had been given a chance for a better life.

Analysis. This well-written book puts the reader into a very different setting, which comes alive in stark realism. The daily struggles of young and old who live on the edge of survival are brought vividly to life. Flavio's asthma, which might have been a very minor problem in other circumstances, was the added burden that almost took his life.

Phillips, Carolyn E. *Michelle.* Illus. New York: New American Library, 1982. 147 pp. Reading Level: Grades 7–12.
Disability: Cancer

Michelle Price's bone cancer of the leg was diagnosed when she was eight. Immediate amputation was recommended, although the doctors said that there would still be a less than 4 percent chance of her surviving the disease. This shock followed only six months after a motorcycle accident that nearly killed the Prices' 20-year-old son. They took Michelle to City of Hope Hospital where her leg was amputated above the knee joint and she received extensive chemotherapy. The young girl accepted her situation with maturity, enduring the pain both of the surgery and of the side effects of the medications. She recovered quickly, learned how to manage on crutches, and eventually was fitted with a prosthesis.

At the time of the writing of the book, Michelle was 12 years old, had become a medal-winning skier in competition for physically impaired people, and an accomplished horseback rider. In addition, she had appeared on national television in such shows as "Good Morning, America." The Prices are a deeply religious family, and all of them were able to trust that God would guide and protect them, whatever the outcome of the crisis they faced.

Black-and-white photographs show Michelle engaging in various activities after her surgery.

Analysis. Michelle joins other narratives that detail the successful treatment of once-fatal bone cancer. It reads smoothly, although the author has taken the liberty of imagining and describing scenes she could not have seen, conversations she could not have heard, and thoughts she could not have been aware of. Therefore, this must be read as a fictionalized narrative. The influence of the Prices' religious philosophy is felt throughout the book, and it might best appeal to readers who share their views.

Poole, Victoria. *Thursday's Child.* Illus. Boston: Little, 1980. 370 pp. Reading Level: Grades 7–12.
Disability: Heart disease (cardiomyopathy)

The author is the mother of Sam Poole, who in 1977 at the age of 18 received a heart transplant at the Stanford University Medical Center. The fifth of six children, Sam had been healthy, vigorous, and athletic until Christmas two years earlier when he came home from prep school looking gaunt and exhausted, and with a startling cough. It was established that he had cardiomyopathy, with an irreversibly and grossly enlarged heart, probably the result of a past infection such as strep or mononucleosis.

As Sam's condition worsened, he and his parents tried desperately to find help. Eventually he was accepted into the Stanford transplant program and after waiting through a tense period, received the heart of a 17-year-old young man who had been killed in an accident. When doctors saw the condition of Sam's own heart, they marveled that he had been able to hold on for so long. When, as predicted by the nurse, Sam's mother saw that his feet were now pink and warm, instead of blue and cold, she realized this was a dramatic sign that his new heart was pumping blood through his depleted body. Sam weathered the inevitable difficulties of convalescence, including rejection episodes; he graduated from prep school and, at the time of the writing of the book, was an active and happy student at Stanford University.

Analysis. Despite the magnitude of the medical problem at the center of this book and despite also her obvious loving commitment to her son, Poole's tone is breezy and humorous. Much of the text concerns the activities, relationships, and antics of a large extended family. The author seems to possess total recall of conversations and incidents central and peripheral to her story. The book offers an interesting picture of the road leading to this relatively new operation, the convalescence that follows it, and the lifelong accommodation that must be made by the patient and his or her family.

Pray, Lawrence M., with Richard Evans III. *Journey of a Diabetic.* New York: Simon & Schuster, 1983. 202 pp. Reading Level: Grades 7–12.

Disability: Diabetes

Pray's diabetes was diagnosed when he was seven years old. He then began the regimen of monitoring and care that accompanies this disease, and at the same time embarked on the journey that would eventually lead, many years later, to acceptance of a chronic, lifelong condition. Pray's family was close, loving, and supportive; they believed in meeting challenges with quiet courage, suppressing anger and anxiety, and it was not until Pray was writing this book that they were all able to sit down and talk about what diabetes had meant in their lives. His parents encouraged him to assume appropriate responsibility for self-care while he was still very young, and they were able to let him lead an active life. After college and graduate school, he became a teacher at a small private school in Maine, where he is now assistant headmaster. He is married and the father of four children.

The book ends with a postscript: three chapters, one for the person with diabetes, one for the family, and one for the doctor. Pray's coauthor is a friend who is a psychiatrist, with whom he had many conversations as he thought through and wrote this book.

Analysis. Pray describes well the various stages he passed through before reaching acceptance of his disease: the denial, magical thinking, and effort of willpower that preceded his recognition that his diabetes could be not his enemy but his teacher. He likens this process to growing up. He says in his introduction that the books about diabetes he found "spoke to my disease but never to my life. . . . Realizing how meaningful acceptance eventually was for me, and thinking I might have benefited if I'd read a true story, I decided to offer my experience in the hope that diabetics and their families could take increased faith in their journey with disease" (p. 12). This book might help any young person who must come to terms with limitations.

Pringle, Terry. *This Is the Child.* New York: Knopf, 1983. 194 pp.
Reading Level: Grades 10–12.
Disability: Leukemia

When Eric Pringle was just over four years old, in January 1980, he was diagnosed as having leukemia. This book is his father's story of the next 20 months. The Pringles took Eric from Abilene, Texas, where they lived, to Texas Children's Hospital in Houston for treatments: bone marrow aspirations, spinal taps, chemotherapy. A three-year program of treatment was planned; the physicians said that Eric had a 50–60 percent chance of survival. Some of the treatments took place in Abilene under the care of Dr. Daniel Pope, whom Pringle first viewed with coolness but later describes as having become a member of the family for whom he and his wife felt enormous gratitude and affection.

Remissions gave the Pringles hope and confidence; relapses filled them with dread. Pringle urged Eric to fight, to think positively about the chemicals that were being used to destroy cancerous cells. Building on Eric's passion for cowboys and guns, he invented all kinds of games to encourage the child to participate actively in his own therapy.

Although the doctors tried different combinations of drugs, by Labor Day 1981, the family (Eric's brother Michael was a year older than he) had to recognize that Eric was not going to achieve another remission and that he was in the last phase of the disease. Pringle took a leave of absence from his job and for the last month of Eric's life stayed at home with his family; in the afternoons, he and Eric would drive into the hills. Two months before his sixth birthday, on October 3, 1981, Eric died. Early in the course of his son's disease, Pringle had promised himself that he would be whatever Eric needed. He thought he had wanted an easy death for the little boy, but the hard fight the child put up in his last 24 hours was like a gift to his father. Pringle kept reliving it, repeating the details and emphasizing that "he never quit, he just wouldn't quit" (p. 178).

In the last chapter, Pringle describes the family's immediate reaction to Eric's death. They spent some days at a ranch after the funeral, rebuilding themselves as a family of three. He describes the subsequent months and the process of grieving they endured, each in a different way and at a different pace. The book closes with two pages of acknowledgments of the help and support given by family, friends, employer, and community. He had not, Pringle says, intended to write this story "until I saw that Eric had left me with one I couldn't stop telling." He had not taken notes during Eric's illness, but his wife had, and these aided his memory.

Terry Pringle changed, as anyone must, during the 20-month course of Eric's illness. Once his concept of God had been "limited to anthropomorphic images"; a fundamentalist Christian, he had asked God for signs. Receiving none, he had become, as he says, a backslider. Now he comes to a different idea of God, one closer to that of Eric's doctor, who believes that God does not control the universe, that evil exists, and that He grieves with us over its presence. Writing of Eric's final weeks, Pringle says, "For a month we lived in a world where everyone we knew acted as though they were straight from God, uncorrupted by the world, wanting to give, not to get, not to invest, not to perform reciprocal favors, but to give unconditionally. They gave to us, we gave to Eric, and he gave back" (p. 182).

Analysis. This is a beautifully moving, intensely felt book. Pringle works for an insurance company and is not apparently a professional writer, but he is clearly a talented one, with a gift for both observation and expression. He captures the moods and spirit of his sons in all kinds of activities. He conveys with precision and economy the anger, grief, powerlessness, and terror of watching a beloved child endure pain and face death. The descriptions of the course of Eric's illness, particularly at the end, are poignant and graphic, leaving little unsaid. Most of the book is written in the present tense.

The most shadowy figure in the book is Pringle's wife, Brenda, perhaps because the author concentrates on his own responses. He does not shrink from picturing honestly his own anger, despair, and impatience. Both Pringles emerge as admirable parents, able to support their sick son as he fought his disease and faced death. They also gave their well son what he needed to cope during Eric's illness and after his death. Terry Pringle convinces us that he truly means the answer he gives to a friend who asks whether they wish they could have had Eric for a long time: "I tell him no, that's not my feeling. What I feel is unspeakable gratitude that he lived with us for six years" (p. 183).

Riedman, Sarah R. *Allergies*. Illus. New York: Franklin Watts, 1978. 64 pp. Reading Level: Grades 4–6.
Disability: Allergies

Part of the First Book series, this text discusses causes, symptoms, and treatment of a number of allergies. After an explanation of what happens in the body when an allergic reaction occurs, the author includes chapters on allergic rhinitis, hay fever, asthma, food allergies, acute reaction to bee stings, and contact allergies.

The text is illustrated with black-and-white photographs and drawings. There is a glossary, a bibliography, and an index.

Analysis. Riedman uses a combination of case histories and exposition to present information; her style is clear and direct. While she does not minimize the severity of certain allergic conditions (such as asthma and sensitivity to bee stings), both the matter-of-fact tone and the factual information will reassure young readers that these problems are manageable.

Riedman, Sarah R. *Diabetes*. Illus. New York: Franklin Watts, 1980. 62 pp. Reading Level: Grades 7–9.
Disability: Diabetes

Riedman opens with a chapter entitled "What's Wrong with Jamie, Doctor?," a short description of the onset of diabetes mellitus in a five-year-old boy. She discusses possible causes of diabetes and its two main types, the role of insulin, conditions of the disease, care (including self-care), and current research.

There are line drawings (including a diet chart) and black-and-white photographs, a glossary, a bibliography, and an index.

Analysis. Like other titles in the First Book series, *Diabetes* is clearly written, informative, and honest. Riedman uses hypothetical case studies of children and adults as well as exposition. At times, she addresses the diabetic child directly, encouraging intelligent self-care based on knowledge and full participation in an active life. The chapter on research points optimistically toward future improved management of the disease. Riedman's book is appropriate reading for all children in this age group, whether they are themselves diabetic, the relatives or friends of people with diabetes, or simply interested in the subject.

Rumney, Avis. *Dying to Please: Anorexia Nervosa and Its Cure.* Jefferson, N.C.: McFarland, 1983. 116 pp. Reading Level: Grades 10–12. *Disability:* Anorexia nervosa

The author is a marriage, family and child counselor in the San Francisco Bay area. She herself had anorexia for more than 17 years, beginning when she was an adolescent, although for much of that time she did not recognize her condition. She did know that she was "chronically obsessed with bodies and food and was discouraged, dissatisfied and depressed" and sought help through psychoanalysis and drug therapy. She found successful treatment at Cathexis Institute, "a transactional analysis-oriented treatment program in Oakland, California." Her book is a combination of an examination of the disease and various treatments and findings by professionals with her own experience.

In Part I, "The Illness," she discusses such topics as the causes of anorexia (for example, perfectionism and competition) and its manifestations in distortion of body image and impeded sexual development as well as in the more obvious disordered eating patterns. In Part II, "The Treatment," she examines ideas of what constitutes a cure and describes varieties of treatment, including behavior modification, drug therapy, psychotherapy, family therapy, hypnotherapy, and the program developed at Cathexis, which "is predicated on a transactional analysis model combined with techniques drawn from behavior modification and use of regressive work" (p. 92). The last chapter details a proposed treatment model.

A directory of organizations dealing with the disorder, a lengthy bibliography, and an index conclude the book.

Analysis. Rumney writes soberly and clearly about the disease, its etiology as presently understood, and varieties of treatment. Often, after describing the findings of professionals and their approaches, she concludes with her own experience as it relates to these topics. Although clearly and understandably most enthusiastic about the therapy that made her recovery possible, she gives other approaches a balanced description, while not hesitating to state her own opinions about their probable efficacy. She is honest about the degree to which she considers that she has achieved health and about the ways in which her illness still manifests itself. Since this is a disorder of teenagers and young adults, *Dying to Please* would be a valuable book for patients, their families, and their friends.

Sanderlin, Owenita. *Johnny.* Illus. New York: Barnes, 1968. 154 pp. Reading Level: Grades 7–12. *Disability:* Leukemia

The author first wrote this story from a mother's point of view, then rewrote it in her son's voice, using his diary and the weekly newspaper he put out for his family. Johnny developed leukemia at age 11. Although his parents were told that he would not live for more than 15 months, a succession of treatments made it possible for him to survive until just before his sixteenth birthday. Johnny's parents did not tell him that he had leukemia when it was first diagnosed. His mother writes in his voice that this was the right thing to have done. Later, after radiation treatment and bone marrow transplant, he questioned one of his doctors and realized from the answers that he was not yet cured and must have "some kind of cancer of the blood."

An ardent tennis player, when in remission Johnny competed successfully. He was a good student and had won a college scholarship before his death in 1963. The book ends with a chapter by his mother and with a memorial written by his classmates that appeared in Johnny's high school yearbook.

Analysis. Johnny Sanderlin comes across as a person of great courage, who, supported by a close and loving family, was able to live fully and happily and to accept the possibility of his death. The book has, however, some elements of fiction, for although Owenita Sanderlin used her son's words, she could not possibly have been inside his head. Only the jacket copy tells the reader that she used Johnny's diary and newspaper.

Seidick, Kathryn. *Or You Can Let Him Go.* New York: Delacorte, 1984. 233 pp. Reading Level: Grades 10–12.
Disability: Kidney disease

The story of eight-year-old Michael is told by his mother, a housewife in her thirties. It begins with the inception of Mike's illness and a mad dash with the convulsing child to the hospital in early morning hours. A succession of hospitalizations and medical procedures followed, after which Michael's parents were told that his kidneys were destroyed and they had three options: dialysis, dialysis and kidney transplant, "or you can let him go." With that diagnosis, the family was to enter the complicated and painful world of those on kidney dialysis.

Seidick describes in minute detail the intricacies of care of a child on home dialysis. She also presents the ordeals the young patient must endure. She describes the pressures on other children in the family as they are forced to defer to their sick sibling, and considers the inevitable neglect they must accept. Finally, Michael was a candidate for a kidney transplant. The family came to realize that they were now confronted with a new set of challenges and uncertainties. The kidney recipient faces the strong possibility of rejection by his body, side effects from necessary medications, and affronts from ignorant or cruel people.

The story ends with Seidick's family united and on a fairly even keel. The family has been forever changed and toughened by their experience. She writes, "We don't 'fit in' anymore. No matter how hard we try to blend in with those around us, the rest of the world won't let us. . . . Now we have to learn to live with our continuing crisis, as well as within this world that so little understands the problems of people like us" (p. 231).

Analysis. This book addresses a rather recent medical situation—the maintenance of children's lives on kidney dialysis and with organ transplants. The themes explored are not new: the anguish of a family with a suffering child, the ambivalence of siblings, the cost and uncertainties associated with extraordinary medical procedures. The author, fueled by anger at her plight, approached the health care experts with a black humor that must surely be enjoyed by anyone who has encountered institutional rigidities and pontifical professionals. Her one-liners will appeal to those who "have been there." In breezy vigorous style (she is a professional writer), she recounts her family's vicissitudes poised on a tightrope between laughter and anger, faith and despair, gratefulness and bitterness. Her fortitude, courage, and honesty are inspiring.

> Silverstein, Alvin, and Virginia B. Silverstein. *Heartbeats: Your Body, Your Heart*. Illus. by Stella Armai. New York: Lippincott, 1983. 60 pp. Reading Level: Grades 4–6.
> *Disability:* Heart disease

The Silversteins, professional writers, have written more than 50 books together. This one begins with a brief vignette about a man who rode a bicycle three thousand miles cross-country five years after he had a heart transplant. They then describe the heart and explain its workings. They explain the operation of the heart in good health and under conditions of disease and discuss measures to maintain cardiac health and to treat cardiac malfunction.

The book ends with a glossary and an index. There are black-and-white drawings.

Analysis. This is an excellent book, clearly written and attractively presented in both text and illustrations. The drawings show people of different races and are nonsexist. Although this book has only one paragraph about a real person with heart problems, it is included because there is very little written for children about heart disease.

Silverstein, Alvin, and Virginia B. Silverstein. *Itch, Sniffle & Sneeze: All about Asthma, Hay Fever & Other Allergies.* Illus. by Roy Doty. New York: Four Winds, 1978. unp. Reading Level: Grades K–3.
Disability: Allergies

The authors explain what allergies are and how they affect the body. They write about food and pollen allergies, asthma, and allergic reactions to drugs, insect bites and stings, and animals. They include a discussion of medical research, the medical treatment of allergies, and what the allergic person can do to make life more comfortable. Doty's three-color illustrations appear on every spread.

Analysis. This is a clear, informative book, well suited to kindergarten and primary school children. The text is direct and lively, the illustrations amusing and educational.

Silverstein, Alvin, and Virginia B. Silverstein. *Runaway Sugar: All about Diabetes.* Illus. by Harriett Barton. New York: Lippincott, 1981. 34 pp. Reading Level: Grades 4–6.
Disability: Diabetes

The authors explain the concept of body energy and the function of the pancreas and of insulin and glycogen. They discuss diabetes in children and in adults, its possible causes and treatment. The text includes descriptions of insulin reaction and diabetic coma, listing the differences, and ends with a glossary of useful terms. Black-and-white illustrations explain the text.

Analysis. Writing clearly and simply, the Silversteins convey considerable information in a short book. Without minimizing the seriousness of the disease or the absolute importance of proper treatment, they emphasize that people with diabetes can lead full, active lives. This is a useful book for children with diabetes and their friends and families.

Silverstein, Alvin, and Virginia B. Silverstein. *The Sugar Disease: Diabetes.* New York: Lippincott, 1980. 111 pp. Reading Level: Grades 7–12.
Disability: Diabetes

The authors begin with a short biographical sketch of Jackie Robinson, the first black major league baseball player, whose diabetes was diagnosed when he was 33; he died 20 years later, of a heart attack, but the heart disease resulted from the diabetes. The Silversteins discuss the characteristics of this disorder, its manifestations and causes. They give some of the history of treatment, with particular attention to developments of the twentieth century. There is a chapter on living with diabetes and another on current research.

A short section called "For Further Information" lists diabetes foundations, gives details on Medic-Alert, and includes a brief bibliography. There is an index.

Analysis. The Silversteins write with conciseness and clarity. Scientific and medical explanations are presented so that they are accessible to the young reader, yet there is no condescension in tone. People with diabetes must of necessity live according to a carefully arranged regimen, but the authors present this as a manageable approach to life and health. It should be noted that Jackie Robinson did not have juvenile onset diabetes.

Simonides, Carol, with Diane Gage. *I'll Never Walk Alone: The Inspiring Story of a Teenager's Struggle against Cancer.* Illus. New York: Continuum, 1983. 183 pp. Reading Level: Grades 7–12.
Disability: Cancer (osteosarcoma and amputation)

Shortly after her fourteenth birthday, in 1976, Carol Simonides's leg was amputated at mid-thigh because of bone cancer. She received a prosthesis and went on to an active high school life that included cheerleading. At one point she described a mystical religious experience, at which her mother was also present, when a faith healer removed nonmalignant cysts from her breast; there was no effect, however, on the bone cancer. The cancer recurred; eventually, she had chemotherapy and surgery on a lung. By the end of the book, she has accepted the fact that she will not survive.

Simonides narrates her story in the first person, with the help of Gage, a professional writer who completed a story about Simonides for *Seventeen* magazine. Two weeks after she completed the book, Simonides died. An epilogue by her mother, LaVonne Simonides, describes their ordeal throughout her daughter's last days and the deep religious faith that sustains them.

Analysis. This is a deeply human, moving story, made even more poignant by Simonides's acceptance of her impending death and by her mother's epilogue. Simonides was courageous, determined, and usually optimistic and cheerful, despite some periods of anger and sadness. She lived her brief life to the fullest, trying to help teenagers in trouble and even marrying her high school sweetheart seven months before her death in 1982 at the age of 20, sustained to the end by her bravery, optimism, and deep religious conviction.

Squire, Susan. *The Slender Balance: Causes and Cures for Bulimia, Anorexia & the Weight-Loss/Weight-Gain Seesaw.* New York: Putnam, 1983. 248 pp. Reading Level: Grades 10–12.
Disability: Anorexia nervosa, Bulimia

Squire, a professional writer, addresses her book to everyone who has gone on more than one diet; to those who feel that being thin is the answer to their problems; to those who think of themselves as fat no matter what their size; and to those who alternate binging with dieting, fasting, exercising, vomiting, or use of laxatives and other drugs; to anyone who has had anorexia nervosa; and to all who need to learn how to eat. She uses personal histories to illustrate various aspects and causes of eating disorders, an increasingly widespread phenomenon in today's culture.

The final chapters discuss ways in which people with such disorders can change their eating and living patterns. There is a chapter that lists places to go for further help, arranged by state.

Analysis. Squire's book, while intended for a nonprofessional audience, is based on research that seems extensive and responsible. Her tone is informal; the narratives move swiftly and compellingly, but the author avoids sensationalism. The material on weight set points provides a healthy corrective for young people to the constant emphasis on fad diets and fashionable slenderness found in the popular media.

Trachtenberg, Inge. *My Daughter, My Son.* New York: Summit, 1978. 271 pp. Reading Level: Grades 10–12.
Disability: Ulcerative colitis

The author, a novelist, tells us that although "this is a true account; true as seen through my eyes; felt and sifted and interpreted by my perceptions," she has given fictitious names not only to the doctors and nurses but also to herself and her family. Trachtenberg is the mother of three children, two with ulcerative colitis, a chronic inflammatory disease of the large intestine that is debilitating and dangerous, with the possibility of perforation of the intestine and of cancer. Her older son, born of a first marriage, escaped the disease; her second son, Sam, first showed symptoms at the age of nine and her daughter, three years younger, became ill at the same age. Although Trachtenberg raised the question of genetic causation, the doctors were unable to give an answer. After many medical consultations and extensive and varied treatment, Sam was operated on. His ileostomy (removal of part of the intestine) was successful, but before he was completely recovered, Rachel's symptoms appeared.

For the next 11 years, Rachel lived under a program of medical management that included the use of powerful drugs with worrying side effects, and then at 20, she chose a controversial surgical procedure called continent ileostomy, performed by the surgeon who was a resident at the time of Sam's operation. At the end of the book, Rachel has returned to college and is beginning the long process of learning to live as a healthy person.

Trachtenberg opens the book as she, her husband, and Sam wait for Rachel's lengthy operation to be over and then alternates between Sam's story (his surgery had taken place almost 12 years earlier) and Rachel's. The text includes poetry by Rachel and information about the National Foundation for Ileitis and Colitis, a group in which Trachtenberg's husband became very active.

Analysis. Although the narrative technique is occasionally confusing, it works well to keep the stories of Sam and Rachel moving and to make the reader aware, as the parents constantly are, of the terrible repetitiveness of their experience and of critical differences. The story is told with passionate involvement and yet with detail about symptoms, treatment, and medication that indicates a certain objectiveness on the author's part. She reproduces conversations that she can hardly have remembered verbatim, but that add immediacy to the narrative. The disease she describes is an agonizing one, not only in its physical symptoms and difficult, problematic management, but in its effect on the patient and family. Trachtenberg writes about complex relationships and reactions with sharp insight, not hesitating to present all the participants—professionals, family members, herself above all—with weaknesses, guilts, and vulnerabilities as well as with skills and strengths.

Both Sam and Rachel appear to be extraordinarily intelligent and perceptive. Trachtenberg's family is economically privileged, able to afford summers at the beach, winter trips to the Caribbean, extensive medical consultation and treatment, private hospital rooms, household help, expensive gifts, and private education for the children. Although this situation plus the relative rarity of the disease (it is one of the group of diseases affecting over 2,000,000 in the United States) might seem to set the Trachtenbergs' experience apart, in fact it could be applied to others living with any chronic disease.

Waller, Sharon. *Circle of Hope.* Foreword by Jordan Wilbur. New York: Evans, 1981. 261 pp. Reading Level: Grades 7–12.
Disability: Cancer (osteosarcoma and amputation)

When Jo Beth (Jobi) Halper was eight, she was diagnosed as having a rare cancer, osteogenic sarcoma, and her leg was amputated above the knee. Doctors in her home city of Minneapolis agreed that further treatment through chemotherapy or radiation therapy was not called for, although the orthopedic surgeon minced no words in telling her parents that in 97 to 99 percent of patients with this condition, the cancer reappeared in the lungs, with fatal results.

As Jordan Wilbur explains in his foreword, treatment of osteogenic sarcoma has changed since 1971, and the outcome can be much more favorable. Jobi's father refused to accept the prognosis and did research on his own that brought the family to the Children's Cancer Research Institute in Palo Alto, California, where Jobi entered an experimental program of chemotherapy supervised by Wilbur. Under his direction, the institute developed a philosophy that demands close cooperation between family and health professional "to form a circle of hope and love around each child." Jobi was one of the lucky ones; she survived and learned to do very well with one leg. This book, by her mother, appeared ten years after the diagnosis.

Analysis. Waller describes not only the course of Jobi's disease and treatment in painfully explicit detail, but also the effect of her illness on other family members, particularly on her older sister. Although she uses pseudonyms for all the medical people except Dr. Wilbur, the author writes graphically about professionals who, either out of self-protection or insensitivity, approached patients and families with what seems harsh coldness. On the other hand, many of the medical people the family met were sensitive and creative. Jobi's parents learned to take an active part in her treatment and to insist on what they believed she needed. On at least two occasions, Waller was helped by the technique of visualization, which involved thinking about and imaging a desired result (raising Jobi's white blood count, seeing her dancing); she never, however, explains why she did not attempt this technique at other critical junctures. Waller writes in a vivid, lively style, and includes a great deal of dialogue that, while it could not possibly have been so accurately and completely remembered, contributes to the readable quality of the text.

Circle of Hope is written for a general audience but might have particular interest for young people either facing a critical illness or coping with an amputation.

Woodson, Meg. *If I Die at Thirty.* Grand Rapids, Mich.: Zondervan, 1975. 148 pp. Reading Level: Grades 10–12.
Disability: Cystic fibrosis

Cystic fibrosis is a congenital, potentially fatal condition that affects in particular the lungs and digestive system. Peggy has cystic fibrosis, as does her brother. Her mother, a minister's wife, recorded conversations that she and others had with Peggy between her daughter's thirteenth and fourteenth birthdays. When Peggy was 13, she picked up in her doctor's waiting room a coloring book designed to explain cystic fibrosis to children. She read a fine-print explanation designed for parents, in which she learned that she did not have a normal life expectancy. Although her parents tried to comfort her with their strong religious convictions concerning faith and afterlife, Peggy began a journey through anger, denial, and bargaining before she came to peace with herself.

Peggy comes across as a lively and lovable girl. She stoically endures much cruelty from her peers at school because of her small size and distended stomach. The descriptions and conversations are sometimes humorous, often profound, but with the child's refreshing point of view.

Analysis. The author honestly chronicles her trials with two very sick but animated and sometimes obstreperous children. This book, like most from Zondervan, comes from a fundamentalist Christian perspective. The dialogues aim at reconciling oneself to a loving God who allows, or wills, suffering. The details of the consuming daily care of a child with cystic fibrosis are interspersed deftly in the story: the prodding to dislodge mucous in the lungs, the pills to help digest food, the small stature and distended stomach, and the mist tent in which the patient sleeps. The hereditary nature of the disease is acknowledged.

Orthopedic/Neurological Disabilities

Baker, Louise. *Out on a Limb.* New York: McGraw-Hill, 1946. 213 pp. Reading Level: Grades 7–12.
Disability: Amputation

Baker was eight years old when the borrowed bike she was riding collided with a car. The accident resulted in injuries necessitating the amputation of her leg across the knee. She was so small that she had to wait for special crutches to be made so she could be "On Foot Again" (Ch. 2). In later life she had colored crutches to match different outfits.

Baker records many anecdotes, such as exhibiting her artificial leg, replete with catsup, as a supposed trophy from an automobile accident. After high school she went to college and married a professor. "From then on he never had a peaceful moment until he escaped via the divorce" (p. 64).

The author dwells on relationships with men while in high school and college, and the kinds of ploys she developed to get along with her crowd. She also had a repertoire of bizarre stories as comebacks for those unfeeling enough to ask "What happened to you?" or "Where's your leg?" She includes a trip to Europe, her career as a journalist, and a stint at a boys' camp with another husband. By the end of the book, she had written a best-seller, *Party Line* (Whittlesey House, 1945).

Analysis. This humorous book is written in a breezy, fast-moving style. The author always goes for a laugh rather than an insight, and the book is full of "one-liners." It was read by a bright eight-year-old who had just had a traumatic amputation, and reported by his mother to be the best therapy she could have envisioned. He was convulsed and shared passages with his parents. It might have been a good one to share with his classmates as well.

Bleier, Rocky, with Terry O'Neil. *Fighting Back*. Illus. New York: Warner, 1976. 268 pp. Reading Level: Grades 7–12.
Disability: Orthopedic injury

Rocky Bleier, former Pittsburgh Steeler and now a television sports commentator, tells the story of his life as a football player for Notre Dame, as a member of the 196th Light Infantry Brigade of the U.S. Army in Vietnam, and as a running back during the Steelers' glory years.

Bleier was injured in Vietnam; a blast of gunfire gashed his foot deeply in three places. Physicians told him that with therapy he would be able to walk, but that he would never play football. He returned to Illinois, where he sold insurance for a time, living in the game room of a friend's home and working out during every spare minute. He eventually went back to the Steeler training camp, won a spot on the starting team, and became a star player.

Analysis. This is a book about college and professional football and about courage and determination. It should not be judged by the television movie made from it. The movie is primarily a love story; the book is primarily a football story.

Bleier recounts his story matter-of-factly and in great detail. He actually tape-recorded the "notes" from which the book was written at the time some of the events took place; for example, the Super Bowl game in New Orleans against the Minnesota Vikings. He does not minimize the pain, anguish, and uncertainty of his recovery years, nor does he turn them into melodrama. Above all, the book is a very good story. The conversation is realistic, including four-letter-words in the usual places.

Brickhill, Paul. *Reach for the Sky*. Illus. New York: Norton, 1954. 312 pp. Reading Level: Grades 7–12.
Disability: Amputation

Douglas Bader, a pilot with the Royal Air Force (RAF), was critically injured in a plane crash in 1931, and subsequently lost both legs; he was then 21 years old. Feisty and stubborn, he recovered from his nearly fatal injuries and was fitted with artificial legs. He learned to swim, dance, play golf, walk without a cane, drive an adapted car, and fly. However, the RAF invalided him out and he worked in civilian life until World War II when he was accepted by the RAF again. He flew fighter planes, became a squadron commander with increasing responsibility, and was decorated. Shot down over France and captured by the Germans, Bader spent the remaining three and one-half years of the war plotting and attempting escape, as he was shifted from one prison to another, until liberated by the American Army at Kolditz. After the war he left the air force and took a job with Shell Oil that involved flying his own plane all over the world. In the United States in 1947, he visited veterans' hospitals to help other men with amputations learn to walk again.

Analysis. Bader's story is full of crises, coincidence, and excitement, and Brickhill tells it well. Bader himself is portrayed as a man of passionate feeling and cocky courage, who accepts what cannot be changed but refuses to allow his sense of himself to be diminished by adversity. The world might term his condition a handicap; he acknowledges it as a disability, makes the necessary accommodations and adaptations, and goes forward.

Brown, Christy. *My Left Foot*. Illus. New York: Simon & Schuster, 1955. 178 pp. Reading Level: Grades 10–12.
Disability: Cerebral palsy

Christy Brown was born in Dublin in 1932, the ninth of 22 children. It was a difficult birth. When he was about four months old, his mother began to notice signs of physical abnormality, such as clenched hands, jaws either locked together or falling open, inability to sit up at the expected time. Doctors said that his case was interesting but hopeless; some said that he was also mentally defective. His parents refused to believe the latter diagnosis and insisted that Christy would be brought up as one of the family. The first vindication of their belief came when the boy was five; with his left foot, he took a piece of chalk from his sister and painfully copied the "A" that his mother drew on the floor. Eventually, she taught him to read and write; he began to paint, still using his left foot, and at 12 he won a Christmas coloring contest.

Brown's childhood was happy despite his disabilities. He was eventually able to sit up, and his brothers took him out in a little cart, including him in their jaunts and games. But adolescence brought consciousness of his difference. He became increasingly unhappy, imprisoned in his constricted body, and envious of others. At age 17, he began to write, but his unhappiness continued. He went to the shrine at Lourdes, hoping for a cure. Help came eventually, not from a miracle of that kind but from a Dr. Collis, who had seen him at a charity film show that Brown attended, carried on his brother's back. Dr.

Collis had a new treatment for cerebral palsy, which Brown first received at home. About this time his mother managed to have built for him a separate little house in the garden where his treatments took place and where he lived. In 1949 he went to London for consultation and examination at Middlesex Hospital, where he was told that with hard work and sacrifice he could be cured eventually. The sacrifice was to give up the use of his left foot, which had been good for him mentally but bad physically because of the strain it created for the rest of his body. Back in Dublin, Brown began treatment at the Cerebral Palsy Clinic.

This period brought new difficulties. Brown was much attracted to a young woman working in the clinic, but was increasingly conscious of his own difference, his emotional needs, and his "lack of really normal human expression and relationship" (p. 128). He had been writing for some years, using his younger brothers as his scribes; his style was based on nineteenth-century writers like Dickens, until he turned to Dr. Collis for help. Under Collis's guidance, Brown began to read widely and to reshape this autobiography that had occupied him for years. The last chapter describes a benefit concert that Brown and his family attended as special guests and at which Collis read the first chapter of this book.

Collis contributed a foreword describing his impressions of Brown and an epilogue discussing cerebral palsy. There are black-and-white photographs of Brown and his family and friends.

Analysis. Brown's story is powerful and moving. He is able to give the reader a firsthand picture of what it is like to grow up with an active mind and zest for experience, trapped in a painfully constricted body. Although he has sometimes felt himself at a distance from his family, especially his siblings as they all grew up, he makes it obvious that he has always been supported by warm and loving acceptance, especially from his parents.

The book is interesting not only in terms of its individual story, but for the picture it gives of the development of treatment of cerebral palsy. It might also be read in conjunction with other personal accounts, such as *New Light of Hope* by Bill Kiser (see this section).

Brown went on to write a best-seller, *Down All the Days* (Stein & Day, 1970), and he became a painter of some note.

Burton, Josephine. *Crippled Victory.* New York: Sheed & Ward, 1956. 144 pp. Reading Level: Grades 10–12.
Disability: Birth defect

In England in 1939, just before the onset of war, Anthony was born with hands that lacked bones, a partially paralyzed face, a convex mouth, and one eye that cried uncontrollably. His mother's first reaction was to pray for her infant son's death, despite the fact that she had tried for 12 years to have a baby.

This is Josephine Burton's story of how she learned to take care of Anthony and how she spent years searching, first for appropriate treatment and therapy, and later for proper schooling. At first, it appeared that little could be done to help him, but due to the war, orthopedic medicine advanced rapidly. He spent many years in casts; eventually, painful surgery did improve his situation. The family was able to send him to good private schools where he did well; he even learned to play tennis.

A convert to Roman Catholicism, his mother drew much comfort and sustenance from her faith, as did Anthony. They spent holidays in France, where one year they visited Lourdes. Anthony felt that he had been helped by the visits; his mother saw no visible improvement.

Analysis. This book is interesting in that it shows what a parent can accomplish almost single-handedly. There were no rehabilitation experts or specialized services offered for Anthony in the England of that era. The author's approach is matter-of-fact; she is neither overly optimistic nor pessimistic in her tone. She does not attempt to view the world through Anthony's eyes but honestly relates the situation from her own perspective.

Campanella, Roy. *It's Good to Be Alive.* Illus. Boston: Little, 1959.
306 pp. Reading Level: Grades 10–12.
Disability: Quadriplegia

In January 1958, Roy Campanella, the famous baseball player, was driving to his home on Long Island from New York City. His car skidded on an icy patch of road, and as a result of his critical injuries he became a quadriplegic. This book was written during his convalescence. After briefly describing the accident and its immediate aftermath, he devotes the next 175 pages to an account of his life up to that point. He was born in Philadelphia in 1921, the son of a white father and a black mother. He began playing professional baseball at 16, on black teams. In 1948, he joined the Brooklyn Dodgers, which had earlier made history by first integrating its team with Jackie Robinson. After the accident, Campanella underwent an extensive period of therapy at Dr. Howard Rusk's Institute of Rehabilitation Medicine; the last third of the book is devoted to his rehabilitation. By the end of the book, he is working with the Dodgers again as a coach.

Analysis. Campanella credits two professionals, Joe Reichler of the Associated Press and Dave Camerer of the Columbia Broadcasting System, with assistance in the preparation of this book. In its artless tone and relaxed, sometimes rambling style, its personal voice and informal syntax, it seems to be Campanella's own work, not an autobiography "as told to" a more accomplished writer. Campanella comes across as a man of courage and honesty who spent years doing what he loved to do most but was able, although not without dark hours, to accept a dramatic turn in his life's direction. As a well-known public figure, his example has inspired others struggling to meet similar challenges, and he has been sustained by his sense of connection. He does speak throughout of "cripples," a word now in disfavor.

Canada, Lena. *To Elvis, with Love.* New York: Everest House, 1978. 178 pp. Reading Level: Grades 7–12.
Disability: Cerebral palsy

Lena Canada, now a legal secretary and author who lives in Los Angeles, grew up in Sweden, where she went to work as a volunteer in a state rehabilitation home in Stockholm. This story is about her life and that of one of the cerebral-palsied children in her charge. The daughter of wealthy but unstable parents, Canada was alone by her late teens. Her authoritarian, abusive father had disappeared from her life after her mother divorced him, and her mother was too preoccupied with a new husband and a new life to have time or concern for her grown daughter. Canada herself had had two years of orthopedic problems and interminable stays in the hospital, facing the prospect of losing her arm. The arm was saved, and she was now healthy. Her mother's new husband was one of Canada's physicians during that ordeal.

The volunteer position was intended to give Canada something to fill the void in her life, but she soon became committed to her job, mainly because of Karen, an eight-year-old girl with severe cerebral palsy. Abandoned by her parents at birth when they learned of her disability, Karen had grown hostile, withdrawn, and depressed. With great effort, Canada won her over and, to the surprise and pleasure of the rest of the staff, became the first person ever to establish real communication with her. She took Karen on frequent outings and eventually managed to bring her home to the fashionable but lonely Stockholm apartment that Canada's mother had given her.

Canada learned that Karen was a great admirer of Elvis Presley, and that, indeed, her interest in him was the girl's only fragile tie to life and hope, except for her newly developed relationship with Canada. Karen, with Canada's help, began to write letters to Presley, to which he did not respond. In desperation, Canada wrote to a Hollywood columnist, who was able to help, and Karen and Presley began a correspondence that changed Karen's personality and even her physical condition until she contracted a severe and fatal case of flu. She died quietly, with Canada at her side.

Canada dedicated this book to Presley, who died a year before it was published.

Analysis. This is a frankly sentimental but never overdone or unrealistic portrayal of a very special relationship between a troubled child, living in a world of both physical and emotional pain, and a young woman whose own world was just as lonely and lacking in love.

Teenaged readers may find this relationship interesting and appealing, and they should like the Hollywood star "subplot" as well. There is some information here for those contemplating careers working with disabled children.

Carlson, Earl Reinhold. *Born That Way.* New York: John Day, 1941. 174 pp. Reading Level: Grades 7–12.
Disability: Cerebral palsy

Cerebral palsy is a syndrome of neuromuscular involvement due to brain damage, which usually occurs before or at the time of birth, often because of a deprivation of oxygen. In 1897, when author Carlson was born in a difficult delivery, little was known about the disorder (called Little's Disease) and few services were available to his poor, working-class family.

It was years before Carlson learned to walk, first with two canes his father carved from branches that the boy had dragged home on hands and knees. He first made his hand do his bidding by stealing an apple from a fruit stand. From this incident he realized that with concentration, will, and persistence, persons with cerebral palsy could help themselves.

Carlson's life through college is described in the first third of the book. He then went to Yale Medical School. The rest of the work describes his illustrious career as a physician who has established clinics and institutions for birth-injured people in parts of the country. He spoke (although it was very labored) at many public occasions as an advocate of disabled people. Carlson ends his book: "I have sometimes been embarrassed by being hailed as an example of what the handicapped person can do if he determines to overcome his difficulties. But what I have accomplished is really due to the help and guidance, throughout my life, of a host of teachers and friends. They kept me struggling against my difficulties and encouraged my belief that, by making the most of my opportunites, I could help other spastics to free themselves from the shackles of their handicap and become useful citizens" (p. 174).

Analysis. This straightforward book is of historical interest. The simply told events depict timeless themes—boys' adventures, struggles in school, and pursuing a career. Carlson's joy of life, more than his frustration over his disability, prevails. The relatively large print should aid the younger reader.

Cleland, Max. *Strong at the Broken Places.* Lincoln, Va.: Chosen Books, 1980. 156 pp. Reading Level: Grades 7–12.
Disability: Amputation

The author was a volunteer in a battle to break the North Vietnamese siege of Khe Sanh in April 1968. A grenade explosion resulted in the loss of both his legs and his right arm. After the war he was appointed by President Carter to head the Veterans Administration, during which time he wrote this book. The narrative begins with his childhood memories and ends with his meeting with President Carter in the Oval Office, only hours after Carter's inauguration.

Cleland discusses the problems he had "getting out in the world," with the knowledge that he would be avoided or pitied. He credits other disabled people, particularly those whose autobiographies he read, with strengthening his resolve to lead a productive life again. He was also sustained by his religious faith.

Analysis. Cleland writes in a terse, straightforward manner. His accounts of his experience in Vietnam and in state and national government are interesting. His insights into the problems of disabled people are informative. His unsentimental story is well written; his courage, strength, and essential optimism shine through.

Cragg, Sheila, with Jim Wilson, Dotty Wilson, and Patty Wilson. *Run Patty Run.* Illus. New York: Harper & Row, 1980. 192 pp. Reading Level: Grades 7–12.
Disability: Epilepsy

Patty Wilson had her first epileptic seizure when she was 11 months old. In the years that followed, she experienced similar episodes, sometimes when in school. The doctor referred to a seizure disorder, and at first the Wilsons did not realize that Patty's condition was epilepsy; when they did, they decided to keep the condition a secret because of the prejudice and shame connected with it.

Patty's father, Jim Wilson, was an enthusiastic runner, and he decided to encourage his daughter to run with him and to compete in cross-country events as a way of combating her clumsiness and building up her self-esteem. Their first long-distance run was 30 miles, from their home in La Palma, California, to Patty's grandmother's house in

Los Angeles. Subsequently, they ran 300 miles from La Palma to Las Vegas in 11 days, 502 miles from La Palma to San Francisco in 19 days, 1,310 miles from Buena Park, California, to Portland, Oregon, in 42 days, and 2,009 miles from Minneapolis to Washington, D.C., in 92 running days. Eventually, Patty developed other goals; starting with the run to Portland, she announced that she was running to help combat prejudice against people with epilepsy, and she was also running to show what a young woman could do. Her efforts have been supported not only by her father but by the rest of her sports-minded family—mother, older brother, and younger sister. There are photographs of Patty and her family.

Analysis. The author, a professional writer, brings a special personal knowledge to this book, since her son also has epilepsy. She concentrates not so much on Patty's disorder as on her running achievements and on the partnership between Patty and her father. Both Patty and Jim Wilson brought extraordinary endurance and perseverance to their running challenges; indeed, it sometimes seems that the effort and the dangers are out of proportion to the goal, as when Patty ran 1,310 miles with a broken bone in her foot.

The book could be enjoyed by sports-minded young readers, by youngsters who have a personal connection with epilepsy, and by those who are intrigued by stories of challenge and achievement.

Crossley, Rosemary, and Anne McDonald. *Annie's Coming Out.* Illus. Australia: Penguin, 1980. 251 pp. Reading Level: Grades 10–12. *Disability:* Cerebral palsy

Crossley was a child care worker/teacher in St. Nicholas Hospital in Melbourne, Australia, where Anne McDonald, with severe cerebral palsy in four limbs, had been committed at age three.

Much of the story involves Crossley's efforts to find a means of communication for the girl. She devised a system in which Anne would guide her hand on an alphabet board. Interspersed in Crossley's text is that written by Annie, describing her reactions in various stages of her life. A bitter battle raged with authorities over whether Crossley actually manipulated Anne McDonald's arm, and the case finally went to court to determine whether McDonald was competent to handle her own affairs and hence sign the book contract. The court ruled in her favor, and, at 18, Annie, with nursing care provided, went to live with her devoted teacher.

Crossley, however, was transferred from the hospital after her unsuccessful efforts to prove that other children there were also intelligent. Parliament did recommend residential care in group homes for the children.

A black-and-white photograph showing the authors opens the book, and diagrams of teaching devices intersperse the text.

Analysis. This book gives an interesting glimpse into educational practices in a country far away. The relationship of Anne to her teacher is somewhat reminiscent of that of Helen Keller and Anne Sullivan. The personalities of the two come across as somewhat blurred. It does seem that Crossley's efforts were made sincerely, and they probably helped to speed her government's progress toward closing large institutions. At any rate, she did effect the deinstitutionalization of Annie, and her story is moving.

Deacon, Joseph John. *Joey.* Illus. New York: Scribner's, 1974. 92 pp. Reading Level: Grades 7–12.
Disability: Cerebral palsy

Joey Deacon, born in England in 1920, has spent nearly all his life in a hospital environment. He lives in a wheelchair, cannot manage any self-care, and his speech is so distorted that only one other person, his friend Ernie, can understand him. This autobiography is a collaborative effort by four devoted friends: Joey Deacon told his story to Ernie, who repeated it to Michael to write it down (Michael's condition is not identified, but it seems to include mental retardation); then Joey read the text, letter by letter, and Ernie, who cannot read or write, read it to Tom, also illiterate, who typed it. The resulting narrative describes Joey's life, his family relationships, his friendships, his illnesses, his work, recreations, outings, and sorrows.

Black-and-white photographs show the four friends.

Analysis. Joey Deacon is clearly an intelligent man who has made the most of his extremely limited physical capacities. Having Ernie as an interpreter has made it possible for him to reach out to those around him. (Today, perhaps electronic developments would enable people like him to communicate more easily.) The narrative is simple and unaffected, without literary shaping or many descriptive details. Deacon wishes he had been born with full capacities and he sometimes feels that the world has a grudge against him, but he makes the most of everything he has; regret does not turn to bitterness, and he appreciates and returns to others the warm love and care that support him.

Donovan, Pete. *Carol Johnston: The One-Armed Gymnast.* Illus. Chicago: Childrens Press, 1982. 44 pp. Reading Level: Grades 4–6.
Disability: Missing limbs

Carol Johnston was born in Calgary, Canada, in 1958 without a right forearm. Despite this disability, she became a competitive athlete;

as a child she was a figure skater and at 12 she began gymnastics. In 1976 she represented Canada in the Junior Olympics at Montreal, and while a student at California State, Fullerton, she won all-American honors at a competition in Seattle. Eventually, two knee injuries caused her retirement from gymnastics, but she had established herself as an outstanding athlete.

Analysis. Johnston's story presents an attractive, determined, hard-working young woman determined "to be treated as a gymnast, not as a one-armed gymnast" (p. 22); her combination of grit and talent propelled her into athletic stardom. The author emphasizes the positive aspects of Johnston's career without any hint that there might have been moments of discouragement and pain. Although Donovan is a professional writer, the book is flawed by a peculiar back-and-forth movement in chronology and by a choppy style that sometimes puts a number of disparate ideas in one paragraph. Nevertheless, young readers might find the story of Johnston's accomplishments compelling; young gymnasts, in particular, might be intrigued by the description of how she uses visualization to help her accomplish exercises.

Eareckson, Joni, and Joe Musser. *Joni.* Illus. Grand Rapids, Mich.: Zondervan, 1976. 228 pp. Reading Level: Grades 7–12.
Disability: Quadriplegia

Joni Eareckson prefaces her book with a consideration of one minute in her 17 years that changed her life forever. She dove into shallow water in Chesapeake Bay and broke her neck. Eareckson details the medical events of the next several years in her arduous process of rehabilitation. She describes the gradual realizations that come to her—that she was paralyzed, that she would never walk, that she would not regain use of her hands. She met many kinds of professionals, from extremely sympathetic and helpful to thoughtless and sadistic.

Along with the physical rehabilitation had to come a psychological restoration. As with many spinal-cord-injury patients, Joni had been an athlete. She had been planning to go to college the fall after her accident. Instead, she was now completely dependent, frightened for her very life. In the depths of her despair, she did not want to live.

Joni's family had a strong Christian orientation. To find meaning and use in her life, she conceptualized her struggle in terms of overcoming her ego and submitting to what she saw as the will of God and His purpose for her life. She studied philosophy and scripture, and received much spiritual help from young religious friends. When finally she became happy and content in her religious belief, she became emotionally independent, and as a mature person achieved some impressive successes. She had learned to draw with pen in mouth, and her artwork began to sell. She began to share her gospel message, and was finally able to do so on national television on the "Today Show." She became a partner in a new religious bookstore, so she had some measure of financial security. She made a home with her sister and her children.

This, her first book, has been translated into many languages. She has written a sequel, *A Step Further* (Zondervan, 1978) and is planning a third.

The black-and-white photographs enhance the story.

Analysis. This book gives a thorough and honest portrayal of the rehabilitation process a person with a spinal cord injury must undergo. The gamut of emotions that Joni felt, from suffering and depression to hope and optimism, are well communicated. The psychological struggle is couched in religious terms. Joni shares enough of her spiritual process that it is understandable to the reader unfamiliar with this orientation. The book is written in an unaffected, simple style and makes fast and interesting reading.

Edgar, Betsy Jordan. *We Live with the Wheel Chair.* Illus. Parsons, W. Va.: McClain Print Co., 1970. 122 pp. Reading Level: Grades 10–12.

Disability: Amputation

Tom Edgar lost his legs during the Battle of the Bulge in World War II. This book by his wife is an account of their life afterward. The nature of his injuries was such that he could not be fitted with prostheses, and he and his wife had to accept the idea that the rest of his life would be spent in a wheelchair. After three years of hospital treatment, including several operations, at Walter Reed in Washington, D.C., Edgar and his wife settled on the West Virginia farm where he had grown up. He went into partnership with his father and became a successful farmer. He also entered politics and for a number of years was a Democratic member of the West Virginia House of Delegates.

From the time of his injury onward, Edgar faced his impairment with courage, humor, and ingenuity. While still in the hospital, he would sometimes take matters into his own hands, contravening doctor's orders—for example, after he insisted that the ward attendant wheel him to the bathroom, in trying to maneuver, he fell into the bowl headfirst. He and a friend developed adaptations that made it possible for him to drive a car before manufacturers had such a device on the market. He made attachments for his jeep so that he could ride around on the farm, overseeing the work; he also hunted from the jeep and campaigned in it.

In the last chapter, the author discusses barriers impeding free access for people with physical disabilities. She has worked with groups to eliminate such obstacles. While in the legislature, after several attempts, Tom Edgar saw passage of a "structural barriers" bill, which contains such provisions as reserved parking spaces for people with disabilities and accessible ramps, elevators, toilets, telephones, water fountains, and doorways in public buildings.

Analysis. Although not a professional or polished author, Edgar writes with sincerity and conviction. She told this story to express her admiration for her husband and his accomplishments and also in the hope that reading it might help others who face similar challenges. In addition, she wants to alert the public to the many barriers to free movement encountered by people with physical disabilities. Although changes in consciousness, building codes, and facilities have taken place since 1970 when the book was published, the need for awareness and implementation continues. Barriers, both in the physical world and in attitudes, still exist for people with disabilities.

Ellis, Frank K. *No Man Walks Alone.* Illus. Westwood, N.J.: Revell, 1968. 128 pp. Reading Level: Grades 7–12.
Disability: Amputation

Lieutenant Commander Ellis now has an "adjustable" height, from 4 feet 11 inches, without his plastic legs, to any required elevation. His story begins earlier as he piloted his ailing jet fighter to sixty-five feet above ground before ejecting. Miraculously his life was saved, but he was left a double amputee. He chronicles his love of flying from his early youth through adventures during training in the navy. The last half of the book is concerned with his efforts to remain on active duty as a pilot, despite his initial official orders to the contrary. Throughout, Ellis tries in his quest to be allowed to fly to show the navy that some of their ideas about the "handicapped" are outmoded. Always he was convinced that God had a purpose for his survival.

While different people in the navy either supported or neglected Ellis's petition, he became "newsbait." His story appeared in newspapers and magazines, and he was awarded the Distinguished Flying Cross for staying with his plane to save a trailer court instead of ejecting earlier.

By the end of the book Ellis has not yet achieved his dream—to be fully reinstated as a fighter pilot, and to be in the space program. However, he is on active duty and able to fly. He also has a new vocation—to be an example of a disabled person who can perform just as well as nondisabled peers.

A number of full-page black-and-white photographs show Ellis preparing for waterskiing, playing with his four children, and fulfilling the navy's endurance requirements.

Analysis. This book is written in journalistic prose. Ellis's style is direct and honest. Relatively large print makes for easy reading. Since it is an old book, it describes aircraft long outmoded and the space program in its infancy. Still, the adventures in the air and the thrill of flying ring true. Ellis's prodigious physical feats after his accident are reflected in the fine action photos as well as in the prose.

Although Ellis dwells on his faith near the end of the book, religion is not otherwise a dominant theme. The main message is acceptance of disabled persons for what they are and can do. Ellis has had experience speaking to young people, disabled and not.

Fiedler, Leslie. *Freaks: Myths and Images of the Secret Self.* Illus. New York: Simon & Schuster, 1979. 367 pp. Reading Level: Grades 10–12.
Disability: Abnormalities

This book is described by its writer, a professional author of some note, as "a meditation, a history, and a continuing dialogue with the world." In it are countless references to and pictures of actual persons who are physically different and bizarre. He also talks about the half-human creatures of fantasy. With regard to human inner reality, he states that through the ages strange, frightful, and contorted beings have been projected into the myths, religions, and arts of all cultures. Embodied in folk tales and legends, scriptures, and art are creatures such as the Medusa, the Sphinx, and countless other half-animal gods and heroes. Most cultures particularly cherish myths of beings who are far smaller or larger than usual. Fiedler notes that tales of leprechauns, elves, trolls, and hobolds are still taken at least half seriously in parts of the British Isles, Scandinavia, and Europe.

The task of separating inner and outer reality is a difficult one, not necessarily mastered even in adulthood. Fiedler suggests that the "myths and images of the secrets," the remnants of childlike archaic thinking, shape our subliminal perceptions of those with actual physical disfigurements or exceptionalities; hence, that confrontations with those who are different evoke our basic and primal insecurities: about scale, sexuality, our status as more than beasts, and our tenuous individuality. Fiedler, in 1978, visited the Circus World Museum in Baraboo, Wisconsin, where a sideshow tent featured plaster replicas of a Congress of Strange People (pictured in his book).

The final chapters discuss contemporary freaks of fact and fiction—speed freaks, those of hallucinogenic drugs, mutants, and robots. He states his thesis: "And most of us most of the time consider theirs to be the better part—except when at the side show and not sure whether we wake or sleep; we experience for a moment out of time the normality of Freaks, the freakiness of the normal, the precariousness and absurdity of being, however we define it, fully human" (p. 347).

A bibliography and an index follow.

Analysis. The author has been criticized for his title because of the pejorative connotation of the word *freaks* in describing those who are unusual or different. Some have felt uncomfortable about looking at human beings as exotica—about looking at the likenesses of disabled and different human beings in a multitude of photographs taken from circuses, medical records, and art. Others find the treatise too imprecise, or simply too wordy and rambling. However, like the few other books of this type (such as Roth and Crome's *Little People,* also this section), it is absorbing and thought-provoking.

Franks, Hugh. *Will to Live.* London: Routledge & Kegan Paul, 1979. 147 pp. Reading Level: Grades 10–12.
Disability: Muscular dystrophy

Muscular dystrophy is one of a number of progressive diseases causing degeneration of muscle tissue. The Duchenne type, which beset Robbie, the hero of this book, begins in childhood, affects mainly boys, and is usually fatal before adulthood. This story was written by Robbie's stepfather, a professional writer in Great Britain.

Three main strands comprise the book. One is a detailed picture of the progress of the disease itself. At the conclusion, Robbie is 20 and physically completely helpless. Another strand is the intellectual and emotional development of Robbie into a mature and compassionate young man. His struggle was not only to come to terms with his disease, for he had been physically and sexually abused by his biological father as a very young child. The final strand is the prodigious strength and patience of the author, which he ultimately transmitted to Robbie, in fighting the disease. He devoted hours and hours of time to Robbie's physical therapy. He was resourceful in anticipating needs and rallying the right support services at the right time. Throughout, Franks showed a lack of bitterness and despair, and a love of life and family, which again his stepson emulated. The setting of the book is generally in rural England and Wales, and the reader gets a glimpse into British school life as well.

Analysis. This book rings true in its optimism in the face of a harsh reality. Franks, however, makes an assumption that was helpful to his situation, but might be troublesome to some readers. Robbie did survive longer than most children with his disease. The author is certain that the regime of exercise, intellectual stimulation, and will to live prolonged Robbie's life, but it does not necessarily follow that the parents and their children who die earlier were themselves to blame for the more rapid course of the disease. With that in mind, this book can be enthusiastically recommended to those interested in understanding muscular dystrophy and one family's success at maximizing their quality of life in the face of adversity.

The writing and vocabulary is British, which could be a hindrance to the less able reader. The word *whilst*, for example, is used liberally. The style is crisp and succinct. There are many humorous stories about Robbie's friends, pets, and school, which add to the upbeat tone.

> Frevert, Patricia Dendtler. *It's Okay to Look at Jamie.* Photog. by David Jonasson and Gordon Dunn. Mankato, Minn.: Creative Education, 1983. 47 pp. Reading Level: Grades 4–9.
> *Disability:* Spina bifida

Jamie is an 11-year-old girl whose major life crisis at the moment is having to give an oral book report in front of her class. Her ongoing life crisis is spina bifida, a condition in which the covering of the spinal cord does not fully develop, although she copes well with it most of the time. She does have periods of depression, which rapidly pass, and she felt particularly bad when she was not well enough to ride the school bus with her brother, Shane, and her friends. When she was younger, she was taken to school in a special van that could accommodate her wheelchair. Now she is able to walk, with the aid of braces; in fact, she plays field hockey in the gym on the fateful day of the book report.

A flashback scene in the middle of the book describes in detail what goes on at Jamie's periodic medical checkups at the children's hospital in St. Paul, Minnesota. The kidney X-ray, which involves the use of a needle to shoot dye into her, upsets her the most, because she has veins that are hard to find. This time, however, the new doctor performs the procedure with dispatch. She has a long orthopedic exam and is fitted for new braces. Simple medical explanations are given in the process of describing Jamie's condition.

Black-and-white photographs of Jamie with her family, at school with her friends, and at physically active play illustrate the book.

Analysis. This is an excellent portrayal of a typical little girl who happens to have spina bifida. Sports, book reports, and friends are as much a part of her life as braces and X-rays. She sometimes feels bad about her disability: "These are the days when she writes in her diary, 'I am handicapped. I don't like it.' These are the days when she stares out the living room window and dreams she's someone else" (p. 20). Being slow and awkward bothers her. Aside from these feelings, she responds and behaves exactly as her peers do.

Frevert knows all the guidelines on handicapism and sexism and abides by them to the letter. The quotation above is the only place where she uses the word "handicapped"; and the usage, given the way Jamie is feeling at the moment, is exactly right. Her doctor is a woman; one nurse is a man. Jamie is interested in rough-and-tumble sports, even though she must be careful when participating in them. The real beauty here is the author's skill; she is not heavy-handed, obvious,or preachy in the process of eliminating sexism and handicapism. Her approach is matter-of-fact; this is the way the world is (not, this is the way I think the world should be and I'm showing you). It must be noted, however, that many children with spina bifida are far more disabled than Jamie.

Goodshell, Jane. *Daniel Inouye.* Illus. by Haru Wells. New York: Crowell, 1977. 32 pp. Reading Level: Grades 4–6.
Disability: Amputation

Army Captain Daniel Inouye lost his right arm at the age of 21 as the result of a wound received in the closing days of World War II. With this loss, his dream of becoming a surgeon was lost, too; instead, he decided to attend law school and go into politics. Neither career path had come easily for him.

Growing up in the slums of Hawaii, Inouye had limited educational opportunity because only students who passed a rigid English-language examination were permitted to attend the English Standard schools, which are far superior to the regular schools. This test served as a vehicle for racial discrimination and segregation; white students who had grown up in English-speaking homes passed it easily, but few Asian-Americans had enough exposure to standard English to achieve a passing score. Inouye, a Japanese-American, was no exception.

During the time he spent in an army hospital, Inouye for the first time had white friends. Some of them encouraged him to abandon his Pidgin English and offered him books they thought he should read. Twenty months later, at the time he was discharged from the hospital, he spoke perfect English. He enrolled in the University of Hawaii and later attended law school at George Washington University in Washington, D.C., which he felt was the best place to learn about politics.

On graduation, he returned to Hawaii and got his first job as a lawyer. A few years later he ran successfully for a seat in the territorial House of Representatives. This was the beginning of a long career as an elected official. When Hawaii attained statehood, Inouye became its first federal congressional representative. In the election of 1962, he was chosen for a seat in the U.S. Senate, where he worked tirelessly to improve the situation of agriculture, on which Hawaii's economy depends, to improve civil rights laws, and to achieve better understanding among nations. He sees population control as one of the major keys to world peace. During the Watergate hearings, his face became familiar to people everywhere. (In 1967, Inouye's autobiography, *Journey to Washington,* was published by Prentice-Hall.)

Black-and-white brushwork drawings illustrate the text.

Analysis. This is an interesting, well-told story. Inouye is portrayed as a man of courage and vision. He not only conquered the social handicaps of racism and unequal opportunity, but he also used his career in government to help effect social change. Ironically, had he not lost his arm, he would have been a physician rather than a politician; this has been the major influence of the disability in his life as it is portrayed in this biography. Whatever adjustment problems and challenges he may have faced because of his disability are not covered.

Gould, Jean. *A Good Fight: The Story of FDR's Conquest of Polio.* New York: Dodd, 1960. 308 pp. Reading Level: Grades 10–12.
Disability: Poliomyelitis

In August 1921, while vacationing at Campobello Island in New Brunswick, Canada, Franklin D. Roosevelt came down with a mysterious illness. At first misdiagnosed, it was eventually correctly described as poliomyelitis, then often called infantile paralysis, and it left Roosevelt with paralysis of both legs. Although author Gould gives background biographical information and tells the story of Roosevelt's political life, she concentrates on his illness and convalescence, and techniques he used to cope with his motor disabilities. Roosevelt was a man of extraordinary courage and strength. Once he understood the extent of the damage caused by the virus, he set himself to do everything suggested by his doctors and everything in his power to recover as much mobility as possible. He refused to dwell on what might have been, or to bow to his mother's efforts to persuade him to lead the life of an invalid.

Sustained by what Gould calls "creative quality in his brave acceptance of the hard blow fate had dealt him" (p. 201), he went on to be elected governor of New York in 1928 and president of the United States in 1932. His own suffering and struggle gave him a new perspective and made him far more sensitive to the lives of others than he might otherwise have been. Gould describes in considerable detail the various courses of treatment and therapy Roosevelt went through and the techniques he developed for getting around, particularly in his public appearances. She also tells the story of the center for people with polio at Warm Springs, Georgia, a site that Roosevelt essentially discovered and built up. The final chapter describes the work of the National Foundation for Infantile Paralysis, the development of Warm

Springs as it continued after Roosevelt's death, and the successful search for antipolio vaccines.

Analysis. Never losing sight of her main focus, Gould handles an enormous body of material with ease. Roosevelt emerges as a dynamic, brilliant leader whose attitude toward his disability contributed to his political effectiveness and also toward public acceptance of impairments.

Although Gould employs the word *cripple*, in use at the time this book was written, for the most part her style is fluent and readable. And although polio has been nearly erased, Roosevelt's experience is transferable to other conditions that dramatically alter lives and expectations.

Graham, Frank. *Lou Gehrig: A Quiet Hero.* Illus. New York: Putnam, 1942. 108 pp. Reading Level: Grades 4–6.
Disability: Amyotrophic lateral sclerosis

Lou Gehrig was a great baseball player for the New York Yankees, rivaling his friend and teammate Babe Ruth. Graham chronicles Gehrig's life beginning with his impoverished early years as the only living child of hardworking German immigrant parents. Gehrig's early love of sports and his triumph in high school football and baseball are detailed. Experiences relating to sports at Columbia University and his recruitment by the Yankees complete the first third of the book. His adventures as a regular with the New York Yankees include successes and failures of the team, friendships, deaths, and the development of Gehrig as a world-class athlete.

The peak of Gehrig's career included assisting his team to win the World Series, establishing good friendships, providing financial comfort for his parents, and enjoying a happy marriage.

The last part of the book deals with the shadows closing around him as he began, without knowing it, to succumb to a rare disease, amyotrophic lateral sclerosis (a form of chronic poliomyelitis) that would take his life at age 38. The quiet courage and forebearance with which he faced his progressive neuromuscular deterioration endeared him to his colleagues and the public. He was an inspiring person as well as a deserving member of National Baseball Hall of Fame in Cooperstown, New York.

Black-and-white photographs illustrate the days of the late 1920s and 1930s.

Analysis. This historical narrative paints Gehrig's life and his baseball experiences in broad brush strokes. The reader is made very much aware of the effect of a serious illness on a great athlete. The book may be somewhat overadulatory of Gehrig, the "half-God" as Graham calls him, but the fast-moving, well-told story should have appeal, particularly to young athletes.

Greenfield, Eloise, and Alesia Revis. *Alesia.* Drawings by George Ford and photog. by Sandra Turner Bond. New York: Philomel, 1981. 59 pp. Reading Level: Grades 4–9.
Disability: Orthopedic injury

When Alesia Revis was nine years old, she was struck by a car while riding a bicycle. Her injuries were so severe that doctors did not expect her to survive and thought that if she did live, she would never be more than a "vegetable." However, Alesia not only did survive, she regained many of her physical and mental faculties.

The book takes the form of Alesia's journal, written between March and October 1980, just after her eighteenth birthday. She still uses a wheelchair and can walk only a few steps without support; however, she attends a regular high school, goes to dances (she can dance if she leans against a wall or on her partner) and to parties, and participates in many other activities. Alesia is part of a close family and has a circle of good friends. Most of the focus is on her present life and thoughts, with occasional reference to the accident, the course of her recovery, and her feelings about her disabilities. At one point she talks about the questions children ask her when they see her in a wheelchair. "I used to get tickled. But it's not funny when grown folks start staring. You expect it from little children, but not from grown folks . . . some people move away from me when they see me in the wheelchair, like they're afraid they might catch my disability. They have disabilities, too—faults and things like that, everyone has them. Mine are just more noticeable, but they don't think about it that way" (pp. 17–18).

There are many black-and-white drawings and photographs.

Analysis. The text reflects close collaboration between Greenfield (an accomplished writer) and Alesia. The voice in this journal sounds like the authentic voice of a bright, lively adolescent who loves clothes and fun, is beginning to think about her future, and is being nudged by her family to do more for herself. Since the book was written eight years after her accident, the pain and rebellion she might possibly have felt then have been muted by time; what the authors give us now is a picture of accommodation, the details of daily life of a young person unselfconsciously working toward increasing emotional and physical independence.

Griesse, Rosalie. *The Crooked Shall Be Made Straight.* Atlanta: Knox, 1979. 240 pp. Reading Level: Grades 10–12.
Disability: Scoliosis

The author's scoliosis—curvature of the spine—was diagnosed when she was 12. The doctor prescribed exercises and a brace, but the curvature progressed. In the meantime, her father was murdered by burglars, leaving her mother a widow with three young children.

Young Rosalie spent many months in Shriner's Hospital in St. Louis where she had two fusion operations before being sent home in a brace. A year later, returning pain and X ray pictures showed that false joints—pseudoarthroses—had formed. Surgery was required, and again after her freshman year at college. Subsequently she married a young Lutheran minister and had three daughters. Then a fall on a freshly waxed floor fractured the fusions and she was operated on again, this time in the Hospital for Special Surgery, part of the Cornell University Medical Center in New York City. Her husband fell ill and had hardly recovered before their orthopedic surgeon recommended another operation because of her continuing pain. This time there were many medical complications, and she nearly died. Then an automobile accident caused a new fracture and fresh pain and, once again, surgery.

By now, Rosalie had been a "scolie" for 31 years. In addition, her experienced eye had detected early signs of the same condition in her oldest daughter; eventually, all three girls were found to have it, as well as her nieces. Treatment with a so-called Milwaukee brace, however, successfully straightened the children's curvatures without surgery. Surgical treatments had also changed, and Rosalie's eighth fusion required only a three-and-a-half week hospitalization without months in a cast. By the end of the book, she is once more going home from the hospital, ready to face a painful convalescence, but trusting her doctors and rejoicing in family and friends.

Analysis. Griesse's book is an absorbing personal account of life with a chronic disorder. It is, as well, in its clinical details, a history of treatment of this condition from 1942 to the 1970s. It also indicates changes in the handling of hospitalization for children; when she was a patient, Shriner's Hospital did not allow parents to visit except on special occasions like the eighth-grade graduation, because it was felt that recurring separations were too upsetting to the children.

Griesse does not hide her moments of self-consciousness, depression, and despair. At the same time, she is convincing when she discusses how she learned to "make friends with pain" or describes the ways in which scoliosis has been a blessing to her, especially in the relationships and insights it has brought her. Most of her doctors and nurses have been the sensitive, skillful practitioners one would like all medical people to be, and she brings them vividly to life with sharp descriptions and humor. She is a woman of many interests who says that long ago, in the large hospital ward in St. Louis, she learned from other children that life is too varied and challenging to be swallowed up by illness. She is able to put her trust in a God who will support her through whatever she is called on to bear.

One possibly discomfiting note occurs in the section dealing with Griesse's experience in Shriner's Hospital. The youngster in the next bed, with whom she became good friends, was a black girl from the South, and the author's attempts to transliterate her dialect may appear to some readers a condescending gesture.

Hacker, Jeffrey H. *Franklin Roosevelt*. Illus. New York: Franklin Watts, 1983. 119 pp. Reading Level: Grades 4–9.
Disability: Poliomyelitis

This is a biography of the only president of the United States elected to office four times. His early privileged life at Hyde Park as an only child, his prep school days, college life, and marriage to his cousin Eleanor are given as background. The bulk of the story describes Roosevelt's adult years, in which his very serious bout with polio figures prominently. When asked later if events at the White House ever worried him, he answered, "If you had spent two years in bed trying to wiggle your big toe, after that anything else would seem easy." Hacker discusses Roosevelt's policies and leadership style as he faced the Great Depression and World War II. The events and controversies of his administration are described and analyzed. His last days and his legacy are discussed at length.

Full-page black-and-white photographs enhance the text.

Analysis. This book is simply, clearly, and objectively written. It does not overburden the reader with facts, but it gives a fine historical view of the first half of the twentieth century. Controversial material is not glossed over; Roosevelt's lifelong relationship with Lucy Mercer and Eleanor's reaction to it are detailed, for example.

Helms, Tom. *Against All Odds*. New York: Crowell, 1978. 277 pp. Reading Level: Grades 10–12.
Disability: Quadriplegia

"Against all odds," Tom Helms recovered from a broken neck, not once but twice. The first time, at age 18, he was in an automobile accident. He had a complete and rapid recovery, effected by his own determination and "hard-nosed" attitude, as his tough and admiring physical therapist, Don Stirewalt, called it. The second break occurred four years later just as Helms had graduated from college and was ready to begin a job in Nashville. Attempting to carry heavy luggage to a car, he lost his balance and fell down stairs and into the parked car, breaking his neck. After the first break, conflicting medical opinions about the necessity versus the dangers of surgery for an anterior fusion had resulted in the young man's decision not to have surgery. The decision had not been based on complete, accurate information, and the second break would probably not have occurred had the surgery been performed.

This second time, Tom Helms was given no hope of ever walking again, even by Don Stirewalt, who was the greatest external force in both recoveries. But after nearly four years of tough, relentless exercise, Helms was able to walk with a cane. And after 18 months of looking for a job, he bitterly realized that all his efforts were not enough to convince employers that he was worth hiring. At that point he decided to write this book. He is now an employment counselor at a state agency.

Tom Helms began his book on one of the blackest days of his life, when the near impossibility of getting people to believe that he was employable had hit him at the same time he was trying to cope with the suicide of Cindy Davis, an incredibly courageous young woman who used a wheelchair after her discharge from the rehabilitation hospital. She struggled through college and had spent months looking for a job. "It just happened one day—a day no different from all others. The courage simply ran out," Tom Helms said to Don Stirewalt (p. 265).

Analysis. Despite the subject, this book is not a downer. It is realistic and funny. It also gives rise to great anger; Tom Helms vividly and graphically describes what potential employers say to him during interviews and how women who appear to be interested in him behave as soon as they see his cane. The littleness and meanness of these people stand in stark contrast to the humanity of Helms, his family, his friends, and many of the people in the rehabilitation hospital. These negative attitudes also are in stark contrast to the tenacity and courage that it required for Helms to walk again.

This book easily ranks as one of the best young-adult selections in this genre. Helms's story is inspiring and enlightening to able-bodied young people, and even for readers who have encountered prejudice, it is an eye-opener.

Heymanns, Betty. *Bittersweet Triumph.* New York: Doubleday, 1977. 191 pp. Reading Level: Grades 10–12.
Disability: Cerebral palsy

The author wrote her account in part, she says, because "so little has been written about personal experiences of the adult cerebral-palsied. Most books covered only the childhood years; many were written through the sympathetic eyes of mothers" (p. 167).

Betty Heymanns was born at home in St. Cloud, Minnesota, in 1932, in a precipitous breech birth. As a baby, she did not sit and crawl at the expected time. When she was 24 months old, a pediatric specialist who examined her "merely shrugged his shoulders and said, 'She won't amount to much' " (p. 22). However, her parents accepted her completely, resisting any suggestion that she be institutionalized, and raised her with love and encouraging support. When she was very young, her father taught her to walk, using a rope strung across the living room. Five years later, when they needed a doctor's report to enroll her in an orthopedic school, they returned to the same specialist, who was stunned by her progress.

Heymanns went to special schools through high school. When she became passionately interested in photography, her mother helped her with procedures too difficult for her to manage alone; after Heymanns took a post–high school vocational course in photography, they ran a studio at home together. Heymanns learned to type on an electric machine, to cook, to sew, to garden; she took public transportation alone; she redesigned her wardrobe so that she could manage her personal care independently; in her thirties, she took courses at the University of Minnesota. Always, she wanted to be accepted as "normal." For many years, her passion for photography absorbed her so intensely that it was a long time before she confronted the fact that in some ways she would never be normal. Her speech was difficult to understand, especially when she was under strain, but she had no idea of how she sounded until she heard a tape recording of her own voice; she was appalled. She could not always control her body movements, and again, the condition was exacerbated by stress. She was immediately identifiable as someone who was different.

For some time in adulthood Heymanns was plagued by poor health, including hepatitis and painful muscle spasms of the back; tumors were found reaching toward her spine, and after they were removed, physical tension and what she calls "that crazy self-conscious phobia that plagued me for years" were relieved. After the surgery, she experienced a brief emotional breakdown. By the end of the book, helped partly by an abortive relationship with a cerebral-palsied young man, she has reached greater acceptance of herself and her life.

A note at the front of the book says that all names and places have been changed. Although many people helped and encouraged her, some were indifferent and others cruel.

Analysis. In her brief foreword, Heymanns writes, "I am no longer the person I write of. This book tells my struggle to emulate 'normalcy'—my ultimate goal. Little did I realize normalcy does not exist." She begins her book with her one-woman photography show when she was 26, a moment that she thought would signal "permanent success." A theme of her autobiography is that there is no such permanence, that her life has been a series of upward and downward movements, although with gradually increasing self-knowledge and self-acceptance. She takes the reader with her, conveying the warm closeness of her family, the bitterness of enduring stares and remarks, the challenges of living as an adult still in her parents' home, the frustrations of physical limitations, the longing to live a fulfilled life as a woman. Some chapters include poetry; as no other author is indicated, one assumes that this is Heymanns's own work.

Although much has changed in the treatment of cerebral palsy, many of the challenges are the same for young patients today as they were for Heymanns, making the book interesting reading for youngsters who have similar conditions, as well as for their friends and families.

Hickok, Lorena. A. *The Story of Franklin D. Roosevelt.* Illus. by Leonard Vosburgh. New York: Grosset, 1956. 177 pp. Reading Level: Grades 4–6.
Disability: Poliomyelitis

More than half of this large-print book recounts boyish escapades of young Franklin Roosevelt. The chapters deal with specific stories, such as the youth's arrest on a bicycle trip in Europe, or the accidental firing of his shotgun. The author covers his college days, marriage, and rise in politics.

The details surrounding Roosevelt's struggle with polio are told in several chapters. His participation in the development of Warm Springs, Georgia, and founding of the National Foundation for Infantile Paralysis are highlighted as important contributions when he was president of the United States. The book ends with anecdotes from the war years and events surrounding his death and funeral.

The black-and-white illustrations recall another era with pictures of square-rigged boats, early twentieth-century costumes, and carriagelike automobiles. Many of these are authentic on-the-spot sketches.

Analysis. This book has an advantage over many biographies in that the author knew the Roosevelts for many years in her capacity as a newspaper reporter and later as a worker on the Democratic National Committee (as Eleanor Roosevelt explains in the preface). Hence, she could know anecdotes about Roosevelt that would especially appeal to young readers. Hickok avoids any mention of political controversy or unpleasantness in the family that would be essential in historical accounts for more mature readers.

Howell, Michael, and Peter Ford. *The True History of the Elephant Man*. Illus. New York: Penguin, 1980. 190 pp. Reading Level: Grades 10–12.

Disability: Neurofibromatosis

The authors have completed a new study of the life of John Merrick, the so-called Elephant Man. His condition, neurofibromatosis or von Recklinghausen's Disease, experienced by an estimated 100,000 people in this country, may result in symptoms as mild as café-au-lait spots or benign skin tumors called fibromas. In Merrick's case, this progressive, untreatable disease was manifested in extreme physical distortion and facial and cranial disfigurement.

Howell and Ford have rectified some earlier misapprehensions about Merrick's mother, who they now believe was compassionate with her affected son in his early years. Merrick became a professional freak, at a time when there was a great interest in human oddities. He was subject to exploitation by his manager and suffered physical abuse and taunts on many sides. He was finally rescued, half-dead, by a physician, Frederick Treves, who later was to write about his charge in "The Elephant Man," included in *The Elephant Man: A Study in Human Dignity* by Ashley Montague (Outerbridge & Dienstfrey, 1971). Merrick was given a little room in the hospital where he would live until his early death.

Although Merrick had been assumed by most to be slow and brutish, he was actually a refined and cultivated man. He acquired as friends distinguished persons of the day and had an audience with royalty. Although he faced an almost unendurable situation, he had a capacity to enrich his world.

Analysis: The authors have done intensive research to document previously unknown areas of Merrick's life. Their conclusions about his mother's love for him make sense. It would be inconceivable that Merrick could have been so unfailingly kind and such a cultured man without the benefit of a good early experience to counteract the hardships and cruelties he endured as a young man.

This account is lucid and interesting. The story of the Elephant Man has been on television, in the theater, and on film.

Jacobs, William Jay. *Eleanor Roosevelt: A Life of Happiness and Tears*. Illus. New York: Coward, 1983. 108 pp. Reading Level: Grades 4–9.

Disability: Poliomyelitis

The author is a historical scholar who has carefully researched the life of Eleanor Roosevelt, who is not depicted just as Franklin's wife and an echo of his career. Rather, her own personal struggle for fulfillment and maturity and her influence on her husband and country are highlighted.

In easily readable prose, her life is detailed from her birth as a homely child, who was "supposed to be a boy," to her triumph in her years alone, without Franklin, as "First Lady of the World" (as Harry Truman called her).

Jacobs emphasizes her role in sustaining her husband and family as polio struck the up-and-coming young politician. As her disabled husband improved, she began her political work to keep him in the public eye so that he could become governor of New York.

Black-and-white photographs from the Franklin D. Roosevelt Memorial Library are well chosen to illustrate the story. For example, the power struggle between Eleanor and her mother-in-law is pictured in a photo of Franklin on the day of his inauguration as governor of New York, January 1929.

Analysis. This book emphasizes the personal motivations and personalities of famous figures rather than historical facts or political analyses.

Judson, Clara Ingram. *City Neighbor: The Story of Jane Addams.* Illus. by Ralph Ray. New York: Scribner's, 1951. 130 pp. Reading Level: Grades 4–9.
Disability: Spinal curvature

The author has made use of Jane Addams's own writings, news reports, and her own acquaintance with the well-known social worker from the first neighborhood house in this country. This biography begins when Jane is a six-year-old, somewhat misshapen child living in a large house in rural Illinois. The year was 1866. Jane's girlhood at home and college experiences comprise a third of the book.

After college, rather frail and ill but most determined, Jane Addams set out to seek her fortune. In 1888, she arrived on the west side of Chicago where new immigrants from many countries were settled. There, at considerable self-sacrifice, she began work on her dream of a "big house," eventually to be a renovated mansion called Hull House. She established programs for the very young and the elderly, and a woman's club, enticing the cooperation of socially prominent women of Chicago. At that time children were employed in sweatshops 14 hours a day. Largely because of Addams and other Hull House residents, Illinois passed its first child labor act in 1893.

The increasing influence of Hull House is depicted. Memorable awards, such as the Nobel Peace Prize, climaxed Addams's 75 years of life. A chronology of important events of her life ends the book. The print is large and the prose easy to read. Some of the black-and-white etchings are precisely executed and attractive.

Analysis. The author took the liberty, she says, of using the fictional form with conversation in order to make the story more vivid. This works well here. The book is not exciting since few conflicts or harrowing events are portrayed, but it does give an interesting look into the life of an influential person of the nineteenth century.

Killilea, Marie. *Karen.* Englewood Cliffs, N.J.: Prentice-Hall, 1962. 314 pp. Reading Level: Grades 7–12.
Disability: Cerebral palsy

This story, written by her mother, begins with a dismal diagnosis that nothing could be done for Karen. With that, the Killileas began their long struggle to help their daughter, who had cerebral palsy, and eventually to help others through their efforts in establishing the United Cerebral Palsy Association, Inc.

The Killilea family of four children, one adopted, was warm and lively. They treated Karen as normally as possible, but for this they were often criticized, as when, for example, they allowed her to receive her first Holy Communion with her class. Karen was an active, spunky child who did not want special treatment. One time the family had gone to the beach and all were enjoying the occasion. As Karen was getting her crutches, an older couple was passing by.

> In an oozy voice the woman said to Karen, "You poor little thing." Karen pulled her crutches back a few inches and straightened to look at them. "It must be awful to wear those braces," said the man. "You poor child," repeated the woman. "Why?" asked Karen inquisitively. "Why—why—well—because—." The woman was obviously off balance. The man took a few backward steps in the direction of the gate. "I'm lucky," said Karen. "You just don't understand." They stared at her. "You see," Karen explained patiently, "I can see with my eyes, hear music with my ears, and I can speak as well as anybody. Mom says better than a lot of grownups." Crouching a little to keep her balance, she lifted a crutch and waved it. "Good-by" (pp. 269–270).

Analysis. This book is written in a somewhat florid, emotional style that appeals to young readers. The lively description of family life and Karen's plucky nature has an immediacy, although the story is an old one.

Two sequels, *Wren* (Dodd-Mead, 1954) and *With Love from Karen* (Prentice-Hall, 1963), continue the story.

Kiser, Bill. *New Light of Hope.* New Canaan, Conn.: Keats, 1974. 223 pp. Reading Level: Grades 10–12.
Disability: Cerebral palsy

When the author was a week old, he stopped breathing for a few minutes and turned blue. (He does not give his birth date, but jacket copy indicates that it was about 1926.) At first the doctor could find nothing wrong with him, but subsequently his motor abilities and speech failed to develop normally. Kiser had had a brain hemorrhage that cut off vital oxygen and left him with cerebral palsy. His parents never gave up hope that he would get well and although of limited means, took him from one doctor to another; most were kind, but one advised them that their child had "no intelligence whatsoever" and that they should put him in an institution and forget him. Since there were no facilities for disabled children available to the Kisers, his parents taught him at home; his mother had been a teacher before Bill's birth. This worked well until he reached high school age; although he got a state high school certificate he had neither the solid academic work nor the social experience that a regular school would have given him.

Kiser's father died when he was 13 and his mother went back to work as a teacher. The youngster felt himself increasingly imprisoned both by his physical condition and by his mother's devotion and their emotional interaction; he thought about suicide and attempted it at least once. Over the years, he had operations and some physical therapy. His mother died when he was in his mid-twenties. He lived on in his house with a woman coming in to help him, became active in a church group, and worked to start a program for adults with cerebral palsy, a job for which he was paid $50 a month by United Cerebral Palsy Association, Inc. (UCP) and another $50 by his church. Due to a number of causes, including Kiser's inexperience and his emotional involvement with a physical therapist, the program was eventually dropped. Kiser then wrote and edited a monthly newsletter for UCP. His income was very small and became more meager when the newsletter was cut off the budget. He became increasingly frustrated in his desire for a normal life, especially a normal sexual and emotional life. In desperation he decided to try brain surgery, which was being done in a Midwestern medical center that Kiser does not name. This experimental procedure with ultrasonic waves not only failed to improve Kiser's condition, but it reduced him to a state of complete helplessness and incontinence. He was forced to life in institutions, and his house was sold.

Long months later, Kiser met a woman interested in spiritual healing, and although he did not himself experience such a cure or become a believer, he says that "some unknown force came into play which helped me regain emotional control and the desire to live. As naive as it may sound to others, and even to me at times, I will always call this a force of God, perhaps never really being able to define my own concept of Him" (pp. 167–168).

Kiser improved physically and began to write a weekly newspaper column, and eventually his "Handicapped Mailbag" column ran in several papers. At the time of the writing of this book, he was living in an apartment that had been modified so that he could manage most details of self-care; he had a high school boy to help him with dressing, and a secretary. In addition to his writing, he was doing some public relations work for Goodwill Industries.

Analysis. Kiser says in his preface that his purpose in writing the book was to "let the layman and professional person alike know how it has been to face life with my limitations, yet with normal drive and aspirations" (p. 8), and that he has not attempted to do so objectively. Indeed, the book is a subjective, often angry, and bitter autobiography, in which he has written about his mistakes and errors of judgment and tangled emotions. Most of the names are pseudonymous, but Kiser warns that the book will probably anger many people, including friends. Students and teachers who work with people with cerebral palsy, as well as those who themselves have the condition or are interested in it, would find the book worth reading.

Kovic, Ron. *Born on the Fourth of July.* New York: McGraw-Hill, 1976. 224 pp. Reading Level: Grades 10–12.
Disability: Paraplegia

The author of this autobiography is a Vietnam veteran whose spinal cord was shattered by a bullet that entered his shoulder and penetrated to his spine. The book opens with a vivid, terrifying description of the battlefield scene. His later description of poor physical care and unsanitary conditions at a New York City veterans' hospital is equally graphic and searing.

Kovic, a patriotic young man from a "typical" American background, whose hero was John Wayne, went to Vietnam to fulfill the ideal of serving his country. After his discharge from the hospital and reentry into civilian life, he endures all the agonizing adjustment problems caused by his disability—problems compounded by his feelings of guilt over his role in the accidental deaths of a sergeant and of some Vietnamese children that occurred in separate, battle-related incidents. He eventually became involved with the Vietnam Veterans against the War. Active as a public speaker, Kovic emerged as one of the movement's leaders and was among a small group who penetrated the Republican National Convention at Miami in 1972 and disrupted President Nixon's acceptance speech with antiwar chants.

Despite his disillusion with national policy, Kovic remains a patriot. He dedicates his book, published during the bicentennial, to "my country and its people." He was born on July 4, 1946.

Analysis. This is a "too good to put down" book; it is moving and deeply disturbing. Kovic forcefully communicates his anger about the course of the war, about the shocking mistreatment and neglect that he and others experienced in the veterans' hospital, and about social attitudes toward disabled people. The horror of his war memories and his descriptions of various incidents in Vietnam are graphic and sometimes unbearable.

Although most of the text is written in the first person, Kovic achieves detachment in certain sections by shifting to third-person narrative. In other sections, he creates the effect of an even deeper involvement by switching to an italicized stream of consciousness. All these devices are effective. Despite the emotional turmoil and tragedy related, the prose is not overwritten or overwrought.

This is a book for mature teenagers able to deal with its powerful emotional tone, violence, grief, and anger. It is as much a commentary on bureaucratic ineptitude, war, violence, and American society's expectations for men as it is on disability.

LaFane, Pamela. *It's a Lovely Day Outside.* London: Gollancz, 1981. 159 pp. Reading Level: Grades 10–12.
Disability: Rheumatoid arthritis

This English author chronicles her battle with rheumatoid arthritis, which caused her to spend over 30 years of her life in institutions. From age 11 to 16, she was treated in hospitals for children, where she could continue her education. After that, she was sent to London to live in a hospital for "the chronically ill" where the majority of the patients were very elderly people and where the medical care was minimal and lacking in attention and concern.

In spite of this, LaFane took correspondence courses and began a career as a writer. A gregarious person, she also made many friends. In 1969, with the help of some of these friends and various others, she left the hospital and took a small apartment of her own, where she has since been able to live independently.

Analysis. This is a story full of perseverance, patience, and courage. The view of the institution for chronically ill people and its indifferent personnel, however, is gloomy and depressing. The contrast between LaFane's spirit and the attitude of those around her is stark, making this an inspiring story of victory over tremendous odds.

Severe arthritis is an uncommon illness among children, but it does occur. These youngsters must be sedentary for long periods, and they may particularly enjoy this book.

Landvater, Dorothy. *David: A Mother's Story of Her Son's Recovery from a Coma and Brain Damage.* Englewood Cliffs, N.J.: Prentice-Hall, 1976. 157 pp. Reading Level: Grades 10–12.

Disability: Brain damage

Seventeen-year-old David Landvater's small car skidded off a curving, rain-slick road on a July night in 1972 and collided with a tree. Although strapped in with a seat belt, he received severe internal injuries and extensive damage to his brain stem, which put him into a deep coma. Physicians immediately told his mother that if he lived, which was unlikely, he would be a "vegetable," unable to walk, talk, or think for the rest of his life. While scores of neighbors, both friends and strangers, rallied to help the family, Dorothy Landvater spent day and night at the hospital for months, determined not to give up hope. Often she saw signs of improvement (the blinking of an eye at her command in response to a question, for example) that medical personnel first denied, then later admitted had occurred.

Still comatose, although somewhat responsive, David was eventually admitted to a rehabilitation hospital, where his improvement was slow but visible. Always his mother was there—pushing him, urging medical personnel to do more, sometimes criticizing their attitudes toward David or their treatment of him. She was not, needless to say, always appreciated.

This book is Dorothy Landvater's account of those early days of her son's injuries and of the three years that followed. During that time, David miraculously regained his memory, speech, and some mobility (he used both a wheelchair and a walker three years after his accident). He even finished his last year of high school, after confrontation with the educational system and with himself. Infuriated by "babyish" learning material and by being consigned to a special school for disabled students, David developed severe emotional and behavioral problems that required psychotherapy.

Analysis. This is an inspiring story of a woman with determination, persistence, and a good dose of common sense, and a son who obviously possessed many of his mother's traits. Although appreciative of the excellent physical care and appropriate approach used by many of the medical people who worked with David, Landvater minces no words in her criticism of hospital bureaucracies and narrow-minded, rigid personnel unwilling to look beyond her son's original gloomy medical diagnosis.

She is also scathing in her criticism of the educational bureaucracy, particularly regarding the problems encountered with special-education personnel in both public and private schools. Her devotion to David's recovery never wavering, she battled them all successfully. Conversely, she is unstinting in her praise of the many individuals in the community who went out of their way to help David and the family during the initial crisis and later on. She also holds in high esteem the rehabilitation hospital where her son spent many months.

Lawrence, Marjorie. *Interrupted Melody: The Story of My Life*. Illus. Carbondale, Ill.: Southern Illinois Univ. Press, 1949. 307 pp. Reading Level: Grades 10–12.
Disability: Poliomyelitis

Marjorie Lawrence was a world-famous opera singer when she came down with polio. Newly married, she and her husband were in Mexico City, where she was to sing with the Mexico City Opera Company. It was 1941, and polio was still a scourge. Lawrence was treated first at Hot Springs, Arkansas, and then went to Minneapolis for the treatment of hot packs and physical therapy developed by Sister Elizabeth Kenny (like Lawrence, an Australian by birth). Despair was succeeded by a determination to sing again. Paralysis had affected her legs, and she also had to learn new ways to use her diaphragm and produce her voice. Eventually, she did perform in public again, in concerts and in operas that permitted her to sing while sitting; ultimately she sang in a standing position, using a device rather like a conductor's podium. During World War II she also sang for troops in American army camps and hospitals and was invited by the Australian government to tour the Southwest Pacific singing to soldiers in that area.

The book is illustrated with photographs, many of Lawrence in her operatic roles. There is also an index.

Analysis. Lawrence's book has two threads: her distinguished musical career and the work that led up to it and her courageous comeback from disabling illness. Although polio is no longer an active illness, young readers should not have difficulty in relating to Lawrence's situation or the persistent effort she describes.

Luce, Willard, and Celia Luce. *Lou Gehrig: Iron Man of Baseball*. Illus. Champaign, Ill.: Garrard, 1979. 95 pp. Reading Level: Grades 4–6.
Disability: Amyotrophic lateral sclerosis

In simple prose, Lou Gehrig's life story is told for young readers. This large-print book is a fictionalized biography of the great baseball player. The first chapter develops Gehrig's life as a six-year-old on New York City's Lower East Side. Subsequent chapters deal with his public school attendance and after-school jobs to allay his constant poverty. Line drawings by Dom Lupo illustrate these years.

Gehrig's baseball career in high school climaxed when the 16-year-old hit a ball out of the park at Wrigley Field in Chicago in the Police Athletic Championship Game. He went on to a successful athletic career and finally joined the New York Yankees. Baseball adventures, with action photos, illustrate the skill, toughness, and warmth of the hero's personality.

The last two chapters deal with Gehrig's diagnosis of amyotrophic lateral sclerosis, the chronic poliomyelitis that benched him and then took his life. The Lou Gehrig Appreciation Day, at which he spoke publicly for the last time to 60,000 people, and his elevation to the National Baseball Hall of Fame culminate the story on a bittersweet note.

Analysis: This large-type book is part of the Americans All series of biographies. Events from Gehrig's life have been skillfully chosen to appeal to young readers. Specific knowledge of the intricacies of baseball is not necessary to follow the story, which is written in an objective style. The events of Gehrig's last days are not sentimentalized—and the events speak for themselves. Although this is the story of an athletic dying in his prime, the reader has catharsis from the sense of a full life well lived. The choice of photographs, full of action and excitement of the game, is excellent.

McCormick, Donald. *The Incredible Mr. Kavanagh.* Illus. New York: Devin-Adair, 1961. 205 pp. Reading Level: Grades 10–12.
Disability: Missing limbs (phocomelia)

Arthur McMorrough Kavanagh was born in Borris, County Carlow, Ireland, in 1831. It was his mother's fourth pregnancy, and although she seemed well, her doctor had a hunch that all was not as it should be. When the baby was born, he had bleeding stumps instead of arms and legs. The physician surmised that the umbilical cord had wrapped around the limbs and severed them; it is now known that this would have been impossible, and the abnormality was probably caused by a hereditary trait or by a virus during pregnancy.

The family was aristocratic and well-to-do. Although many people living at that time might have felt that young Kavanagh's impairments were caused by God's wrath for wrongdoing and although others certainly connected the abnormality with a superstition about the family's fortunes, his mother said, "Thank God he was born to me and not to anyone else." She raised him without pity and with as little special treatment as possible, although she never discussed his impairments or permitted anyone else to do so in her hearing.

The doctor who had delivered him and became his lifelong friend gave him his first horseback ride when he was two. Kavanagh learned to ride; he got around by a mechanical chair, by hopping on his stumps, or by being carried on someone else's shoulders. Later, he fished, hunted, and chopped down trees. His mother taught him to paint, draw, and write by holding a brush or pen in his mouth; a letter written when he was 11 shows a clear, beautiful script. He also used hooks, but attempts to fit him with artificial limbs failed. His education as planned by his mother (his father died when Kavanagh was young) was strict and demanding. As a young man he traveled extensively in Europe and the Middle and Far East, sometimes with his mother and family, sometimes with an older brother and their tutor. Because of the early deaths of his two older brothers, he became manager of the family estate. He married and had six children. From 1868 to 1880, he represented his Irish constituency as a Member of Parliament, living in his yacht on the Thames during sessions of Parliament. He lived a vigorous, active life, spending much time outdoors except when in London; in his fifties, however, his health began to fail, and he died at age 58.

Black-and-white illustrations show, among other subjects, Kavanagh as a child and in midlife. There is a bibliography and an index.

Analysis. McCormick's book is a lively, readable, informative account of the life of a remarkable man. Although people of today might think that the refusal of Kavanagh's mother to discuss or openly acknowledge his abnormalities could have negative results, he grew up to be a healthy person of high achievement. Others expected much of him and he apparently expected no less of himself. In addition to detailing the story of a fascinating man, the book offers an interesting picture of the period, especially in Ireland and in the countries where Kavanagh traveled. Readers might find it worthwhile to compare his adaptation to his disabilities with current accounts of children born with truncated limbs, for example, *Don't Feel Sorry for Paul* by Bernard Wolf (see this section).

Mack, Nancy. *Tracy.* Photog. by Heinz Kluetmeier. Milwaukee: Raintree, 1976. 31 pp. Reading Level: Grades K–3.
Disability: Cerebral palsy

Using Tracy's voice, the text describes her disability and life: "I was born with cerebral palsy. My legs don't work right. I have a little trouble with my arms too." Her condition circumscribes some of her activities, of course, but Tracy goes to "a regular school with kids who can walk" and participates in the program as fully as possible. Twice a week she has therapy sessions after school. At home, where she is part of a large family, she sets the table, reads, listens to music, and plays with her brothers and sisters.

The book is designed so that every spread includes at least one large picture, some in color; the text is simple and the type large.

Analysis. Mack has succeeded in making Tracy's voice sound authentic, direct, and spunky; after introducing herself, Tracy says, "I know what you're thinking. You're looking at the wheelchair and you're thinking 'What happened to her?' " She is honest and forthright about what she can and cannot do, what she wishes she could do, what is scary, and what is fun. The emphasis in both text and illustrations is on a child who is being helped to be as active and independent as possible. Recommended for children with cerebral palsy and their siblings and for fostering understanding among all children.

Mee, Charles L., Jr. *Seizure.* New York: Evans, 1978. 216 pp. Reading Level: Grades 10–12.
Disability: Brain tumor

This book concerns a neurosurgeon, whose story was told to the author, and Kathy, a young student of voice. The story begins when Kathy is hospitalized with a seizure due to a benign brain tumor. The climax is the drama of the operating room where the surgeon conducts a long and unsuccessful operation, after which he gives his patient up for dead.

Miraculously, Kathy slowly recovers. She sustains another, more successful operation by the same surgeon and regains enough function to become a successful singer in a night club. Throughout the book, the reader is given simple but effective explanations of what is and what is not known about the structure and operation of the brain.

Analysis. This fast-moving story is an engrossing account of hospital life and what really goes on in the operating room. The doctor-patient relationship is explored from the perspective of both parties. The insights into the surgeon's psychology were perhaps more interesting than those of the patient, possibly because the former are so seldom elucidated. The reader comes away with an enormous respect for the brain, both in its complexity and its regenerative power.

Miers, Earl Schenck. *The Trouble Bush.* Chicago: Rand McNally, 1966. 342 pp. Reading Level: Grades 10–12.
Disability: Cerebral palsy

Miers was born with "the shakes," as a result of a very difficult protracted home delivery in the early part of the century. By the time he was a teenager he could ride a tricycle, but his use of his hands was limited. During his boyhood in Brooklyn, New York, his family treated him as normally as possible. "If all of life's troubles were hung on a bush, you'd still pick your own," said his mother, Muz, giving him the title of his autobiography. Miers eventually went to Rutgers College School of Journalism, although one professor tried to keep the brilliant student from graduating because "he could never get a job."

The second half of the book is an account of Miers's life and loves as he became a successful magazine editor, and finally free-lance writer of many books for children and adults. His ongoing experiences of frustration and prejudice because of his disability made him a champion for the civil rights of the oppressed. Up into the Kennedy years, he worked with many well-known people in American literature and politics, whom he describes in rich detail.

Analysis. Miers reveals himself as a boisterous advocate of fair play and excellence and as an early activist for civil rights for minorities and disabled people. With enthusiasm and cussedness, he forged an inspiring and deeply fulfilling personal and professional life, always tempered by the exigencies of his considerable disability. In a robust literary style, he shares an insider's view of American life and thought in his time. The book is considerably longer than most cited in this bibliography, but each chapter is entertaining in itself and the book is worthy of the attention of an able young reader.

Milam, Lorenzo W. *The Cripple Liberation Front Marching Band Blues.* San Diego: Mho and Mho Works, 1984. 218 pp. Reading Level: Grades 10–12.
Disability: Poliomyelitis

In 1953 Lorenzo Milam, at the age of 19, had a severe case of polio. He was the second in his family to contract the illness; a year earlier, his 29-year-old sister had died from it.

Milam was sent to Hope Haven, the pseudonym of a hospital in Florida that was the antithesis of hope; he suggests that the sign over hell in Dante's *Inferno*, "Abandon all hope, ye who enter here," would have been most appropriate at the hospital entrance, next to the name "Hopeless Haven." Milam describes his stay there, in surreal nightmarish prose, as a true piece of hell where not a vestige of human dignity is preserved, and where, he learns later, the treatment is outdated, brutal, and only minimally therapeutic. Then he is transferred to Warm Springs, Georgia, to which he gives the highest accolades and where his true rehabilitation begins, complete with a love affair with a young woman who is also a patient. He learned to walk again with aids.

After his release, he must cope with the pity of family, friends, and strangers, with the inaccessibility of bathrooms and friends' upper-story apartments, and with the severe limitations of life-as-is compared to life-as-was.

Milam went on to attend Haverford College, married for a brief period, fathered a daughter, attempted to found community radio stations to promote nuclear disarmament and world peace. In the process of the latter venture, he learned for the first time that he was a wealthy man as the result of his family estate, which was much larger than he had realized. Disillusioned after a two-year struggle in Washington, D.C., over a radio station, he sailed to Europe for a long hiatus, which involved several homosexual love affairs. He accepted his homosexuality after years of struggle.

Analysis. This is a searing, frank, no-holds-barred portrait of disability. The minute personal details of daily life and survival are candid and graphic, as is the language. Fecal imagery is frequently employed, and the discussion and description of sex, as well as its problems for physically impaired people, are both frank and detailed.

This is, however, a very funny book, at least within the genre of "black humor." It is also a very angry, bitter cry, and it presents a set of militant and just demands. Some degree of reader maturity is recommended. Young adults who are not attracted to the usual level of YA writing are likely prospects for this book.

A review in *Booklist* (August 1984) described the prose as "frequently overwrought and overwritten," but the work itself as one by a major talent who brings us a "provocative if uncomfortable view of the world." The "cripple" (Milam's chosen word) as real human being is paramount here from beginning to end. This is a prime example of the new wave of frank, unvarnished, angry books about disabilities that smash the old icons.

Nasaw, Jonathan Lewis. *Easy Walking.* Philadelphia: Lippincott, 1975. 224 pp. Reading Level: Grades 10–12.
Disability: Paraplegia

When he was 20, Jonathan Nasaw—nicknamed Willie—was in an automobile accident that left him paralyzed from the waist down. The doctors operated to fuse his shattered spine, and eventually he was moved to a rehabilitation center where his condition deteriorated until his uncle arranged for him to go to a veterans' hospital; from this facility, he went to another, much better rehabilitation center. Eventually, his muscles were built up and his bladder function restored through painful therapy. He then was able to walk out of the hospital on braces and crutches. Using this orthopedic equipment, plus a wheelchair and a specially adapted car, he became an independently functioning person again. At the end of the book, he had enrolled again in the college where he had studied before the accident.

Analysis. Nasaw was born in 1947, and this book is very much a product of the 1960s in tone and language. Although he shapes his material imaginatively, he writes as the reader assumes he speaks, with the slang of that period and free use of expletives. Nearly everyone in the book smokes pot, and Nasaw responds to painkillers as he does to the dope he is accustomed to taking. He chronicles his slow recovery, with its agonizing setbacks and occasional days of black despair, with a rough honesty and considerable insight. As he recovers more mobility and begins to move out of the encapsulated world, he is often dogged by an inner voice he names Cripple Willie. Cripple Willie thinks everyone is looking at him with pity, he imagines endless disasters, he wants to stay at home and hide under the bed. When Nasaw can use a parking slot set aside for "Handicapped Driver" because it is the most convenient and sensible thing to do, he has accepted both his condition and his challenges, and he vanquishes Cripple Willie. However, neither Willie nor his physician-roommate expresses any regret about the fast driving that led to their accidents and neither indicates that more caution will be used in the future.

Nicholson, William G. *Pete Gray: One-Armed Major Leaguer.* Illus. by Ray Abel. Englewood Cliffs, N.J.: Prentice-Hall, 1976. unp. Reading Level: Grades 4–9.
Disability: Amputation

Born in Nanticoke, a small coal-mining town in eastern Pennsylvania, Pete Gray lost his arm in an accident at the age of six. He loved baseball, and when the other children would not let him play, he practiced hitting stones with a stick. He soon became so proficient that children began to play catch with him, and he became the best baseball player in the area.

After playing in the best semipro league for two years, he became a professional player for the minor league team in Memphis, where he was highly successful and winner of the league's most valuable player award for the 1944 season.

The St. Louis Browns of the American League bought his contract. Gray was a popular player and started out well in the 1945 season. However, major league pitchers soon discovered his weakness; he could not easily change his swing after the pitcher threw the ball, so if they tricked him on the kind of pitch they were going to throw, he was an easy out. Gray remained very popular with the fans despite his failing batting average; in fact, a quiet, shy person, he was embarrassed by all the attention. He was released by the Browns at the beginning of the next season, and he spent several succeeding years playing minor league baseball.

The text is illustrated by drawings in tones of brown, gray, and black.

Analysis. The focus of this book is on the formidable task that Pete Gray accomplished. While he was not a success in the major leagues, the fact that he even played there for a year is remarkable, as is the success of his minor league career. He is portrayed as an ordinary person, not a larger-than-life hero.

Opie, June. *Over My Dead Body.* New York: Dutton, 1957. 265 pp. Reading Level: Grades 10–12.
Disability: Poliomyelitis

June Opie, a young, attractive New Zealander, came to London to study. Within a few days she became ill with what proved to be polio; almost overnight she was totally paralyzed, unable to move anything but one eyelid. She spent two and a half years at St. Mary's Hospital in London struggling with her illness.

This book is a factual, detailed account of those years, at the end of which she achieved a remarkable recovery.

Analysis. Opie tells her story with both humor and drama. Her sense of detail is flawless, and her characterization of the medical personnel, patients, and other people who come in and out of her confined life is excellent. Although she does not portray herself as a dramatic heroine, but rather as clearly human, her courage and determination are obvious.

Panzarella, Joseph J., Jr., with Glenn D. Kittler. *Spirit Makes a Man.* Illus. New York: Doubleday, 1978. 134 pp. Reading Level: Grades 10–12.
Disability: Multiple sclerosis, Paraplegia

Panzarella noticed the first symptoms of multiple sclerosis (MS) when he was still a student in medical school. His fiancée insisted that her feelings for him were unchanged by this diagnosis and their uncertain future, and they were married. Initially, he practiced as an anesthesiologist. Ten years after the onset of the disease, he was in an automobile accident and subsequently the MS flared up. One of the specialists he consulted suggested that since not all his symptoms pointed conclusively to MS, he might have a tumor at the back of his neck. The only way to find out was to operate, and the operation was risky. Panzarella went ahead with the procedure; there was no tumor, but he woke up from the operation to find himself a paraplegic.

He could no longer manage the physical demands of his anesthesiology practice and had to give it up. By now, he and his wife had six children and they subsequently had a seventh. The generosity of family and friends and the determination of his wife kept their life going, but he had to contend with inevitable depression, especially when he tried to change his specialty and get back into practice. Eventually, rehabilitation medicine was suggested to him. He did a three-year fellowship with Dr. Howard Rusk at the Institute of Rehabilitation Medicine and went on to a successful career in this field, setting up programs for a number of hospitals and for the Continental Insurance Company. He has received many awards in recognition of his work, including the Handicapped American of 1976 Award from the Presidential Committee on the Employment of the Handicapped.

The Panzarellas endured not only his progressive disease, but his two heart attacks and the sudden death of one of their sons. This young man had become his father's assistant and attendant; on the night of Panzarella's second heart attack, Jeffrey was following the ambulance to the hospital when his car crashed into a telephone pole. At the end of the book, Panzarella describes symptoms in one of his daughters that point to MS.

An appendix listing some of the organizations across the country whose services are available to people with disabilities ends the book. Black-and-white photographs taken over the years show Panzarella in both private and public life.

Analysis. The Panzarellas emerge from this book as people of great courage, determination, and persistence. While he does not ignore the difficulties of his physical situation, Panzarella's tone is optimistic and energetic. For example, he says that he has long since gotten over his embarrassment at having to be fed, even when eating in a restaurant.

Patterson, Katheryn. *No Time for Tears.* Illus. Chicago: Johnson, 1965. 109 pp. Reading Level: Grades 10–12.
Disability: Epilepsy, Hydrocephalus

When she was 19, author Katheryn Patterson and her husband, a young black couple with a three-year-old daughter, had a son, whom they named after his father and called Junior. By the time he was eight weeks old, the baby's head had grown several inches. The diagnosis was hydrocephalus (commonly known as water on the brain); the neurosurgeon said that nothing could be done for the child, that if he lived he would be "an imbecile," and that his parents should look for institutional care. Although they worried about the reactions of family and friends and wanted to hide both the infant and themselves, the young parents decided almost immediately to keep their son at home.

At first Patterson had to force herself to touch or look at him; they hated taking him out because of the reaction of strangers. But, guided by her grandmother, who felt that Junior had his place in the family, they persisted, enduring the cruelty of others and loving their child. Katheryn Patterson had had epilepsy, and had already been exposed to stares and hostility. The epileptic seizures had stopped during her second pregnancy, but a blood clot during her second month had required the administration of an anticoagulant drug—a possible cause of Junior's abnormality.

Contrary to the prediction of the specialist, the child made progress and by the time he was two, his hydrocephalus had been arrested. He had an engaging personality and normal intelligence, but because of his physical disabilities (chiefly difficulty in standing and walking), ordinary public education was not possible. When Junior was eight, his parents took him to the Illinois Children's Hospital School in Chicago, 200 miles from their home in Canton, Illinois. There, with physical therapy and a good teaching program, Junior has made excellent progress. His family—parents, older sister, two younger brothers—miss him, but he spends vacations at home and they visit him once a month. His mother writes of the school with high praise and looks forward with confidence to her son's future.

Black-and-white photographs show the family together.

Analysis: Katheryn Patterson does not minimize the pain and anxiety she and her husband have experienced since the birth of their first son. Nevertheless, supported by the wisdom and affection of their family (especially her maternal grandparents and her mother), and by their own inherent strength, this young couple has been able to accept their hydrocephalic child as wholeheartedly and lovingly as they welcomed their other children. They have always discussed Junior's physical difference openly, and he has accepted it unselfconsciously. Fluently written, the book reflects the Patterson's religious faith and acceptance; the author makes clear that Junior has contributed to his family in full measure. She concludes by saying that their son has made "a miraculous adjustment to his handicap and has two healthy brothers and a devoted sister to help him through life. These are prayers answered; even when we did not realize it God had his hands on us. My handicapped child is my blessing. I have no time for tears" (p. 95).

A useful and informative appendix, "Hydrocephalus: A Medical Definition," is reprinted by the School of Medicine, Loma Linda University, Los Angeles. Readers who are interested in the subject might want to read further to see what progress has been made in the treatment of this condition since 1965. Also, now the public school system is obliged to provide for all handicapped children and in the least restrictive environment. Since there is a dearth of books about minority families coping with disability, *No Time for Tears* may be of particular interest.

Pieper, Elizabeth. *Sticks and Stones: The Story of Loving a Child.* Syracuse, N.Y.: Human Policy Press, n.d. 88 pp. Reading Level: Grades 10–12.
Disability: Spina bifida

Spina bifida in its extreme manifestation is a congenital condition in which the spinal cord has grown out of a split in the spinal column, resulting in paralysis from that point down the body, and often hydrocephalus as well. It is a fairly common birth defect, generally fatal until recently, but medical advances have enabled many babies with this condition to survive.

Pieper begins her book with the story of the birth of her first child in 1961, who had a diagnosis of spina bifida myelomeningocele. She and her baby were generally the targets of neglect on the part of the medical establishment. The procedures necessary to save her baby's life were not explained, and physicians were unresponsive to the family's distress at mounting medical bills.

Following are chapters devoted to trying to find help for Jeff—both therapy and school. He had hydrocephalus at birth, and there were problems with the shunt that had been implanted to relieve the pressure of the cerebral spinal fluid. He was thought, therefore, to have sustained some brain damage.

Special education was not yet a right for all handicapped children in upper New York State, so Pieper sought help from charitable agencies such as the Albany Cerebral Palsy Center. The constant runarounds due to bureaucratic indifference and mismanagement made Pieper into a civil rights activist on behalf of disabled children. Her legal efforts were precursors of the Right to Education Consent Agreement in Pennsylvania and Public Law 94-142, The Education of All Handicapped Children Act, signed into law in 1975.

Pieper ends her story as Jeff, happily enrolled in a special school, has become a real friend to his mother.

Chapter 8, "Institutions," raises questions about the fate of elderly or disabled persons when families are no longer able to care for them.

Analysis: Pieper's is a well-written account, and one of the few addressed particularly to the problems of raising a child with spina bifida, although this is a not uncommon condition. She writes in a vivid and angry tone. Her insights into the ambiguities of social institutions and the prejudices and carelessness of people at large in dealing with disabled persons are penetrating and informative.

Plummer, Beverly. *Give Every Day a Chance.* New York: Putnam, 1970. 221 pp. Reading Level: Grades 7–12.
Disability: Osteogenesis imperfecta (brittle bones)

Osteogenesis imperfecta (OI) is a metabolic disorder in which collagen, necessary for bone formation, is defective. Children born with this problem have brittle bones that are subject to multiple fractures and poor growth. They will always be of short stature, may have problems with ambulation, and eventually, with hearing (because the tiny bones in the middle ear are involved). An arduous medical procedure is done today to insert metal tubes through the bones to provide strength and allow growth. The child is in the greatest jeopardy during the period of highest growth rate, but the condition becomes stabilized with maturity. OI is transmitted by a recessive gene and is relatively rare.

The book tells the story of Roxanne up to the time that she can drive a car and is about to enter college, as related by her mother. The title, *Give Every Day a Chance,* was Roxie's philosophy throughout all the bad and good times that she experienced. The reader becomes familiar with the consequences of OI: repeated hospitalizations, pain, institutional problems, people's insensitivity, and interrupted lives. However, the enduring pluckiness of this little girl, supported by a loving family, prevails.

The reader rejoices with her when she is strong enough to take a hike in summer camp, when she gets such pleasure from small things in nature, and when she becomes healthier in adolescence.

Analysis. This easy-to-read, exuberant book is by a professional writer. It explores emotions from bitterness and sadness to joy and love, telling the story with compassion and reverence for life, without being maudlin. While the disease depicted is rare, the kinds of experiences the affected child and family face as a result are unfortunately common to physically disabled children. Since this book was written, there has been a growing interest and networking on the part of families and physicians involved with OI.

Roth, Hy, and Robert Crome. *The Little People: An Illustrated Look at Some of the World's Most Engaging Men and Women.* Introduction by Irving Wallace. Illus. New York: Everest House, 1980. 173 pp. Reading Level: Grades 7–12.
Disability: Short stature

Hy Roth is an illustrator who does magazine and film work. He collected photographs from many sources in this country and abroad of little people. Since many of these black-and-white pictures are from newspapers, magazines, and posters, entertainers from world's fairs, circuses, and theaters comprise most of the subjects. Little people were often objects of fascination for royalty and thus some photos show famous people of normal stature as well.

Crome, a well-known writer for television and magazines, has supplied a text tracing the history of attitudes toward many little people of history and today, and their varied fates. He discusses the fascination and fear that people have had toward actual little people as well as toward mythological small beings through the ages, always in a sympathetic and compassionate manner. Many funny and some tragic incidents are related, such as Hitler's relegation of the performer Lya Graf and many more little people to the death camps.

The book ends with an account of the founding of Little People of America. There are pictures of the founder, 3-foot-9-inch Billy Barty, of several contemporary actors and athletes, and of a smiling young schoolteacher who is 4 feet 2 inches.

Analysis. The photographs in this book are fascinating. Action shots of normal-sized athletes, actors, and circus performers are entertaining to people of all ages. When miniature adults are shown, and often next to more ordinary people, the effect is startling. A number of little people themselves have greatly enjoyed the text and pictures of the book and are inclined to see it as a positive and respectful look at the joys and difficulties of their uniqueness.

Rubin, Robert. *Lou Gehrig: Courageous Star.* Illus. New York: Putnam, 1979. 160 pp. Reading Level: Grades 7–9.
Disability: Amyotrophic lateral sclerosis

Henry Louis Gehrig was born in 1903 in New York to German immigrant parents, poor and hardworking. His mother, to whom he was always very close, was determined that her son would get the education that would enable him to break out of poverty. Gehrig enjoyed sports from early childhood and in high school played soccer, football, and baseball. Columbia University wooed him as a football player, but during his undergraduate years he was spotted by a Yankee baseball scout.

After college, he became a famous professional baseball player with the New York Yankees. In the next 14 years he played a record 2,130 straight games at first base. Then physical difficulties started to dog him; he dropped things and began to walk with a shuffle. When he went to the Mayo Clinic, the doctor who waited for him in the lobby diagnosed his illness as Gehrig walked toward him: The ball player had amyotrophic lateral sclerosis, a disease in which the myelin sheath covering the nerve fibers is destroyed and replaced by scar tissue, preventing impulses from traveling through the nerves and causing paralysis. There is no cure. On July 4, 1939, Gehrig was given a tremendous tribute at Lou Gehrig Appreciation Day in Yankee Stadium. He spent the rest of the season on the bench and the following year, at Mayor LaGuardia's invitation, he worked on the New York City Parole Board. He died in June 1941.

Black-and-white photographs show baseball scenes. There is an index.

Analysis. Rubin begins with Gehrig's first game for the Yankees, in 1925, and with a summary of his baseball record and his response to fatal illness. He then goes back to Gehrig's birth and traces his life and career. Gehrig's quiet, courageous character is emphasized as much as his extraordinary athletic prowess and baseball career, although the latter is given far more space. This biography presents a hero who remains credible as a human being.

Rudolph, Wilma, and Bud Greenspan. *Wilma: The Story of Wilma Rudolph.* Illus. New York: New American Library, 1977. 172 pp. Reading Level: Grades 10–12.
Disability: Orthopedic birth defect

Wilma Rudolph at the age of 16 ran with the 1956 U.S. Olympic team. She had worn leg braces until only four years before this competition. She would go on to win three gold medals and set new world records at the 1960 Olympics.

The twentieth of 22 children, Rudolph was born into a close-knit black family in Clarksville, Tennessee. She was premature and born with a crooked right leg, with a foot twisted inward. In addition, a series of severe childhood illnesses kept her sick and thin for the first decade of her life. She did not attend school until second grade. Braces provided by the Maharry Medical School in Tennessee eventually rehabilitated her leg, and her teen years brought her better general health.

Rudolph attended a segregated high school and went on to Tennessee State, a black college. At both schools, athletic competition for women was the norm, and Wilma, a natural athlete and an especially good basketball player and runner, participated eagerly. She relates the details of how this participation led her to the Olympics in 1956 and again in 1960, as well as the events of these two competitions.

After the 1960 Olympics, where she became the first American woman ever to win three gold medals, she received a hero's welcome in major cities across the United States, and her welcome-home parade in Clarksville broke the color barrier. Her life since then has been quiet and ordinary, and the struggle to earn a living has not always been easy. Black-and-white photographs are included.

Analysis. Rudolph and Greenspan relate the narrative in a conversational, colloquial style that makes for easy, pleasant reading. The story is inspiring. Rudolph not only had to conquer her disabilities; she also had to contend with poverty and racism, which looms as a large, pervading theme throughout the book. She stopped the continuous wearing of leg braces in 1950, but wore them intermittently for two years afterward. The disabilities are dealt with early on and they are never mentioned again, nor are her health problems. While her approach to her health problems and braces is matter-of-fact and offhand, her comments on racism and poverty are acerbic and pointed.

In addition to the indicated reading level, this book is also a possible choice to motivate fifth- and sixth-graders.

Sands, Harry, and Frances C. Minters. *The Epilepsy Fact Book.* Illus. New York: Scribner's, 1977. 116 pp. Reading Level: Grades 7–12. *Disability:* Epilepsy

In five chapters the authors discuss the nature and treatment of epilepsy, living with the condition, the child with epilepsy, and where to find help. They describe different types of seizures and the examinations and treatment that a patient undergoes, and discuss societal attitudes and cite statistics to show how these are changing, giving information about activities that can be safely engaged in by a person with seizures. They describe the experience of children and teenagers with this disorder.

The book concludes with a list of epilepsy terms, a bibliography, and an index.

Analysis. Sands and Minters have written a careful, detailed, and informative book. Without minimizing the effects of epilepsy, they emphasize the degree to which it can be controlled and the wide range of activities and experience open to a person with the disorder. This excellent source book is valuable for self-understanding by a young person with epilepsy; it could also be helpful for classmates and siblings to allay their concerns and foster understanding. Readers should bear in mind that this book was published in 1977 and that there are continuing advances in the treatment of this disorder.

Savitz, Harriet May. *Wheelchair Champions: A History of Wheelchair Sports.* Illus. New York: Crowell, 1978. 118 pp. Reading Level: Grades 7–9. *Disability:* Orthopedic injury

As the subtitle makes explicit, this is a history of wheelchair sports from the beginnings in the 1940s up to the late 1970s. The initial impetus for such activities came from disabled veterans of World War II, those with amputations, paraplegia, and quadriplegia. Medical advances of the period made it possible for a far greater number of injured military men to survive than ever before; the "lightweight, collapsible, metal wheelchair" designed by engineer Harry C. Jennings, Sr., gave the person using a wheelchair new maneuverability. The work of Howard Rusk in developing rehabilitation medicine and programs for military hospitals and later for civilian institutions changed the treatment and prognosis of people with disabilities. All of these conditions made possible the growth of wheelchair athletics from the first impromptu pick-up basketball games to the highly organized teams and events of today.

The book concludes with a page titled "If You Were Suddenly Disabled . . ." that suggests provocative questions; there is also a list of organizations and publications related to disability and wheelchair sports, and an index.

The book includes black-and-white photographs.

Analysis: Savitz has written a readable history that manages never to sink under the weight of its comprehensive, precise details. Personal stories of many of the people involved in the movement, disabled and nondisabled alike, keep up the reader's interest. Savitz's philosophy is clear throughout; she believes in the fullest possible activity and participation in life for all people.

Segal, Patrick. *The Man Who Walked in His Head*. Trans. from the French by John Stephens. Illus. New York: Morrow, 1980. 254 pp.
Reading Level: Grades 10–12.
Disability: Paraplegia

The French author was a 24-year-old physical therapist in training when a stray bullet lodged in his spine and nearly killed him. After medical rehabilitation, he goes to China for acupuncture treatments. He describes the strange and alluring attractions of Canton. "It's true I'm not in good physical condition as I leave China . . . so in my body I'm thin and weak . . . but in my head, in my head I have begun to walk" (p. 37).

In alternating chapters, the author describes first his depressing experiences in various hospitals and clinics in his initial year of rehabilitation, and second, his many adventures as he travels around the world. His emotions ride a roller coaster from elevation to despair and back many times. He tries many activities, from being a volunteer

counselor to injured children in war-torn Vietnam to being a professional photographer in Venezuela. He meets a host of friends. Although recurrently short of money, he has the wherewithal to buy
cars, plane tickets, and other necessities for living. He travels the world
attempting to find a place for himself.

In his epilogue, Segal elucidates his resolution to his quest. He has
decided to bear witness as a photo journalist. At the conclusion of the
book, he had just turned 29. .

Analysis. This book was the winner of the Prix de la Presse in its
original French version. The translation by John Stephens is smooth.
The story, unlike many other autobiographies in this bibliography,
appears almost allegorical. Segal's quest is for control of his life and a
right to useful work and happiness. The kaleidoscope of visions from
his travels, which he describes so vividly, is a descant to the ups and
downs of his search for personal meaning in his life.

Particularly noteworthy is the spiritual quality of the book. However, the differentiation between fact and impression is not always
clear. The author tells, for example, of being in his uncle's apartment
alone and without food for three days because he could not negotiate
the stairs, disclaiming any particular discomfort from the experience.
The reader might be cautioned to consider such instances hyperbole
rather than fact.

A literal-minded reader might become confused by the alternation
of the narrative between events of the year of rehabilitation and subsequent travels. Stream-of-consciousness prose flows within both story
lines, heightening and highlighting Segal's inner life, while giving the
adventures a transcendental quality.

Segal's perceptions of social discrimination against disabled people, especially from caregivers, are subtle. In his travels he learned the
anguish of his disabled confreres over the denial of their basic sexuality
and need to be useful. He obviously had the means and connections
that provided opportunities not available to most people. Nevertheless,
his struggles, his courage, and his good will come across as authentic.

Silverstein, Alvin, and Virginia B. Silverstein. *Epilepsy*. Illus. Philadelphia: Lippincott, 1975. 64 pp. Reading Level: Grades 4–9.
Disability: Epilepsy

The authors discuss epilepsy as a misunderstood disease and give
its history as "probably the oldest known disease of the brain" (p. 15).
They describe the condition itself, with its varied manifestations and
probable causes. Chapters on research, treatment, and societal attitudes bring the subject up-to-date. A short section describes well-
known people of past and present with epilepsy. The chapter called

"Living with Epilepsy" is illustrated with pictures of such epileptics as Caesar, John Considine, a professional hockey player, and a high school wrestler. Another short section tells the reader what to do if he or she is with a person who has a seizure.

Addresses are given for sources of pamphlets on the disease and there is an index. Black-and-white photographs and drawings illustrate the text.

Analysis. Epilepsy is a condition that can produce fear and apprehension. Writing in a quiet, nonjudgmental tone, the Silversteins go far to counter this attitude. Their book is clear and informative, guided throughout by their conviction that epilepsy is a controllable condition and that people with it need to be accepted as fully functioning members of society. The drawings and photographs are helpful. Since the book was published in 1975, readers might want to look further for more up-to-date information.

> Stein, Sara Bonnett. *About Handicaps: An Open Family Book for Parents and Children Together.* Illus. New York: Walker, 1974. 46 pp.
> Reading Level: Grades K–3 and adult.
> *Disability:* Amputation, Cerebral palsy

This book is part of a series, the Open Family Books. Each has black-and-white photographs and words in large print for the child reader; a running commentary is provided for the adult, who is encouraged to discuss with the youngster feelings and questions that the story raises.

The simple story is told from the point of view of Matthew, an average child, who is uneasy about Joe, his friend with cerebral palsy. Matthew imitates Joe, worries that he might become like him, and becomes concerned about his own small physical imperfection, a crooked toe, which he hides in his boots. Matthew even pushes his friend down and does not want to see him anymore. He tries to avoid a man who has a hook for a hand. At this point Matthew's father intervenes and introduces his son to the man, a friend of his, who explains his war injury and demonstrates his prosthesis deftly. The man recounts his initial feelings of embarrassment about his artificial limb and his worry that he would not be accepted; now he is used to his prosthesis and knows that people like him. Matthew is finally able to talk with his father about Joe's legs and the one-armed man. He becomes reconciled to Joe; they talk about Joe's crippled legs and Matthew can share the secret of his funny toe. Together the boys build a wonderful structure of blocks.

Analysis. This may well be the best book in the series. It does not dwell only on children's fears and anxieties, but honestly expresses the ambivalences, feelings, and thoughts that the young child may have regarding physical differences and disabilities. The adult narrative is sensitive and perceptive. The illustrations are well integrated with the story and the message. The photographs show both Matthew and Joe to be winsome children, and Joe's legs, in shorter pants, are obviously spastic. The explicit pictures are introduced gradually; for example, the one-armed man is first shown at a distance, so that his prosthesis is scarcely visible. In the five shots of him, Matthew and the reader come closer and closer to the hook hand. The last shot shows a close-up of Matthew's finger grasped in it. The book has a happy ending, with childhood fears put to rest, each boy accepting his own and the other's differences while creating a structure in mutual friendship. A fine book in a unique series.

Stingley, Darryl, with Mark Mulvoy. *Happy to Be Alive.* Illus. New York: Beaufort Books, 1983. 237 pp. Reading Level: Grades 7–12. *Disability:* Quadriplegia

Darryl Stingley was a professional football player with the New England Patriots when, in August 1978, during a preseason exhibition game, he received a spinal cord injury that resulted in quadriplegia. In this book, Stingley describes his life as a young boy growing up in a black Chicago ghetto, as a football player at Purdue, and as a National Football League (NFL) team member.

After his injury, months of painful treatment while immobilized in bed, and a near brush with death from pneumonia, he faced the challenge of "getting to know the new Darryl"—"Darryl the quad" not "Darryl the athlete." In addition, he had to deal with national publicity at a time when coping with the changes in his daily life was a sufficient problem. He also had to determine his approach to the legal issues surrounding his injury, inflicted by Jack Tatum, then of the Oakland Raiders. His family was also in turmoil for some time.

Stingley wrote this book partially as a response to Tatum's *They Call Me Assassin* (Everest House, 1979), in which Tatum graphically describes many of his "hits" on NFL players, including Stingley, in accord with a vicious and violent style of football that certain professional players and teams were using at that time. Stingley deplores this situation and speaks out strongly against it, against violence in sport in general, and against league policies that did little to prevent or stop this type of play.

Black-and-white photographs of Stingley's life illustrate the text.

Analysis. This is foremost a good story. It reads well, abounds in description, and has a lot of football talk in addition to talk about the hard realities of life with quadriplegia. Stingley discusses his difficult period of emotional adjustment, including a bout of depression and a brief moment when he seriously considered suicide, with great candor and insight. He speaks against violence in sport persuasively and with fervor.

Family members, friends, and teachers are sometimes confronted with the return of a young person after a life-altering accident or illness. This book would be helpful to them, and to the disabled person, and could increase everyone's understanding of the adjustment problems involved.

Booklist included this title on its list of Best Young Adult Books of 1983.

Sullivan, Margaret W. *Living with Epilepsy.* Illus. by Robert Loomis. New York: Nellen, 1979. 127 pp. Reading Level: Grades 7–12.

Disability: Epilepsy

The author experienced her first epileptic seizure one night at the age of 23. Her parents, who were present, would not discuss what had happened and cautioned her not to tell anyone. She followed their advice until she had her first daytime seizure in public. Now she teaches and counsels people with epilepsy, and her book is addressed directly to this audience. She begins with a brief description of her own experience and refers to it again at intervals. She discusses the history of epilepsy, its types and manifestations, emergency care, causes, drug therapy, medical tests, and nutrition, with one chapter speaking directly to the parents of epileptic children. Sullivan talks about the effect of negative public attitudes on personality development, driving and employment for people with seizures, and details of daily living.

Resource material includes vitamin and mineral charts, footnotes, a glossary, suggested readings, and an index. Black-and-white sketches illustrate the text.

Analysis. Drawing on personal experience, the accounts of her students, and research, Sullivan highlights the extent to which epilepsy is feared and misunderstood by the general public. The medical profession is not exempt from misguided attitudes. Sullivan describes her encounters with a doctor and nurse at an institution she visited, both of whom exhibited appalling insensitivity. For example, the doctor proudly displayed a lobotomized patient to her.

This book is intended not only for people with epilepsy, but for their families, counselors, and teachers. While acknowledging that seizures are frightening to the onlooker and upsetting to the person who has them, and acknowledging also that the disease is still incompletely understood, the author presents information to foster a rational understanding of epilepsy and its implications. Unfortunately, while there is

142   Physical Problems

much good material here, the text is marred by numerous errors in English usage.

> Thomas, Henry. *Charles Steinmetz*. Illus. by Charles Beck. New York: Putnam, 1959. 126 pp. Reading Level: Grades 4–6.
> *Disability:* Kyphosis (orthopedic abnormality)

Steinmetz was born in Breslau, Germany, in 1865, inheriting his deformity from his hunchbacked father. In addition, he was scarcely 4 feet tall and had an unusually large head and a limp. Always a brilliant student, particularly in mathematics and physics, Steinmetz studied in Breslau and Zurich, and in 1889 came to the United States. Four years later he joined the General Electric Company, where he spent the rest of his working life. Despite his deformities and a weak heart, he worked and played with enormous energy; he made many contributions to the study of electricity and improved and invented devices for electric generators and motors. The author makes it clear that Steinmetz's extraordinary accomplishments were due not only to his innate brilliance, but to his determination not to be defeated by his physical abnormalities.

The book is illustrated with black-and-white drawings.

Analysis. The story of Steinmetz is interesting and could be inspiring to young readers. In this account, the narrative is marred by stilted dialogue unlikely ever to have been spoken. Chapters are headed by half-page black-and-white drawings that fail to add much to the text and that carry mysterious smoky smudges even when they do not include Steinmetz's famous omnipresent cigar. However, until a better biography of the scientist comes along, this one can serve as an introduction to the subject.

> Trull, Patti. *On with My Life*. New York: Putnam, 1983. 144 pp. Reading Level: Grades 10–12.
> *Disability:* Cancer and amputation

Pattie Trull was a normal, active 15-year-old when a malignant tumor was discovered in her right femur, which the doctors first treated with chemotherapy and radiation. Another tumor was found in her right lung and was successfully removed. Eventually, after much pain from a necrotic ulcer in an unhealed incision in her leg, she had to face amputation of the entire limb at the hip. Although she had never been particularly interested in studying before her illness, she went on to college and to special training as an occupational therapist. She went back to Children's Hospital in Seattle, where she had received most of her treatment, to work through the Hematology-Oncology Department with young cancer patients and their families. When funding for her job was cut off, she went into medical sales, but continued to run a children's group on a volunteer basis.

Fifteen years after her illness was first diagnosed, Trull remains free of the disease; she has an artificial leg, which she uses only some of the time, but with or without the leg, she is extremely active, skiing, swimming, riding a bike (with one leg); "I've found—or created—a way to do most everything I've wanted to do, with the one exception of jogging" (p. 142). Writing of the way people often shut themselves off from hearing about work such as hers, Trull says, "What people didn't understand were the positive things these children had to offer and their ability to enjoy and live life in spite of everything. It was something many fifty-year-olds never learned and ten- and fifteen-year-old kids were teaching us" (p.117).

Analysis. Trull writes honestly, neither hiding nor dwelling on her reactions to illness and disability. The chapters describing her work with children are heart-wrenching but restrained, particularly when she writes about those who must meet death. Material on the changes in treatment of osteogenic sarcoma since her own illness is informative and interesting. This is a book to recommend to young people considering a career similar to Trull's as well as to teenagers and their families who must face the challenge of possibly mortal illness.

> Valens, E. G. *A Long Way Up: The Story of Jill Kinmont.* Photog. by Burk Uzzle and others. New York: Harper & Row, 1966. 245 pp.
> Reading Level: Grades 10–12.
> *Disability:* Quadriplegia

Jill Kinmont was an accomplished skier, a future Olympic contender, until an accident at a race in Utah in 1955 severed her spinal cord and left her paralyzed, without feeling from the shoulders down. In a few minutes, her life and that of her family changed dramatically. This book, based on the writer's extensive research and conversations with Kinmont, her family, friends, and teachers, tells her story BC (her phrase for Before the Crash) and afterward. Months of hospitalization were followed by months of rehabilitation; eventually, Kinmont was able to achieve a degree of physical independence, although she will always need assistance in managing daily life. The near-fatal accident at 18 altered not only her physical life but her spiritual and intellectual existence; the young woman, who had hardly thought about her future beyond skiing or about education beyond high school, graduated from UCLA and went on to postgraduate work in education. She has become a remedial reading teacher accredited to teach on the elementary and secondary levels. Black-and-white photographs enhance the text.

Analysis. In a sense, this is a fairy tale. Attractive, gifted, young princess suffers an abrupt change in fortune that completely alters her life, but, through her own efforts and the support of those around her, she wins for herself a life completely different from the one she had anticipated. Moreover, the comfortable circumstances of Kinmont's family and her many connections made possible arrangements that are beyond the reach of most quadriplegic people. Valens is successful in keeping up the pace of Kinmont's story and in making the details of her rehabilitation compelling. Throughout the book he recreates conversations as if he had been a witness to them, but this artistic license does not detract from the essential authenticity of the account. This book inspired the movie *The Other Side of the Mountain*.

Viscardi, Henry, Jr. *A Man's Stature.* New York: John Day, 1952. 240 pp. Reading Level: Grades 10–12.
Disability: Missing limbs

Henry Viscardi, Jr., was born in 1912 with underdeveloped legs, a condition described in medical terminology as "arrested development of the lower limbs resulting in incomplete growth of the bones and spasticity of the immature, ill-formed muscles." Treatment at the New York Hospital for Deformities and Joint Diseases eventually made it possible for him to walk and even run, wearing orthopedic boots on his stumps. But because his lower legs and feet were lacking, he was dwarfed in stature; his upper body was normally developed, but his arms hung nearly to the ground. When he came back to his neighborhood to live after years in the protective environment of the hospital, he encountered stares, pity, and the taunts of other children, who called him ape man.

Bright and energetic, Viscardi managed to work his way through Fordham University until lack of funds forced him to leave before completing the undergraduate course. He found a job with a law firm and went to law school at night, then switched to work with the federal government's Home Owners' Loan Corporation. When he had nearly worn out his attenuated legs, his doctor persuaded him to take a leave of absence and consult a maker of prosthetic limbs. Many painful weeks later, he walked in on his astonished family, a man who had grown from 3 feet 8 inches to a height of 5 feet 8 inches. Viscardi's subsequent career included work with the Red Cross during World War II, a job in radio, and a position as personnel director of Burlington Mills. Finally, he took the directorship of a new organization, Just-One-Break, or J.O.B., whose sponsors included Dr. Howard Rusk, Eleanor Roosevelt, Conrad Hilton, Bernard Baruch, and Bernard Gimbel. J.O.B. is dedicated to finding work for disabled people who have been rehabilitated.

Analysis. Viscardi writes with energy and flair and without self-pity. He is skillful at setting scenes, describing people and events. Although it is unlikely that he can have remembered all the dialogue he reproduces, one cannot doubt the essential truthfulness of his account. Supported by the staff of the hospital where he spent most of his early years, by his parents and sisters, and then by his wife, he has been able to draw on great inner strength as well as physical endurance; he wastes no time in bitterness. Both his personal life and his work at J.O.B. have been shaped by a belief that we must think of ability rather than disability.

Warren, Mary Phraner, and Don Kirkendall. *Bottom High to the Crowd.* New York: Walker, 1973. 222 pp. Reading Level: Grades 10–12.
Disability: Poliomyelitis

Don Kirkendall contracted polio at the age of four and nearly died; he survived with paralysis in both legs and one arm. This book recounts the next 40 years of his life and tells how he coped with the physical problems of the disability and the emotional problems caused by an unaccepting society. A fighter and not one to feel sorry for himself, Kirkendall has led an active life, including several business careers and three marriages.

Analysis. The writing is amusing and detailed, and the story is interesting. Kirkendall's courageous struggle, humor, and spunk appeal to teenaged readers.

Wheeler, Kathryn. *Tanya: The Building of a Family through Adoption.* New York: North American Center on Adoption, 1979. 36 pp. Reading Level: Grades 10–12.
Disability: Scoliosis

This paperback book is written by the mother of a physically disabled seven-year-old girl named Tanya. In journal style she describes the trials and tribulations of going through the adoption process, even though the child's race, age, and "normalcy" were not issues for the couple. Tanya was "Sunday's Child" available for adoption as featured in the newspaper. When the parents-to-be met her in her foster home, very tiny, with her leg in a cast, " 'Hi' she says in a teeny-tiny voice. 'My boy friend says my nose is very soft. Would you like to feel it?' " And thus Tanya won the hearts of her new father, mother, and little brother.

Tanya's orthopedic problems had been variously diagnosed—or misdiagnosed. She did have scoliosis and was much improved after wearing a brace. She had also been physically very sheltered in her foster homes and had almost never been taken out, so she was culturally deprived.

The author tells of sometimes amusing, sometimes wrenching moments describing the stages involved in building a family. In addition, the help and hindrance of professional agencies became particularly important because of Tanya's special physical problem. The compelling personality of Tanya always shines through as she charms those around her. For example, at one period Tanya was getting a stomachache each day in her regular school class. It turned out that she was exacting her friends' desserts for the privilege of sitting next to her at lunch and she was accommodating at least three or four friends a day.

The story ends happily with Wheeler writing, "Last winter an acquaintance of ours, on learning that Tanya was adopted, expressed surprise: 'But she looks like your daughter,' the woman exclaimed. Of course. She is." (p. 34).

A brief appendix has suggested readings.

Analysis. This is one of the very few books that addresses the experience of the adoption of a disabled child. The kinds of problems encountered, the red tape, disapproving professionals, and the sudden impact of a brand new family member are not different in kind from the adoption of a child without disabilities; the difference is one of degree. Therefore, this book might have a special appeal to adopted children, disabled or not, and their families. It could also be recommended for siblings of disabled children since their challenges are very similar to those of Tanya's brother.

The diary style in which the book is written is clear, poignant, and humorous.

White, Paul. *Janet at School.* Photog. by Jeremy Finlay. New York: Crowell, 1978. unp. Reading Level: Grades K–3.
Disability: Spina bifida

Five-year-old Janet is a tiny, pretty, and bespectacled girl with spina bifida. A simple explanation of the condition of open spine is provided in the text and in the illustrations, and the limitations it imposes are described in a matter-of-fact way. The very simple prose and colored photographs appearing on every page show Janet in her wheelchair at school and on the playground, participating in activities with her able-bodied friends, learning to walk using leg braces and a walking frame, and with her family at home and at a camping site.

Analysis. Janet is clearly a bright, active, alert child who is being encouraged to participate in life to her fullest capacities. The tone of the text is straightforward and unsentimental; Janet's difficulties are not usually minimized in either the text or the illustrations, although the sentence "Janet has spent a lot of time in the hospital, but now she only has to go there four times a year" does seem to gloss over reality. The book ends with a direct remark to the reader: "If you meet Janet, you may want to know how her wheelchair works. If so, just ask. She'll probably be very pleased to show you."

The text can probably be read by a second- or third-grader, but its interest level makes it appropriate to be read aloud to preschoolers. Although the writer covers many details in a short space, the young reader may have further questions and may be distressed by Janet's unusual appearance in some of the photographs; this is a good book for children and adults to share together.

White, Robin. *Be Not Afraid.* New York: Dial, 1972. 222 pp. Reading Level: Grades 10–12.
Disability: Epilepsy

The author is a professional writer with many books and articles to his credit. He weaves a verbal tapestry of his family and work life, with the main focus on his elder son, Checkers, through his twenty-first year. The Whites' California home in the mountains was the center of their life, and their challenging treks into the high mountains offered them spiritual cleansing and relief periodically throughout the years of the story.

Checkers was a winsome, energetic, and generous boy who, at age eight, began to experience major convulsions, which triggered his downward course toward mental, emotional, and physical degeneration. The causes of his disease and progressive deterioration remain obscure, but there is some evidence that the massive doses of medication needed to keep blackouts, psychomotor seizures, and grand mal attacks from overwhelming him may have been contributing factors.

White places much emphasis on the bad, good, and indifferent medical people who tackled Checkers's complicated problems. As well, he describes the school personnel's response to Checkers's bizarre behavior as ranging from sympathetic to punitive. The reaction of Checkers's classmates to his disability contributed to his anxiety and withdrawal. The father went so far, in a somewhat successful effort to change their cruel behavior, as to stalk a young gang who taunted and beat up his son on a school bus. White thinks that epilepsy is the least understood and most neglected major health problem of children.

In one joyous Christmas season, the family went back to White's boyhood home in southern India, where Checkers found his greatest measure of social acceptance and warmth. Also, the backpacking each summer restored his energy for the ordeal of the school year ahead.

Career, school, and health ups and downs of the parents, Checkers, and his young brother and sister punctuate the years. About Checkers, White wrote, "His mind, like a light bulb in a storm, would dim and brighten and we never knew when it would go out altogether, when we would no longer be able to hold back the night" (p. 184). At age 21, Checkers had been medically stabilized and was functioning well enough to live at home, with participation in a sheltered workshop for mentally retarded persons.

When the book ends the reader knows the story is not finished and that the family will endure much more sadness and joy. There is the promise that they will share treks in the high and remote Sierras many times again.

Analysis. The center of this beautifully written saga is really Robin White, who pits himself against fate and the elements to protect each member of his family and to nurture his children through the successive stages of childhood. That is not to say he is egotistical; his own obviously successful career as a talented writer is definitely secondary to the focus of the story.

Willis, Jack, and Mary Willis. "*. . . But There Are Always Miracles.*" New York: Viking, 1974. 181 pp. Reading Level: Grades 10–12. *Disability:* Quadriplegia

In 1970, at age 36, Jack Willis was a film director and a television producer. Handsome and vigorous, he was engaged to Mary Pleshette, a beautiful young reporter/researcher for *Newsweek.* They planned to marry in a few months, and their lives lay happily before them. In a split second, everything changed. Jack was critically injured while bodysurfing on Long Island. He broke and dislocated his sixth and seventh vertebrae and was paralyzed from the neck down. He spent the next nine weeks in a Stryker frame in the hospital; he had two operations, one to clean out the injury to his vertebrae and assess the damage, the other to fuse bone from his hip to the damaged vertebrae in his neck. Because the doctors could not determine the extent of injury to his spinal cord, they could not make accurate predictions about his recovery. The consulting neurosurgeon who did the first operation thought he would never walk again; the attending physician, although all along hesitant to commit himself, was more optimistic. Gradually, Willis's condition improved, from the first exciting moment when he found he could wiggle a toe through the slow revitalization of other muscles. The narrative, which is told in alternating sections by

Jack and Mary, covers the period from the accident until they are being driven away from Southampton Hospital in an ambulance, heading for Rusk's Institute of Rehabilitation Medicine.

A postscript by Jack tells us that three months later he was able to walk out of the institute on crutches; for the next five months he went to the institute in the mornings and to work in the afternoons. A year after the accident, "I quit Rusk altogether, threw away the crutches, and started to get around on a cane. I joined an exercise class and had hopes of a slow but almost total recovery." The last two sentences of the book, by Jack and Mary, announce their marriage in September 1971 and the birth of their daughter three years after the accident.

Analysis. This absorbing account explores for young people what challenges and rewards an intimate relationship can involve. While this book certainly shows how courage, persistence, and excellent medical care can contribute to rehabilitation, one cannot always hope for such optimistic results in cases of this sort. Both authors are accomplished professional writers who describe their experience with immediacy and vivid detail.

Before the accident they enjoyed a warm close relationship, untried by challenges or suffering. Abruptly, they faced pain, loss, and uncertainty, not only about Jack's physical future but about the quality of their relationship. The honesty that existed between them made it possible for them to share the suffering, understand each other's reactions, and support each other. Both are very explicit in describing their anxieties about the future of their sexual life and their relationship with their families (both sets of parents, while warmly supportive, tended to want to pull their children back into more dependent patterns in an effort to protect them from what had happened).

Wilson, Dorothy Clarke. *Handicap Race: The Inspiring Story of Roger Arnett.* Illus. New York: McGraw-Hill, 1967. 278 pp. Reading Level: Grades 7–12.
Disability: Paraplegia

In 1930, Roger Arnett was a track star at Michigan State Normal College in Ypsilanti, considered a prospect for the next Olympic games. Coming from a painfully poor family, Arnett combined work, studying, and athletics in a grueling schedule that allowed only a few hours of sleep a day. Driving to South Bend to participate in a meet at Notre Dame, he was caught in a blinding snowstorm, had an accident, and fractured his back. He confounded the doctors by surviving his injuries, but he was left paraplegic. He did finish college, and after much discouragement, found work in a welfare office. He married a young woman mildly disabled as the result of childhood polio, and they adopted three children. He was successful as a gladiola grower, and later became a preacher ministering chiefly to the elderly and disabled. He was active in efforts to improve the lives and opportunities of people with disabilities.

Analysis. Wilson bases her story on extensive information, including tape recordings, obtained from Arnett and his family, friends, physicians, and associates. Although there is no reason to doubt the authenticity of her account, her heavy use of synthesized conversation places it close to fictionalizing. Arnett led a positive life, even against terrible odds and at a time when treatment available to paraplegics was less sophisticated than it is today. He drove himself relentlessly and survived many medical crises arising from his physical condition. The author emphasizes Arnett's determination and his personality, while not omitting reference to family difficulties that arose at least in part from limited understanding. Wilson herself sometimes displays limited sensitivity, as in her use of the words "victim" and "afflicted."

Wilson, Dorothy Clarke. *Take My Hands! The Remarkable Story of Dr. Mary Verghese.* New York: McGraw-Hill, 1963. 216 pp. Reading Level: Grades 10–12.
Disability: Paraplegia

Mary Verghese was a medical resident in her native India when in 1954 she was involved in an automobile accident that left her with a disfiguring facial scar and with paraplegia of her legs. Eventually, she fought her way back to professional activity, but she could not stand in order to practice gynecology and obstetrics as she had planned. Instead, she learned to do extremely delicate reconstructive surgery on the hands and faces of leprosy patients while sitting down. She went to Australia for a course on rehabilitation for herself and later to New York; there, at Dr. Howard Rusk's Institute of Rehabilitation Medicine, she was both a patient and a doctor studying Rusk's techniques. She went back to India to establish the Department of Physical Medicine and Rehabilitation there.

Throughout her illness and subsequent convalescence, she was sustained by a strong Christian faith; she had been born into the Syrian Christian Church of South India. Her experience after her accident strengthened her beliefs, and they sustained her as she weathered physical crises and professional challenges.

Analysis. Wilson's style is to write biography like a novel. She apparently did considerable research, studying Verghese's life during the time the doctor spent in the United States. However, her continuous use of invented dialogue makes her biographies read like fiction, and while many biographers share this practice to some extent, such an extensive use tends to undermine the credibility. The subject (a woman physician from another culture) does make the account attractive.

Wolf, Bernard. *Don't Feel Sorry for Paul.* Photog. by the author. Philadelphia: Lippincott, 1974. 96 pp. Reading Level: Grades 4–6. *Disability:* Missing limbs

The author, a professional photographer, captures two weeks in the life of seven-year-old Paul, who was born without a right hand and right foot and with only parts of the left hand and foot. The book begins with Paul dressing himself and putting on three prostheses. Text and pictures then go on to show him having a riding lesson, working and playing with his family and at school, and celebrating his seventh birthday with a party. He is also portrayed having therapy and a checkup at the Institute of Rehabilitation Medicine and going to the Eschen Laboratories for repair to his prostheses. In the final pages Paul participates in a horse show and wins a red ribbon for second place from a judge who does not know that he has a disability. The book's title comes from a conversation Paul's mother has with another mother at the horse show: "Paul's father and I are awfully lucky people. I don't know what we ever did to deserve a son like Paul. He gives our lives a special kind of lift. If I could have one wish come true, I would wish that Paul could be as happy for the rest of his life as he is right now. I know that when he grows up, a lot of people won't be as concerned with him as we are. But that's life, and I think he'll be ready when those problems come. No . . . don't feel sorry for Paul. He doesn't need it" (p. 94). Black-and-white photographs enhance every spread.

Analysis. Don't Feel Sorry for Paul is cited frequently where children's books about disabilities are listed and discussed. It might be argued that young children, to whom this book is addressed, do not necessarily share the pitying attitude of older people and that the title makes an unnecessary assumption.

The author describes Paul's life and his family's loving support in matter-of-fact narrative. The explanations and close-up photographs of Paul's impairments, his prostheses, and his management strategies are detailed and clear. Paul is a smart problem-solver; his occasional impatience and frustration are not overly emphasized. An understanding black child is shown helping him to accept an unkind remark made by another youngster at his birthday party; this may have been staged, but most of the story appears to be straightforward.

This book can be recommended for elementary-school readers and particularly for classes that include children with impairments. Preschoolers and kindergartners, who have much interest in stories of daily life, would enjoy seeing the pictures and hearing the narrative read aloud.

6

Books Dealing with
Sensory Problems

This chapter contains titles classified in three sections: Deaf-blind; Hearing Impairments; and Visual Impairments.

■ Citations are alphabetical by author in each section.

Deaf-blind

Bigland, Eileen. *Helen Keller*. Illus. by Lili Cassel Wronker. New York: Phillips, 1967. 192 pp. Reading Level: Grades 4–6.
Disability: Deaf-blind

Originally published in England and enlarged and revised for the American edition, this biography begins with the Keller forebears and a brief story of an ancestor who was "the first man to work out a system of teaching the deaf in the city of Zurich to speak, read, and write." The first chapter includes some rarely reported details of Keller's life before Anne Sullivan's arrival, including Mrs. Keller's efforts to train her multiply impaired daughter. Keller's life through her graduation from Radcliffe takes up two-thirds of the text; the remaining third covers the years from 1904 to her death in 1968.

Analysis. Bigland handles Keller's compelling story with a lively style, good choice of details, and vivid narrative of her heroine's situation and experiences. Unfortunately, she uses the word "dumb" to describe the muteness of profound early deafness. While it is true that Keller herself used the word ("I am not dumb now!" she said repeatedly when she first learned to speak), it is no longer acceptable, at least in the United States.

The black-and-white drawings enhance the text attractively, both in charming small designs around the initial letter of each chapter and in larger illustrations.

Crist, Lyle M. *Through the Rain and Rainbow: The Remarkable Life of Richard Kinney*. Illus. Nashville, Tenn.: Abingdon, 1974. 224 pp. Reading Level: Grades 10–12.
Disability: Deaf-blind

Richard Kinney lost his vision at the age of seven; 13 years later, he lost his hearing. Unable to finish his sophomore year at Mount Union College, he returned to his home in nearby East Sparta, Ohio. At first, his family and friends communicated with him by the use of taps; later, by a white glove with letters marked along the fingers in black ink. At the instigation of a blind social worker, he learned communication by the manual alphabet.

Always interested in literature, he began to write poetry and to take courses from the Hadley School, a correspondence school for blind persons in Winnetka, Illinois. After eight years at home, he reentered Mount Union College with the help of the American Foundation for the Blind, as well as a number of interested individuals. When he graduated in 1954, he became the third deaf-blind person in the United States to graduate from college.

Even before he graduated, the Hadley School negotiated to employ him as an instructor, and he began work immediately on receiving his degree. Through his correspondence teaching, he became acquainted with Evelyn Davis Warmbrodt, a teacher who was blind and taught in a Catholic school in St. Louis. They eventually met, immediately fell in love, and were married. Their son, Clark, was born with full vision and hearing. Just three years later, however, Evelyn Davis Kinney died from a return of the cancer that had caused her blindness as a child. With his mother-in-law's assistance, Kinney stayed in the house where he and his wife had lived and raised his son himself. A prominent participant in worldwide activities to promote the welfare of deaf-blind persons, he also continued teaching, and then began to perform administrative work at Hadley. At the close of the book, he had become director of the school.

Black-and-white photographs of Kinney's life are included.

Analysis. Richard Kinney is a courageous, resourceful, talented person, and the author warmly portrays the details of Kinney's life, its triumphs and its tragedies as well as its humorous events. The title, *Through the Rain and Rainbow*, a phrase taken from one of Kinney's poems, serves as a theme for the story and as a metaphor for his life.

The author writes excellent description and narrates events in Kinney's life with close attention to detail and authenticity. The narrative sometimes suffers, however, from jumps back and forth in time that may be confusing to readers.

The use of the terms "the deaf-blind" and especially "a deaf-blind" (the latter in reference to a person who is deaf-blind) are jarring to a reader sensitized to current-day attitudes and practices regarding language referring to people with disabilities, but this usage is understandable in the context of the date of publication of this book. Despite this flaw, the work presents a positive portrayal of disability; for example, both the Kinneys were very much a part of mainstream society, having received all of their education in schools not designed exclusively for blind or deaf persons. In addition, Evelyn Kinney taught in the Roman Catholic school system in St. Louis, not in a school for blind children. Nor is Kinney pictured as a saintly type; his participation in college pranks and some of the ways he adapted to being deaf and blind (for example, his method of making telephone calls to Evelyn when he was courting her) are narrated with humorous realism.

Davidson, Margaret. *Helen Keller*. Illus. by Vicki Fox. New York: Hastings, 1971. 95 pp. Reading Level: Grades 4–6.
Disability: Deaf-blind

This biography for young readers concentrates on Keller's childhood and education by her teacher, Annie Sullivan. The last two chapters touch on her years at Radcliffe College and, very briefly, the work of her adult life. The book is illustrated with black-and-white drawings, two photographs of Keller, and a drawing of the American manual alphabet.

Analysis. Davidson covers some of the well-known points of Keller's development, describing events in a clear, vivid style. She has chosen to omit much, but the biography can serve as a first introduction for elementary-school readers; slightly older children could be encouraged to read some of the other books on Keller and Sullivan (see this chapter).

Graff, Stewart, and Polly Anne Graff. *Helen Keller: Toward the Light*. Illus. by Paul Frame. Champaign, Ill.: Garrard, 1965. 80 pp. Reading Level: Grades 4–6.
Disability: Deaf-blind

This is a retelling of the familiar Helen Keller story, the content of which is given in other annotations (see this chapter). This particular version contains ten chapters covering Keller's life. It is illustrated by color drawings that brighten the text and are appropriate for young readers.

Analysis: The narrative is well written and interesting, and could possibly be read and enjoyed by second- and third-graders who are good readers, as well as by fourth- to sixth-graders. The story is faithful to the facts of Helen Keller's life and portrays her not as a martyr or a saint, but as an unusually determined person.

Hickok, Lorena A. *The Story of Helen Keller.* Illus. New York: Grosset, 1958. 154 pp. Reading Level: Grades 4–6.
Disability: Deaf-blind

The often-told tale of Helen Keller, blinded and deafened before age 2, is here recounted in simple language. The story begins with Helen, uncomprehending, angrily tipping over her baby sister's crib. The author describes the thoughts in Helen's head and quotes dialogue. With Anne Sullivan's arrival when Helen is 7, the arduous power struggles and slow process of socialization begin. The stranger (as Helen thought of Anne Sullivan) ensconced herself with her charge alone in a cottage, away from the overprotection of Helen's parents. There Helen learned the manual alphabet (shown in the book). Finally she comprehended at the water pump that the manual symbols stood for things. This event also marked the beginning of Helen's real love for the woman she called Teacher. Helen would be able to read, write, typewrite, lip-read, and talk by the time she was 11.

Helen, accompanied by Sullivan, eventually went to a regular school and to college. Her book about her life was published when she was a junior. Hickok describes the postcollege career of lecturing, writing, and vaudeville that Keller shared with Sullivan and, briefly, Sullivan's husband. Anne Sullivan died in middle age, but Helen had another companion in Polly, her secretary. The book ends with Helen in the midst of good works at home and abroad.

Analysis. This large-type book tells the story of Helen and Sullivan in simple but interesting prose. It highlights the kind of events that would appeal to a young school-age child: the death of Helen's dog, her narrow escape from fire, her worries about being accepted at school. Insights into what it would be like to be deaf and blind are skillfully woven into the story. That this is an old book is perhaps evident from the rather stilted drawings, but it remains a good one.

Hickok, Lorena A. *The Touch of Magic: The Story of Helen Keller's Great Teacher, Anne Sullivan Macy.* Illus. New York: Dodd, 1961. 184 pp. Reading Level: Grades 4–6.
Disability: Deaf-blind, Partially sighted

The author became interested in Anne Sullivan when she interviewed Helen Keller, since Sullivan's name always came into the conversation. After extensive research, she wrote this biography for young readers. The story opens with the inauspicious journey of partially sighted nine-year-old Anne and her four-year-old crippled brother to the state alms house in a hearse. There she was to comfort Jimmy until he died of tuberculosis. Anne's vision had been affected by trachoma.

After several chapters about Anne Sullivan's unusually depressing four years in the alms house, the story moves to her experiences in the Perkins Institution for the Blind in South Boston, where she avidly pursued her education, although like Helen Keller, her later pupil, she was only "half tamed" at the beginning of her attendance at Perkins. Twenty years old, she ended up valedictorian of her class and received the invitation to teach "deaf, dumb, and blind" Helen Keller, with whom she would stay the rest of her life.

The middle section of the book describes Sullivan's efforts to socialize Helen and their continued association throughout Helen's college days. The last section describes Sullivan's romance with John Macy and her close relationship with Helen during their tumultuous adult years. Their days on the road as lecturers and entertainers are detailed as well as Sullivan's subsequent rift with her husband. Throughout the book the reader has been kept cognizant of the effects of trachoma and the lessening ability of physicians to treat Sullivan's condition. Her deteriorating eyesight and autumn years culminating with her death and funeral are described in the final chapters. Sullivan's ashes were placed in the National Cathedral in Washington, D.C., the first time such an honor was accorded any teacher or any woman. A space beside her was reserved to receive the ashes of Helen Keller.

Analysis. Parts of this book might seem redundant to those who have read Hickok's companion book about Helen Keller (see preceding annotation) but it is refreshing to have the story from Anne Sullivan's perspective. The writing is clear and accurate. The one illustration is a most attractive black-and-white photograph of Sullivan and Keller as young women.

Hunter, Edith Fisher. *Child. of the Silent Night: The Story of Laura Bridgman.* Illus. by Bea Holmes. Boston: Houghton, 1963. 124 pp. Reading Level: Grades 4–6.
Disability: Deaf-blind

This is a biography of the first deaf, blind, and mute person to be successfully educated in the United States. Laura Bridgman was born in New Hampshire in 1829. When she was a toddler, a raging case of scarlet fever left her deaf, blind, mute, and almost without the senses of taste and smell. Her parents recognized her superior intelligence, but they found it increasingly difficult to control her.

Through a series of circumstances, a report on Laura reached Dr. Samuel Gridley Howe (see Meltzer's *A Light in the Dark* in this section), director of the first school for blind children in the United States. He had been waiting for someone like Laura in order to demonstrate that a multiply handicapped child could be given the key to learning. When she was of school age, Bridgman's parents brought her to the New England Asylum for the Blind, later to be called the Perkins School for the Blind, and left her with Dr. Howe and his sister. She learned to read books in raised type and became the star attraction of the open-house sessions held by Howe in order to acquaint the public with his work. In 1842 Charles Dickens visited the school and wrote an account of Bridgman in *American Notes;* Helen Keller's mother was to read that description 40 years later, prompting the Kellers to turn to Perkins for help. Laura Bridgman lived at Perkins until her death at 60, helping to educate succeeding generations of blind children. The book is illustrated with line drawings.

Analysis. This biography is well written and easily accessible to young readers. Although some of the dialogue sounds fabricated to adult ears, it will probably not trouble children; in any case, most of the book is in the form of expository narrative. The chief focus is on Bridgman's childhood in the period from her illness through her first four years at Perkins. Hunter gradually introduces the reader to Bridgman's disabilities, making clear the extent to which they cut her off from normal communication. The description of Dr. Howe's educational program for Bridgman is equally clear. Difficulties are hinted at but never emphasized. Howe called Bridgman's education a "sort of triumphal march," and this is what Hunter emphasizes.

In the illustrations, Bridgman is always shown wearing a small eye mask, but this is never mentioned in the text—a puzzling omission.

Keller, Helen. *The Story of My Life.* Illus. New York: Doubleday, 1954. 382 pp. Reading Level: Grades 10–12.
Disability: Deaf-blind

This book, edited by John Albert Macy, Anne Sullivan's husband, first appeared in 1903. It falls into three parts: Keller's "The Story of My Life"; "Letters," most of them written by Keller, a few written to her, arranged in chronological order from 1887 (when she was seven) to 1901; and "A Supplementary Account of Helen Keller's Life and Education," written by Anne Sullivan and John Macy in informal letters and formal reports. The last section includes material relating to the so-called Frost King affair, when 11-year-old Helen sent a story to the director of the Perkins Institution and Massachusetts School for the

Blind, and was subsequently accused of plagiarism. This was a shattering accusation for both Helen Keller and Anne Sullivan; an investigation eventually determined that she had been read a similar story in 1888 by another woman, in Sullivan's absence, and that without remembering it consciously, she had reproduced much of the original language. All three sections chronicle Keller's life until 1903, when she had finished her first two years at Radcliffe College. Ralph Barton Perry's introduction gives in brief form information about her life after graduation from college.

Analysis. Helen Keller's story is widely known and many of the details are familiar. Repetition and familiarity cannot, however, dull the effect of this remarkable life. To read her account and Sullivan's of the early years is to enter into their world, so vividly do both women write. Sullivan's notes on her teaching methods are of particular interest. For example, she decided to teach the child Helen language by communicating with her as one does with a two-year-old—"I *shall talk into her hand as we talk into the baby's ears* [italics in original]. I shall assume that she has the normal child's capacity of assimilation and limitation. I *shall use complete sentences in talking to her* [italics in original], and fill out the meaning with gestures and her descriptive signs when necessity requires it; but I shall not try to keep her mind fixed on any one thing. I shall do all I can to interest and stimulate it, and wait for results" (p. 258). High school students might want to read this book in conjunction with the play *The Miracle Worker* by William Gibson, and particularly able readers might wish to follow these with a book such as Joseph Lash's *Helen and Teacher* (see following annotation).

Lash, Joseph P. *Helen and Teacher.* Illus. New York: Delacorte, 1980. 811 pp. Reading Level: Grades 10–12.
Disability: Deaf-blind, Partially sighted

Drawing on extensive archival materials—principally those at the American Foundation for the Blind, the Perkins Institution, and the Alexander Graham Bell Association for the Deaf (the Volta Bureau)—Lash has written a double biography of exhaustive detail. He divides his book into seven parts: "Annie," "Teacher and Helen," "Helen and Teacher," "Helen and Teacher and John," "Helen and Teacher and Polly," "Helen and Polly," and "Helen."

There are many photographs, a bibliography, and an index, and the endpapers provide a chronology. In his acknowledgments, Lash explains that he has omitted detailed footnotes, but that annotated copies of the book can be found at the American Foundation for the Blind, the Perkins School for the Blind, the Alexander Graham Bell

Association, and the Schlesinger Library at Radcliffe. The book is one in the Radcliffe Biography series.

Analysis. Lash has done a superb job of mastering and presenting an enormous body of material. A fluent and expressive writer, he is able to sustain a sophisticated young reader's interest through a detailed exposition of the lives of these two remarkable women. His insights and deductions draw judiciously on psychiatric knowledge and his approach, particularly in dealing with controversial episodes and interpretations, is fair and balanced. This book could be read either in whole or in part. Young adults who are able readers should not be daunted by the size of this beautifully printed study.

Meltzer, Milton. *A Light in the Dark: The Life of Samuel Gridley Howe.* New York: Crowell, 1964. 239 pp. Reading Level: Grades 7–9.
Disability: Deaf-blind

Samuel Howe (1801–1876) grew up in Boston, studied at Brown College and Harvard Medical School, and in 1824 went as a volunteer to help the Greeks in their struggle against the Turks. He spent the next seven years in Greece as army surgeon, soldier, organizer. When he came back to Boston, unsettled about his future, he accepted the offer to become director of an institution still in the formative stage, the New England Asylum for the Blind, later renamed the Perkins School for the Blind. Here Howe put into effect programs for teaching blind people derived from his study of European methods and from his own experience.

In 1837, a child was brought to Perkins who, as a toddler, had had such a severe attack of scarlet fever that it left her without sight or hearing and with impaired taste and smell. Howe took the child, Laura Bridgman (see Hunter, *Child of the Silent Night,* this section) and taught her to communicate by means of raised letters as well as the manual alphabet. Unusually bright and lively, Bridgman became his most famous pupil and lived at Perkins all her life. A man of outstanding energy and creativity, Howe joined with Horace Mann to urge the use of oral methods in teaching "deaf-mutes," supported Mann's efforts to establish training schools for teachers, was active in prison reform, became general superintendent for the Massachusetts School for Idiotic and Feeble-Minded Youth (*sic*), and worked for the abolition movement.

Analysis. Meltzer writes clearly and powerfully, conveying Howe's energy, courage, and creativity. The book is compelling not only for its attention to the special subjects of education and disabilities, but for its picture of nineteenth-century American life as reflected in the experiences and ideas of someone who was part of so many important events of that century. At times, because Meltzer is compressing so much activity into a relatively short space, the chronology may be confusing to the young reader, but this is a minor flaw. The book compels and rewards attentive reading.

Peare, Catherine Owens. *The Helen Keller Story*. Drawings by Jeanyee Wong of the one-hand alphabet. New York: Crowell, 1959. 183 pp. Reading Level: Grades 4–6.
Disability: Deaf-blind

Beginning with Keller's babyhood, the author traces the now-familiar story of Keller's extraordinary development from half-savage child, locked in terrible mute isolation, to brilliantly accomplished woman with international fame and immense influence. She describes Anne Sullivan's tireless, imaginative teaching that, building on the work of Samuel Gridley Howe with Laura Bridgman (see also titles by Hunter, Meltzer, and Wilkie, this section), saved Keller from a life of tragic waste. Half the book is devoted to Keller's career after her graduation from Radcliffe in 1904. Peare describes her efforts to speak intelligibly and her experiences on vaudeville stages and lecture platforms, her work for the American Foundation for the Blind, her tireless worldwide travels on behalf of blind and disabled people, and her writing. A brief section, "How to Behave with a Deaf, a Blind, or a Deaf-Blind Person," is followed by an illustration showing the manual alphabet. There is a selected bibliography of books, magazine articles, and pamphlets—almost 50 titles (all published before 1960); also included is an index.

Analysis. Focusing on Keller's point of view, Peare succeeds in giving the reader a sense of what Keller's life was like, even before she learned to think with language. The dialogue is sometimes stiff and unnatural, at other times more successful; characters come alive and information is conveyed clearly. Young readers will gain an appreciation of what Sullivan and Keller accomplished together. The short "How to Behave with a Deaf, a Blind, or a Deaf-Blind Person" makes suggestions that are both sensitive and practical for children and adults.

Waite, Helen Elmira. *Valiant Companions: Helen Keller and Anne Sullivan Macy*. Philadelphia: Macrae Smith, 1959. 224 pp. Reading Level: Grades 7–9.
Disability: Deaf-blind, Visual impairment

The book opens with Anne Sullivan's graduation as valedictorian from the Perkins Institution and Massachusetts School for the Blind. By the third chapter Sullivan is traveling to Tuscumbia, Alabama, to become governess to seven-year-old Helen Keller, deaf and blind since an illness at 19 months. Cut off from the usual avenues of sensory perception and human intercourse, the child was wild and angry, and her loving but powerless family were unable to manage her.

Sullivan met her with firm, consistent, and affectionate discipline, with physical and moral strength, and with an imaginative teaching program. In the portentous scene at the water pump, Keller at last understood that the letters being spelled by Sullivan into one hand symbolized liquid rushing over the other hand. Her terrible isolation was breached and her bright, inquisitive mind set free. Anne Sullivan was determined that her charge would not live Laura Bridgman's protected but isolated life (see Hunter, *Child of the Silent Night,* this section). She supervised Keller's education at home, at the Perkins Institution, at the Wright-Humanson Oral School for the Deaf in New York, and eventually at Radcliffe College.

Keller's adult life was devoted to the cause of improving the lives of blind and deaf-blind persons, and she used the international fame that had come to her even in childhood to further these ends. When Anne Sullivan Macy died in 1936, Polly Thomson, who had joined their household in 1914, became Keller's companion, but no one could ever replace Teacher.

There is a short bibliography.

Analysis. The narration moves quickly and compellingly, with skillful use of details gathered from authoritative sources. The conversations, which are realistically re-created, are, says the author, "based upon the writings of Helen Keller, Anne Sullivan Macy and other firsthand sources." Two especially painful passages in Keller's life—the accusation of plagiarism over her short story "The Frost King," written when she was 11, and an abortive love affair when she was 36—are described with sensitivity. Unfortunately, the book is marred by occasional racist notes, such as reference to a black child as a little pickaninny or description of black servants "watching her with their eyes rolling in awe."

Wilkie, Katherine E., and Elizabeth R. Moseley. *Teacher of the Blind: Samuel Gridley Howe.* New York: Messner, 1965. 191 pp. Reading Level: Grades 7–9.
Disability: Deaf-blind, Visual impairment

Samuel Gridley Howe was born in 1801 and died in 1876. After graduation from Brown College in Providence, R.I., and from Harvard Medical School, Howe went to Greece to aid the cause of their democracy. He spent seven years abroad. On his return to Boston, he was offered the directorship of the newly organized New England Asylum for the Blind. He then went back to Europe to study methods of teaching blind people; there, he became involved in trying to get aid to Polish refugees and was imprisoned in Berlin. After being freed, he came back to work at his school, now called the New England Institution for the Education of the Blind, and later (after the gift of his house and gardens by Colonel Thomas Perkins) named the Perkins Institution.

Howe carried on his educational work at Perkins for 44 years. He believed that his students should be taught both intellectual and mechanical subjects and that programs should be fitted to the child's abilities. Probably his best-known work came from his teaching of Laura Bridgman (see Hunter, *Child of the Silent Night*, this section), who was brought to Perkins as a little girl for her schooling. As a toddler she had lost sight, hearing, and most of her taste and smell as a result of scarlet fever. Under Howe's direction, Laura was taught to read, write, and sign, as well as to do many domestic tasks. She lived her whole life at Perkins. Charles Dickens's description of her in his *American Notes* led Helen Keller's parents to approach Perkins when they were searching for a teacher for their daughter, and Anne Sullivan consulted with Bridgman before going to Alabama. In addition to his work with education for blind students, Howe was associated with Dorothea Lynde Dix, who fought to reform treatment of people with mental illness, and with Horace Mann, the educator. He was married to Julia Ward Howe, author of "The Battle Hymn of the Republic," and both were strong advocates of the abolition of slavery.

The book ends with a bibliography and an index.

Analysis. The authors have done a skillful job of presenting Howe, his personality, life experiences, and accomplishments. In addition, they describe well the sometimes difficult marriage between Samuel and Julia Ward Howe. Young readers of this biography would get a clear picture of Howe's work as well as an idea of some salient features of this period in American history.

Yoken, Carol. *Living with Deaf-Blindness: Nine Profiles.* Washington, D.C.: National Academy of Gallaudet College, 1979. 175 pp. Reading Level: Grades 10–12.
Disability: Deaf-blind

Yoken's purpose in writing this book was "to introduce students and professional workers to issues in the lives of deaf-blind individuals" (p. 3). After finding subjects for her study through the help of professional agencies and obtaining their consent, Yoken interviewed them and people associated with them—family, neighbors, agency workers. She used a variety of methods, necessitated by the double disability, to communicate with the deaf-blind individuals.

Of the nine people profiled, four were born with impaired hearing and gradually lost all or most of their sight; two were both hearing and vision impaired suddenly; two had severe vision impairment in childhood, regained some sight, and then developed hearing impairments; one lost most of his vision from glaucoma as a young man and in his forties developed severe hearing impairment as a result of Ménière's syndrome. Some of the respondents had Usher's syndrome, "a genetic condition with the predominant symptoms of hearing loss and vision impairment. It is characterized by deafness or lesser hearing loss, most often present at birth, accompanied by a specific restriction of vision due to *retinitis pigmentosa* . . . [which] causes slow deterioration of the retina, resulting in early night blindness and progressive loss of peripheral vision" (p. 26). This condition is the most common cause of deaf-blindness. People with Usher's syndrome often experience a special degree of isolation and confusion, since their visual impairment is frequently not recognized or understood by those around them.

The respondents ranged in age from 23 to 71, varied in educational background, and had very different work experiences. Each profile describes the person as she or he appeared to the interviewer and gives information about family background; onset of the disability, adjustment, and past and present life patterns are described. Much of the material appears in the respondents' own voice and language, as recorded by the interviewer. Each respondent was interviewed in ways best suited to her or his preferences and needs—for example, Yoken asked questions by writing, finger spelling, signing, printing on palm or shoulder; and respondents answered by typing, signing, finger spelling, speaking, or by combining methods. In many profiles, names of people and places have been changed.

The book ends with a chapter of conclusions and with appendices giving the interview questions in English and in American Sign Language and copies of the authorization forms used in the study.

Analysis. Yoken is a sensitive interviewer. She framed her questions with care, and the format allows the person and voice of each respondent to come through. She seems to have approached each person with dignity and respect. In one profile, however, she repeatedly uses the term "feeble-minded," a loaded phrase. As she notes in the conclusion, people who are deaf-blind often experience isolation and dependence and exhibit anger and resentment, "but for no one are they [these conditions and emotions] so all consuming to completely control and define the person" (p. 157). Yoken notes that the interviewees all shared the same aim: They wanted "to work and to love." Society, Yoken believes, must help them achieve that aim.

This is a valuable book, not only for the audience of students and professionals Yoken is primarily addressing, but for all readers who would like to gain more insight into the world of the person with both visual and hearing impairments.

Hearing Impairments

Albronda, Mildred. *Douglas Tilden: Portrait of a Deaf Sculptor.* Illus. with photog. Silver Spring, Md.: T. J. Publishers, 1980. 144 pp. Reading Level: Grades 10–12.
Disability: Deafness

Douglas Tilden, born in Chico, California, in 1860, lost both his hearing and speech at the age of five after a prolonged and severe case of scarlet fever. At the age of six, he enrolled in the California School for the Deaf in San Francisco. Three years later, the school moved to Berkeley, where it remains today. Tilden, a good student from an educated, middle-class family of California pioneers, graduated from the school and then taught there for eight years, during which time he published articles about educating children who are deaf.

During summer vacation in 1882, Tilden spent a month studying drawing and painting at the California School of Design, and the following summer he became intrigued with sculpting when, on a visit home, he saw one of his brothers modeling clay. He visited his brother's teacher, who in one month taught Tilden all he could about sculpting. Seized by a great passion for this art form, Tilden launched himself into a lifelong career as a sculptor. He moved into a deserted laundry shed on the campus of the California School for the Deaf, and for four years he continued to teach, while he modeled in clay during his free time. In 1887 he resigned his teaching position and spent the next seven years in New York and Paris perfecting his sculpting skills. In Paris he won recognition as an outstanding sculptor, including an honorable mention for his sculpture *Baseball Player,* from the Salon des Artistes Françaises, a body whose approval was necessary for the attainment of public commissions and prominence in the art world.

Financial problems forced Tilden to return to San Francisco in 1884, just at the time that commemorative sculptures were nearly an obsession with its citizens. He enjoyed many years of prominence and good fortune as an artist and a teacher of art, although his later years were marked by personal and professional adversity. During his artistic career, he continued to write and to work in behalf of education for the deaf and for their integration into the mainstream of American society.

His works still standing in the San Francisco Bay area include *The Mechanics, California Volunteers, Admission Day, Football Players, Father Junipero Serra, The Bear Hunt,* and *Baseball Player.*

Useful items appended to the text include notes to each chapter, a bibliography, a chronology of Tilden's life, a list of his major exhibitors and displays, and an index. Photographs of Tilden, his family and associates, and his works are included.

Analysis. This work meets all the criteria of appropriate treatment of persons with disabilities. Albronda emphasizes Tilden's accomplishments as a sculptor and portrays him as typically human, pointing out, for example, the stubbornness and irascibility for which he was well known. He does seem to be a remote, distant person; somehow, his personality never really emerges. This is not a fictionalized biography. The writing style is spare, tight, and sometimes a little tedious, with emphasis on the facts of Tilden's life and his accomplishments. The researcher has obviously been thorough and precise, and has utilized primary source material to a great extent.

Allen, Elizabeth Cooper. *Mother Can You Hear Me?: The Extraordinary True Story of an Adopted Daughter's Reunion with Her Birth Mother after a Separation of Fifty Years.* Illus. New York: Dodd, 1983. 208 pp. Reading Level: Grades 10–12.
Disability: Deafness

The author was 50 years old when she became intensely interested in her family of origin, about whom she knew almost nothing. Beginning with some information from her adoptive sister, she started out on a search for her mother, which quickly led her to the nearby residential training school for retarded persons. Her natural mother, Almeda, was deaf. For four months mother and daughter learned to communicate with and love each other. Frail, elderly Almeda died peacefully and was buried in the small town from which she came. The funeral was a moving end of life as well as a beginning of Cooper's acceptance into her biological family. From them and from records she pieced together the facts of her mother's life:

Almeda was born the fifth child in a large family in rural New Jersey. Between two and four, she evidently was deafened by scarlet fever or meningitis. At nine she was sent to a school for the deaf in New Jersey. In 1917 she was raped by a migrant worker and became pregnant with Elizabeth Cooper, the author. A few months after she had her baby, she gave her up and was committed to North Jersey Training School for retarded persons, which was to be her home for 50 years.

An appendix to the book gives Allen's testimony for a State Assembly Bill to Open Adoptions Records (New Jersey, 1981).

Analysis. A number of books have been written of late by people searching for their natural parents, or by people disturbed by hindrances to their learning of their families of origin. Moreover, spurred by professionals in the family therapy movement, people are becoming interested in extending their knowledge of their own genealogies in order to better understand themselves.

This book is unique because the long-lost mother was disabled—a fear that must beset many offspring who do not know their parentage. For Allen, her mother's disability turned out to be basically unimportant, except as it showed her mother's courage and tenacity in the face of adversity. A practicing psychologist, Allen experienced great personal growth through this experience. She no longer had a sense of loss about her natural mother, and she developed a greater compassion for her adopting parents and her sister.

Not really resolved in this book is the problem of a father rapist (who apparently was sentenced to prison and deported to Mexico). Nevertheless, Allen's warmly told tale is powerful and the resolution gratifying. Her prose is honest and uncomplicated.

Benderly, Beryl Lieff. *Dancing without Music: Deafness in America.* New York: Doubleday, 1980. 302 pp. Reading Level: Grades 10–12. *Disability:* Deafness

Benderly is a professional writer with training in anthropology and linguistics. She says, "This book is about holy war"; the war is the "passionate disagreement" between the two principal camps of education for the hearing impaired, between the oralists and the manualists. The disagreement has gone on for more than two hundred years, and Benderly uses it as a recurring theme. She asks questions like "Who are the deaf?" and "What is hearing loss?" She describes what it is like to grow up deaf and discusses speculations about how people learn to think if they do not learn language aurally.

Several chapters cover the history of the controversy between oralists and manualists, an explanation of how different modes of training work (including what is called "total communication"), and the subject of mainstreaming. The book ends with footnotes, a list of source material, recommended further reading, a list of organizations, and an index.

Analysis. Benderly's book is engrossing and very well written. She says in her preface that she has written "as honest, as disinterested, as open-minded and open-hearted a study" as she was able to do and that in examining the great debate she reached the conclusion that "there is no single truth." Readers will get a fair-minded picture of this complex subject. Although the book is long, and occasionally technical, it is for a lay audience and accessible to mature and able high school students.

Blatchford, Claire H. *Listening: Notes from a Kindergarten Journal.* Washington, D.C.: Alexander Graham Bell Assn. for the Deaf, 1973. 111 pp. Reading Level: Grades 10–12.
Disability: Deafness

Author Blatchford, who herself became profoundly deaf at the age of six, taught at the Lexington School for the Deaf in New York. For one year she kept a diary in which she recorded the events in her kindergarten, with emphasis on the individual characteristics of the children, their interaction with the other children as well as with her, and her relationship with the parents of these children. She comments at length on behavior problems and on the problems that hearing parents have when interacting with their deaf children. Although she does come down heavily on the side of oral education, she stresses the importance to parents of nonverbal communication and gestures, but stops short of discussing or advocating sign language.

Analysis. This is a sensitive, perceptive description and analysis of the inner dynamics and external relationships of a group of very young children who are deaf. Each child has at least one chapter dedicated to her or him, and is also mentioned elsewhere. Teenagers who are considering careers in which they would work with young children, either disabled or able-bodied, might find this book enlightening as well as interesting.

Bove, Linda. *Sesame Street Sign Language Fun.* Illus. by Tom Cooke. New York: Random House, 1980. unp. Reading Level: Grades K–6.
Disability: Deafness

The author is a deaf actress who has been associated with "Sesame Street" and with the National Theatre of the Deaf. In this book, a double-page spread introduces a cluster of signs from American Sign Language by means of colored photographs of Bove signing and colored cartoonlike drawings. This is followed by a spread featuring Bert and Ernie, with the question, "How many things in this picture can you 'sign'?" At the bottom of the spread, a strip of photographs illustrates complete sentences using the concepts that have just been introduced. The topics include subjects such as morning preparations, school days, the farm, the playground, verbs indicating activity, jungle animals, the seasons, and colors. The front endpapers illustrate the sign alphabet in color photographs; the back endpapers present numbers up to ten.

Analysis. Like the "Sesame Street" television program, this book is cheerful, jaunty, fast-moving, and informative. The signs are clearly illustrated, with arrows showing how to move hands and fingers. Although directed toward elementary-school-age children, the book would serve well to raise interest in learning sign and could be used by a whole family.

Braddock, Guilbert C. *Notable Deaf Persons.* Ed. by Florence B. Crammatte. Washington, D.C.: Gallaudet College Alumni Assn., 1975. 210 pp. Reading Level: Grades 10–12.
Disability: Deafness, Hard of hearing

The material in this book appeared originally between 1937 and 1946 as a series in the *Frat,* the publication of the National Fraternal Society of the Deaf. The author, who died in 1972, lost his hearing at the age of four and a half; he became a minister and was also a free-lance researcher and writer. He wrote nearly one hundred profiles for the series, arranging them in roughly chronological order. European as well as American figures appear. In her introduction, the editor notes that the life span of Braddock's subjects ends in the early years of the twentieth century and that no one has continued his work.

The people about whom Braddock wrote include relatively well-known names such as Sophia Fowler Gallaudet (for whose husband Gallaudet College was named) and Alice Cogswell (Gallaudet's first student), as well as others who may be more obscure to the general public, although no less interesting.

An alphabetical list of profiles appears at the front of the book and a general index at the back.

Analysis. Braddock writes in an engaging, often humorous style—for example, in mentioning the death of George Dougherty, a successful deaf chemist and assayer, he says, "He departed on December 2, 1938, to take up some higher duties, such as the assaying of golden harps and halos" (p. 203). This is the kind of book that can be used either for specific reference or for browsing. It could be recommended to hearing-impaired readers and their classmates, as well as to young students of history.

Charlip, Remy, with Mary Beth and George Ancona. *Handtalk.*
Illus. New York: Four Winds, 1980. unp. Reading Level: Grades
K–12.
Disability: Deafness

This picture book introduces readers to finger spelling and signing. Each spread includes the finger sign for a letter (in alphabetical
order) photographed in black and white; a finger-spelled word, also in
black and white; and a large full-color photograph illustrating a signed
word or phrase. The front endpapers repeat the finger alphabet and
the back endpapers illustrate more than two dozen signs.

Analysis. Through its attractive design, lively models, and high-
quality photographs, *Handtalk* presents voiceless communication in a
stimulating way that invites readers to participate. The emphasis is on
sharing, rather than on a language that is limited to the hearing-
impaired alone, making this an excellent introduction to the subject for
people of all ages.

Communicative Skills Program. *A Basic Course in Manual Communication.* Illus. by Donald W. Lacock. 2nd ed. Silver Spring, Md.:
National Assn. of the Deaf, 1973. 161 pp. Reading Level: Grades
7–12.
Disability: Deafness

This is a basic textbook for sign language and finger spelling. It
contains 45 lessons, the first dealing with finger spelling, the others
with signs. Each sign is drawn with a combination of solid and dotted
lines and arrows show the directions of the hand motions. No written
description of the hand motions is provided. Practice exercises for each
lesson are in a separate section following the illustrated text. An appendix supplies signs for pronouns, affixes, articles, contractions,
prepositions, conjunctions and related terms, and the verb "to be."

Bibliographies include "A Manual Communications Bibliography";
"A Selected Annotated Bibliography of Books, Films and Teaching Media on Sign Language"; "Films and Teaching Media"; and "A Selected
Bibliography of Books About or Related to Deafness." There is an
index of words.

Analysis. The illustrations are clear and easy to follow, and the
exercises provide continuous practice in all signs that have been
learned to that point. The bibliographies are useful, although one
would need to look for current material also. The absence of a written
description for the hand motion of each sign is not detrimental because
the illustrations are clear. However, books that provide a description
and a note on the origin of the sign (such as Riekehof, *The Joy of*

Signing, this section) provide a more interesting introduction to sign language.

> Craig, Helen B., Valerie A. Sins, and Sandra L. Rossi. *Hearing Aids and You!* Illus. by Robert Neisworth. Beaverton, Oreg.: Dormac, 1976. 118 pp. Reading Level: Grades 4–9.
> *Disability:* Deafness, Hard of hearing

At the time of writing, Craig was research director and Sins and Rossi were speech tutors at the Western Pennsylvania School for the Deaf. Addressing the reader directly, the text begins by posing and answering such questions as "What is a hearing aid?" "How does a hearing aid help you?" "Why do you wear a hearing aid?" and "When do you wear a hearing aid?" A section is devoted to the body hearing aid, another to the ear-level hearing aid. The final section has checklists for both types of aids and a glossary of hearing-aid words. Many of the pages are followed by a page of multiple-choice questions.

Black-and-white drawings illustrate every page.

Analysis. This book is specifically directed toward the child whose hearing impairment can be helped by a mechanical aid. The workbook format means that it is most valuable if each youngster can have his or her own copy. Information is clearly presented, and the drawings—in a lively cartoon style—illustrate and further develop the text. The authors discuss the care as well as the operation of hearing aids. Questions, answers, and statements guide the young reader through the text; the tone is cheerful and informative without being preachy.

> Curtis, Patricia. *Cindy: A Hearing Ear Dog.* Photog. by David Cupp. New York: Dutton, 1981. 55 pp. Reading Level: Grades 4–6.
> *Disability:* Deafness

Curtis follows the story of the dog Cindy from an animal shelter to the New England Education Center where she is trained in the Hearing Ear Dog Program. The book closes when Cindy goes home with her new owner, a deaf teenaged girl. Both text and black-and-white photographs detail the steps of the dog's training as she learns to respond to buzzing alarm clocks, ringing doorbells and telephones, whistling tea-kettles, smoke alarms, and noises in the street. The book ends with a list of some of the organizations that have similar training programs, plus the name of one that teaches deaf people to train their own dogs. There is also an index.

A three-page section gives information about the number of deaf people in the United States, the history of the program to train hearing-ear dogs, and the funding situation for this effort.

Analysis. Straightforward and informative, *Cindy* presents a clear picture of this specialized training. Names of all people mentioned are fictitious except for the director of the Hearing Ear Dog Program, D. P. MacMunn, but both the excellent photographs and the text appear factual in other respects.

DeGering, Etta. *Gallaudet: Friend of the Deaf.* Illus. by Emil Weiss. New York: McKay, 1964. 177 pp. Reading Level: Grades 4–6.
Disability: Deafness

Born in 1787, Thomas Gallaudet grew up in Connecticut and graduated from Yale. He tried law and business before becoming a theological student, but discovered his life's work after he casually taught Alice Cogswell, a nine-year-old child who could neither hear nor speak, to write and read the word *hat.* At that time there were no schools for deaf people in the United States. Gallaudet went on to make a career of the education of deaf persons. Short, nearsighted, and plagued by fragile health, he was unusually sensitive to the needs of others with impairments.

After teaching Alice Cogswell, Gallaudet traveled the state looking for deaf children and adults. Alice's father, a doctor, led a committee in Connecticut that raised money to send Gallaudet to England, Scotland, and France to study the methods used in schools for deaf students. In 1817 Gallaudet became the director of an institution which is now the American School for the Deaf in Hartford, Connecticut. He married Sofia Fowler, one of his deaf students, and had eight children, all of whom were hearing. Two of his children carried on his work. The youngest, Edward, became superintendent of the National Deaf-Mute College in Washington, D.C. (renamed Gallaudet College in 1889, 38 years after Thomas Gallaudet's death in 1851).

A bibliography lists books about Gallaudet, related titles and background material, magazine articles and papers, and books by Gallaudet.

Analysis. Like her biography of Louis Braille (see this chapter under Visual Impairments), DeGering's story of Gallaudet's life is clearly written and informative, and moves at a good pace. Dialogue for the most part is natural and believable. Weiss's pleasantly lively line drawings reflect the tone of the text. Both writer and illustrator emphasize the sunniness of Gallaudet's life and world. Although his difficulties are not omitted, pain is not dwelled on. There is some discussion of Thomas and Edward Gallaudet's belief in the "combined system," using oral communication, hand signs, and finger spelling.

Ferrigno, Lou, and Douglas Kent Hall. *The Incredible Lou Ferrigno: His Story.* Illus. New York: Simon & Schuster, 1982. 208 pp. Reading Level: Grades 7–12.
Disability: Hard of hearing

Ferrigno is an award-winning body-builder (Mr. America, Mr. Universe, and other titles) and the actor who played the Incredible Hulk in the television series. More than half the book consists of his picture portfolio in various body-building poses and in his Hulk role, followed by a detailed, step-by-step training program and special body-building techniques. Ferrigno the body-builder does not, however, overshadow the young Ferrigno, a small, quiet boy known in his Brooklyn neighborhood as "Tin Ear," "Deaf Louie," and "Deaf Mute."

Ferrigno lost a large proportion of his hearing from severe ear infections during infancy. He attended a neighborhood Catholic school, but his hearing was extremely limited and he required a hearing aid and lipreading. (He now wears two hearing aids.) His speech was not clear either, and as a child he suffered at the hands of both his peers and his teachers because of his disability. His father, a policeman who was determined that his son should not be treated as a "handicapped" child, always worked out with weights to keep himself in condition. Lou followed in his footsteps, except that he soon found his way to a gym and to the magazines of professional body-building.

Although, at his father's insistence, he worked for a time as a sheet metal worker, his love of body-building eventually won out and he turned to it full time. One of his great disappointments was that although he was filmed for a sequence on ABC's "Wide World of Sports" after the conclusion of a major international contest, the segment was not run. His father had to tell him that his comments were so unclear that it would have made him look bad. The book recounts this and other incidents, often humorous, concerning the influence of his hearing impairment on his life. He relates that he finally learned to accept his disability and admit it to people rather than hide it.

Analysis. This is a clear, simple, moving story that very directly connects the effect of a disability on one's life to societal attitudes toward that disability. For example, Ferrigno says that his body-building activities in the gym started as a way out of his problems and worries, and ultimately became a successful career that in turn from time to time was still influenced by his impairment. A strong message is that only when he was able to be open about his hearing loss—an openness that his early experiences had taught him would bring negative results—was he able to function as a fully integrated person.

Ferris, Caren. *A Hug Just Isn't Enough.* Illus. Washington, D.C.: Gallaudet College Press, 1980. 93 pp. Reading Level: Grades 10–12.
Disability: Deafness

Ferris is a professional who works with deaf children and their parents. At the time of writing, she was Educational Diagnostician at the Maryland School for the Deaf. She has divided her material into ten chapters, with titles such as "Goals Parents Have for Their Deaf Children," "Deaf Awareness and Further Acceptance," and "Multihandicapped Hearing Impaired Children." Each chapter opens with a short preface, followed by material drawn from interviews with both hearing and deaf parents. The children are identified by their first names and the parents by their children's names; as the same names keep appearing, the reader puts together a picture of children and families from the parents' words.

An appendix tells readers that the 29 participating families were taken from the rolls of the Maryland School for the Deaf Preschool Parent Counseling Program; the Maryland School is a total communication institution, but parents do discuss other approaches. Each spread is illustrated with black-and-white or color photographs.

Analysis. Ferris's approach is unusual and intriguing. Her topics are well chosen to reflect the range of interests and concerns of the parents of hearing-impaired children. Both the quotations and the attractive photographs bring the youngsters vividly before the reader. The title comes from a mother who remarks, "My sisters still won't learn to sign. . . . A hug just isn't enough" (p. 68). Through her own material and her selection of quotations, Ferris presents a realistic picture of the choices, challenges, and unanswered questions facing the parents of hearing-impaired children. Her book could be read not only by these parents and by those who work with the hearing-impaired, but by young people with both impaired and normal hearing.

Gannon, Jack R. *Deaf Heritage: A Narrative History of Deaf America.* Illus. Silver Spring, Md.: National Assn. of the Deaf, 1981. 483 pp. Reading Level: Grades 10–12.
Disability: Deafness

This monumental history of Americans who are deaf begins in 1816 with the voyage from France of Thomas H. Gallaudet, an American minister, and his friend, Laurent Clerc, a 30-year-old deaf teacher of deaf persons at the National Royal Institution for the Deaf in Paris. Together they planned to start the first American school for deaf people. Seventeen chapters later, the book ends in the twentieth century with "deaf awareness" and "deaf rights" in the forefront and with accounts of deaf Americans who are active in all aspects of life. In between are ten chapters that detail the cultural, social, and educational milieu for Americans who are deaf, decade by decade from the 1880s through the 1970s. Interspersed are chapters dealing with artists, humor, publications of deaf persons, sports, American Sign Language, and the National Association of the Deaf.

Chapter notes, a detailed bibliography, and an index are included. There are plentiful black-and-white photographs and numerous charts, tables, and chronologies. All chapters are interspersed with boxed biographical sketches relevant to the topics under discussion in the text.

The author is director of Alumni and Public Relations at Gallaudet College and executive secretary of the Gallaudet College Alumni Association.

Analysis. Despite its imposing size and scholarliness, this is an inviting and attractive book. The text is well written and lively, and the layout is superb. The charts, graphs, photographs, lists, and boxed biographies are vital in making the work as appealing physically as intellectually. Because of the numerous bibliographic aids and the detailed table of contents, it is also useful as a reference work. More important, however, it is an accurate and painstakingly detailed account of the history of a hidden minority of Americans whom traditional history has neglected.

Glick, Ferne Pellman, and Donald R. Pellman. *Breaking Silence: A Family Grows with Deafness.* Illus. Scottdale, Pa.: Herald, 1982. 187 pp. Reading Level: Grades 7–12.
Disability: Deafness

Craig and Carson Glick, identical twins, were born in 1956. This book is written by their mother and their cousin. Although the family suspected before the children turned two that something might be wrong, their deafness was not diagnosed until they were two and a half; one of the professionals they consulted believed that they were suffering from receptive aphasia (inability to use words), and this diagnosis was the basis of their early training. Subsequent examinations by other audiologists did not confirm the aphasia, which is usually caused by a brain lesion. The Glicks enrolled the boys first in special schools for the hearing-impaired and later sent them to Mennonite schools. Emphasis there was always on oral communication rather than on signing, although Carson later became fluent in sign.

At the time of the writing of this book, both young men had achieved independent lives, Carson working in a department store and studying to become an interior designer and Craig still in college. Glick discusses not only the family's response to their situation, but various approaches to the training of deaf children.

Analysis. The title of this book can be understood on two levels, for Glick describes not only the experience of raising deaf children but also a family unaccustomed to communicating deep feelings. Eventually, all the members learn to "break silence" in their various ways. Without bitterness, she discusses mistakes in diagnosis, education, and training made by both professionals and parents. Thus, the Glick experience, in both its positive and negative aspects, could be helpful to others with similar challenges. Glick's coauthor, a cousin, has had considerable writing experience; the text is eminently clear and readable.

Goss, Madeleine. *Beethoven: Master Musician.* Illus. by Karl Schultheiss. New York: Holt, 1966. 364 pp. Reading Level: Grades 7–12. *Disability:* Deafness

The author covers Beethoven's life from his birth in Bonn in 1770 to his death in Vienna in 1827. Chapter XIII, "The Approaching Tragedy (1802–1803)," describes the composer's loss of hearing and his response to it. Although Beethoven did not discuss his condition with those around him, he did write to two friends, describing it; the author quotes at length from these eloquent letters. Later chapters describe occasions on which Beethoven attempted to conduct his own music, although he could not hear it.

Each chapter is headed with a black-and-white line drawing. The book ends with appendices including a short bibliography, a list of Beethoven works and recordings, material on Beethoven's world, and an index.

Analysis. Although the author has relied rather heavily on invented dialogue and imagined scenes—a style of fictionalized biography less prevalent now than when the book was written—this is a full and readable account of Beethoven's life for junior and senior high school readers.

Harris, George A. *Broken Ears, Wounded Hearts.* Washington, D.C.: Gallaudet College Press, 1983. 174 pp. Reading Level: Grades 10–12. *Disability:* Deafness

Jennifer, born two months premature, weighed only 3 pounds 2 ounces at birth. After six weeks in an incubator she underwent heart surgery. This account, by her father, tells of the struggle of her 19-year-old parents, who were college students, coping with a difficult baby, school, and financial problems. By the time Jennifer was 19 months old, she was diagnosed as not responding to sounds, and was eventually treated as a deaf child. She also had scoliosis and a peculiar complex of cognitive and social strengths and weaknesses.

The story line is chronological, depicting the many struggles of these young parents to find sympathetic and knowledgeable professionals to help them understand and nourish their strange child as well as to fulfill themselves in their career preparation. The marriage, a result of Jennifer's impending birth, finally dissolved, but both parents continued to participate in her upbringing. The book ends on a reasonably happy note; Jennifer, at 12, is progressing in a special class in her residential school for deaf children and showing a delightful if unusual personality through her manual communication with her parents and her winning ways.

Harris is frequently introspective, giving a father's deep ambivalent feelings over his fate. His last thoughts about his daughter are illustrative: "Her choice to acknowledge but not live in the past seems altogether wise. It is a decision that seems sensible for me to follow as well, when memories crowd their way to the surface" (p. 174).

Analysis. Harris, a professor of psychology, writes in a clear and personal style. Jennifer becomes intriguing to the readers through his eyes. Harris's descriptions of professional and bureaucratic bungling are appalling. He is honest enough to make the reader see that *he* could be perceived as a demanding parent by these professionals, but the parents' efforts finally secured what Jennifer needed.

This book would be of interest to young people contemplating the responsibilities of marriage and parenthood as well as readers drawn to stories about unusual and appealing children.

Hlibok, Bruce. *Silent Dancer.* Photog. by Liz Glasgow. New York: Messner, 1981. 64 pp. Reading Level: Grades 4–6.
Disability: Deafness

Ten-year-old Nancy, who is deaf as are her parents and brother, lives in a suburban area of New York City. One day in her life is shown, beginning with breakfast, where the family members communicate by sign language. The children are bused each day to Lexington School for the Deaf in New York City. Several pages describe Nancy's school day, where she has speech lessons along with the usual academic subjects, but her mind is on what will occur after school. Every Friday Nancy and some of her friends attend a ballet class for deaf children at the Joffrey School of Ballet in Greenwich Village. The story recounts in great detail the events that occur in the ballet class—how their teacher, Meredith Baylis, works with them assisted by an interpreter/aide, Marianne Gluszak; how they learn the ballet routines; how on this particular day a television crew arrives to videotape them for a network news program.

The group dances to classical ballet music that some, including Nancy, can hear assisted by hearing aids; all of them feel the music through the special sound system that vibrates through the floor. During the course of the lesson, Nancy and the other children experience joy, discouragement, exhaustion, and exhilaration, but no boredom. They engage in some mischief, such as imitating the teacher behind her back. When Nancy is interviewed for the news show, she is asked her dream for the future. Her response is that she wants to be a dancer and to dance again at Lincoln Center, where, as accounted earlier in a flashback scene, her class had once participated in a special benefit concert.

The book is illustrated with large, clear, black-and-white photographs, which are a real asset to the text.

Analysis. The author of this well-written book is Nancy's older brother, who is an actor, dancer, director, and playwright. It is matter-of-fact and at the same time imaginative, giving a real feeling for Nancy's involvement in dance, whose routines are described with precision, employing exact technical terminology. The world of a deaf child who uses both sign and oral language in the course of her day is interwoven with the dance theme. The use of total communication is naturally and very subtly integrated into the story, but it could possibly trigger the request for more detailed information as to why Nancy signs, wears a hearing aid, attends a speech class, and so on. Enough is given in the narrative, however, so that confusion should not result. Nancy emerges as a lively, energetic little girl with big dreams.

Hyman, Jane. *Deafness.* Illus. New York: Franklin Watts, 1980. 64 pp. Reading Level: Grades 7–9.
Disability: Deafness, Hard of hearing

A title in the First Book series, *Deafness* uses a combination of anecdote and exposition to describe the condition, causes, and treatment of deafness and hearing impairment. Hyman explains how the normal ear functions, what types of medical treatment are available for impairments, and how hearing aids work. She discusses the effect of a hearing impairment on a child's development and on her or his family, and gives a survey of the various methods that make it possible for the deaf person to communicate and the kinds of educational programs available to hearing-impaired young students.

The text includes a glossary, a bibliography, and an index, and is illustrated with black-and-white photographs.

Analysis. For the most part, the text is clear and informative. Hyman does not shrink from describing professional controversies over the best way to educate hearing-impaired children. The anecdotal material is well written and realistically illustrates some of the different stages of the deaf child's development, from infancy to adolescence. However, young readers may be frustrated by the way characters are introduced and then dropped. For example, the first chapter begins with a description of an infant whose impairment is suspected by his parents and diagnosed definitely when he is 20 months old; this baby's story is never continued.

Ireland, Karin. *Kitty O'Neil: Daredevil Woman.* Illus. New York: Harvey House, 1980. 77 pp. Reading Level: Grades 4–6.
Disability: Deafness

Kitty O'Neil lost her hearing as the result of illness at the age of four months. The loss was discovered by her parents when she was two, and they began immediately to encourage her to speak and engage in all kinds of physical activities. She went first to special schools and, at the age of eight, to public school. She used her athletic ability as a way to find her place with hearing children, and became a successful competitive swimmer, diver, and racer, and a professional stuntswoman.

Black-and-white photographs show various aspects of O'Neil's life.

Analysis. Written in a breezy, fast-paced style, this biography moves over the external events of O'Neil's life. Setbacks and challenges are lightly described; O'Neil's physical courage and energy are emphasized, with scant attention paid to pain, discouragement, and despair.

Komroff, Manuel. *Beethoven and The World of Music.* New York: Dodd, 1961. 183 pp. Reading Level: Grades 7–12.
Disability: Deafness

This biography chronicles the entire life of the great composer. The author discusses the deafness that began when Beethoven was in his twenties and that gradually worsened. By the time he was 47, he was profoundly deaf. The biographer writes about the effect of his impairment on Beethoven's work and personality. He points out that when Beethoven began to lose his hearing, he knew that he could not continue as a concert pianist and then, "with a heart weighted with sorrow, he turned to composition" (p. 38). The book includes a select list of Beethoven music and recordings and an index.

Analysis. Of the three biographies of Beethoven reviewed here (see the titles by Madeleine Goss and Reba Paeff Mirsky, both in this section), this is the most scholarly and relies most completely on authentic sources. A well-written account, it is accessible to mature readers of junior high and high school age, and should attract those with an interest in music, in German and Viennese life of the period, and in the effect of a hearing impairment on a musical genius.

Levine, Edna S. *Lisa and Her Soundless World.* Illus. by Gloria Kamen. New York: Human Sciences Press, 1974. 30 pp. Reading Level: Grades K–3.
Disability: Deafness

The first seven pages, amply illustrated, discuss how children use their senses to hear music, to smell cookies baking, to see television. Then eight-year-old Lisa, who is severely hearing-impaired, is introduced. The author explains that Lisa is able to do all things other children can do except that she cannot hear well, and therefore she did not learn to talk when other children did, so she had no friends.

Her impairment was undetected until her parents took her to a doctor to find out why she could not talk. Diagnosed as deaf, she was given a hearing aid and sent to classes in lipreading and speech. Lisa has also learned sign language. She has made good progress in all these areas and has become a happy, gregarious child.

Illustrations with golden brown and black tones, a positive addition to the text, are used on almost every page; there is also a diagram of the ear. The title page and the conclusion of the text feature a drawing of Lisa's name in finger spelling.

Analysis. This is an excellent and realistic portrayal of deafness. Lisa is able to hear with a hearing aid, she is good at lipreading, and her speaking is progressing so well that she will some day have clear speech. The author stresses throughout the book, however, that not all deaf persons can hear with an aid, become proficient at lipreading, or learn to speak well.

The combination of narrative and expository text is well balanced and designed to appeal to young readers' imaginations as well as to teach them facts about deafness and its treatment.

Lipa, Karel, and Pavel Les. *We Have Overcome: Deaf, Blind and Great.* Illus. Czechoslovakia: Lipa & Les, 1971. 155 pp. Reading Levels: Grades 10–12.
Disability: Deafness, Hard of hearing (also Blindness, Deaf–blind)

In this book are vignettes of 27 notable persons who were hard of hearing, deaf, blind, or deaf-blind. Among these are Julius Caesar and

Thomas Edison. Many are persons from middle and eastern Europe, active in diverse fields.

The illustrations are black-and-white postage stamps printed by different countries to honor their famous compatriots.

Analysis. This quaint book is briefly noted here for several reasons. Although uneven in its descriptive vignettes, both in length and thoroughness, it highlights some interesting people over the centuries and in many lands, united only by their sensory infirmities and acknowledged contributions. Further, the perspective is that of authors in the Soviet bloc, so that young readers may have an opportunity to read of someone like Konstantin Tsiolkowski, an inventor of rockets (deafened at age 11).

The book is, however, severely flawed. It is highly selective in its detail; for example, Smetana's death is described without reference to the fact that he took his own life. Originally printed in Czechoslovakia, it was translated with printing and spelling errors, non-English grammatical constructions, and nineteenth-century usages, such as "my dear reader." There is no table of contents and no index or bibliography documenting the often intriguing quotations and tales. Archaic terminology, such as references to "the deaf and dumb," could reflect either present practice or faulty translation. Nevertheless, these exotic accounts may interest readers who are drawn to the study of differences and exceptionalities. It is, at least, a place to start in the study of noted people who are deaf, deaf-blind, or blind.

Mirsky, Reba Paeff. *Beethoven.* Illus. by W. T. Mars. Chicago: Follett, 1957. 176 pp. Reading Level: Grades 4–6.
Disability: Deafness

This biography for young readers takes Beethoven from the age of nine to his death in 1827, at the age of 57. The composer began to lose his hearing as a young man of 28. Doctors suggested a variety of treatments, none successful. At first, Beethoven attempted to keep his impairment a secret, but eventually he could no longer hide it. He did continue to compose. The author explains, "Although his ears were sealed to the outer world, in his head he could hear music perfectly" (p. 121).

Analysis. This is a readable account of Beethoven's life and work, illustrated attractively with line drawings. The theme of deafness is, of course, only a part of the story, but it could make the book especially interesting to youngsters who themselves have a hearing impairment. The reader should be cautioned to keep in mind that deafness acquired in adulthood is a quite different, and actually less serious, disability than congenital deafness. Long before the onset of deafness, Beethoven had mastered his native language and the language of music.

Neimark, Anne E. *A Deaf Child Listened: Thomas Gallaudet, Pioneer in American Education.* New York: Morrow, 1983. 116 pp. Reading Level: Grades 7–9.
Disability: Deafness

The story begins with Thomas Gallaudet at age 15, in 1802, about to leave his home in Hartford, Connecticut, to go to Yale. After college, he spent some years in a variety of activities; he studied law in a Hartford firm, peddled goods in Kentucky and Ohio, and studied theology. His life's work came to him when he taught nine-year-old Alice Cogswell that the letters H A T named the object he wore on his head. Alice had been deaf since contracting scarlet fever at the age of two, and her parents had been unable to educate her. A committee that included Dr. Mason Cogswell, her father, wanted to establish a school for teaching deaf children in the United States. They sent Gallaudet to Europe to study methods developed in England and France. English education for deaf people was dominated by one family that kept its methods of strictly oral teaching a secret, which they would not share with Gallaudet; the French, on the other hand, used sign language and were very helpful.

The book details the rest of Gallaudet's life as head of an institution for the education of deaf persons, which is now known as the American School for the Deaf in Hartford, Connecticut. He taught the use of sign language and developed an approach similar to total communication, which combines oralism and sign. Gallaudet, frail since childhood, which perhaps made him unusually sensitive to people in difficult circumstances, also served as chaplain for prisoners and mentally ill patients.

He married Sophia Fowler, one of his deaf pupils, and they had eight children (all hearing). The youngest of their children, Edward Miner Gallaudet, became head of the Columbia Institution in Washington, D.C., later called the National Deaf-Mute College and now Gallaudet College, the only college for a disability group in the world.

The book ends with a bibliography, a list of service organizations and centers for deaf people, and an index.

Analysis. The author tells Gallaudet's story with style, bringing to life his personality and his world. The magnitude of Gallaudet's accomplishment is made clear and the material on deaf education, with its two often opposing philosophies, is well presented. The book would be of interest to a general audience of middle-school readers, whatever their connection with hearing impairments. Some deaf students may be below grade level in reading ability. This book, with a reading level of grades 7–9, does not talk down to its audience, so it may be most appropriate for deaf students at the high school level. Teachers and librarians in a mainstreamed school might keep this in mind.

Neisser, Arden. *The Other Side of Silence: Sign Language and the Deaf Community.* New York: Knopf, 1983. 301 pp. Reading Level: Grades 10–12.

Disability: Deafness

The author says in the prologue that she first became aware of deaf life when she heard a research paper on American Sign Language (ASL) at an academic conference. Until recently there has been little focus on ASL by academic linguists. The thrust of American deaf education for about one hundred years had been dominated by oralism and by the effort to teach deaf students to speak and lip-read, despite the fact that few succeeded. ASL had not been considered a true language; it had not been taught, and signing had been actively discouraged.

Neisser spent five years on the research that led to this book. She investigated the history of education of deaf people, visited residential schools and special education classes, talked to teachers and parents and to deaf and hearing-impaired people. She observed deaf children in school and at home. One chapter is devoted to a discussion of efforts by research groups to teach language to chimpanzees. The author has painstakingly investigated at least some of the studies on teaching ASL to chimps, reporting rather negative results. Other researchers, however, have reported more positive results. Another chapter focuses on artistic, athletic, and intellectual activities of deaf people, with emphasis on the National Theatre of the Deaf. The last chapter examines the impact of mainstreaming on deaf education.

There are footnotes, a bibliography, and an index.

Analysis. This is a fascinating, perceptive, skillfully written book. The author makes no attempt to hide her astonishment at the attitude of many professionals toward sign language, which she sees as the native language of deaf people, but which has been viewed by many as a kind of debased, imprecise mode of communication. She makes clear the difference between American Sign Language, a language with its own grammar, syntax, and conventions just like any other language, and signed English, which follows the structure of English. She also makes clear her immense admiration of and respect for the culture of deaf people.

In conclusion, the author talks about the effort of deaf people to escape from being classified as retarded or deranged (it should perhaps be noted that although she is a very sensitive observer, she uses the phrase "the feeble-minded and the insane") and says that "the story of the deaf is about the development of culture and language of a high order. . . . Deaf children with ASL are intellectually, emotionally, and linguistically indistinguishable from hearing children with English" (pp. 281–282). Despite the strength and richness of deaf culture, "educational policy in the past has done much to discourage deaf culture, and now appears actively trying to destroy it" (p. 282).

Each chapter forms an integral whole and could be read separately. Mature high school students who are interested in deaf education, deaf culture, and linguistics could find this absorbing reading, whether or not they have any experience with hearing impairments.

North, Sterling. *Young Thomas Edison.* Illus. Boston: Houghton, 1958. 182 pp. Reading Level: Grades 4–6.
Disability: Hard of hearing

This great American inventor was born in 1847 and died 84 years later, in 1931. In boyhood, Edison lost some of his hearing after an incident that occurred when he was trying to climb aboard a moving train, where he sold newspapers; to save him from falling under the wheels, a trainman lifted him "by the ears" into the car. Edison heard something "snap" in each ear, and the pain for a time was intense. "Earache came first, then a little deafness, and this deafness increased until . . . I could hear only a few words now and then" (p. 47). Although he later said that he had not heard a bird sing since he was young, Edison also described his loss of hearing in positive words: "From the start I found that deafness was an advantage to a telegrapher. While I could hear unerringly the loud ticking of the instrument, I could not hear other and perhaps distracting sounds" (p. 53). Deafness shut out distractions of all kinds and gave him a quiet world in which he could concentrate on the reading, thinking, and inventing to which he devoted his long and active life.

At the end of the book is a list of Edison historic sites and an index. Drawings, photographs, and diagrams illustrate the text.

Analysis. This is a well-written biography that appears based on careful research; it presents a lively, readable account of a fascinating genius, recreating Edison's world without fictionalizing. Little attention is paid to his hearing impairment, probably an accurate reflection of the inventor's own attitude.

Panara, Robert, and John Panara. *Great Deaf Americans*. Illus. by Kevin Mulholland. Silver Spring, Md.: T. J. Publishers, 1983. 145 pp. Reading Level: Grades 7–12.
Disability: Deafness

This collection of biographies relates life stories of 33 deaf people, living and dead, selected by the authors as representative of deaf Americans "who have followed the American dream of fulfillment through opportunity," and who have contributed "to the cultural development of America" (p. v).

Arranged chronologically by order of birthdates, the subjects range from Laurent Clerc, a pioneer teacher born in 1785; to Juliette Gordon Low, founder of the Girl Scouts, born in 1860; to Donald Ballantyne, a medical scientist born in 1922; to Linda Bove, star of "Sesame Street," born in 1945; to Lou Ferrigno, the "Incredible Hulk," born in 1951. Each chapter is three to four pages long and narrates the life story and achievements of the individual. A five-page bibliography of books, articles, and videotapes is included. Black-and-white drawings illustrate each chapter.

Analysis. Here is a valuable account of people who have achieved success in a wide variety of careers. Their achievements are as diverse as their personalities. Most have had to overcome a variety of difficulties in addition to deafness. The stories are short, snappy, and interesting.

Peters, Diana. *Claire and Emma*. Photog. by Jeremy Finlay. New York: John Day, 1976. unp. Reading Level: Grades K–3.
Disability: Deafness

Four-year-old Claire and her sister Emma, two, were born deaf; Claire, who is "slightly more aware of loud sounds," wears one hearing aid and Emma wears two. The writer, the children's mother, explains and illustrates the components of these aids. She describes the girls' daily activities, both those common to all children and the special situations and training experienced by deaf youngsters. Claire and Emma are shown with their brother, who has normal hearing, and with hearing friends; Claire goes to a special class for deaf children, but much of the time these students are integrated with hearing youngsters. At several points the writer addresses the reader directly, suggesting helpful responses to a deaf person: "Claire cannot always make herself understood, as her speech is not very clear. If you don't quite understand her, try to help her explain. Don't be in a hurry and don't walk away if you cannot understand at first. Just give her a little longer."

Analysis. Peters's text is direct, clear, and informative. She describes the handicaps caused by the impairment: not only difficulty in making oneself understood and in understanding others, but inability to hear a knock or ring at the door and to talk on the telephone, difficulty in following television, and impaired sense of balance. Although the typical reader would be at the primary level, older children could respond to the information and to the excellent color photographs.

Powers, Helen. *Signs of Silence: Bernard Bragg and the National Theatre of the Deaf.* Illus. New York: Dodd, 1972. 176 pp, Reading Level: Grades 10–12.
Disability: Deafness

Bernard Bragg is the deaf son of deaf parents, a relatively rare occurrence. During his first three years, he lived in Brooklyn, where he rapidly learned to play with hearing children. When he was four, his parents separated, just a few weeks before his mother took him to the residential New York School for the Deaf; she gave him no explanation about where he was going or what would happen there. He found it difficult at first to adjust to deaf playmates, life without both parents, and the total absence of a home. His mother, who had a room with a relative, had no place for him to stay, so although she visited him weekly, he had no home to go to for several years. Eventually, his parents reunited, but it was many years before they could afford to have their own apartment again. His father had become a lithographer and encouraged his son to follow the printing trade because deafness was a minimal problem in such an atmosphere and employment was secure.

Instead, Bragg graduated from the New York School for the Deaf, where he was greatly influenced by his deaf English teacher and friend, Robert Panara, and went on to Gallaudet College. Bragg's father had been an actor, and a love of the stage, as well as a love of literature, inspired the young Bragg. He was active in theatrical and literary endeavors throughout his school years. After graduation, he took a job teaching at the School for the Deaf in Berkeley, California, where he spent considerable time at the theater. He attended a performance by the famous French mime Marcel Marceau and knew immediately that he had found the medium by which he could reach both deaf and hearing audiences. His meeting with Marceau after the performance launched him on a theatrical career that eventually led him to become a highly acclaimed actor in the National Theatre of the Deaf.

Besides detailing Bragg's personal and professional life, the author conveys much information about the lives and education of people who are deaf, as appropriate within the context of the biography. For example, in discussing Bragg's early schooling, she devotes five pages to explaining how deaf children are taught to speak, why sign language is the natural language of deaf persons, the differences in the philosophies of education for deaf persons, why the term "deaf-mute" is totally pejorative, and other similar information. She also devotes five pages to a discussion of sign language, its development, use, and place in the education of deaf children, and suggests why hearing educators and parents of deaf children have so strongly (and wrongly) opposed it. Other informational sections are integrated into the story at appropriate spots.

The text is illustrated with black-and-white photographs of various events in Bragg's life and career.

Analysis. In this absorbing, fast-paced book, Powers not only chronicles the facts of Bragg's life and career, but also reveals his personality, his periods of questioning and depression, and his love affairs. She draws a portrait of a full human being. The didactic/informational material integrated into the text is sometimes a little jarring because it interrupts a very good story, but it is nonetheless useful, educational, and pertinent.

Quinn, Elizabeth, and Michael Owen. *Listen to Me: The Story of Elizabeth Quinn.* Illus. London: Michael Joseph, 1984. 232 pp. Reading Level: Grades 10–12.
Disability: Deafness

Elizabeth Quinn played the part of Sarah Norman in Mark Medoff's *Children of a Lesser God* during its two-year run in London. Previously, she had been Phyllis Frelich's understudy for that role during part of the play's run in New York. This biography/autobiography recounts her life from her birth in upper New York State in 1948 to her work in the London theater in 1983. Quinn and coauthor Owen alternate in the writing, with Quinn telling parts of the story directly in the first person and Owen narrating the rest.

Quinn lost her hearing at age two as the result of a succession of mumps, measles, and an unnamed viral infection. Her family, who by then had moved to Connecticut, sent her at the age of six to the American School for the Deaf, where she lived during the week, returning home on weekends. She was left there with no explanation from her parents as to what was happening. Consequently, her transition from a hearing to a deaf environment was very difficult.

Quinn had a strained relationship with her mother, the only person in her family who refused to learn to sign until Quinn was in her thirties. No less problematic was her relationship with her warm, lov-

convince investors and the public that the invention was more than a toy.

One of the backers of the harmonic telegraph was Gardiner Greene Hubbard, who engaged Bell to improve the speech of his hearing-impaired daughter Mabel, deaf as the result of childhood scarlet fever. Bell and Mabel fell in love, and when her father became convinced of the value of the telephone, they had his consent to marry. Immediately after their marriage, they went to London so that Bell could lecture and help the English develop a telephone system; he also demonstrated his invention to Queen Victoria. Back in the United States, Bell had to defend himself in many lawsuits brought by others claiming to be the inventors of the telephone. The system flourished, and in 1915 there was a ceremony celebrating the joining of the east and west coasts by telephone. Bell sat in New York, Watson in California, and using replicas of their original instruments, Bell said, "Mr. Watson, come here. I want you," as he had said 39 years earlier from one room to another with their first successful experiment.

Analysis. Despite some awkwardness of style, the narrative moves quickly and the details of Bell's invention are presented clearly. As in most biographies for young readers, the author has taken the liberty of inventing dialogue; when she records the presumed thoughts of the figures in her narrative, she uses a formal language that one can hardly imagine passing through any brain, even the most brilliant, but the conversation is more natural and believable. Mabel Hubbard Bell's story is peripheral. We are told briefly of her illness and resulting deafness, that her parents had her taught lipreading both in America and Germany, and that she could speak and read lips without difficulty. The illustrations, in brown, black, and white, are undistinguished, and while some add to the interest of the text, at least one picture bears little relation to the words on the facing page.

Spradley, Thomas S., and James P. Spradley. *Deaf Like Me.* New York: Random House, 1978. 280 pp. Reading Level: Grades 10–12. *Disability:* Deafness

When Louise Spradley was a few weeks pregnant, she came down with what looked like rubella (measles), contracted from her small son. Doctors in both California, where the family was vacationing, and Illinois, where they lived, said abortion was illegal and therefore impossible. At her birth, in April 1965, their daughter Lynn seemed perfectly well, to her parents' enormous relief. When the baby was a few months old the Spradleys began to worry about her hearing, but they were reassured by their doctor. A specialist thought she might have nerve damage, but gave no advice. The audiologist whom they consulted at the John Tracy Clinic in Los Angeles when Lynn was 17 months old confirmed a hearing loss and suggested that the Spradleys use the clinic correspondence course.

The John Tracy Clinic is committed to the oral approach to hearing loss, and for the next few years, the Spradleys provided as richly oral an environment for Lynn as possible. She learned to lip-read with ease and also to read written words, but despite intensive work, her voice production was disappointing and her spoken vocabulary limited to a few words. By the time she was four and a half, she was attending kindergarten in a special public school in Sacramento, where the family now lived; the school was committed to a pure oral approach. When some parents petitioned to have a class in which the teacher used signing in addition to speech, the Spradleys began to face some of their own doubts and disappointments, as well as their anxiety because they were so cut off from real communication with their daughter. With material given them by new acquaintances, they started to use sign language at home, with extraordinary results. This contravened all advice given them at Lynn's school. When the book ends, in 1974, Lynn is a fluent signer, the whole family communicates in sign, and her school has begun to accept and teach signing.

Lynn's story was written by her father, Thomas, and by her uncle, James. The book ends with an appendix giving resources on deafness.

Analysis. Although the authors come down clearly on the side of total communication, they present the oralist argument fairly and in detail. For years, oralists have emphasized that if hearing-impaired people are not to be isolated, they must learn to communicate with the speaking, hearing world. They have insisted that this is possible and that deaf people can be taught to lip-read and to speak with fluency and comprehensibility. When the Spradleys are able to admit to themselves that Lynn is not succeeding and that lack of communication is leading to unsocial behavior at school and to frequent frustration, they can begin to examine the implications of the oral approach. Although they regret the time lost and ask why the oralist organizations and publications ignored evidence about the effectiveness of signing, the authors do not convey bitterness or resentment. Their account is reasoned and yet passionate, especially when they point out that by forbidding sign, oralism told Lynn that she was forbidden to learn her native language. There are moving moments in the book, especially toward the end; for example, when Lynn learns to sign "I love you" to her parents and brother and when she recognizes her own name in finger spelling. *Lynn* is a word impossible to lip-read. "Of all the injuriès that oralism had inflicted on Lynn," the authors write, "the most insidious had been to rob her of a name. . . . Without an accepted symbol for herself, her capacity for self-awareness and self-control had failed to take root and grow" (p. 243).

Deaf Like Me is a fascinating account of a deaf child in a hearing family, and it is also an enactment of the conflict between the oralist and signing schools of thought. It could be read with interest by high school students of both normal and impaired hearing as well as by the parents of hearing-impaired youngsters. Readers might like to look at *Breaking Silence* by Glick and Pellman (see this section) for another account of a family learning to communicate across the barrier of hearing impairment.

Star, Robin Rogoff. *We Can!* Illus. Washington, D.C.: Alexander Graham Bell Assn. for the Deaf, 1980. 2 vols. 88, 98 pp. Reading Level: Grades 4–9.
Disability: Deafness

The biographies of 33 contemporary Americans who are deaf are presented in this two-volume work, designed as a career education series for children who are hearing-impaired and can read at least at the fourth-grade level. Each section is five to ten pages long. The beginning page of the biographical sketch contains a black-and-white photograph of the person, name, cause of hearing impairment, age at onset, and degree of hearing loss. Men and women are equally represented. The careers cover a wide range.

Analysis. The biographical sketches are well written and could be of interest to hearing children as well. Each person lip-reads and speaks rather than using any sign language. In the biographical sketches, the use and importance of oral communication is emphasized as are the special challenges that hearing impairment has brought to each person's life. These are all people who have handled the challenges well and have had success with oral communication skills. The explanation of each person's career is detailed enough to give children a good idea of what goes on in that particular occupation, and, again, would be equally useful to nonhearing impaired children. The argument for oral education, which is a subtly recurring theme, is well presented, but it is only one aspect of a complex picture. Books dealing with the values, benefits, and skills involved in sign language and the use of total communication are readily available and could be used for another perspective. An explanation and discussion of both sides of the oralist-manualist controversy appears in Benderly, *Dancing without Music* (see this section).

Sternberg, Martin L. A. *American Sign Language: A Comprehensive Dictionary.* Illus. by Herbert Rogoff. New York: Harper & Row, 1981. 1,132 pp. Reading Level: Grades 10–12.
Disability: Deafness

Approximately 5,000 words and phrases are listed in this pictorial dictionary. Each includes a pronunciation guide, a grammatical note, and an illustration accompanied by a description of how the word or phrase is communicated in American Sign Language (ASL). Some entries also give other words that are related, and in some cases the meaning of the components of the sign is explained. For words that require different signs for different meanings, the various signs are given.

There are several useful appendices including a comprehensive bibliography of over 1,200 current references and seven foreign-language indexes.

Analysis. This is a basic reference book for anyone working with ASL. *Choice* called it a first priority item for all libraries. Although its price (about $40) makes it prohibitive for purchase by many teenagers, it is well within an appropriate range for a reference book and should be made available in high school and public libraries where it will be easily accessible to young people.

Sullivan, Mary Beth, and Linda Bourke, with Susan Regan. *A Show of Hands: Say It in Sign Language.* Illus. by Linda Bourke. Reading, Mass.: Addison-Wesley, 1980. 96 pp. Reading Level: Grades 4–9.
Disability: Deafness

Using cartoonlike drawings in black and white with brief text, the authors introduce both sign language and finger spelling. Some characters appear throughout the book: a boy who initially sees no point in learning to talk with his hands, a hearing-impaired girl, and another boy who signs because he has a hearing-impaired brother.

The book ends with an index of the 150 signs shown. The attractive drawings, which fill most of the space on every spread, show both black and white people.

Analysis: Sullivan and Bourke have produced a lively, amusing, and informative book. Directions for making signs and letters are clear, and hearing readers will find the idea of a manual language appealing whether or not they have contact with hearing-impaired people.

Warfield, Frances. *Keep Listening.* New York: Viking, 1957. 158 pp. Reading Level: Grades 10–12.
Disability: Hard of hearing

The author was hard of hearing as a child and her condition, otosclerosis, was progressive. The impairment was not acknowledged by family and friends, all of whom pretended that nothing was wrong, although the otologist mentioned lipreading and hearing aids. Warfield rejected the hearing aid vehemently. She describes such coping mechanisms as talking incessantly to her teenaged friends so that she would not have to try to hear their conversations. When she was in her thirties, she went surreptitiously to lip-reading classes at the Nitchie School of Lip-Reading in New York. It was her first step toward confronting her disability, to be followed eventually by use of hearing aids, work with the New York League for the Hard of Hearing, and two operations: a fenestration procedure on one ear in 1948; mobilization of the stapes in the other ear in 1955. Surgery restored her hearing, but she continued to think, write, and speak about the experience of being hearing-impaired.

Analysis. A professional writer, Warfield has a clear, lively style with an engaging touch of self-deprecation. She is acutely conscious of the psychological harm done by the kind of pretending that she grew up with and internalized, yet her account is not accusatory or self-pitying. Information about hearing impairments, surgical procedures, hearing aids, and attitudes toward hearing disabilities is well presented. The book would be of interest to young people seeking information about past medical and societal treatment of hearing impairments as well as those attracted by a discussion of the psychological implications of disability.

Wolf, Bernard. *Anna's Silent World.* Photog. by Bernard Wolf. Philadelphia: Lippincott, 1977. 48 pp. Reading Level: Grades K–3. *Disability:* Deafness

Anna, a first-grader living in New York City, was born with "profound hearing loss," but with the help of hearing aids she can hear some sounds. The book, illustrated with large black-and-white photographs on every page, shows Anna in various activities interacting at home with her family, receiving special testing and training at the New York League for the Hard of Hearing, going to first grade with hearing children, attending ballet class, playing with her best friend, and celebrating Christmas at home. The writer explains such concepts as decibels, speech therapy, lipreading, and the operation of Anna's hearing aids.

Analysis. This fine book well deserves its reputation for excellence. Anna and her family, friends, and teachers are attractive, vibrant people whom the photographer has captured in an unposed and natural way. Anna's disability and its effect on her life are clearly explained. Every effort is being made to help her live in the world of hearing people. Explaining her situation to Anna's best friend, Anna's mother predicts, "It will take her longer to speak clearly, but she'll catch up." The last photograph shows Anna with her favorite Christmas present, a recorder. "Now," writes Wolf, "she can add her own music to the sounds of her silent world."

Wolf does not discuss the possible origin of Anna's disability, a question that some young readers might raise. No mention is made of sign language, which is evidently not part of Anna's education.

Wright, David. *Deafness*. New York: Stein & Day, 1969. 213 pp. Reading Level: Grades 10–12.
Disability: Deafness

David Wright, South African by birth, lost his hearing in 1927 as a result of scarlet fever. He was then seven years old, and had learned to read, write, and count in kindergarten. His mother took him to England to consult specialists, and he became the private pupil of a woman who taught deaf people; she used oral methods and drilled him in enunciation. When he returned to South Africa, he was taught by a governess who had been an assistant to his first teacher. He then had several years at a "hearing" school, after which his mother took him back to England and enrolled him in the only school in the British Commonwealth that offered education up to the university level for deaf students. This was an oral school, although the boys used a private language of sign plus spoken words when they were alone. Wright has never learned sign language. After his secondary education, he went to Oxford. He is a writer of both prose and poetry.

The first section concentrates on Wright's personal experience of deafness. In the second half he discusses current (as of 1969) education of deaf children and the integration of deaf people into hearing society, noting changes that have taken place since his childhood. He gives a history of the origins and development of the education of deaf people, with attention to the battle between the oral and nonoral schools of education. There is an appendix, "Hearing, Deafness, and Recent Research," by K. P. Murphy, deputy director of the Audiology Research Unit at the Royal Berkshire Hospital in Reading, England.

Analysis. A professional writer, the author is skilled in transmitting ideas, impressions, and experience. He is always cognizant of the fact that, because he was old enough to have a good grasp of language before his illness, he is particularly fortunate, and he makes frequent comparisons between people like himself and those who are born deaf. He has known both worlds, although at the time of the writing of this book he had been deaf for more than 40 years; moreover, he has functioned well in the hearing world.

Although Wright discusses both approaches to deaf education (oral and sign), he comes down quite solidly in support of the oral approach. For example, although he recognizes the difficulties, he thinks that deaf youngsters should be isolated as little as possible, lest they form their own separate world: "If deaf children are herded together it must inevitably accentuate those idiosyncrasies and mannerisms created by the condition of being deaf. Having no other models the children naturally imitate one another. This intensifies little peculiarities of speech and demeanor, which in turn helps the segregation process" (p. 80). Writing without self-pity or egotism, he offers valuable insight into the deaf experience. This book could be read by mature high school students, hearing and hearing-impaired alike, and by professionals.

Note: Wright uses the term "deaf-and-dumb," which is no longer acceptable in the United States.

Visual Impairments

Barry, Henry. *I'll Be Seeing You.* New York: Knopf, 1952. 239 pp.
Reading Level: Grades 7–9.
Disability: Blindness

As a young man living near Boston before World War II, from a large and poor family, the author had quit school to go to work. Barry married at the age of 20, and he and his wife had two sons, Donny and Henry, Jr. In time, Barry and his wife separated.

Somewhat at loose ends when the war broke out, he enlisted. As his group fought its way through a German town, Barry received a severe head wound. He was shipped to a hospital in Paris, where a doctor removed his right eye and told him that the hemorrhage behind the left eye would take a long time to clear up. From France, Barry was flown to a hospital in England and then on to the United States. Eventually he was sent to Valley Forge Hospital in Phoenixville, Pennsylvania, where all military eye cases were eventually referred. His doctor told him that he was blind in both eyes.

The rest of the book describes how Barry overcame frustration and despair, and developed ways of coping with his condition. He learned braille, had mobility training, and did leather crafts. He has come to appreciate life and to live fully again.

Analysis. This is a very simply written, straightforward work that does not require a highly sophisticated reader. It specifies in clear detail some techniques helpful to blind people, such as the clock system for eating, which imagines the plate as a clock face with food positions described by numbers. This introduction to blindness and such techniques would help classmates share the perspective of a blind peer.

Ching, Lucy. *One of the Lucky Ones.* New York: Doubleday, 1982. 323 pp. Reading Level: Grades 10–12.
Disability: Blindness

Lucy Ching is a social worker in Hong Kong, where she works with people who are blind and those who have other disabilities. Born in Canton in the 1930s to a large, well-to-do family (her father was an architect), she became blind as the result of an herbal treatment applied to her eyes to relieve a fever contracted at the age of six months. As was customary then, her family believed that blindness was a curse brought on by some offense to God. The usual practice was either to abandon blind children to die or to sell them into slavery. However, Ching's family kept her, although they never included her in family outings, and education for her was unthinkable.

Her brother, a ham radio operator, learned from a physician in the Philippines about a way that Lucy could learn to read and write. The physician mailed Ching the basic information and materials that she needed, and with them, she taught herself braille. She persuaded her family and officials of a local school that she could attend classes with sighted students. She proved to be an outstanding student and continued her education, even during World War II, when her family was forced to flee to Macau, where they lived in poverty.

After the war, Ching studied in Hong Kong and was eventually awarded a scholarship to the Perkins School for the Blind in Boston. Some of the Chinese schools she had attended were run and staffed by Christian missionaries from the United States, and many times during the course of her education, her way was eased or doors were opened to her through her contacts with them (she had converted to Christianity as a young girl). Besides this, her greatest source of help came from her own incredible will to work and study for long hours, to walk for miles from the home of one reader to the next, or from home to school, and to spend hours compiling what turned into mountains of braille notes.

None of this would have been possible, however, without Ah Wor (to whom this book is dedicated), one of four family servants when Ching was an infant. Ah Wor stayed with the family and with Ching, taking special care of her and teaching her the living skills she needed. When Ching was in school, Ah Wor helped to pay for her expenses by doing piecework sewing. She has never left her.

Analysis. This is a dense book, factual and full of interesting details about life in China during the past 50 years and about Lucy Ching's life, which is a testimony to the ability of will and determination to overcome all obstacles. It is a good story, exciting in a quiet way, sometimes understated, highly realistic and always interesting.

Clifton, Bernice. *None So Blind.* Illus. Chicago: Rand McNally, 1962. 253 pp. Reading Level: Grades 7–12.
Disability: Blindness

The author begins her autobiography with her trip to the doctor who told her she was losing her sight. The book is dedicated to her mother, with whom she lived and to whom she attributes part of her subsequent good adjustment.

Clifton describes her acquisition of a dog guide, new ways of taking care of herself and her apartment, adventures, bad and good in her life, and her successful career as a lecturer and fund-raiser. She became engaged to a young army doctor, but he died of pneumonia. By the end of the story, her dog guide, Karla, and her mother—her "two little old ladies"—had also died. Always resilient, Clifton went to The Seeing Eye for Karla Reincarnate, and continued to look forward to the future with contentment.

Analysis. With quite large print and simple prose, this book moves quickly. As is often true in older books, Clifton is perhaps over-resolutely cheerful and thankful for her blessings. However, her sense of humor and optimism make this entertaining and diverting general reading.

Curtis, Patricia. *Greff: The Story of a Guide Dog.* Photog. by Mary Bloom. New York: Dutton, 1982. 53 pp. Reading Level: Grades 4–6.
Disability: Blindness

The mother of the dog guide Greff was chosen for breeding by the Guide Dog Foundation for the Blind in Smithtown, New York, because of her superior qualities. This book takes us from the puppy's birth through the end of his training with his new master, Peter. The author describes the dog's first year with his foster family (called "puppy walkers"), the six months of training at the foundation, and the three weeks' training session with his future owner.

There are many black-and-white photographs. The book ends with a list of training centers for guide dogs and an index.

Analysis. Curtis's book is attractive in format and clearly written. Without sentimental anthropomorphism, she successfully focuses on Greff's point of view in much of the text, then emphasizes Peter's point of view once dog and man begin working together. Young readers who want a more detailed description of the training carried out at the foundation might prefer *Tom & Bear* by Richard McPhee (see this section).

Davidson, Margaret. *Louis Braille: The Boy Who Invented Books for the Blind.* Illus. by Janet Compere. New York: Hastings, 1979. 80 pp. Reading Level: Grades 4–6.
Disability: Blindness

Louis Braille, born in 1809 in a village about 30 miles from Paris, was the son of a saddle and harness maker. When he was three, he had an accident while trying to use his father's awl, and lost his eyesight. Although it was not customary at that time to teach blind children, Braille had lessons first from the village priest and then in the village school. When he was nine, his parents were persuaded to let him go to Paris to the Royal Institute of Blind Youth. There, at last, he learned to read, using cumbersome raised-letter books.

When Braille was 15, he heard of a method devised by an army captain for sending night messages, which used a system of raised dots to represent sounds. Although much more efficient than raised letters, this method was still unsatisfactory for transcribing books for blind readers. For the next three years Braille worked to improve it, and at last developed the braille alphabet based on variations of a six-dot pattern, or cell, that is still used today. Official opposition to Braille's invention hindered its acceptance, although blind boys in the Royal Institute immediately began to use it. In spite of recurrent tuberculosis, Braille continued to work for acceptance of his invention. Before his death in 1852, its use was spreading; the first braille printing press was made in 1847. Six years after his death, the first school for blind children in the United States adopted the alphabet; 30 years later nearly every school in Europe used it. In 1952, Braille's coffin was reburied in the Pantheon in Paris.

Analysis. The author tells Braille's story sympathetically and clearly in a style that should be appealing to elementary-school readers. The line drawings are attractive, and the explanation and illustrations of the braille alphabet are clear. One point the author does not cover, however, is that when braille is written with stylus and paper, the writer must work backward.

The book would be appropriate for reading aloud to youngsters below the fourth-grade level.

DeGering, Etta. *Seeing Fingers: The Story of Louis Braille*. Illus. by Emil Weiss. New York: McKay, 1962. 115 pp. Reading Level: Grades 4–6.
Disability: Blindness

Frenchman Louis Braille lost his sight when a young boy as the result of an accident. At the age of nine he went to a boarding school for the blind in Paris where the few books available were huge tomes with the text embossed in large capital letters, which blind students read with their fingers. Braille was dogged by the nagging desire to find a better way to translate books into an alphabet that would be easily accessible to blind people. A system of embossed dots worked out by an army captain for reading messages in the dark gave Braille the key he needed; by the time he was 15, he had developed the method into a six-dot system that could be mastered in a very short time. Slow-moving bureaucracy and political disruption of the school delayed official recognition of Braille's system until 1844. His health eroded by poor living conditions and overwork, Braille died of tuberculosis in 1852, but he had the satisfaction before his death of knowing that succeeding generations of blind people would be able to read with their fingers, using the system in use today, which we call braille.

The book is illustrated with adequate if not distinguished line drawings.

Analysis. The author tells Braille's story with enthusiasm and optimism, conveying her affectionate admiration for him and her appreciation of the magnitude of his accomplishment. She uses historical material skillfully to convey a sense of the period and employs dialogue both to transmit information and to reveal personality. Her explanation of the six-dot system is very clear, although it is too bad that the symbols are not embossed as well as printed, so that sighted readers could try to read braille. The difficulties Braille encountered both in his childhood and in his career as teacher and inventor are described, but the tone is cheerful and the pace rapid, so that the full sense of these obstacles is muted. Young readers could come away from *Seeing Fingers* with a strong feeling for life's possibilities even under adverse conditions, and they might gain as well an understanding of blindness and an appreciation of Braille's brilliance.

Readers who enjoy this book might also like *Louis Braille: Windows for the Blind* by Kugelmass (see this section). Some of the biographical details differ, as do the emphasis and tone.

Dyer, Donita. *Bright Promise.* Grand Rapids, Mich.: Zondervan, 1983. 174 pp. Reading Level: Grades 10–12.
Disability: Blindness

Chung Syn Yang was born in Korea in 1920, the fifth daughter in a once well-to-do family, now poor because of the father's political dissidence with the Japanese military government that ruled Korea at the time. Chung's mother tried to smother her after she was born because she was yet another girl, but the child survived because of her grandmother's intervention. As a youngster, she became ill with a high fever; she miraculously recovered, but was left completely blind. Shortly afterward, some local Christian missionaries began to visit her. She soon was attending the local church and, while still a child, became a lay evangelist. Her strong religious faith never left her.

Chung was able to attend a school for blind children, whose director happened to seek shelter in the family's home during a storm. She was a good student, but because of her family's poverty she had to work incredibly hard to earn enough money to offset tuition and living expenses. Eventually, she went to Japan to study music, but studied medicine instead. During World War II, Chung was interned for some time in a Japanese prisoner of war camp because she was a foreigner and had refused to convert to Shintoism. Her braille notes from medical school were used as evidence of her participation in a spy network. She was beaten, tortured, and forced to live in a filthy cell. Eventually, the head of the medical school was able to free her. She finished medical school, and, rejecting a proposal of marriage from a long-time Japanese friend and fellow student, returned to Korea to keep her promise to serve God there. She set up a clinic that ministered to both physical and spiritual needs. She also earned a degree in theology. Forced to flee by military unrest in North Korea, she moved to Inchon, South Korea, where she did educational work with blind children, work with orphans, and, always, religious work. She studied for several years in California, earning education degrees there in 1960. She then returned to Inchon, where she does preaching, counseling, and work with prison inmates.

Dyer wrote this book from braille notes kept by Chung Syn Yang and translated into English by her adopted son, Henry Syn.

Analysis. In this very interesting and well-written book, the historical setting is clearly explained, as are Korean cultural and social traditions. The author employs colorful, descriptive language that paints vivid pictures with words. She takes a bit of novelist's license—for example, in her exact description of what Chung Syn Yang's mother was doing just prior to her daughter's birth, as well as the birth scene, but this occurs only sporadically and adds color, life, and a sense of reality. There are many conversations where direct quotations are employed, but considering that the book was written from Chung Syn Yang's notes, this is a permissible departure from rigorous nonfiction. The main themes of this book are heroism and faith, and both are very real. Chung Syn Yang's achievements are truly remarkable, beyond anything realistically set for either a woman or a blind person in her society.

Edwards, Audrey, and Gary Wohl. *The Picture Life of Stevie Wonder.* Illus. New York: Franklin Watts, 1977. unp. Reading Level: Grades K–3.
Disability: Blindness

The life of the famous black songwriter, singer, and instrumentalist is told in simple prose and illustrated with black-and-white photographs. The first shows the young blind boy standing before the microphone singing, arms outstretched, wearing the dark glasses that have become his hallmark. Young Stevie is shown at the school for blind children he attended when not touring, and reading braille books. Later photographs capture the excitement of the rock groups, the fans, and the rich expressiveness of Wonder's personality. His identity as a black American is evident, but it is not addressed as an obstacle; rather, it is his blindness that makes him an object of attention here.

Analysis. This simply written story escapes a patronizing or maudlin attitude. Responding to its optimistic tone, young readers will be encouraged to think that they, too, can overcome obstacles and grow up to achieve.

Frank, Morris, and Blake Clark. *First Lady of The Seeing Eye.* Illus. New York: Holt, 1957. 156 pp. Reading Level: Grades 10–12.
Disability: Blindness

Morris Frank lost vision in one eye in an accident when he was six and in the other, again accidentally, ten years later. In 1927, when he was 20, a newspaper vendor drew his attention to an article by Dorothy Harris Eustis, describing how the Germans had trained shepherd dogs to act as the eyes of blind people. Eustis lived in Switzerland and trained dogs for work with the army, the police, and the Red Cross; she had never trained a dog to lead a blind person.

Frank went to Switzerland and persuaded her to train a dog for him. The dog he received there was to change his life from one of angry dependence and frustration to one of activity, fame, and proud independence, save for the bond of mutual trust and interdependence uniting man and animal. The book tells the story of Frank's own training and of his participation in the subsequent development of The Seeing Eye, Inc. This organization, through its philosophy, training, and dogs, was to offer to hundreds of blind adults the same exhilarating freedom that Frank enjoyed with Buddy and with her successors. The authors also describe Frank's career as a lecturer promoting The Seeing Eye.

Black-and-white photographs supplement the text.

Analysis. Frank and Clark tell the story in a rapid, easy style, complete with conversations that, while they could not possibly be remembered so accurately, help to sustain the pace. Details of the training are clearly presented. Occasionally a sexist note crops up, as when Frank talks about the importance of making it possible for blind men to hold various jobs and for blind women to be housewives and mothers. Although such attitudes date the book, young readers interested in the subject should still find it absorbing; they might want to go on to compare training procedures used in the early years of The Seeing Eye with current programs.

Fraser, Ian. *Whereas I Was Blind.* London: Hodder & Stoughton, 1946. 169 pp. Reading Level: Grades 10–12.
Disability: Blindness

Fraser was 18 when he was wounded while fighting with the British forces in France in World War I and lost his sight. During an initial period of bitterness and despair, he received a letter from Sir Arthur Pearson, who had become blind in middle life and had subsequently founded St. Dunstan's, a privately funded organization to train blinded military personnel. Fraser went to St. Dunstan's, where he learned to accept his condition. He became Pearson's assistant and ultimately his successor. He also married the young woman who, as Sir Arthur's assistant and guide, had originally brought him the letter from Pearson.

Fraser describes both the work of St. Dunstan's and his own rehabilitation. He explains how he manages his life—for example, he deals with such topics as going out alone and with a guide, riding horseback, handling written material; discusses various aids that were available to blind people in the early 1940s; and writes about the greatly expanded work of St. Dunstan's. His book was published in 1942, in the first years of World War II, and reprinted just after the war. In addition to his work with St. Dunstan's, Fraser served for many years as a Member of Parliament and was at one time the governor of the British Broadcasting Company.

Analysis. Fraser's story is interesting both as personal history of adaptation to adventitious blindness and for the information it gives on resources available to the blind in Great Britain between 1916 and 1946. It would probably have a rather specialized appeal.

Frevert, Patricia Dendtler. *Patrick, Yes You Can.* Photog. by Sally DiMartini. Mankato, Minn.: Creative Education, 1983. 48 pp. Reading Level: Grades 4–9.
Disability: Blindness

Patrick Neazer was born with glaucoma. After corrective surgery he still had poor vision and needed special training at school. At the age of eight, he was struck in the eye by a football and became completely blind. After traveling teachers provide some mobility training and braille lessons to him at home, his parents decide he should return to St. Cyril's, the school near his Long Island home that he had attended before the accident. Apprehensive, Patrick thinks he cannot do it; how will he get around crowded halls and survive on the playground full of active, rapidly moving, and sighted schoolmates? " 'I can't do it,' he said. Mr. Neazer looked up. 'Patrick,' he said, 'Yes, you *can.* And you will' " (p. 23).

Buoyed by his parents' confidence in him, Patrick returns to school and discovers that not only must he learn ways of adapting to his disability, but he must also teach others. Classmates have to learn how to guide him correctly. A substitute teacher speaks to the class about him in the third person and refers to him as "the blind boy" when she calls on him. He teaches her that he is there, can communicate, and has a name. Part of the story is told as a flashback sequence. At the time the book opens, Patrick has adjusted to his loss of vision and is living in his home, school, and community much as he did before the accident. He uses braille, a braillewriter, and an Optacon. He can again participate in football and baseball, and he and his family are in the process of building a deck for their swimming pool just in time for Patrick's swimming party.

Black-and-white photographs illustrate the text.

Analysis. This is a positive, realistic, and happy account. Patrick's fears and apprehensions are there, along with his victories and accomplishments. Negative attitudes of other people are brought out, as are the positive ways he deals with them. The author stresses that Patrick still sees with his mind and lives in a bright, colorful world. Explanations about braille, the braillewriter, and the Optacon are useful, as are explanations about the ways that sports and games can be adapted so Patrick can participate. This book is one of a small number dealing with black people who are disabled. The photographs are particularly well chosen to illustrate the facts and the spirit of the text.

Fukurai, Shiro. *How Can I Make What I Cannot See?* Trans. by Margaret Haas and Fusako Kobayashi. Illus. with photog. by Kenji Ishiguro. New York: Van Nostrand, 1974. 127 pp. Reading Level: Grades 7–12.
Disability: Blindness

Shiro Fukurai had no special training for his work as a teacher of the visually impaired in Japan when he was a young man, and only gradually developed teaching methods. In this book he describes his work with clay and with linear painting, and, employing drawings, dialogue, and exposition, talks specifically about particular sculptures and how the children made them. Chapter 3 is a series of vignettes about the students and himself.

Fukurai's first success with the children came when he gave them red clay to model; he has also used "Craypas," paint, and india ink. He points out that children without sight can feel their drawings if the lines are traced in glue and filled in with sand or if dotted lines are made with a tracing wheel. The work of his young artists has been shown in exhibitions and reproduced in a booklet distributed around the world; a documentary film, *What Is It Like to See?*, won a prize in a television drama festival in 1961. In the early days of his teaching, most of his students were completely blind, but by 1965 partially sighted children had become the majority.

The book is illustrated with photographs of the children's sculpture and reproductions of their brush paintings.

Analysis. Fukurai's book is a moving account of his work. He describes the children and their art with compassion and understanding but without sentimentality. The translation appears to be excellent and the illustrations clearly show powerful art. The book could appeal to teachers of both sighted and nonsighted children, giving them ideas about their work; it could encourage nonsighted students in their artistic activities and help sighted youngsters understand a bit more about the world of their visually impaired peers.

Hall, Candace Catlin. *Shelley's Day: The Day of a Legally Blind Child.* Photog. by the author. Hartford, Conn.: Andrew Mountain Press, 1980. 24 pp. Reading Level: Grades K–3.
Disability: Partially sighted

Shelley is a seven-year-old girl with very little vision. Along with her brother, she attends the local public school, where she has been mainstreamed into a classroom of sighted students. Black-and-white photographs on each page and a simple text show a typical day in Shelley's life, during which she goes to school, performs various activities in class, eats lunch, and comes home to watch her fish, play with her doll, and try hard to remember to put her toys away. She is shown reading *Hansel and Gretel* with a special magnifier light, as well as playing games with her family, drying the dishes, and watching television. The narration closes on the only spread without photographs by asking the question, "Was your day like Shelley's day?" (p. 23).

Analysis. This is a simple, effective presentation and an appropriate way to introduce younger children to the concept of mainstreaming. Shelley's life is indeed very much like that of any schoolchild her age. Photographs showing the special adaptations she must make to maximize her vision, such as putting her head very close to the page when she reads and writes, using a telescopic lens for viewing television, and using magnifier light for reading, are particularly useful. The quality of paper, print, and photographs in this small-press publication is good, although the photographs are rather small. A library would find the thin paper cover a drawback in the children's collection (there is ample space for binding or reinforcement of the original lightweight paper covers).

Hartman, David, and Bernard Asbell. *White Coat, White Cane.* Illus. Chicago: Playboy, 1978. 182 pp. Reading Level: Grades 10–12.
Disability: Blindness

Hartman, a practicing psychiatrist, lost his sight at the age of eight when the retinas peeled off the backs of his eyes. The book begins with a sketch of himself as a medical resident, attending two patients, one of whom demands, "Where is the Real doctor?" He describes what it is like to be blind, including his frustrations, regrets, and wishes, and moves to a chronological account of his life. In boyhood he had two unsuccessful eye operations within a couple of months of each other, and after the second he was completely blind. In some ways, this outcome liberated him; in an attempt to save the retinas, his physical activity had been restricted, but once there was no more need to move carefully, he played and roughhoused vigorously. He was educated for four years at the Overbrook School for the Blind outside Philadelphia, and then went into public junior high and classes of sighted students. After high school he attended Gettysburg College, where he worked hard to maintain his grade average so that he would qualify for medical school, a goal he had held for many years. He also became engaged to the woman who is now his wife.

The process of applying to medical school was discouraging, sometimes humiliating. Despite his credentials, which put him on a par with able-bodied applicants, most schools refused even to consider him. One school (Tulane) even sent back his application money. A few did grant him interviews, and nearly everyone tried to persuade him to get a Ph.D. in psychology instead of an M.D. At last he was accepted by Temple University. The final chapters describe his medical training and the methods he devised to master the material. He also looks back at his experience and at education of blind people in general and makes criticism and suggestions.

Black-and-white photographs illustrate the text.

Analysis. Hartman's book is funny, realistic, tough. Although he has been described in the media as brilliant (his struggle to go to medical school was dramatized in a television program), he disclaims unusual intellectual powers. Rather, he says, he was persistent, determined to get what he wanted (as he had been since childhood when he learned how to push his parents), willing to work hard, and equally determined to be judged on his merits. He credits his warm, supportive parents and his older sister (who always insisted that he shoulder his share of responsibility and learn to be independent) with giving him a sense of self-worth as well as endless practical assistance, and a doctor uncle who inspired his career choice, and describes the effect various teachers had on him. Passages describing a wrestling match, a visit to an amusement park, and his efforts at dating are richly humorous.

Hartman's book can be read on several levels: as a picture of growing up in America in the 1950s and 1960s, as a story of successful achievement, and as commentary on what it means to be blind. Early in the book, Hartman talks about how he hates to *feel* blind, to be forced into popular stereotypes of which the blind beggar is the extreme example. The Bible, he remarks, "is merciless to the blind" (p. 16). *Treasure Island* has a malevolent blind character. "In stories for children, why is disability, like Captain Hook's missing limb, so often connected with evil?" he asks (p. 16). Hartman's book goes a long way toward correcting that misshapen image.

Hasegawa, Sam. *Stevie Wonder.* Illus. by Dick Brude. Mankato, Minn.: Creative Education, 1975. 31 pp. Reading Level: Grades 4–6.
Disability: Blindness

Stevie Wonder, born in Saginaw, Michigan, in 1950 and raised in a Detroit ghetto, has been blind from birth. He demonstrated musical talent very early and made his first record for Motown when he was ten years old. From then on, he was a professional musician, and although his career has had fluctuations, he has enjoyed remarkable success.

Analysis. Although some mention is made of Wonder's experiences as a blind person, the author concentrates on his musical life and on detailed descriptions of some of his compositions and performances.

Haskins, James. *The Story of Stevie Wonder.* Illus. New York: Lothrop, 1976. 126 pp. Reading Level: Grades 7–9.
Disability: Blindness

Born Steveland Morris in Saginaw, Michigan, in 1950, Stevie Wonder was blind as the result of receiving too much oxygen after his premature birth. At the age of two he was beating out rhythms with spoons, and progressed to cardboard drums, harmonica, real drums, and the piano. Music—making it, composing it, listening to it—has been the center of his life. He made his first record at the age of 10, became a star at 12, and has been a professional musician ever since. This biography includes a discography and an index.

Analysis. Haskins is successful not only in describing Wonder's music and career, but in helping the reader share Wonder's experience as a blind person and as a black man. The dialogue uses quotations from Wonder and others; the narrative has an authenticity that comes from the writer's skillful presentation of Wonder's personality and accomplishments.

Hocken, Sheila. *Emma & I.* New York: Dutton, 1977. 211 pp. Reading Level: Grades 7–12.
Disability: Familial blindness

Hocken, an Englishwoman, has impaired vision because of congenital cataracts and also retinal damage, which she and her brother inherited from their father. Their mother was also visually impaired because of childhood illness. Childhood surgery cost her brother the use of one eye and was unsuccessful for her. Their parents resisted having the children sent away to a school for blind children as the father had been because they felt that such an education made it so difficult for a person to cope with the sighted world. After secondary school, Hocken was trained to be a switchboard operator; she had nothing to do with this decision, which was made by her guidance counselor.

Her sight had deteriorated to the point where she had learned braille and where she found it increasingly difficult and frightening to get around, particularly in city traffic. Then she was given the opportunity to be trained to use a dog guide, and Emma—a beautiful, intelligent brown Labrador—changed her life significantly. She moved out of her parents' home, shared an apartment with a sighted friend, and then lived on her own. Although social relations with men had always been difficult for her, she met, fell in love with, and eventually married a sighted man.

Hocken and her family had not thought of trying surgery again until her brother consulted an ophthalmologist and sent Hocken to him. With no promises except that if surgery failed she would be no worse off than before, the surgeon operated successfully, and Hocken's sight was restored when she was 29 years old. In the weeks after her surgery, she learned to live as a sighted person and Emma gradually adapted to her new role of nonworking dog. The next year Hocken gave birth to a daughter, and, knowing that the ophthalmologist had warned that the baby had only a 50-50 chance of perfect vision, the parents were relieved and joyful when at six weeks the baby imitated her father and stuck out her tongue.

Hocken had accepted her blindness because that was the only way to get on with her life. But at some level she always resisted blindness; "underneath, like blind people, I had *never* accepted it. There is always a small voice somewhere at the back of the mind insisting, *I've got to see. I can't go on living like this* [italics in original]. But that voice always has to be strangled, suppressed, put out of mind, because if you heed its message you will never be anything more than a ragbag of regret, and unable to take your part in the world, a part limited by the fact that you can't see" (pp. 149–150).

Analysis. Hocken writes fluently and vividly, concentrating on her experience in a dark world, her life with Emma, and the startling burst of color, light, and shape brought her by her corrective surgery. She is particularly good at describing the adjustments necessary once her sight was restored, when her perceptions and her thinking were so dramatically altered. For most blind people, such a sight-restoring operation is not possible. If this book is used to help young blind people and their peers, it is important to prevent false hope. Although her account of the dog-guide training program is not as detailed as that in *Tom & Bear*, it might be interesting for readers to compare her description with the account by Richard McPhee (see this section).

Hocken has continued her story with two more books: *Emma V.I.P.* and *Emma & Co.* (Gollancz, 1980, 1984).

Keitlen, Tomi, with Norman M. Lobsesy. *Farewell to Fear*. Illus. New York: Geis, 1960. 286 pp. Reading Level: Grades 10–12.
Disability: Blindness

At the age of 32, Keitlen was an active worker for the Anti-Defamation League of B'nai B'rith, a mother, and a housewife enduring an incompatible marriage. Her life began to change when she stabbed her eye with a pencil and began to lose her sight from an infection that resulted from the injury. Eventually she became totally blind. Surviving a bout of deep despair and anger, she reaffirmed her positive and energetic approach to life, and determined to live alone and independently. She had many inventive ideas that helped her gradually to resume normal living. Quite soon, she was accepted by The Seeing Eye, Inc., to train with her superb dog guide, Duchesse.

Keitlen's feats after her blindness were prodigious. She became an expert skier and mountain climber. She also became a celebrity in the United States and abroad, interviewing for newspapers and television.

Keitlen resumed her job with B'nai B'rith, but became increasingly interested in the cause of blind people following negative experiences not only with society at large, but with the very organizations that were intended to serve blind people. She became managing director of the Physical Fitness Institute and promulgated programs for blind children and adults. She expresses her philosophy in a situation in which her presence had been deeply reassuring to a man who feared he was going blind, stating that if it was true that she had had a positive influence on him, "then I myself had finally made friends with life—a much more satisfactory accomplishment than mere triumph over it."

The black-and-white photographs, many the author's own and taken ingeniously after her blindness, depict her many activities and reinforce the feeling of her love of life.

Analysis. This very well written story creates suspense and interest as Keitlen describes conquering her fear and accepting ever greater challenges in her life. She shares her doubts and fears as well as her successes, and her clever ways of managing both success and failure. The book is dated in that general attitudes toward blindness and dog guides are more positive today than in Keitlen's young adulthood, but this situation is probably due in large part to her own energetic efforts both in the United States and abroad. Her ideas on sexual relationships outside marriage date the book as well.

This may well become a classic in the literature of blindness, in part because it deals with the recent history of changing attitudes toward blind people.

Krentz, Harold. *To Race the Wind.* New York: Putnam, 1972. 282 pp. Reading Level: Grades 7–12.
Disability: Blindness

This is the autobiography of a young man who has just taken a job in a law firm and who married his girlfriend of long standing. Since his birth, author Krentz has been almost totally without sight due to retro-lental fibroplasia. His story begins with the circumstances surrounding his premature birth and his parents' determined efforts to make his life as normal as possible. He describes his early life at home and his joy in "racing the wind" as a preschooler, and relates his many adventures as he grows up in the context of a seeing world. He recalls his humiliation when young schoolmates laughed at the strange glasses that allowed him to detect letters and words when he was in elementary school, and his despair at the moment when the last bit of light perception disappeared during his college years. Krentz is inclined to emphasize humor in difficult situations. For example, he was called up by the draft, and the draft board was unmoved by his protestation of blindness. Finally, his predicament was related on a radio show on which he often played the guitar, and his story inspired the fictionalized play and film *Butterflies Are Free*. The ups and downs of life at Harvard College and Law School are chronicled with careful attention to the strategies with which he compensates for his blindness in order to succeed in his studies.

Analysis. This well-written book is funny, touching, and inspiring. Krentz makes us aware that he was endowed with brains and charm and an affluent and supportive family—everything *but* sight. He is not an average or typical blind person any more than he would have been an average or typical seeing person. He has received many honors as an achieving disabled person. He is exceptionally witty, does not hesitate to tell jokes on himself or stories of adventures that were humorously disastrous. The book is full of amusing one-liners. For example, he writes of concluding a speech before an audience of high school students saying that he would rather fall down an open manhole than feel his way along. "The following day I fell down a manhole," he ends wryly. However, he describes his agonies, frustrations, and loneliness in realistic fashion, avoiding self-pity or sentimentality.

The book is a fine example of literature that can help "normal" young people learn from and appreciate a disabled peer.

Kugelmass, J. Alvin. *Louis Braille: Windows for the Blind.* Decorations by Edgard Cirlin. New York: Messner, 1951. 160 pp. Reading Level: Grades 7–9.
Disability: Blindness

Louis Braille was born in 1809 not far from Paris, where his father was a saddle and harness maker. At age three, he injured his eye with one of his father's awls as he tried to cut letters out of scraps of leather. Within a few days he was blind in both eyes. At the age of nine, he went to a school for the blind in Paris; the founder, Valentine Hauy, had begun instruction with an alphabet made of twigs, but by the time Braille entered the school, Hauy used books printed with embossed letters. It was a cumbersome method, but at least it permitted blind people to become literate at a time when most were consigned to a life of beggary. Through a wealthy patron, a musician who himself was blind, Braille was given organ lessons and became an outstanding musician on both this instrument and the cello.

Unsatisfied with the embossed alphabet, Braille searched restlessly for a better method. A newspaper item led him to a French army officer who had developed a system of communicating at night with code punches in paper. Three years later, in 1829, Braille's persistent efforts resulted in the braille cell, in which letters and numbers are characterized by a pattern made from three pairs of embossed dots yielding 43 braille symbols. The directors of his school resisted all ideas of changing to Braille's system, and the government establishment was at first indifferent. When he was offered a government grant, Braille refused it because he did not want to be directed by the Royal Institute. Braille died of tuberculosis in 1852, fearful for the continued acceptance of his system, but publicity given it two years later by Emperor Louis Napoleon at the Paris International Exposition secured the attention Braille had sought in vain. The braille system used today is essentially the same as the one developed more than one hundred years ago.

There are black-and-white chapter decorations and an index.

Analysis. Braille's personality, passionate and brilliant, and his reactions, intense and often bitter, come through in this biography. The author has also been successful in giving the reader some sense of what it must be to know the world without sight. Occasionally the dialogue, which the author has tried to render with French flavor, seems awkward and unnatural, but the narrative descriptions are vivid.

Lusseyran, Jacques. *And There Was Light.* Trans. from the French by Elizabeth R. Cameron. Boston: Little, 1963. 312 pp. Reading Level: Grades 10–12.
Disability: Blindness

The author was born in Paris in 1924. Nearsighted as a child, he was almost eight years old when he was injured in an accident at school; he fell against the teacher's desk and one arm of his glasses tore his right eye away so that it had to be removed; sympathetic ophthalmia caused loss of sight in his left eye. He made a swift recovery, both physically and emotionally, and soon was walking, running, playing, and reading braille. He describes his surprise at finding himself blind, for people told him that blindness meant not seeing, and yet he saw and his world was bathed in light. He says he saw colors also, and that everything had a characteristic color. Light and joy faded only when he was afraid. Hearing assumed a much more important place in his life, and his hands moved in a way independent of him.

Supported by wise and loving parents, Lusseyran grew up a bright, energetic, purposeful boy, one who attracted and led his fellows. He went to regular school, using braille books and a braille-writer. In discussing schools for blind children, he acknowledges their place and accomplishments, but is deeply grateful that his parents chose not to put him in such an institution. "The only way to be completely cured of blindness, and I mean socially, is never to treat it as a difference, a reason for separation, an infirmity, but to consider it a temporary impediment, a peculiarity of course, but one which will be overcome today or at least tomorrow. The cure is to immerse oneself again and without delay in a life that is as real and difficult as the life of others. And that is just what a special school, even the most generous and intelligent of them, does not allow. Even if the school has the ingenuity and the understanding not to block this course forever, at least it slows it up" (p. 36).

When World II began, Lusseyran's father, a chemical engineer, was called to Toulouse. After the fall of France, when the Germans took over the northern part of the country leaving the southern section to a puppet government, Lusseyran and his family returned to Paris. There he finished his secondary education and entered the university. There also he and a close childhood friend, Jean, became leaders in the underground Resistance and worked for it until July 1943. Betrayed by a traitor, Lusseyran, Jean, and other friends were arrested by the Germans. Eventually, Lusseyran was transported to the concentration camp at Buchenwald where he survived unspeakable horrors; Jean and most of his other friends and comrades perished.

Lusseyran ends his story with the liberation. An epilogue tells the reader that at the time of writing he was living in the United States, married, a father, professor, and writer.

Analysis. Lusseyran's book is an extraordinary account of adventitious blinding. Written in a poetic, abstract style, it tells the reader little of the techniques of everyday living developed by the blind author; rather, it concentrates on emotional, psychological, intellectual, and spiritual experiences and responses. At the beginning, Lusseyran explains why he is grateful to have been made blind in childhood, while he was still a supple, malleable child "ready to settle with life as it is, ready to say yes to it" (p. 14). Acceptance and strength seem to have marked Lusseyran's personality and life. It is interesting to see that he was mainstreamed in another country and that he is such a strong advocate of this kind of integration.

And There Was Light would attract young readers interested in the psychology of blindness as well as in a firsthand account of World War II as experienced by a young French Resistance fighter imprisoned by the Nazis.

McPhee, Richard. *Tom & Bear: The Training of a Guide Dog Team.* Photog. by the author. New York: Crowell, 1981. 149 pp. Reading Level: Grades 7–12.
Disability: Blindness

Richard McPhee is a professional writer, a television film producer, and a photographer with a long-time interest in the relationship between blind people and their dog guides. This book is the result of his stay at Guiding Eyes for the Blind, Inc., Yorktown Heights, New York, where he followed 12 students and their dogs through the 26-day training program. McPhee focuses on Tom, a 24-year-old totally blind young man with diabetes who had lost his sight a couple of years previously, and on Bear, his 19-month-old golden retriever. We are taken through the day-by-day training that begins with assessment of the students and their needs in order to make the most appropriate match between humans and dogs, and then continues with a careful, intensive program. The students vary in their degree of visual disability and the time of onset, as well as in personality, age, sex, and work. The dogs vary in personality, response, and work ability.

This book is written as a journal; McPhee interweaves the description of training with Tom's own story, which he learned gradually. "Tom's Journal," describing his first few days back at home, and brief accounts from the other participants conclude the narrative. In the final pages, McPhee describes the Guiding Eyes' Sixth Annual Walk-A-Thon, gives advice on how to help a blind person with a dog, names the eight dog-guide schools listed by the American Foundation for the Blind in their *Directory of Agencies Serving the Visually Handicapped in the United States,* and gives a glossary of terms.

Analysis. The journal form gives McPhee's narrative immediacy and makes it possible for the reader to absorb detailed information without feeling overwhelmed. McPhee is interested and empathetic but never sentimental. He does not omit the hard parts of the training, the discouragement, irritation, and tears, but he is always conscious of the accomplishments made possible by the mutual efforts of trainers, students, dogs, community organizations, and the families who keep the puppies for their first year. A charming and appealing young man, Tom makes an excellent subject for the author's focused attention. The account of his initial reaction to his approaching blindness and eventual loss of sight is honest and unsparing. He went through what is probably a typical pattern of denial, isolation, anger, and depression (a pattern that follows knowledge of impending death as well as the experience of loss) until he was able to reach acceptance of his condition. His training at Guiding Eyes was built on that acceptance; at the end of the time there he was able to say, "Bear and I are a team now. We're one" (p. 106).

Young people who are animal lovers might be particularly intrigued by the vivid descriptions of dogs.

Malone, Mary. *Annie Sullivan* Illus. by Lydia Rosier. New York: Putnam, 1971. 62 pp. Reading Level: Grades K–3.
Disability: Partially sighted

In a biography designed for beginning readers, the author tells Annie Sullivan's story, beginning with her arrival when she was ten years old at the Tewksbury, Massachusetts, poorhouse with her younger brother. The book follows her through her education at the Perkins Institution and her life as Helen Keller's beloved "Teacher"; most of the focus is on the years of Keller's childhood.

The illustrations are black-and-white line drawings, some of which have areas of blue. There is a list of key words.

Analysis. The author has been successful in writing an informative biography in a graceful style, with characters and events that should be interesting to very young readers. The plentiful, well-drawn illustrations are true both to the text and to frequently reproduced photographs of Sullivan and Keller. *Annie Sullivan* could be recommended for classroom or home reading and could serve as a valuable adjunct to books for young readers about both Laura Bridgman and Helen Keller (see this chapter).

Marcus, Rebecca B. *Being Blind.* Illus. New York: Hastings, 1981. 119 pp. Reading Level: Grades 4–6.
Disability: Blindness

After inviting her readers to try to imagine what it is like to be blind and to try to simulate the condition, Marcus discusses society's treatment of blind people from antiquity to the present. She describes both earlier and current devices used by blind people; how a baby learns, how blind children have been educated in the past, and how they are educated now; how sight is lost; and how blind people get around, manage daily life, and earn a living. She closes with a chapter on how sighted people can help those with visual impairment and a final section on new devices for blind people.

There is a short bibliography and an index.

Analysis. Marcus writes with clarity and directness, taking the reader with her as she explores the world of blind people. Without sentimentality or illusion, she emphasizes the wide range of experience open to those with visual impairment. The photographs of active, happy children reinforce her theme. Although written for children, the book could interest more mature readers.

Mathis, Sharon Bell. *Ray Charles.* Illus. by George Ford. New York: Crowell, 1973. 33 pp. Reading Level: Grades K–3.
Disability: Blindness

Mathis concentrates on the early life of pianist and composer Ray Charles, who lost his sight at the age of seven. He was educated by the St. Augustine School for the Blind in Florida. He had started to play a neighbor's piano before he was four, and at school learned to read and write music in braille and to play every instrument in the school band. His mother died when he was 15, leaving him without any family. He left school, made his way to Seattle, and began a career as a nightclub entertainer. Eventually, he became enormously successful as a performer on alto sax and piano, as a singer, and as a composer. He owns a record company and lives happily with his family.

The book is illustrated with black-and-white drawings, some of which are printed on tawny colored paper.

Analysis. Mathis, a talented black writer, tells Charles's story in simple but powerful language. She does not gloss over the hurts experienced by the child who is different. Well-chosen details from painful times in his early years emphasize the extent of his accomplishment. Young readers will probably not see the irony of separating blind children by skin color, but they can understand when Mathis writes, "His parents . . . tried to find doctors to save his eyesight. But it was hard for Black families in the South to get good medical care." And they can respond to her description of the singer's "rich, black voice" and her account of what he has done and is doing for his people. The section of the book that describes Charles's school experience allows the young reader to see taunts and teasing from the victim's perspective; the book could be used very effectively to help children think about how their disabled peers would like them to act.

Mehta, Ved Parkash. *The Ledge between the Streams*. Illus. New York: Norton, 1983. 525 pp. Reading Level: Grades 10–12.
Disability: Blindness

At 51, this staff writer on *The New Yorker* magazine has sorted through his memories and written about the very different world of his native India.

When he was three years old, Ved Mehta became blind as the result of meningitis. The central themes of this work are loss of sight, loss of home (when he went thirteen thousand miles away to a school for the blind at age five), and eventual loss of country. He recounts his years in the Bombay School for the Blind and ends before the 1947 partition of India when his family lost everything and had to flee for their lives. Trying to keep up with his brothers and sisters left him scarred with bruises, bumps, and broken teeth. Mehta also describes what blindness really meant for an Indian person in the 1940s—becoming a beggar of alms or a caner of chairs.

After an education as a rich boy in the school for the blind in the slums of Bombay, he was admitted to the Arkansas School for the Blind in Little Rock. Although he had typed out his own many letters of application, he knew little English and was quite unsocialized.

Mehta flourished academically in high school and college, but suffered loneliness. At Pomona College in California, he wrote a youthful autobiography, *Face to Face* (Little, 1957), in order to have a girl he secretly liked take dictation. Although his ploy was a failure, his book sold 45,000 copies. Then he went off to Oxford University to read history. He thrived in the atmosphere of social tolerance and began his long and distinguished career as a writer. He joined *The New Yorker* staff at age 26.

This is the fourth book of a large autobiographical work that includes *Daddyji* (1979), *Mamaji* (1979), and *Vedi* (1982), all Oxford University Press.

Analysis. These are not fast-moving books, and they do require excellent reading ability. Prose that is poetic and sensuous with evocative visual descriptions gives the reader a wonderful picture of Mehta's life and times. The later books are delightful to read aloud.

The author's writings have evidently been important in helping him resolve his problem of accepting blindness. Therefore, disability is a central theme and honestly portrayed. Young readers might find the first book of the series, *Face to Face*, most appealing.

Montgomery, Elizabeth Rider. *W. C. Handy: Father of the Blues.* Illus. by David Hodges. Champaign, Ill.: Garrard, 1968. 95 pp. Reading Level: Grades 4–9.
Disability: Blindness, Partially sighted

Born in Alabama in 1873, the son of a minister in the black African Methodist Church, William Christopher ("W. C.") Handy had to learn to play instruments behind his father's back because the elder Handy considered all music except church music sinful. Nothing, however, could keep Handy from his music.

Handy's first full-time job was working in the mills of Bessemer, Alabama, and it was there that his eyes, injured by work over molten metal, bothered him for the first time. He ultimately became a musician and popularized black folk music, which became known as the "blues."

Traveling with a band on lurching trains, Handy wrote musical scores and took care of correspondence, activities that strained his eyes. He also spent time composing music by dim lamplight far into the early hours of the morning. For a time both his band and his music publishing business were successful; then an economic recession forced him to do long hours of paperwork himself. At this point the eye pain he had endured periodically all his life became worse. Consulting a physician for the first time about his eyes, he was told that he would lose his sight completely. He went through a period of hopelessness and despair; then he returned to his music and gained new hope.

An operation restored his sight, but he lost it again soon afterward and was blind for the last 13 years of his life. This time, however, he accepted his condition with calmness and continued to work until a few years before his death at the age of 84.

Drawings and black-and-white photographs illustrate the book.

Analysis. This is a simply told story that should appeal to youngsters. Handy's career in music is the main theme; his disability is dealt with briefly, with emphasis on the period of pain and despondency when he lost his sight for the first time and how, when the loss recurred, he was able to accept it because of the great faith and peace of mind that had resolved his initial depression. Medical details of his loss of vision are not discussed.

Neimark, Anne E. *Touch of Light: The Story of Louis Braille.* Illus. by Robert Parker. New York: Harcourt, 1970. 180 pp. Reading Level: Grades 4–6.
Disability: Blindness

While playing in his father's harness shop at the age of three, Louis Braille injured his eyes and became totally blind. During his years as a student at a school for the blind in Paris, he became engrossed with the idea of developing a way to make books accessible to blind persons. He created and perfected the method of raised dots that carries his name and is used worldwide today.

Analysis. This simple and well-narrated tale gives young readers a picture of a person of courage and determination, as well as a brief historical introduction to braille.

Petersen, Palle. *Sally Can't See.* Illus. New York: John Day, 1977. unp. Reading Level: Grades 4–6.
Disability: Blindness

Sally, now 12, was born blind. Showing a black page in the book, the author explains the darkness in which Sally lives and invites readers to try to understand this by closing their eyes and covering them with their hands. At a special boarding school for blind children, Sally learns to use her fingers to know objects and her ears to recognize people and to have fun with music. She masters braille, typing, swimming, and jumping. She takes care of her pet parakeet, does puzzles, listens to tapes, records her own stories, has riding lessons, and participates in art projects. At home she goes out on her own, using a long white cane. She is also shown playing the organ from braille notes and going to the seashore with her parents.

Color photographs illustrate almost every page and there is a chart showing the braille alphabet and numbers. The book was translated from Danish.

Analysis. Petersen successfully describes Sally's life and helps the reader understand how she functions in her dark world; the photographs enhance and extend the text. The author emphasizes the point that Sally is learning to take care of herself and that she wants "to be treated as much like other children as possible." Little if anything is made of the difficulties and frustrations encountered by a person with a disability. It is too bad that the braille chart is not punched out in true braille, so that readers could share Sally's experience in this activity. The book would also have been improved had the writer discussed, even briefly, the cause of Sally's blindness, as this is a question that may occur to young readers. The text is rather simplistic and would be appropriate to readers several years younger than Sally.

Potok, Andrew. *Ordinary Daylight: Portrait of an Artist Going Blind.* New York: Holt, 1980. 290 pp. Reading Level: Grades 10–12.
Disability: Partially sighted

In his early forties, Andrew Potok was facing approaching blindness from congenital retinitis pigmentosa (RP). He had had the condition since his youth in Poland, but now the degeneration had become disabling. Potok was a painter, so loss of sight meant a dramatic readjustment. Four years earlier he had undergone a training period at the St. Paul's Rehabilitation Center in Newton, Massachusetts; now he was active as friend and counselor in a group of people who shared his condition. Still unable to accept his diagnosis, Potok went to London to try a treatment with bee stings developed by a woman named Helga Barnes. His daughter, who also has RP, joined him there for treatment. After six months, he realized that there was no improvement in either his condition or his daughter's. He returned to Vermont to work as a writer. Still not totally blind, he is now able to accept his situation and, in addition, to accept his wife's success as a potter. When he suggests to his daughter that when she is ready to have children, she adopt them, she says, "Papa, how can you say that? You're nearly blind and you're doing damn well" (p. 290).

Analysis. Potok is a vivid, expressive writer and a tough, unconventional person. He makes no attempt to disguise his anger at his condition and his resistance to accommodation to it; at one point, he remarks on the slowness of his rehabilitation. He does not seem to resent Barnes for claims of cure, and his descriptions of her are lively and funny. Indeed, the whole tone of the book is fast-paced and humorous. This book might be of particular interest to a young person wrestling with the acceptance of a hereditary disability.

Putnam, Peter. *"Keep Your Head Up, Mr. Putnam!"* New York: Harper & Row, 1952. 171 pp. Reading Level: Grades 10–12. *Disability:* Blindness

Six months after he was blinded by a gunshot wound while an undergraduate at Princeton, Putnam went to the The Seeing Eye, Inc., in Morristown, New Jersey. There he underwent the rigorous training that would enable him to use a Seeing Eye dog. With occasional flashbacks to his convalescence and to college scenes, Putnam focuses on the weeks spent in Morristown, describing his experiences in detail. His book is the story not only of his training with Minnie, his dog guide, but of the changes produced in him by his accident and resulting disability and also by the program and people at The Seeing Eye.

Analysis. Putnam writes without sentimentality or self-pity. Since his training course took place in 1941, it may not be an accurate picture of current practices, but this does not invalidate its appeal. Although published as an adult book, it could be read by high school students and even by some in junior high, as is true of his subsequent work (see following annotation).

Putnam, Peter. *The Triumph of The Seeing Eye.* Ed. by Walter Lord. Illus. New York: Harper & Row, 1963. 178 pp. Reading Level: Grades 4–9.
Disability: Blindness

In November 1941, Peter Putnam went to The Seeing Eye, Inc., in Morristown, New Jersey, to get his first dog guide. An author of other books about blindness (see, for example, the preceding annotation), Putnam here presents a history of the founding in the late 1920s of The Seeing Eye, Inc., the first American organization to train dog guides.

After giving the details of the organization's establishment and early days, Putnam explains, step by step, the selection and early upbringing of dog guides and the subsequent training given to the dog and its future blind owner. He tells the story of a group of dogs and then a class of individuals and their new dogs who are being trained by Harold Coleman of the school. The group includes a strong, overconfident young man, still in high school, who lost his vision as the result of an athletic injury; a passive, frightened woman who withdrew from physical and social activity as she lost her sight; and a lawyer, a musician, and two businesspeople who are returning for new guide dogs.

The dogs are assigned according to the physical and temperamental characteristics of both the animal and the person, and the long, rigorous training begins. The instructor and the class members are fictional people, but the sequence is based on a composite of people and incidents to create a typical class at the school. Putnam says that "any similarity to real persons and real events is strictly intentional" (p. xiii).

Black-and-white photographs of people and dogs in the process of training are interspersed throughout the text.

Analysis. Putnam tells a vivid, realistic story, and an interesting one, and in spite of the publication date (1963), the book still holds reader appeal. The language at times is a problem; for example, the statement that being in Paris, where Morris Frank could not speak or understand French, was like being "deaf and dumb," and having one of the workers at the school greet a boy who had sprained his ankle with the comment: "How's my cripple?" This language is not intentionally pejorative; it is simply dated. It does not mar the message of the book, which is first to recount the development of dogs as remarkable mobility aids for people who are blind, and second to underscore the fact that "blindness was neither more nor less than the lack of eyesight" (p. 39).

Rappaport, Eva. *"Banner, Forward!": The Pictorial Biography of a Guide Dog.* Photog. by the author. New York: Dutton, 1969. 127 pp. Reading Level: Grades 7–12.
Disability: Blindness

The book begins with the birth of Banner, a golden retriever puppy bred to be a guide dog. After the first weeks in the kennel, which included extensive testing to determine her suitability for the work, Banner was sent to a 4-H foster home. There she was raised by a boy named Jesse in a household that included other dogs, a Siamese cat, a Siamese rabbit, and an otter. Jesse continued the dog's training for some months, after which Banner was returned to Guide Dogs for the Blind in San Rafael, California.

Now the training became even more specific and intensive, until Banner was ready to join a blind young woman who was returning for her fourth dog guide. The book follows Banner and her mistress back to their home in San Francisco, where they are shown working, shopping, playing, going to the museum, and entertaining guests. Meanwhile, Jesse, who had come back to Guide Dogs for the graduation, has been given another golden retriever puppy to raise.

The book is illustrated with many black-and-white photographs and concludes with a bibliography.

Analysis: In this detailed, well-written account of the intensive training necessary to prepare a dog for guide work, Banner's personality comes through clearly in both text and photographs. The author's afterword tells the reader that the book "is a blend of realities—fictional only in bringing together the pictures and experiences of several dogs under a single Banner" (p. 125), but it has the ring of authenticity.

Young readers interested in the subject might also want to read other accounts about guide dogs, for example, *Tom & Bear* by McPhee (see this section). A reading level beginning at Grade 7 is indicated here, but younger children might enjoy hearing the book read aloud and looking at the excellent pictures.

Russell, Robert. *To Catch an Angel.* New York: Popular Library, 1963. 206 pp. Reading Level: Grades 10–12.
Disability: Blindness

Russell gradually lost his sight from the age of five after an accident in which a splinter became lodged in his eye. He was old enough to have a rich visual memory of the world and young enough to make the adjustment to blindness with relative ease. The darkness came gradually, over the period of a year: "I was too young to be firmly committed to living in a world of light; and so, as I wandered through the land of evening and at last crossed its borders, my ears became accustomed to the darkness; and as my dependence upon them grew, so did their power. So gradually did they accept the function of my eyes that there was no specific time when I knew the change had been completed. There was no crisis. I did not know when I became a citizen of the night" (pp. 16–17).

When he was seven, Russell's parents sent him away to the New York Institute for the Blind in the Bronx. After he had completed high school there, he went for two years to Hamilton College, transferred to Yale where he earned both his B.A. and M.A. in English literature, and did further graduate work for three years at Oxford University, England. At the time of the writing of this book, he was an associate professor at Franklin and Marshall College, Lancaster, Pennsylvania, married to an Englishwoman whom he met at Oxford, and the father of four children.

Analysis. Russell writes with power and perceptiveness, and without self-pity. He describes vividly his schoolboy and college life. His games and occupations were no less vigorous and mischievous than those of sighted children, and he was almost always encouraged by his parents and his teachers to participate fully in both the sighted and the nonsighted worlds. Yet underlying everything was the constant sense that he was part of a separate community, a white crow amidst a majority of black crows, and that it would take continual effort to decide where he wanted to spend his life and then to achieve that choice. He was happy at the Institute for the Blind, yet being there meant repeated and painful separations from his family.

Russell describes honestly, but without bitterness and often with humor, some of the common perceptions held about people with visual limitations. Swept along by the power of his story and his writing, the reader shares Russell's triumph each time he enters more fully into the community of black crows, each time he is acknowledged not only as a blind person (with the adjective describing the impairment coming before the noun), but as a person who happens to be blind.

To Catch an Angel can stand on its own as a literary work and would be appropriate reading for a high school English class.

Sewell, Ray, and Gloria Sewell, as told to Renate Wilson. *House without Windows.* Illus. Toronto: Peter Martin, 1974. 231 pp. Grades 10–12.
Disability: Blindness

Gloria Mortimore Sewell and Ray Sewell are a Canadian couple, both blind. She had had minimal sight since early childhood due to juvenile glaucoma; her right eye was removed when she was five and eventually the other eye as well. Ray Sewell was severely injured in an automobile accident as an adult and as a result lost his sight, most of the hearing in one ear, and most of his sense of smell. Gloria was educated in a school for blind children until she went to McMaster University in Toronto. Her first job was as a home teacher in Ontario for the Canadian National Institute for the Blind (CNIB). Later she became home teacher and secretary for CNIB on Vancouver Island, and it was there that she met Sewell, who had been sent to her as a trainee field secretary. They fell in love and married, despite the prevailing sentiment in such organizations as CNIB, which opposed marriages between blind people; "There should be windows on one side of the house," was an organizational axiom. The Sewells have lived in many places in Canada and have held a variety of jobs; Gloria has spent much of her professional life as a social worker dealing with sighted clients.

Although both Sewells are blind, they have discovered many differences between them stemming from the different origins of their impairment—Gloria's congenital condition and Ray's adventitious blindness in adulthood. For example, as a newly blinded adult, Ray received mobility training, but at her special school Gloria had had practically no such help toward attaining independent movement. They have had disappointments and difficulties, for example, Gloria's near-fatal rupture of the aorta due to Marfan's syndrome. Ray had professional difficulties with the hidebound CNIB and experienced disappointment with a computer programming course. Nevertheless, they have made a good and satisfying life for themselves. They now live in Victoria, on Vancouver Island, where the mild climate makes getting around easier for them. Ray runs a CNIB concession stand selling candy and soft drinks, and Gloria has begun to work as a private counselor, seeing clients in her home and giving courses.

Most of the book is told in Gloria Sewell's voice. Coauthor Renate Wilson met the couple when she was doing research for an article on disabled housewives. She became their friend and collaborator. Black-and-white photographs illustrate the text.

Analysis. This detailed book is a fascinating, explicit picture of what it is like to grow up blind, what it is like to suddenly become blind, and what it is like to live as a blind person. The Sewells include material about how they manage daily routines, what they particularly enjoy doing, how they have developed as individuals. As Wilson points out in her introduction, it is also the story of the 28,000 blind people in Canada. "Moreover, the Canadian National Institute for the Blind kept intruding in the narrative. The Sewells alternately praised many of its staff members, services and functions, and damned it as a paternalistic, dictatorial and anachronistic organization. The fact that they themselves have been part of the organization as well as its clients, gives their views added weight" (p. x).

House without Windows would be of interest to sighted high school readers who would like to know more about what it is like to live without vision, to visually impaired young people who would find the Sewell's experience particularly pertinent, and to professionals working with blind people who are concerned with their clients' perspectives.

Sullivan, Tom, and Derek L. T. Gill. *Tom Sullivan's Adventures in Darkness.* Illus. New York: McKay, 1976. 106 pp. Reading Level: Grades 7–9.
Disability: Blindness

To save the lives of some premature babies, oxygen must be administered; the amount needed may be too much for the immature retinas of the baby's eyes, and blindness may result. That is what happened to Tom Sullivan, but he has still managed to lead an active life. He describes his boyhood games with sighted and nonsighted friends; his education at the Perkins Institution and then at Providence and Harvard colleges; his participation in sports (including skydiving and water skiing); his successful musical career; and his marriage and fatherhood. Although his parents initially overprotected him, they encouraged and supported his activities. He describes himself as obstinate and says, "When people tell me that I can't do something because I'm blind, that makes me more determined than ever." Photographs show a vigorous, cheerful child and a handsome, athletic adult.

There is also a young adult version of this biography, entitled *If You Could See What I Hear* (New American Library, 1976).

Analysis. Sullivan's style is clear and energetic, his attitude optimistic. His gifts, especially in sports and music, and his determination have enabled him to overcome the isolation that people with disabilities often feel and to become a fully participating member of the larger world. Without preaching, Sullivan suggests both through his tone and through the narrative of his accomplishments that others can enjoy similar satisfactions, that like him they can find life an adventure. The book is weakest in its attention to Sullivan's musical career.

Swieringa, Marilyn. *See It My Way.* Illus. by Robin A. Jensen. Grand Rapids, Mich.: Institute for the Development of Creative Child Care, 1973. unp. Reading Level: Grades 7–12.
Disability: Blindness

Author Marilyn Swieringa became blind in 1969 at the age of 38 as the result of diabetes. Based on her experiences during her first years without vision, this book is a guide to help sighted people interact positively with blind people. The left page of each spread gives an example of a typical situation in which a sighted person and a blind person are interacting socially, such as at a wedding reception, in a restaurant, in a store. The example is followed by a brief summary, set off in a box and labeled "Rule: Please See It My Way," of how to handle the situation appropriately, such as "Be more specific in your seating instructions. Better yet . . . help me to get my hands on the chair itself." The opposite page consists of a black-and-white line drawing depicting the situation accompanied by a second brief summary of appropriate behavior for sighted persons, as "Take a person up to a chair that is in the open. Make sure that her hands come in contact with it."

The Lions Club of Holland, Michigan, supported the publication of this book.

Analysis. This is a creative, lively approach to teaching sighted persons appropriate behaviors when interacting with blind persons. The writing is succinct but not dry because of the plentiful use of illustrative examples, always told from a humorous point of view. The typography, page layout, and large, simple cartoon drawings heighten eye appeal.

In addition to recommending this book to older children and teenagers, teachers, librarians, and parents could use the cartoons and captions with younger children.

Thomas, William E. *The New Boy Is Blind.* Illus. New York: Messner, 1980. 64 pp. Reading Level: Grades 4–6.
Disability: Blindness

Ricky, a blind boy about eight or nine years old, joins a classroom of sighted children. He sits next to the classmate-narrator, who tells the story of what Ricky, the other children, the teachers, and Ricky's parents do and learn during the school year. Ricky has never played much with other children and does not understand when they tease and are mean. His classmates have never met a blind person. With the help of the classroom teacher and two special teachers, Ricky does his academic work and learns to find his way around the classroom and then around the school. The other children are taught to act as "sighted guides" for Ricky and are eager to quiz him on his lessons.

As he watches Ricky and helps him in the classroom and on the playground, the young narrator begins to understand some of the skills that a blind child must acquire and some of the battles he must fight, not only with the disability itself but with its effect on others. The narrator sees the teacher making hard demands on Ricky while his mother babies him at home. He recognizes the truth of the teacher's assertion that Ricky is not helpless, only blind. He understands too that the teachers really care about Ricky and want him to develop the skills and the sturdy self-confidence that will enable him to live a more independent life, one that is integrated into the seeing world.

The book is liberally illustrated with photographs, at least one to each two-page spread, which enhance and extend the text.

Analysis. The author's effort to acknowledge the difficulties and setbacks of a mainstreamed blind child is admirable and largely successful, even though the shift in the mother's attitude seems to happen too quickly and with inadequate motivation. The young narrator's voice is authentically breezy and colloquial, conveying much information without didacticism. Thomas makes vivid for the reader the gaps between the sighted and blind worlds, at the same time showing the extent to which sighted and blind children can share their experiences. Ricky is shown as a normal boy who can enjoy jokes, wants to participate as fully as possible in all activities, but is not immune to frustration and despair. However, the narrator never asks some of the worrying questions that might occur to sighted children reading the book, such as, how did Ricky become blind? could it happen to me? Nonetheless, this is an excellent book to use if a blind child is to enter an elementary-school class.

Thornton, Walter. *Cure for Blindness.* London: Hodder & Stoughton, 1968. 221 pp. Reading Level: Grades 10-12.
Disability: Blindness

In June 1944, Thornton was injured by a "buzz bomb" in London and lost his eyesight. At the time he was 29 years old, an officer in the air force, and married, with a baby daughter. Very soon after his injury, he was transferred to a hospital with a St. Dunstan's Unit (St. Dunstan's is the privately funded organization that for years has provided training for blind people in Britain). Under their auspices, Thornton's rehabilitation took place. He describes this process in detail, beginning with the braille watch presented to him in the hospital and the impact of his first contact with Sir Ian Fraser and Lady Fraser. Fraser (see *Whereas I Was Blind,* this section), who had lost his eyes in World War I, directed St. Dunstan's for many years, and his life became an inspiration to Thornton. After recovering from his wounds, Thornton found a job with Cadbury, the British chocolate manufacturer. No one was too clear about the work he could do there, but he carved out his own sphere by developing programs for Cadbury's junior male employees.

It seems clear that although he knew despair and frustration, Thornton's inner resources and determination to make the best of things, plus the wise support of his family (especially his wife, to whom he often refers), his friends, and his professional associates all combined to make possible his many accomplishments. He never hesitates to acknowledge the help given him, and feels he has been fortunate.

Thornton describes in specific detail his accommodations to blindness in domestic family life, in professional activities, and in outside interests. He has taught lifesaving to boys and young men, has led groups of young people on trips, and has helped in the development of sensory aids for those with visual impairment. He became interested in mobility training, and in the mid-1960s spent some weeks in the United States observing programs and learning how to use the long cane. The book is indexed.

Analysis. Thornton has written a compelling, detailed book that is both a personal account of blindness and a picture of British rehabilitation resources available to those with visual disability. His tone is modest and honest. *Cure for Blindness* would appeal to the general reader as well as to those with a closer connection—personal or professional—to blindness. It might well be read in conjunction with Ian Fraser's book.

Ulrich, Sharon. *Elizabeth.* Introduction and commentary by Selma Fraiberg and Edna Adelson. Illus. Ann Arbor: Univ. of Michigan Pr., 1972. 122 pp. Reading Level: Grades 10–12.
Disability: Blindness (retrolental fibroplasia—RLF)

If too much oxygen is administered to a premature baby, blindness may result because of a condition known as retrolental fibroplasia (RLF). Elizabeth was such a baby, born three months early, weighing 2 pounds 4¼ ounces. Most of the story is her mother's account of Elizabeth's life until she is five. There is a commentary written by two professionals who worked with and learned from Elizabeth when she entered the Child Development Project at Ann Arbor, Michigan, which had research funding to investigate the development of young blind children.

Elizabeth was not known to be blind until she was four months old. From that time, Elizabeth's family, professionals in the project, understanding teachers, and friends began her education as a blind child with patience and resourcefulness. The story ends with Elizabeth as a happy, competent child. However, she must look forward to education in a special school because the neighborhood school is not yet prepared to handle a blind child.

Black-and-white photographs of Elizabeth show her first as a tiny baby in the incubator and last as an active preschooler.

Analysis. The author shows great sensitivity and knowledge about early child development. That professionals learned insights and practices from her is not surprising. She explores the feelings of her other four children about their disabled sibling with tact and sympathy.

Weiss, Malcolm E. *Blindness.* Illus. New York: Franklin Watts, 1980. 84 pp. Reading Level: Grades 4–6.
Disability: Blindness

One in the series of First Books, *Blindness* begins with a chapter, presumably fictional, about a child named Sarah who has been blind since birth. Weiss later introduces Sarah's sighted friend, Margot, and alternates the narrative description of Sarah's life with nonfictional presentation of information. He explains how we see, some of the causes of visual impairment, the methods that blind people use to live in a self-sufficient manner, and the devices available to them. The sections featuring the two girls give the author an opportunity to explore Sarah's relation to her world, the way her parents have treated her, and the relationship between Sarah and Margot, a relationship that has grown from Margot's initial anxiety and discomfort to a friendship between peers.

The book includes a short glossary and a bibliography, as well as an index. The photographs and diagrams are a useful graphic addition to the information in the text.

Analysis. As in his earlier book for older children, *Seeing through the Dark* (see following annotation), Weiss presents a clear, honest, realistic picture of the condition of blindness. He has a gift for conveying factual information; skillfully chosen examples and analogies are an intrinsic part of the exposition. Quietly and firmly, he advocates the right of blind people to be accepted for themselves, as people who happen to be blind but who exhibit the same range of gifts and personality traits as the sighted population, and to be integrated into the larger society. *Blindness* is a well-written book that does not condescend to its young audience.

Weiss, Malcolm E. *Seeing through the Dark: Blind and Sighted—A Vision Shared.* Illus. New York: Harcourt, 1976. 78 pp. Reading Level: Grades 7–9.
Disability: Blindness

Weiss begins by emphasizing that there are many ways of "seeing," that is, of knowing and understanding. He goes on to explore these approaches, describing the use of the other senses, of physical activity, and of mental powers. He explains such physical phenomena as the way sound and light travel, the difference between vision in daylight and in darkness, and how the ear functions. The subtitle of the book runs as a motif throughout the text. The children he describes and whose pictures appear in the illustrations are in school with sighted youngsters, functioning as equals. The blind young people whom he quotes live fully active lives and have learned to counter some of the misapprehensions of sighted people with skill and humor.

The book includes an index and a bibliography.

Analysis. Weiss writes with clarity and force. He has chosen to focus on the ways in which we all—blind and sighted—learn to know our worlds and on the partnership that is possible between these groups. He is particularly skilled at drawing the analogies that can help his readers understand how they perceive the world. Implicit throughout is his belief that we are best defined not by our complement of senses, but by the way we use our gifts and develop our competencies.

Wilson, Beth P. *Stevie Wonder.* Illus. New York: Putnam, 1979. 63 pp. Reading Level: Grades K–6.
Disability: Blindness

This book tells of the boyhood of popular black musician Stevie Wonder, who was born blind. Divorced when her sons were very young, Stevie's mother raised her children in a rundown section of Detroit. Wonder and his brother are shown riding a bike together, climbing trees, and swimming.

Stevie Wonder started playing the harmonica when he was about four years old and learned to play drums and the piano. He began making records when he was in elementary school. Enrolled in a high school for blind children, he made excellent grades even though he already had a career. After he graduated, he became a singer, holding concerts and giving the proceeds to worthy organizations. He is still making music and has received many awards. The book ends with Wonder now married and with children. Photographs show Wonder in various stages of his life.

Analysis. This helpful book would enable young children to better understand what a blind child can and cannot do. Wonder is shown in an active and creative life. The book is consistently upbeat, but apparently so is its well-known hero.

Wolf, Bernard. *Connie's New Eyes.* Photog. by the author. Philadelphia: Lippincott, 1976. 96 pp. Reading Level: Grades 4–6.
Disability: Blindness

Blythe, a golden retriever puppy, spends her first year of life on a small farm in New Jersey where she is cared for by Alison, a 15-year-old girl who is a member of the Seeing Eye 4-H Puppy Club. The dog gets her initial training from Alison and from an adult instructor. Then, as part of the program, Alison must give Blythe up, and the dog is sent to The Seeing Eye, Inc. (an institution for blind people) for a three-month intensive training period.

The focus of the book shifts to Connie David, a young woman from Iowa, blind since her premature birth due to the administration of too much oxygen in the incubator. She has dreamed of having a dog guide ever since she heard the story of Morris Frank (see *First Lady of The Seeing Eye*, this section). The rest of the book describes the training that Connie and Blythe undergo, separately and together, to prepare them for their life as a team.

Black-and-white photographs illustrate every spread.

Analysis. Wolf writes with clarity and restraint. Never sentimental, condescending, or pedantic, he moves the reader simply by describing and photographing what he has observed, never intruding himself into the narrative. For example, after getting Blythe, Connie goes to work at a school for children with impairments; there, one of her students is Gloria, a 16-year-old with cerebral palsy so severe that she must be tied into her wheelchair to keep her from falling out. One spread shows teacher and student at rest time: Connie is reading Wilder's *The Long Winter* from braille text; Gloria is on a mat, her body contorted in spasms but her face alert as she listens.

Wolf's work achieves a high degree of professionalism and sensitivity. This book is targeted for elementary school children, but it can be interesting reading for all ages.

Zook, Deborah. *Debby*. Scottdale, Pa., and Kitchener, Ontario: Herald, 1974. 128 pp. Reading Level: Grades 7–12.
Disability: Blindness

Zook lost the sight of one eye at the age of eight; her remaining sight gradually deteriorated until, after her freshman year at college, she had become legally blind. When she wrote this book, she was teaching braille at a vocational school in Hazard, Kentucky; it is simultaneously a description of a visit she made alone to see a rehabilitation center in Louisville and an account of her reluctant acceptance of her visual disability and of the training she received to enable her to cope with it.

Analysis. Zook has chosen a rather self-conscious and artificial structure, using a short trip as the framework for her analytical look backward. She comes across as a religious person, for whom God is a powerful and ever-present force, but her consistently optimistic tone might make it hard for some readers to relate to the book. Some of the material she presents, for example, the steps in learning to use a cane, is informational and potentially helpful to readers.

7

Books Dealing with Cognitive and Behavior Problems

This chapter contains titles classified in four sections: Emotional Disturbances, Learning Disabilities, Mental Retardation, and Speech and Language Impairments.

- Citations are alphabetical by author in each section.
- Books under Emotional Disturbances cover such disabilities as autism, chemical dependency, mental illness, psychosis, and schizophrenia.
- Learning Disabilities includes dyslexia and perceptual and other problems.
- Books that deal with brain injury, developmental disability, and Down's syndrome are annotated in the section on Mental Retardation.
- Speech and Language Impairments contains titles dealing with such disabilities as aphasia and stuttering.

Emotional Disturbances

> Axline, Virginia. *Dibs in Search of Self: Personality Development in Play Therapy.* Boston: Houghton, 1965. 186 pp. Reading Level: Grades 10–12.
> *Disability:* Emotional problems

This volume is an account of play therapy with a five-year-old boy, mostly drawn from recorded sessions of Dibs and his mother, using actual conversations. Dibs was about to be expelled from a small private kindergarten for behavior ranging from withdrawn to violent. With various diagnoses of mental retardation, brain damage, and emotional disturbance, he was a puzzle to his teachers. His mother was a remote, precise woman who was explicitly convinced of the boy's mental retardation. She had not wanted to bear Dibs and had given up a career as a surgeon. She had also removed herself from friends when Dibs appeared to be subnormal. The situation created a strain on her marriage to an introverted scientist.

However, even in the early therapy sessions, it was evident that Dibs could read and had some knowledge far beyond his years, although in other respects he was infantile. It was only after many sessions that he began to reveal his intelligence at home—an intelligence that his mother had unconsciously suspected and fostered since he was very young by reading to him extensively. Finally, Dibs began to make a social adjustment at school, going so far as to feign ignorance to be like his peers. The therapy ended with the boy's last visit to his therapist and to the playroom where he said a nostalgic goodbye to all that had helped him find himself. The story concludes with several chance meetings of Dibs and the author. An epilogue discusses Dibs when he was 15 and, according to his mother, a brilliant boy, full of ideas.

Analysis. Intended by the Rogerian (client-centered therapy) psychologist as a professional book, this account is well and simply written, so is accessible to young people. A sense of immediacy is heightened by the use of actual conversation. The reader learns to know and sympathize with the little boy who works so hard to achieve a sense of selfhood and a place in the world. Axline gives a running account of the reasons for what she did with Dibs and his mother. Her respect and gentleness are always evident.

That this is also an old book is evident from several themes, such as the dilemma of Dibs's mother. At that time it apparently was accepted that she would renounce her career as a surgeon because she had become a mother. But the mother did grow in her ability to communicate and express herself, and seemed contented in the epilogue. Another somewhat dated theme is the family's deep humiliation at producing what they believed to be a retarded child, a function of the negative attitudes of the time. Although these feelings still exist, such extreme responses as isolation and hiding the problem are less prevalent. Such a troubled family today would probably be treated by a therapist as an entity.

Baruch, Dorothy W. *One Little Boy.* Medical collaboration by Hyman Miller, M.D. New York: Messner, 1952. 242 pp. Reading Level: Grades 10–12.
Disability: Emotional problems, Asthma

Kenneth's mother first consulted Baruch because it had been recommended that her seven-year-old son repeat second grade. He was a good little boy, she said, and she had always felt that he was bright.

His only other problem was asthma. Baruch, a psychotherapist, began to treat Kenneth. She would continue to do so, through play therapy at first and later through talk, for the next two and a half years, followed for the next three years by intermittent appointments at Kenneth's request. Baruch recognized in Kenneth "a child so hungry for love that he wanted to slip back to the beginning of his life in order to make up for what he felt he had lacked. He wanted a second chance at being a baby so that he might gather into him the sense of being loved for himself, not for what he did or accomplished" (p. 14).

Born with an allergic tendency, Kenneth used asthma as a way of working out emotional difficulties. Over a period, Baruch helped Kenneth find other, healthier ways to meet his anxieties and needs, other ways to express himself. She also treated his parents, who were themselves troubled people as a result of unsatisfying parenting and a poorly established marital relationship. By the time Kenneth was 12, he had developed into a physically and emotionally healthy boy; his parents had also made great progress. Kenneth's story is a true one with sufficient alteration to disguise identities and was written with his and his parents' permission.

In a postscript, Baruch addresses parents who may have wondered what the book has to do with their children or themselves. She emphasizes that all children share the kinds of thoughts and feelings experienced by Kenneth—for example, an interest in their bodies and body feelings and angry feelings with fantasies of killing. Parents who understand this can communicate their understanding to their children and facilitate healthy development.

Analysis. Baruch's book is now a classic case study with application for ordinary, nontreatment situations. Extremely well-written, it is at times moving and always clear. Her orientation is Freudian, but the text is free of jargon or difficult scientific language. The book would be of interest to young people looking forward to parenthood as well as to young readers exposed to situations that are similar to those of Kenneth and his family.

Berger, Gilda. *Mental Illness.* New York: Franklin Watts, 1981. 136 pp. Reading Level: Grades 10–12.
Disability: Mental illness, Neurosis, Psychosis

Berger is a professional writer with a number of informational books for young readers. In eight chapters, she looks at the history of attitudes toward mental illness, discusses who might be so described, and explains the different types of professional specialists who treat it. She also describes neuroses, psychoses, and other types of mental illness, discussing the variety of treatments used in the past and today. She talks about aftercare and rehabilitation, and concludes with a chapter on the rights of mental patients. Appendices include a bibliography, a suggested reading list, and supplementary numerical tables, as well as lists of pertinent organizations, names of advocacy and self-help groups, and publications by ex-patient organizations. There is a glossary and an index.

Analysis. This is a clear, informative book, written with sensitivity. Berger is particularly good at presenting a balanced picture of the diverse theories and practice of professionals in the field and at describing the effect of recent laws mandating deinstitutionalization. She makes complex subjects accessible without trivializing them and without condescending to the reader. Brief patient histories appear at intervals in the text and work well to illustrate the condition being discussed; these are most effective when the author includes some indication of the outcome of treatment.

Copeland, James. *For the Love of Ann.* Illus. London: Arrow, 1973. 156 pp. Reading Level: Grades 7–12.
Disability: Autism

When Ann Hodges was six and a half, her parents, who lived near Manchester, England, were told that she was "a schizophrenic and a psychopath," that she was uneducable, and that she would probably never be able to recognize them as her parents. Much later, they learned that Ann's disability was autism. As an infant, the child had not followed expected developmental patterns; she did not gurgle or coo, did not want to be picked up, showed no recognition of family members but was passionately attached to her bottle. In early childhood she became increasingly difficult to manage; she resisted socialization, had long screaming bouts, and rocked obsessively in a special chair. All change seemed to upset her and caused extreme reactions. Her two brothers, one older and one younger than Ann, were growing up normally.

The Hodgeses refused to consider institutionalization and would not give up hope that they could reach their daughter. On a couple of occasions, accidental violent contact with something resisted and feared (water in a puddle, sand at the seashore) had brought about changes, and Jack Hodges decided to try to use deliberate violence to teach Ann. He started with forcing her to feed herself, smacking her every time she resisted. The Hodgeses kept this technique to themselves, for they were ashamed of using physical punishment, but it succeeded. Eventually, as they established connection with Ann, the parents were able to abandon punishment. They pinpointed her fears (for example, she was terrified of the color red) and slowly brought her to see that these were groundless. They taught her to respond to their voices, to identify letters, and to speak. Then they fought to get her accepted into a special elementary school. They helped her manage processes of daily living that other children learn almost without effort. Ann started as a student in a special secondary school, but it was an unhappy experience and she finished her education with home tutors.

An epilogue brings Ann to the age of 20. She has learned office work and works at a modeling agency; she has a boyfriend and her own front door key; she has traveled, can drive a car, and has appeared on television and radio. Her parents are active in the Society for Autistic Children and Ann herself is very interested in people with her disorder. She is still not entirely "normal," but is a functioning member of her family and of society.

The book is based on a diary kept by Ann's father. After he showed it to a newspaper writer who also had an autistic child, James Copeland, another writer on the same paper, interviewed the Hodgeses and wrote an article.

Family photographs illustrate the text.

Analysis. Copeland writes in an easy style often found in popular journalism. Ann's story is a narrative of parents who doggedly refuse to accept a negative medical prognosis and who, through love and persistence, find a way to reach their child and redeem her life. (This kind of happy outcome is not always possible.) High school students might find it interesting to read this book in conjunction with some of the other studies of autistic children, for example, those by Greenfeld and by Pinney (see this section).

Craig, Eleanor. *One, Two, Three: The Story of Matt, a Feral Child.* New York: McGraw-Hill, 1978. 294 pp. Reading Level: Grades 10–12.
Disability: Feral child

Although the child in this story is actually a composite, the book is listed as nonfiction because it is based on cases and clinical reports about real children.

At six, Matt's only communication was a babyish, often excruciating scream. He liked to be naked and to be carried like an infant. Craig took on the task of treating the troubled mother and boy. The parents both were abused and neglected as children. Some one hundred relations were traced by a social worker, all of whom had been associated with the state as prisoners, foster children, violent criminals, and the like. Craig, therefore, had to deal with a deprived mother of a low economic and social class who was in a desperate and degrading symbiotic relationship with her animal-like child. The story recounts the gradual socialization of Matt and the emergence of language and skills, as professionals worked patiently with him and his parents. The book ends with the boy and his family coping more maturely.

The daily activities of a child guidance clinic are depicted throughout the book.

Analysis. Craig's earlier book describes her experiences as a teacher (see following annotation). This title concerns her new career as a counselor in a center. Her references to her personal life and thoughts give an interesting look at what goes on inside the head of a therapist. The compassion and effectiveness of therapists and teachers are clear in this work. The story is well told and fast moving. The mother's conversations are all written in the dialect she speaks, which might be a problem for some young readers.

Craig, Eleanor. *P.S. You're Not Listening.* Illus. New York: NAL, 1973. 224 pp. Reading Level: Grades 10–12.
Disability: Emotional problems

The title was taken from a note that one of Craig's five anguished young students in her new transitional class left on top of the wastebasket for her to see. Craig had responded to the challenge of teaching in the new program to serve troubled, antisocial, and often violent young people, and she did indeed listen with remarkable empathy, humor, and patience.

The story describes the progress of the class over an entire school year. Craig's tumultuous school experiences are counterbalanced by the normalcy of her busy, close family. The highlight of the year for her small class was a bake sale that they planned and conducted to raise money for a children's hospital. This event demonstrated that they had achieved the ability to cooperate as a group, and it gained them new prestige in the eyes of their schoolmates. The book ends with two children returning to their neighborhood schools and the prospect of new classes being formed for the next year.

The illustrations are pictures and written work by the children.

Analysis. The *Washington Post Book World* says about this book: "Recorded with the radar of a born teacher and rendered with a novelist's ear for dialogue." Craig's vivid prose brings each of her charges to life. Her own feelings of warmth, frustration, and humor permeate her writing (see also preceding annotation).

Although this book would have obvious appeal to future teachers, it does not address Craig's pedagogical, as contrasted with her psychological, work with the children, but it is clear that she had good success in both areas. Since the prose is straightforward and most of the events school-related, it might be advantageous in the reading curriculum of underachieving or disturbed young people. It could certainly spark discussion around school-related problems.

Edwards, Henry. *What Happened to My Mother (Not to Mention the Rest of Us)*. New York: Harper & Row, 1981. 175 pp. Reading Level: Grades 10–12.
Disability: Geriatric depression

The author, a film writer, begins with the very sudden mental illness of his 62-year-old mother, Esther. He recounts a long and frustrating battle with institutions, one of which came close to destroying his mother and devastating his father, Sam, in their clumsy effort to treat her deep depression.

In a new hospital Esther's former lively character begins to reassert itself. She becomes the Jewish mother to an assortment of disturbed young people who soon count her a dear friend. The final rehabilitation involves nurse/companion Mrs. Pordy, an elderly, frail black woman who is as much in need as Esther.

The story culminates as ever-supportive Sam and Esther join Mrs. Pordy in a wonderful Sunday service and dinner at the Star of Zion Baptist Church. Son Edward's film script for "Sgt. Pepper's Lonely Hearts Club Band" has been a success, and his parents are again well and happy.

Analysis. This breezy, fast-moving account was written by an adult who is a loving and frustrated son, in partnership with his father to regain the mother he knew. In readable, sometimes sad, often humorous detail he presents the kinds of dilemmas faced by elders in our society, and mentally ill persons as well.

Greenfeld, Josh. *A Child Called Noah: A Family Journey*. New York: Holt, 1972. 193 pp. Reading Level: Grades 10–12.
Disability: Autism

In diary form, this book recounts the first five years of Noah's life, as seen through the eyes of his father. The lives of Karl, Noah's older brother, and Foumi, his Japanese mother, unfold, all profoundly altered by Noah's developmental strangeness.

Noah had seemed normal when he was born and he was, in fact, a beautiful child. Although his motor development was slow in his first year, he did begin to talk, but lost his speech by the time he was two and a half. He engaged in self-stimulation, remained somewhat incontinent, and showed behavior such as lint catching, thread pulling, blanket sucking, and bursts of giggling, crying, and incoherent babbling addressed to his flexed hand.

The parents went to the usual experts who gave the usual equivocal diagnoses of Noah's problem. Certainly he exhibited autisticlike behavior, for which a number of treatments were tried without much success.

Greenfeld closes his book on a positive note, feeling that his family had made their peace with the child called Noah.

Analysis. Greenfeld is a novelist; his descriptions are crisp and vivid. The diary is written as if the prose were spoken—in a stream-of-consciousness style that enables the reader to get inside Greenfeld's head. Greenfeld is painfully honest about his and his wife's despair. Because it is often a great relief to know that others share and understand such feelings, the book might help family members and friends who must deal with negative as well as positive reactions toward a mentally disturbed person (see also following annotation).

Greenfeld, Josh. *A Place for Noah.* New York: Holt, 1978. 310 pp.
Reading Level: Grades 10–12.
Disability: Autism

Here Greenfeld, a professional writer, continues the story of his brain-damaged son from his earlier *A Child Called Noah* (see preceding annotation). He says in his introduction that he no longer considers Noah autistic. "My son Noah was—and is—brain-damaged. He suffers from severe developmental disabilities and acute deprivation in his fine motor processes; he is definitely mentally retarded and naturally has a behavior problem. We have yet to discover the exact reasons—which area of the brain and what perceptional faculties are not functioning properly" (p. 2).

The book takes the form of journal entries from July 1971 to January 1977, when Noah was ten and a half. At that time, he could not speak or communicate in more than a minimally meaningful way; he had tantrums, chewed fabric, woke frequently at night, had imperfect bladder and bowel control, and could not accomplish intellectual tasks. Greenfeld records the daily minutiae of life with such a severely disabled child, the difficulties of finding adequate and appropriate schooling, the frustrations and limitations that Noah places on family life, the tug of love and responsibility that he presents, and the constant awareness that some day he will have to be institutionalized. Although Greenfeld says repeatedly that soon he and his wife will have to make some kind of decision about this, by the close of the book Noah is still at home and the future is as hazy as ever. The last chapter is the factual report written by Greenfeld's 12-year-old son, Karl, for his health class; it is about Noah.

Analysis. The journal form gives Greenfeld's account immediacy as he charts and describes the ups and downs—mostly downs—of living with Noah. Greenfeld faces his own ambivalent feelings honestly, not attempting to disguise the many moments when he wishes only to be free of this unending, cruel burden and its attendant responsibilities. While he makes poignant and clear the effect of Noah on family relationships and on the development of his older son as well as on his wife's professional life, he also shows occasional redeeming moments of love and joy. However, Greenfeld is not a Pollyanna. Noah has not changed anyone's life for the better. Moreover, Greenfeld writes that "had I known at his birth the extent of the brain-damaged condition Noah suffers, and therefore the quality of life in store for him, I certainly would have preferred his not living. And even now, I must honestly admit, I find his death a valid solution to the problems posed by his existence. I mean that if a society does not care it might as well kill, directly and swiftly and kindly, rather than indirectly and slowly and cruelly" (p. 166).

Over the years, the Greenfelds consulted many professionals and tried many different approaches for Noah. By the time he writes this book, they have come to reject the psychiatric approach, operant conditioning, and mega-vitamin therapy. They see Noah's problems as organic, not psychological, and they desperately want to find a permanent situation for him that will provide nonpunitive, comfortable, custodial care where their son will be as happy as possible.

Greenfeld does not disguise his anger at medical professionals and health care and education specialists, nor his scorn for those who do not confront the problems honestly. High school readers who have had personal experience with brain damage or who are thinking about a career in special education or the health professions could find this book interesting. Readers familiar with the author's first book about Noah can follow his story further.

Hayden, Torey L. *Murphy's Boy.* New York: Putnam, 1983. 324 pp.
Reading Level: Grades 7–12.
Disability: Mutism

While working as a research psychologist at a clinic, Hayden was asked to take on an adolescent boy, Kevin Richter, who was institutionalized in a nearby facility. Kevin was almost 16, had spent 7 years in institutions, and had been mute for more than 8 years. He was afraid of almost everything and because he habitually barricaded himself under tables ringed by chairs, he was called "Zoo-boy." Hayden began by crouching under the table with him, reading aloud, and urging him to read at least one word from the book. Quite soon, the boy began to speak—single sounds at first, forced out with incredible effort, and finally complete, fluent speech. Initially, he spoke only to Hayden, but eventually began to talk to others. However, unlocking his voice was only the beginning. Kevin's folder carried very little information about his history. He had many behavioral difficulties, many bizarre phobias, and a potentially murderous rage. Over the next two years his story emerged, a story of inhuman brutality and neglect at the hands of a monstrous stepfather who beat him and tortured and killed his sister, and a mother who stood by, unwilling or unable to defend her children against attack. After many ups and downs, many traumatic setbacks, and several different placements, Kevin is at last able to lay the ghosts of his past at rest. At the end of the book, he is living in a group home, going to public high school; his sessions with Hayden have come to an end. Along with Kevin's story, Hayden writes about her relationship with Charity, the Native American eight-year-old assigned to her under the big-sister program.

As a therapist, Hayden finds herself unable to subscribe to any particular school of thought. When confronted by a friend and colleague, a psychiatrist who works with her on Kevin's case and who demands to know if she has any theory, she answers that she guesses she uses the theory of probability. " 'What's that mean?' 'That if I keep trying long enough, sooner or later, the probability that the odds will be in my favor has to occur' " (p. 186).

Analysis. Hayden writes extremely well. Everything she describes becomes vivid—for example, in a little Frosty-Freez restaurant "the humid, greasy warmth greeted us like a fat auntie's kiss" (p. 136). She recreates scenes and dialogue like a novelist, and while it does not seem possible that she can have remembered all these conversations, her account feels authentic. Grim though most of this book is, Hayden writes with considerable humor, particularly in her descriptions of Charity, the irrepressible little sister.

Hayden, Torey L. *One Child.* New York: Putnam, 1980. 251 pp.
Reading Level: Grades 7–12.
Disability: Emotional problems

Torey Hayden was teaching a class of eight severely disturbed children, the maximum number allowed by Iowa law, when the director of special education told her in January that she would have to take a new child into her room. Sheila was six years old. Two months before, she had burned a three-year-old boy, injuring him critically, and she was to be sent to the state hospital as soon as a place was available. So she comes into Hayden's class, a wild, filthy little girl, sometimes sullen and withdrawn, sometimes seized by ferocious, destructive rage. She stinks of urine, she fights against control, she does shocking things, like gouging out the eyes of the class goldfish with a pencil.

Slowly, with patience and exasperation and love, Hayden coaxes her out of her shell, insisting that she conform to class standards of civilized behavior and that, bit by bit, she join in class activities. The child who emerges is not crazy (although Sheila herself calls their group the class for crazy kids), nor any more disturbed than anyone who had had her experiences would be; moreover, she is extraordinarily bright, has learned to read by herself, is gifted in math, and tests off the charts. Eventually, Hayden and the school go to court and are successful in keeping her from being sent to the state institution. During the spring of the year she spends in Hayden's class, she is brutally raped by an uncle and spends some weeks in the hospital, but with incredible courage and self-control, she survives this trauma as she has survived abandonment by her mother and whippings by her father. By the end of the year, Sheila can accept separation from Hayden, painful though it is, and agrees to go into a regular third-grade class in the fall.

The Little Prince becomes one of Sheila's favorite books, especially the part where the prince and the fox tame each other and in doing so become responsible for each other—an emblem for the relationship that develops between teacher and child.

Hayden has profound respect for the children she works with. Others call them the "garbage class," but at the end of her book she writes, "My work with the emotionally disturbed had deeply impressed upon me their resilience. Despite many popular notions, they were far from fragile. To have survived at all was testimony of this. Given the tools that so many of us take for granted, given love and support and trust and self-value that we often do not notice when we have it, they go beyond survival to prevail. In Sheila this was self-evident. She would not give up trying" (p. 236). The epilogue is a poem that Sheila sent to Hayden after the teacher had moved to another state. The final lines are clear proof that Sheila has indeed prevailed (p. 251).

Then you came
With your funny way of being
Not quite human
And you made me cry

And you didn't seem to care if I did
You just said the games are over
And waited
Until all my tears turned into
Joy

Analysis. This is Hayden's first book, written in eight days (see also preceding and following annotations). She is, to judge from this account, a gifted, creative teacher who, contrary to all professional wisdom, let herself become involved with her students. She writes well—bringing the children, her two assistants, and the world of their classroom vividly before us, carrying us through the months of her life with Sheila. She is at once tough and vulnerable—tough enough to survive, vulnerable enough to feel—like Sheila.

Hayden, Torey L. *Somebody Else's Kids.* New York: Putnam, 1981. 331 pp. Reading Level: Grades 7–12.
Disability: Emotional problems

The author is a teacher in a resource room that has been established for four misfits who cannot be mainstreamed in regular classes: autistic Boo, a racially mixed, seven-year-old boy who does not speak except to repeat weather facts or other people's words; Lori, brain-damaged from parental child abuse when she was a baby, who tries so hard to learn to read; abused Tomaso, who witnessed the murder of his father by his stepmother and has been shunted from one foster home to another; 12-year-old Claudia, the "normal" student, dismissed from her parochial school because she is pregnant. Children and teacher begin to grow together and in this classroom find the love and understanding denied them elsewhere.

Analysis. This frankly sentimental book tells a tough story in attractive, simple prose. As in Hayden's other books (see two preceding annotations), the writing rings true and the reader identifies with both teacher and her charges in their joys and sadness. Hayden comes across as an inspiring teacher and a fine model for future teachers. *Somebody Else's Kids* could be used in class to motivate children who themselves are troubled. It would also increase understanding of the perils many children face.

Horwitz, Elinor Lander. *Madness, Magic, and Medicine: The Treatment and Mistreatment of the Mentally Ill.* Illus. New York: Lippincott, 1977. 191 pp. Reading Level: Grades 10–12.
Disability: Mental illness

This history of the treatment of persons who are emotionally disturbed covers eras from the Old Testament and ancient Greece and

Rome up to the present. It focuses on Western Europe and the United States, except for the early history, which deals with the ancient world of the Middle East and Southern Europe. Surprisingly, some of the attitudes and treatments found in these regions more than one thousand years ago are very contemporary. The physician Rhazes, chief of the hospital at Baghdad in the ninth century who was greatly influenced by the Roman physician Galen, recommended therapy that included proper diet, adequate rest, baths, massages with oil, a calm, agreeable environment, and recreation, particularly the game of chess.

Music therapy was also used, as in the story of Saul in the Old Testament, whose writers reflect a society that believed madness came from God. Therefore, persons who exhibited unusual behavior were not bothered in any way; in fact, some were viewed as prophets. The Talmud distinguishes between emotional disturbances of mental or physical origin and mental retardation, and recommends recreational therapy and what we would call psychotherapy, having the person talk about his or her problems. The New Testament views emotional problems as a punishment for sin. During the Middle Ages in Europe, possession by the devil became the explanation, and any cure lay in the hands of religious officials.

The Renaissance, however, saw "possessed" persons as heretics, labeled them witches, and burned them. Those who were not burned were confined to prisons or cellars, or lived as wandering outcast beggars. Such was the treatment of the emotionally disturbed people in early colonial America as well. At this time, however, the medical profession again became interested in the treatment of emotional problems. Benjamin Rush, a Philadelphia Quaker, physician, and signer of the Declaration of Independence, founded the practice of psychiatry in America. Communities established asylums, where physicians attempted cures by bleeding, various types of restraining devices, and sometimes light manual labor. These institutions soon fell into deplorable condition, which nineteenth- and twentieth-century reformers attempted to alleviate.

The development of contemporary treatment is also chronicled—phrenology and mesmerism, psychoanalysis, electroshock therapy, psychopharmacology, psychosurgery, and various current treatments such as behavior modification therapy, couple therapy, family therapy, sex therapy, primal therapy, and orthomolecular therapy. The last chapter, "The Full Benefits of Our Society," deals briefly with abuses of commitment to institutions, the current emphasis on community care as an alternative, and some of the ramifications of this change.

The text is illustrated with black-and-white drawings from the Bettman Archives, the National Library of Medicine, and the American

Psychiatric Association, in addition to a few contemporary photographs. It has a three-page annotated list of suggestions for further reading, both fiction and nonfiction, and an index.

Analysis. This is a readable, popular treatment of a serious subject, appropriate for a mature high school student. The author is straightforward and matter-of-fact when dealing with the horrors that have been inflicted on emotionally disturbed people. She has avoided the pitfalls of being either euphemistic or lurid in the descriptions. The organization of the material, a combination of chronologic and geographic, is well planned and executed. The treatment of emotional disturbances is always related to the beliefs, customs, and mores of the period being described. Horwitz is clearly an advocate of humane, fair treatment.

The Library of Congress uses a "juvenile literature" subdivision as an option for its first subject heading. While this book is not inappropriate for younger children, the vocabulary and concepts are advanced enough that only a mature child who is an excellent reader would find it manageable.

Hyde, Margaret O. *Is This Kid "Crazy"?: Understanding Unusual Behavior.* Philadelphia: Westminster, 1983. 96 pp. Reading Level: Grades 7–9.
Disability: Emotional problems

The author narrates brief case histories to explain the symptoms and causes of schizophrenia, depression, autism, and eating disorders. Most of the persons in these case histories are children or teenagers, whose symptoms will be familiar to some young readers. Ways of helping family members and friends who are emotionally disturbed or under stress are discussed.

Sources of information are appended: a glossary, a bibliography, and a list of associations and clinics.

Analysis. This useful introduction to the topic of emotional disturbance contains clear and simply stated facts presented in an interesting style. The viewpoint is a positive one, with emphasis on the fact that although emotionally disturbed persons are certainly different, they are not, as the popular stereotype would have us believe, always dangerous to themselves or others. Some illustrations would have made the book more attractive.

Jones, Ron. *Kids Called Crazy.* Illus. by Tom Parker. New York: Bantam, 1982. 150 pp. Reading Level: Grades 7–12.
Disability: Emotional problems

The author has been a teacher for many years, and this book is the story of a summer program he directed for teenagers in a dilapidated mental hospital. Five disadvantaged kids were paid to attend school with an equal number called "crazy."

Two themes run throughout. One is the progress of an alliance, at first fragile but at last deep, between the inside patients and the "outside" kids, to their mutual benefit. The other is the influence of the stultifying, dehumanizing bureaucracy of the mental hospital in which the school operated. The book climaxes with the story of a wonderful roller skating party that the class planned. The hospital staff tried to prevent the trip, which was beyond the limits allowed for patients to go from the grounds, by saying no conveyance was legal for transportation. However, the insurance regulations of the hospital permitted the legal use of a mortuary vehicle, so the students hired a long black limousine with blue flags over the fenders to escort their group in style.

In the end, however, the institutional practices and policies surrounding the closing of the entire hospital contributed to the suicide of one of the students. The others built an outrageous, electronically wired spaceship in the crumbling hospital, before all left to go their own ways. Jones ends by saying "This wonderful statue of life [the space ship] in a house ruled by death" (p. 149).

Black-and-white drawings illustrate the story.

Analysis. The chapters of this slim book are written in the present tense, so the author seems to be narrating the events like a newspaper reporter. Conversations are quoted verbatim, catching the flavor of street language and dark humor. Each chapter is a story unto itself, with fast-moving events. The reader is drawn to the charm and desperation of the ward kids and the inherent generosity and resourcefulness of their counterparts from the outside.

Kaufman, Barry Neil. *Son-Rise.* New York: Warner, 1977. 221 pp.
Reading Level: Grades 10–12.
Disability: Autism

When their son Raun Kahlil was 17 months old, Barry and Suzi Kaufman recognized without being told by medical professionals that he was autistic. Although seemingly strong and alert at birth, the infant troubled his parents by his crying and irresponsiveness. A severe ear infection, compounded by dehydration caused by heavy doses of antibiotics, sent him to the hospital at four weeks. Over the next months he showed increasing signs of abnormal withdrawal and insensitivity to sounds, sights, and human activity. When their own diagnosis was confirmed by doctors, the Kaufmans sought help for their baby's condition but were disappointed everywhere. Then, influenced by something called the Option Method, which is based on the Option Attitude "To love is to be happy with," they began a home program of complete acceptance of Raun and constant stimulation of him. His mother was the chief teacher, but she was joined by the rest of the family and by others. Their aim was to draw him out of his encapsulated state, to show him that although they loved and accepted him as he was, it would be worth his while to make the tremendous effort necessary to learn the responses that come so naturally to normal infants. When the book ends, Raun is two and a half. Although he is "still working twice as hard as another child would while performing the same task . . . still volatile and vulnerable," he has made astonishing progress, almost unbelievable to the medical people who have evaluated him at intervals.

Analysis. Kaufman gives a detailed account of Raun's condition, treatment, and progress. While many families would not be able to duplicate the program, which demands both money for materials and an enormous investment of time (Suzi Kaufman sometimes spent nearly all of Raun's waking hours working with him, making arrangements for others to help with the household and with the two older children), the philosophy and components of the program compel attention. The book is marred by lush overwriting that could detract from Kaufman's message and might make some readers question its validity.

Lane, Harlan. *The Wild Boy of Aveyron.* Cambridge: Harvard Univ. Pr., 1976. 351 pp. Reading Level: Grades 10–12.
Disability: Autism

The provenances of this book are various historical reports, including those of the efforts of Jean-Marc-Gaspard Itard, a French doctor. In 1877, Victor, a boy of 10 or 11 years, was captured by hunters in the forest of Aveyron in Southern France. He is generally judged to have been mentally retarded, and he certainly acted like an animal in his movements, lack of speech, reliance on sense of smell, and disregard of heat and cold. Some current experts have suggested that Victor was actually an austistic child who may have run away from or been abandoned by his family. This book chronicles the five-year experiment in educating the boy by the young physician, Itard, through patient and consistent stimulation and instruction. As Itard's techniques and successes are described in detail, the reader rejoices with him in the slow but sure development of Victor's personality.

The physician-author's first account was printed in France in 1801 when he had worked with the wild boy for several years. A final report was published in 1806.

Victor did not achieve normalcy, so Itard considered his experiment a failure. In retrospect, however, his work with Victor demonstrated the potential of a disabled child to learn and socialize when taught by a dedicated, skilled teacher. Itard's student, Eduard Sequin, continued Itard's methods, which were to influence special education in Europe and the United States.

Analysis. This book and older treatments of the same subject are considered classics in special education, the first documentation of an educator's ideas, successes, and failures with a disabled child, and the first in the rich treasury of readings about exceptional individuals. The edition is not as prolix as some previous ones; however, the somewhat verbose prose, characteristic of the eighteenth and nineteenth centuries, requires patience on the part of the reader.

Lane, Harlan, and Richard Pillard. *The Wild Boy of Burundi.* Illus. New York: Random House, 1978. 188 pp. Reading Level: Grades 10–12.

Disability: Feral child

The authors set out to find an eight-year-old wild boy, who, it was claimed, had been adopted by a troop of gray monkeys. He was spotted by soldiers patrolling an isolated area in a dense tropical forest in Central Tanzania, jumping, chattering, and trying to climb like his primate companions. However, detective work by the authors and others revealed that the "wild boy" was a runaway from an orphanage, probably suffering from infantile autism. As the meeting and examination of the boy and the quest for his origin are described, the reader is introduced to a culture and land totally different from that of Western society. The authors tentatively conclude that the plight of the wild boy is a metaphor for the troubles of Burundi.

Analysis. The narrative is fast moving in a journalistic style. The black-and-white photographs are helpful supplements to the descriptions of this remote third-world area. The condition of infantile autism, the wild boy's actions and his past, as well as his eventual medical workup, are described. Although there is justifiable pessimism about the boy's fate, the authors believe that his life will be best in the small orphanage where he has been cared for in the past. The wild-boy legend seems to have a universal fascination, and this book offers a well-told saga of a journey from that fantasy to hard reality.

Langone, John. *Goodbye to Bedlam*. Boston: Little, 1974. 168 pp.
Reading Level: Grades 7–12.
Disability: Mental illness

Langone is a medical journalist and the author of a book for
young people called *Death Is a Noun* (Little, 1972). In *Goodbye to
Bedlam*, he begins with a chapter on understanding abnormality and
goes on to look at neuroses, character disorders, schizophrenia,
retardation, psychosomatic disorders, and brain dysfunction. He devotes a chapter to various therapies such as psychoanalysis, psychotherapy, group therapy, behavior therapy, shock treatment, hypno-
sis, art therapy, and medication. A short bibliography and an index
conclude the book.
Analysis. Langone's opening historical survey, brief but clear, gives
perspective to this sober, detailed, but eminently readable discussion.
This book, with its objective yet compassionate tone, supplies the kind
of information and understanding that are much needed on the subjects of mental disturbance and retardation.

Liston, Robert A. *Patients or Prisoners? The Mentally Ill in America*.
New York: Franklin Watts, 1976. 119 pp. Reading Level: Grades
10–12.
Disability: Mental illness

Robert Liston has written a number of books examining American
institutions. Here he focuses on "the problems associated with the
various institutions for treating mental illness and mental retardation"
(p. vii). In the first chapter, "A Search for Perspective," he discusses
mental illness as a personal tragedy and as a public, medical, and legal
problem. In succeeding chapters he looks at how people are committed
or commit themselves to mental institutions, how competence or in-
competence is assessed, and past attitudes toward mental aberration.
Liston discusses the medical model, the right to treatment as established by law, and varieties of treatment. The last two chapters examine deinstitutionalization and predict future approaches to management and probable future issues. Reference notes, a list of suggested
readings, and an index complete the book.
Analysis. This informed and skillful writer presents his material
clearly and fairly. Although the book is a sophisticated examination of
a complex subject, it could be read by high school students, especially
those who have had some prior contact with the topic. Adults working
with young people might like to use parts of the book as a basis for
group discussion of issues raised by the author.

MacCracken, Mary. *A Circle of Children*. Philadelphia: Lippincott, 1974. 239 pp. Reading Level: Grades 10–12. ⸱
Disability: Emotional problems

MacCracken uses Edwin Markham's poem "Outwitted" to describe the heretic rebel children she encountered in her classroom (see also following annotation). She began her long teaching career as an aide, and learned tenderness, compounded with strength, from her teacher, Helga, who had a knack with children that MacCracken would someday find useful with her own class. Patience, strength, and love were Helga's keys to unlock the door and reach the rebels, and understanding kept the door open until Helga entered their circle. When Helga retired, MacCracken volunteered at another school for a day, and later took over the class because the teacher never returned. She was not qualified educationally to teach these children, but instinctively she fitted their needs.

MacCracken knew that she must start where the children were and progress from that point to gain their trust and confidence, always with love. She tried to draw a circle around them and protect them from outside fears. She had to cope with four boys who differed in stature and appearance and yet were so alike in hate and anger. Her goal was to make the children independent so that they could gain confidence in themselves. One child of potentially normal functioning level used diapers, bottles, and baby food, which MacCracken was able to persuade him to give up. Her philosophy was that every child was to be treated with respect and dignity. MacCracken tackled each difficult problem with the conviction that to try was the best any teacher could do.

As time passed, she acquired a new class and became a staff teacher instead of a substitute. She and another teacher, Dan, decided to team teach, combining their classes of four children each into one room, one circle. Along with the problems of eight rebels enclosed by four walls, the teachers faced problems with the administration over books, appropriations for materials, and furnishings. They both believed the children should be exposed to the world, so they took them on outings and trips. These adventures opened new doors for the children and enabled them to include Mary and Dan in their circle. Because of the love and trust MacCracken and her colleague bestowed on the children, they in turn began to open their hearts to their teachers.

Analysis. This book was cited in *Booklist* (October 14, 1983) in the Young Adult Services Division's bibliography "Best of the Best Books for 1970–1982." It has the same kind of appeal as Craig's *P.S. You're*

Not Listening (see this section) and other classroom-focused books. The style is moving, powerful, and engrossing. It is recommended highly for leisure-time reading or as a point of departure for classroom discussion about the problems of growing up and parenting.

> MacCracken, Mary. *Lovey: A Very Special Child*. Philadelphia: Lippincott, 1976. 189 pp. Reading Level: Grades 10–12.
> *Disability:* Emotional problems

The author recounts her experiences during one school year as a teacher of four emotionally disturbed children in a private setting. Into her group of three boys came Hannah, filthy, alternatively screaming and withdrawing to the closet. Most of the book describes the gradual transformation of Hannah, who came to be known as Lovey, and the mutual growth of love, understanding, and self-respect that occurred in the classroom. Hannah's story climaxed as the whole school and her overjoyed mother celebrated her ninth birthday at a picnic on the last day of classes.

A subplot runs throughout. Teacher Mary has been trying to find her own identity through her commitment to these special children. By the end of the book, the children of her class have become strong enough to move on. She has been able to make the hard decision to leave the school to complete her college education and to pursue needed state certification in special education.

Analysis. This adds another to the genre of books written by sensitive, gifted teachers about children in their charge, and one of several that MacCracken has written (see also preceding annotation). Her descriptions and anecdotes bring to life some characteristics that are very typical of emotionally disturbed children: their bizarre defenses, their extreme vulnerability, and often a deep and painful wisdom beyond their years. Although the course of Lovey's development was almost miraculous, MacCracken fairly describes her less successful efforts with other students as well. This is a well-written, fast-moving book that might attract young people to the teaching of children with special needs.

> Park, Clara Claiborne. *The Siege: The First Eight Years of An Autistic Child with an Epilogue, Fifteen Years After*. Illus. Boston: Little, 1982. 328 pp. Reading Level: Grades 10–12.
> *Disability:* Autism

Elly was the fourth child born into an academic family. Although the pregnancy was not wanted, as her mother had planned to go back to school, the baby was accepted into her warm and loving family. She was a healthy, alert infant, but by two years of age she was exhibiting the classic symptoms of infantile autism. Her mother's story is of her determined efforts to lay siege to her daughter's "willed isolation." The Parks sought counsel from many professionals and received much conflicting advice about this mysterious disorder. Accounts of Park's day-by-day efforts reveal her to be a born teacher. Elly's personality gradually unfolded, and by the time she was eight, she had mastered self-care activities and useful, albeit very concrete, speech. She also displayed extraordinary intellectual capabilities in narrow areas, such as geographical memory.

The epilogue, comprising about one-fifth of the book, describes Elly 15 years later. With continued perseverance on the part of her family, various helpers, and school, she had progressed to the extent of holding down a part-time clerical job and painting beautiful abstract pictures at home. She had, by the end of the story, developed enough language both to share her enormously rich although unrealistic fantasy life, and to engage with family and friends in work and play.

Park ends her account with a philosophy born from her struggle: "I write now what fifteen years past I would still not have thought possible to write: That if today I were given the choice, to accept the experience, with everything that it entails, or to refuse the bitter largesse, I would have to stretch out my hands—because out of it has come, for all of us, an unimagined life. And I will not change the last word of the story. It is still love" (p. 320).

The black-and-white photographs are charming additions to the text.

Analysis. Park tells a moving, honest story about her strange and fascinating daughter. Her insights and teaching techniques would be of interest to the professional; for the general reader they are entertainingly woven into the narrative. She undergoes considerable introspection throughout the book, and the reader senses that she has honestly faced the many ambiguities of her situation. She had reported when Elly was eight that her daughter had no inner mental life—she certainly amended that opinion forthrightly 15 years later.

Pinney, Rachel, with Mimi Schlacter, assisted by Antea Courtenay. *Bobby: Breakthrough of an Autistic Child.* London: Harvill, 1983. 250 pp. Reading Level: Grades 10–12.
Disability: Autism

The book begins with a description by Bobby's father of the child's first four years. Bobby's birth in 1972 was difficult; the umbilical cord had tangled around his neck just before delivery and the doctor had to use forceps. He seemed perfectly well afterward and during his early infancy. Before he was a year old, however, his mother noticed that he seemed to look through her instead of making eye contact. Soon his parents observed that he related to things rather than to people and that he showed, in his father's words, "an emerging pattern of repetitive or perseverative conduct." Bobby's brother Billy was 11 ½ months younger. Although he did not show all of the same characteristics, both boys became increasingly hyperactive and difficult to manage. By the age of two, Bobby's expression had changed and had become thoughtful and withdrawn. His earlier smile was gone, he hardly spoke, and he resisted attempts at socialization. A pediatric neurologist diagnosed autism and recommended that the parents consult the director of a residential program stressing behavior modification, a program they found very distasteful.

Eventually, they were put in contact with Dr. Rachel Pinney, an Englishwoman who had worked at a clinic in Toronto. There she had treated disturbed children using a program of giving the child "an Hour." During that time the therapist gave the child total attention, recapitulating her or his activities as they occurred and, within the limits set by "DDI—Danger, Disturbance, and Impropriety," allowing the child to initiate and continue activities at will. "During an Hour," Dr. Pinney writes, "the child has the experience of having his activity listened to without the intervention of adult views and values; an experience granted to few children, but for those lucky enough to have received it the experience causes a removal of tension, a restoration of emotional growth, and is a source of happiness" (p. 12). All children, she feels, can benefit from this.

Dr. Pinney undertook treatment of both Bobby and Billy, but she concentrated more on Bobby. Although Billy took his cues from Bobby and exhibited disturbed behavior, he was not autistic. Bobby was judged by those who met him and worked with him to be an extraordinary child. For example, he was fascinated by subways and buses and very early in treatment had mastered the New York City transportation system.

Dr. Pinney worked with the boys from March 1972 until the following December. Looking for different experiences of physical freedom, she took them (with their mother and baby sister) to Cape Cod for a couple of weeks. On another occasion, she and Schlacter took the boys across country with the intention of spending time in a California commune supposedly devoted to the interests of healthy child development; Pinney found within hours that she and the commune adults had fundamental differences, and they left precipitously. Over the course of the nine months of treatment, both boys showed great development. Both achieved a degree of inner-directed control; Bobby began to perceive other human beings as people rather than objects.

The book is written chiefly by Pinney and Mimi Schlacter, who became her chief assistant. She gave the boys what were called "Special Times" and also acted as their baby-sitter. The father and mother contribute sections as well. A postscript describes two visits made by Bobby to London after Dr. Pinney had returned there, one in 1978 when he was six years old, and the other a year later. He had continued to make progress; at seven, he was exploring London on his own. When he was ten, his father wrote to Dr. Pinney that he was doing well at a special school, was fitting in better socially, and would move to a regular school within the next year or two. A select bibliography acknowledges the influence of Dr. Margaret Lowenfeld and directs the reader to her unpublished papers collected at the University of Cambridge as well as to books by other writers.

Analysis. Bobby is a fascinating study of the treatment and development of an autistic child as well as a detailed demonstration of the treatment itself. Without undue proselytizing or egoism, Pinney makes clear her absolute conviction about the merit of children's hours as an approach to children, disturbed or well. The reader may feel occasional anxiety about the kind of freedom given to Bobby; Pinney understands this uneasiness and has shared it herself. She was apparently able to gauge Bobby's growth and give him appropriate responsibility, so that he never came to any harm. Pinney never directly answers the question of the causes of Bobby's disturbance, but at various points seems to suggest that parental handling contributed to its etiology. She mentions several times the measures adopted by his parents in an attempt to control his early unmanageable activity, and his mother's emphasis on orderliness and appearance. There is also an oblique suggestion that a move from Brooklyn to Manhattan early in Bobby's life may have played a part, in that his freedom became more limited. Nevertheless, she says more than once that whatever reservations the parents may have had about her methods, they trusted her with their children, whom they obviously loved very much.

The other voices in the book add to the detailed texture of the narrative, giving varied views of what was happening. No information is given about Dr. Pinney's educational or professional background, save for some reference to her work in Toronto; this seems an unfortunate omission.

Bobby should be of interest to adults dealing with autistic children and to mature high school readers exploring the subject. British terminology is used throughout, although most of the writers and speakers are American—for example, *lift* for *elevator*, *nappies* for *diapers*, *cot* for *crib*; this is an understandable editorial decision, since the book was published in England.

> Quinn, P. E. *Cry Out*. Nashville, Tenn.: Abingdon, 1984. 205 pp.
> Reading Level: Grades 10–12.
> *Disability:* Emotional problems, Child abuse

The author, a former minister and hospital chaplain, is now a speaker and educator for International Child Advocacy and Resources Enterprises (ICARE), a program focusing on the prevention and treatment of child abuse. Quinn has written this story in the third person about his own experience as a severely abused and neglected child. Some chapters are preceded by a short summary of how he felt and thought at the particular time in his life described in the following account.

Quinn was the third of five children born to a couple married in England during World War II. The father was a Native American who brought his English bride to live in a small community near his reservation, where he reentered college. The marriage disintegrated, and Quinn was shunted to eight foster homes between ages six and eight. He reports that his one goal became survival, and he feels that only this saved his life.

Eventually, he was reunited with his two younger brothers on a backwoods farm, where they slaved as underfed laborers for their foster parents. Four years later, the children were abruptly given to a young couple in Middle America. Having adjusted to farm life, he was suddenly asked to adapt to city life and a new family, which was more than he could endure. "Everything was different and strange. Everything except those old familiar feelings of being unloved and unwanted. They never changed" (p. 123).

Punished and scorned at home, Quinn was befriended by the librarian in the suburban school he and his brothers attended. She directed him to a good adventure story, which marked the beginning of his love of reading. In his seventeenth year he was literally thrown out of his adoptive home, a deeply emotionally disturbed young man let loose on the street. After several weeks, near starvation, he was taken in by some hippie bikers, "Satan's Saints."

An epilogue to the story tells that Quinn lived with the bikers two and a half years while managing to graduate from high school. The turning point in his life came after a fight with another group of bikers that left his best friend dead on the beach. Shortly after, he met his wife-to-be, made it through college, and had two children. His story ends with the author again single, but near his children, and in his present work. The book ends with several essays on child abuse.

Analysis. In this period of increasing concern about child abuse and neglect, this book is timely. The author hopes that his account, with the accompanying bibliography and lists of regional resource centers, will make a difference in the lives of children at risk.

The book makes ample use of quotations; and the language used against Quinn is vicious and vituperative. The story is most vivid in the parts that tell of the author's life up to age 17. His adult development is touched on only briefly. Readers in middle school and high school could be directed to this book.

Rothenberg, Mira. *Children with Emerald Eyes: Histories of Extraordinary Boys and Girls.* New York: Dial, 1977. 293 pp. Reading Level: Grades 10–12.
Disability: Autism, Behavior disorders, Schizophrenia

Most of the chapters describe the author's experiences with different groups of children or with various individual children over many, many years of conducting therapy. Her first assignment was an internship, while she was at Columbia University, working with seriously disturbed orphans born in concentration camps during the Nazi holocaust. In the context of a special school, a camp, a residential treatment center, and therapy sessions, Mira, as the children know her, works, plays, and teaches mentally ill children with such diagnoses as delinquency, retardation, childhood schizophrenia, and autism. A preface and an appendix of comments by professionals about the author's work complete the book.

The author makes few moral judgments about her patients (or their parents). Rather, she tries to see their reasons for the wanton destruction, self-mutilation, regression, and isolation that have earned them such labels as retarded, psychotic, autistic, criminal. She acknowledges their insanity as their best coping mechanism and her therapy as breaking through this defense.

Analysis. The prose in this work is vivid and passionate. One has a sense of immediacy in each account. The book is not a presentation of case studies with erudite explanations of a therapeutic methodology. Rather, each child or groups of children are brought to life with descriptions, conversations, and intuitive inferences, with the author assuming the vantage point, perspective, logic, and fears of each of the deeply disturbed children and youths who have come into her care.

The book can be appreciated on several different levels. It is engrossing as a collection of adventures in which the protagonist enters the nightmare worlds of insane and tormented minds in order to free each child's loving soul. The battles are formidable, often won by Rothenberg, with whom we rejoice, and sometimes clearly giving victory to the demons.

The book is a well-told anecdotal report by a person who works as teacher, therapist, and camp director, chronicling experiences with very sick but ingenious children whom, through the author's eyes, we learn to care about. It is probably on this level that most young people would enjoy it. One could take a professional look at the author's methodology, as did the physicians in the preface, to attempt to ascertain what this therapist and her associates *did* to accomplish such often impressive results.

Shapiro, Patricia Gottlieb. *Caring for the Mentally Ill*. Illus. New York: Franklin Watts, 1982. 90 pp. Reading Level: Grades 7–12. *Disability:* Mental illness

The author, a professional writer and social worker, begins by discussing concepts of mental illness, giving a brief profile of a person with schizophrenia. She describes past and present attitudes toward and care of people with mental illness. One chapter, "From Freud to Electroshock," discusses treatment, and another, "Resources within the Community," goes into some of the effects of deinstitutionalization of mentally ill people. Chapter 5 asks whether community care is working, and Chapter 6 talks about legal rights of patients, a theme throughout the book. All sketches of patients are composite profiles, drawn from the characteristics of several people, and all names are fictitious. In her conclusion, she poses a number of difficult questions about deinstitutionalization, the responsibility of society to provide treatment, and the responsibility of doctors to their patients, particularly those who cannot make decisions for themselves.

There is a glossary of terms, a brief bibliography, and an index. Black-and-white photographs illustrate the text.

Analysis. Shapiro writes clearly and compassionately about this complex and emotionally charged subject. She presents material in the hope that readers will draw their "own conclusions about the kind of care that is not only humane for this troubled minority but also fair to society" (p. 10). This is a thoughtful, provocative book, one that could be read by both young people and adults and that would serve effectively as a springboard for group discussion.

Vonnegut, Mark. *The Eden Express.* New York: Praeger, 1975. 214 pp. Reading Level: Grades 10–12.

Disability: Schizophrenia

Vonnegut graduated from Swarthmore College in 1969. After a year of working and wandering, he and a group of friends went to British Columbia to buy land and establish a group living arrangement. At first, the project was successful and Vonnegut himself felt satisfied. In 1971, however, his behavior became increasingly bizarre and frightening, both to himself and his friends, who called his father in the East. Mark was hospitalized with a diagnosis of schizophrenia. No one there gave him much of an explanation of his condition or help in learning how to live. A few weeks later, when the doctor in charge of his case was away, he left the hospital. Before long he was back, having—as he put it—cracked again; a third crackup occurred during his hospitalization. After his release, he left British Columbia and went East. At the time of the writing of this book, he had gone back to school and was trying to get into medical school.

Several factors in Vonnegut's life had come together at once to put him under stress: His parents separated, his woman friend had sexual relations with another man, and his father, novelist Kurt Vonnegut, was becoming increasingly famous. However, in the last section, "A Letter to Anita," written to a person suffering similar symptoms, he makes it clear that he believes that schizophrenia is a disease caused by biochemical abnormalities and that it can be controlled by orthomolecular therapy. Although he recognizes that his environment and background affected him, he believes that psychological theories about the origin of schizophrenia and psychological therapies used to treat it result in placing blame on someone. If the condition is biochemical in origin, such an approach is of no use and may indeed be harmful. Vonnegut recommends two books on schizophrenia, as well as the resources of the American Schizophrenia Association and the Huxley Institute.

Analysis: Vonnegut is very much a product of the 1960s and 1970s in his language and attitudes. Although not apparently a heavy user of drugs, he makes frequent reference to marijuana smoking and describes experiences with stronger substances, which were sometimes very frightening. The "Letter to Anita" is written in a more sober style and does not reflect to the same degree his counterculture life-style and his disturbance. At one point in the letter he remarks that cracking in "very hip surroundings," while it can be advantageous "in terms of people being willing to go the extra mile, having more respect and sympathy for the terrors you're going through, . . . can also add some new problems. . . . Many of the things that were happening to me were things I was supposed to like: ego death, communicating with the supernatural, hypersensitivity of all sorts" (pp. 209–210). Young readers might find this book dated.

Wilson, Louise. *This Stranger, My Son: A Mother's Story.* New York: Putnam, 1968. 247 pp. Reading Level: Grades 10–12.
Disability: Paranoid schizophrenia

Louise Wilson is the mother of four children, the oldest born during World War II, while her husband was serving as a surgeon with the navy. Tony was handsome and alert, but from the beginning seemed high-strung; he did not sleep well, was bothered by noise, and cried a great deal. Later, he could not bear to have his mother leave him and did not want to play with other children. When he was about two, Wilson had to go away abruptly when her father died, and two weeks later, left Tony to go to the hospital to have a second child. The family moved to another house and twins were born—many changes for a young child.

Tony became increasingly difficult and different. He did well in school, but he had no friends and was always a loner; he was often violent with his younger siblings. At his request, his parents sent him to camp for the summer when he was 11. On the trip home after visiting him, Jack Wilson told his wife that Tony was psychotic, that he had schizophrenia. Although they did not mention those words again, they did seek professional help, and over the following years went on seeking it, but it was not until Tony was 19 that this same diagnosis was pronounced by a psychiatrist.

Eventually, they had to make arrangements for Tony to live away from home, first in a special school and then with two psychiatrists, husband and wife, who took a few disturbed young people to live with them. At the end of the book, this is where Tony is living; he has not wanted to see his parents for three years.

The cost of this illness to the family has been incalculable—in emotional strain, in despair, in guilt, in money. Most of the professionals the Wilsons consulted emphasized that parents are in some way responsible for a child's schizophrenia. Only one doctor, whom Louise Wilson went to see when Tony was nearly grown up, spoke of schizophrenia as a physical illness for which the family is no more responsible than if the patient had diabetes. This comforted her to some extent, although she was frustrated by the resistance of the established medical community to this kind of thinking and to the possibility of chemical therapy.

Analysis. In the last chapter, Wilson asks herself why she wrote the book. Her answer is multifold: to sort things out, to tell other families that they are not alone, to say that there are no answers to the terrible question "Why our son?" and no insurance against fate. She and her husband have learned to accept what has happened to them, as well as to take joy in their other children and in their lives. All of them have learned both toughness and compassion. They still love Tony, and they have faith that in his clear moments he is conscious of that love.

Wilson writes extremely well. Although she concentrates principally on Tony, her husband, and herself, all the figures in the book come alive in her descriptions—the other children, the doctors (a note under the copyright information says "All names in this book have been changed," presumably that of the Wilsons as well). While not hesitating to draw presumably accurate and unflattering portraits of some of the professionals, she is not bitter or angry, only tremendously sad, and she is honest in presenting equally unflattering pictures of episodes in their family life. The book could be of value not only for its description of a particular and terrible disability, but for its account of the effect on a family of a chronic and disturbing illness. It should be noted that in the 16 years since the book was written, treatment philosophies have changed a great deal with respect to schizophrenia, but problems for the families remain very much the same.

Learning Disabilities

Clarke, Louise. *Can't Read, Can't Write, Can't Takl Too Good Either: How to Recognize and Overcome Dyslexia in Your Child.* Illus. New York: Walker, 1973. 280 pp. Reading Level: Grades 10–12.
Disability: Dyslexia

Clarke, a professional author who writes here under a pseudonym, describes the first 20 years of the life of her son Mike. As a toddler, he frequently mispronounced words. Difficulty in expressing himself continued, and in grade school he had a great deal of trouble with reading and writing; except for swimming, he was clumsy at sports. When he was 17, his problems were identified as due to developmental dyslexia, or specific language disability.

In the years before this diagnosis, Mike and his parents struggled to find reasons and solutions for his learning difficulties. The Clarkes sent Mike to private schools in New York City. The first, Collegiate, was not a happy place for him; his second, Saint Bernard's, provided more of what he needed. Then he went away to boarding school and ultimately, against the advice of parents and teachers, to Harvard. He flunked out after his sophomore year, but was readmitted after working for a year as copy boy and clerk with an advertising agency. Eventually, he graduated from college and went on to earn a Ph.D. in science. Twenty years later, Clarke goes back to the schools Mike had attended, to see what progress has been made in the recognition and treatment of dyslexia; she also visits public schools.

In addition to Mike's story, Clarke discusses the condition of dyslexia, with special attention to the work of those who have contributed to its understanding and treatment. She discusses significant characteristics that parents can be alert to and describes specific programs. Mike himself contributes a chapter, which he recorded on tape before reading his mother's manuscript. Clarke brings a personal perspective to the subject, since she realized after living with Mike that she and other members of the family have mild dyslexia also.

The book concludes with a section on sources of information and materials, an appendix listing public and private schools and referral centers by state, a bibliography, and an index.

Analysis. Clarke brings to her account both the involvement and commitment of personal experience and the objectivity of a reportorial writer. She recognizes that Mike was fortunate: Without understanding his problems clearly, his parents and teachers were able to supply much of what he needed, and he himself brought courage and persistence. Other children are not as lucky, and Clarke makes the reader understand the frustration and waste involved in their lives. The material on the history and treatment of dyslexia is clearly presented, and the illustrations aid the reader's understanding. Much has changed in the educational field since Mike was a child, and also since Clarke's book was written. Still, teenagers who have learning problems would find much to interest them here, as would young people contemplating a career in special education.

Gardner, Richard A. *MBD: The Family Book about Minimal Brain Dysfunction.* Illus. by Alfred Lowenheim. New York: Aronson, 1973. 185 pp. Reading Level: Grades 4–6.
Disability: Minimal brain dysfunction

Gardner, a physician, addresses the first part of his book to parents, covering such topics as the concept of minimal brain dysfunction (MBD) and primary and secondary signs and symptoms. In the second half of the book, he speaks to youngsters, and primarily to those with a learning disability. Here the print is larger and there are many black-and-white cartoonlike illustrations. He explains what the brain does and what happens when part of it malfunctions; he goes on to a discussion of how children with MBD can be helped and how they can help themselves. A section on worries gives practical suggestions about what to do in specific situations, for example, when other children taunt with cruel names.

Analysis. Gardner's approach is direct and supportive in both sections of the book. He believes in being honest with children, and he stresses the importance to both parents and children of accepting a diagnosis of MBD once it has been confirmed by specialists. He discourages doctor shopping and prolonged denial. A child psychiatrist who has worked with learning-disabled children, he believes strongly that such youngsters can be helped through medication, education, parental guidance, and psychotherapy where indicated. In addressing both parents and children, he emphasizes that MBD involves only part of the brain and only some functions; although youngsters need to understand that some learning tasks will require greater effort on their part than may be demanded of their peers, they must also be helped to recognize that everyone has some deficits and that they may be very adept in some areas. Gardner supports the idea of placing children with similar problems together in school classes, where they get the special attention they need and are not humiliated by having to compare themselves with students for whom learning may be easier and faster. He is optimistic about the extent to which youngsters with MBD can, with proper guidance, achieve fulfillment. Gardner's style is clear and noncondescending, and the cartoons are lively and amusing. Some of Gardner's ideas and statements are controversial. Since 1975, people have become much more inclined to mainstream such children.

Hampshire, Susan. *Susan's Story: An Autobiographical Account of My Struggle with Dyslexia.* Illus. New York: St. Martin's, 1982. 168 pp. Reading Level: Grades 7–12.
Disability: Dyslexia

Susan Hampshire, a successful actress on stage, in motion pictures, and in television, has won three Emmy awards. Born in London in 1942, she was the fourth child of a mother who was pursuing a successful career as a dancing teacher. Her workaholic father was already living apart from his family at his place of employment in the north of England. Susan enjoyed a happy, unorthodox early childhood, much of it spent in her mother's dance studio while her siblings were away at boarding school.

When it was time for Susan's formal education to begin, her mother formed her own school, the 1947 version of an alternative school. Susan, accompanied by a number of other children, received much of her education under the tutelage of her mother and a sister.

Susan's mother had recognized that her youngest daughter was different—a difference rooted in the inability to read or spell words correctly. At first she thought it might be mental retardation. Susan also had other problems: inability to remember numbers, inability to distinguish left from right, some bedwetting. All of these symptoms are associated with a condition that today has been named dyslexia.

In her midteens Susan felt herself unfit for preparation for any career, nor did she want to lose her freedom by marrying. She had always enjoyed theatricals of any sort and loved to act. She applied for and got a job with a British repertory company when she was 15. She tells in detail of her various experiences over the years as an actress, including the ways that her dyslexia influenced her life negatively until she decided to go public about it. Many facts and feelings about dyslexia are interspersed in this story about her acting career, her family, her two husbands, and her two children (one of whom died shortly after birth). Included are two appendices, "Assessing for Dyslexia" and "Sources of Information on Dyslexia."

Analysis. Susan Hampshire tells the story of her unorthodox and interesting life in a warm, entertaining, and humorous fashion. She manages to make some of her most embarrassing moments, brought about because of dyslexia, absolutely hilarious. In addition, she gives good, solid information about the causes of dyslexia and the symptoms and problems associated with it. There was ample opportunity for melodrama here—miscarriages, her baby's death, her divorce, various career situations—but she has completely avoided it and presents the story in a straightforward manner, returning again and again to the recurring theme of the influence of dyslexia on her life.

Hart, Jane, and Beverly Jones. *Where's Hannah?* Illus. New York: Penguin, 1980. 255 pp. Reading Level: Grades 10–12.
Disability: Brain injury

Jane Hart is Hannah's mother and Beverly Jones has been her teacher at the Leaf Center for Learning in Cincinnati. Hannah has had a number of labels applied to her, among them brain-injured, brain-damaged, perceptually handicapped, badly brought up, aphasic, naughty. Her parents recognized fairly early that she was "special," but they felt that some of the diagnoses failed to evaluate their daughter's true potential; they were sure, for example, that she was bright, not "trainable retarded." They consulted experts and tried a variety of educational situations, most of which either did not accept

Hannah or were unacceptable to the Harts. When she was nearly eight years old, she entered a special-education class taught by an experienced teacher and in the three years she remained there, showed much growth. Specialists in visual development provided help. Ray H. Barsch, who has developed a theory called Movigenics, recognized Hannah's potential, and his ideas became the basis for much of the program developed by Hart to help Hannah.

Hart's book explains normal development, moving through sequential stages, and shows the ways in which a child like Hannah deviates from the usual pattern. She describes the specific ways in which she helped Hannah find herself, locating herself in space and time, something the child had been unable to do before; she gives the exercises and games they used, for example, to help Hannah eat by herself, function in social situations, deal with stress, and master academic tasks.

A preface brings the reader up to date on Hannah's progress in the years between 1968 (first edition) and 1980 (Penguin edition). An appendix charts Hannah's development from infancy to 11½ years of age; it also has a list of resources for parents and teachers and a bibliography. There is an index. Black-and-white sketches illustrate the text.

Analysis. Hart presents both Hannah's situation and Barsch's theories in clear prose accessible to the lay reader. She also moves from Hannah to a more general picture of children like her. This is a parent's book, growing out of immediate and deeply felt experience, but it is also a book by someone who has been able to stand back and observe both herself and her child with a certain amount of detachment. She addresses herself most particularly to the parents of other children like Hannah, with the hope that they may gain support and specific help. Teachers and young people interested in pursuing a career in education will also find provocative material here. Readers of high school age who have similar problems might relate to this book. The Harts have a son who functions normally, but he does not figure much in the text. It would have added to the value of the book if Hart had discussed more fully his reactions to the intense attention demanded first by Hannah's aberrant behavior and then by the program developed to help her.

Hayes, Marnell L. *The Tuned-In, Turned-On Book about Learning Problems.* Illus. San Rafael, Calif.: Academic Therapy Publications, 1974. 63 pp. Reading Level: Grades 4–9.
Disability: Learning problems

Hayes is a professor in the Department of Special Education at Texas Woman's University. She is also the parent of a daughter who is a good visual learner but a poor auditory learner; this youngster, 12 years old at the time of the writing of the book, served as editorial consultant to her mother and wrote a brief introduction. Hayes begins by explaining who she is and why she is writing this book. She takes it for granted that any young person reading it has been having trouble in school. Addressing that reader directly, she emphasizes that whatever the nature of the difficulty, the student is not "dumb." Chapter 2 gives a sampling of learning problems and some typical, familiar adult responses, such as "He doesn't try." Using questions and two checklists, Hayes in the third chapter invites the reader to analyze her or his difficulty. The author follows up with specific suggestions for auditory and visual learners. The sixth chapter presents activities that will help people without learning disorders (especially parents and teachers) understand the difficulties faced by students with learning disabilities. The last chapter, "Work to Assign Your Parents and Teachers," lists organizations, journals, and books that might be helpful for adults. Black-and-white drawings illustrate the text.

Analysis. Hayes says that she has tried to write so that the book is "interesting to read, and not *too* 'preachy' " (p. 7), and for the most part she has succeeded, achieving a tone that is neither condescending nor too intimate. Her clear, practical suggestions should help all students handle schoolwork more successfully, and the games in Chapter 6 should be valuable in conveying some of the difficulties and frustrations experienced by youngsters with learning problems. Hayes's consistent and repeated emphasis on the innate abilities of her audience could be reassuring to children with learning disabilities and to their parents.

Simpson, Eileen. *Reversals: A Personal Account of Victory Over Dyslexia.* Boston: Houghton, 1979. 246 pp. Reading Level: Grades 10–12.
Disability: Dyslexia

The author is a psychotherapist and a writer. She begins her story with her realization, when she was nine years old and in fourth grade, that there was something wrong with her brain. Unlike her older sister and her friends and classmates, she could neither read nor spell. The astonishment and impatience of those who tried to teach her only made things worse; reading aloud was a special horror. The Simpson children were orphans who lived with two aunts, one an assistant principal. Auntie tutored Eileen at night, in sessions that were increasingly painful to them both; she took her to doctors, who could find nothing wrong with her sight or hearing; she devised games that were supposed to make learning easier. After a year of this, the lessons stopped. The summer she was 12, Simpson's sister got her to read most of *Little Women* by threatening not to speak to her all summer if she did not do it; she skipped long chunks, but she did read. This was a milestone. Another was the discovery that her mother had also had difficulty in learning to read.

Devising stratagems to avoid exposure, clowning, participating in extracurricular activities, Simpson got through grade school and high school and entered Hunter College, in New York City. She had begun to read for pleasure after picking up a popular novel that was largely dialogue. After college she got a job and her own apartment, and met and married the poet John Berryman. With him and their friends, she continued her literary education. Eventually, she went to graduate school and became a clinical psychologist and a writer. Over the years, she has learned the nature of her disability. She is not cured, she says, for there is no cure for dyslexia. Some days are better than others when it comes to spelling, calculating, following a map, finding her way. Simpson prefaces her chapters with quotations from other people who have battled with dyslexia—some well known, like Flaubert and Agatha Christie, others unknown and unnamed. Informational material about dyslexia, its causes, manifestations, and treatment, is woven into the text with Simpson's own story. The book ends with a list of resources and a selected bibliography.

Analysis. Simpson is a vivid writer, skilled at conveying character, setting, and situation. She describes her dyslexia and its effect on her without self-pity or bitterness, even when writing about the acute miseries of her childhood. She presents technical information with great clarity and balances personal narrative and exposition effectively. This would be an excellent book for a high school reader with a learning disability, as well as for young people considering work in special education.

Mental Retardation

Agress, Hyman. *"Why Me?"* Wheaton, Ill.: Creation House, 1974. 201 pp. Reading Level: Grades 10–12.
Disability: Mental retardation

Hyman Agress, a rabbi, is the father of a disabled son. He and his wife, Frances, were told at Michael's third annual pediatric checkup that he was brain-damaged, hyperactive, and retarded. Seeking further medical diagnosis and advice, they were amazed at the cold, uncaring attitudes they encountered, especially the tendency to "blame" their son's problems on them. By chance, they were referred, by a member of Agress's congregation, to a diagnostic center that was helpful and that ran a nursery school program.

The Agresses moved from New York City to Aurora, near Chicago, when Michael was five, and found an excellent school for children with disabilities. A few years later they decided that Michael was ready for more challenge, but after nearly two years of frustrating experiences with other schools, Michael returned to the original school.

Michael got along well with his younger brother and sister, and his development proceeded satisfactorily. His father began teaching him Hebrew, and at 13 he participated in an abbreviated Bar Mitzvah. He performed so well that Agress decided to conduct another full-length ceremony at a later date when Michael had time to prepare properly for it.

Analysis. Agress's anger at society's callousness in dealing with retarded persons is real and deep. His pride in his son's achievements is great. This book is an exposition and a justification of his search both for an answer to his philosophical and religious questioning (why me?) and for appropriate training and education for Michael. There are many anguished moments and a satisfactory resolution.

Anders, Rebecca. *A Look at Mental Retardation.* Foreword by Muriel Humphrey. Photog. by Maria S. Ferrai. Minneapolis: Lerner, 1976. unp. Reading Level: Grades K–3.
Disability: Mental retardation

Part of the Lerner Awareness series, the book is aimed at children in the primary grades. Each double spread has a black-and-white photograph on the right and a very brief text on the facing page. The photographs are attractive, showing both normal and mentally retarded children in a variety of activities, most of them in a school setting. The text describes retardation and discusses some of the causes. The writer emphasizes the ability of retarded people to learn, however slowly, and points out their need for love, encouragement, and acceptance.

Analysis. Unfortunately, the author is not specific in her suggestions to readers of normal intelligence. Facing a picture showing children doing calisthenics on a playground are these sentences: "If there are mentally retarded students in your school, you can do much to help them. With friendship and encouragement, your mentally retarded classmates will find it easier to learn." The young reader would be hard put to decide which children in the illustration are normal and which retarded or to describe just what kind of helping is going on. Moreover, the text does not address the very real uncertainties children may have when they first associate with people who are different. In failing to acknowledge characteristics sometimes associated with retardation, such as odd speech, outbursts, drooling, lack of motor coordination, the writer seems to imply that these do not exist. Even seven- or eight-year-old readers could understand a simple explanation of different behavior and thus be better able to associate creatively with retarded children in mutual enjoyment.

It is interesting that all the adults in the photographs are female. While it is an indication of progress that the medical person with a stethoscope shown examining an infant is a woman, the absence of male figures reinforces the old stereotype of the exclusively female caretaker/teacher.

Anderson, Kay Wooster. *Don't Forget Me, Mommy!* Illus. San Rafael, Calif.: Marin, 1982. 118 pp. Reading Level: Grades 7–12.
Disability: Down's syndrome

Jay T. Wooster, "Buddy" to his family, was the third of five children. He was obviously "different" from the other Wooster newborns, but medical personnel refused to discuss any details about the infant. In the fall of 1940, when Buddy was seven months old, the family moved from Chicago to San Francisco. Before the trip, his mother, the author, took Buddy to the well-baby clinic at Children's Hospital, hoping they would not confirm the diagnosis of another physician, who had told her that Buddy had "Mongolian slowness" but offered her no further explanation. Buddy was examined by the chief physician and a group of residents. Kay was told: "Your baby is a Mongoloid! He is mentally retarded! He will never be normal! On your way to California, I suggest you drop him off in an institution and forget about him" (p. 9).

Kay's husband refused to deal with Buddy or with his problem and gradually withdrew from the family. She spent the next 36 years caring for Buddy, just as she cared for her two older children, and the two younger ones who were born in California. Obtaining education and training for Buddy and finding and keeping the right school and/or program for him created an unending struggle. The struggle intensified when the father left, and Kay found herself the single parent of a family of five children in the 1950s, when support for single parents was as lacking as support for families whose members included a mentally retarded person.

When in his thirties, Buddy developed an illness that prevented him from absorbing food and ultimately led to his death at the age of 36.

Black-and-white photographs show Buddy and his family at various stages.

Analysis. This is a well-told story, both factual and moving. Although there is a strong undercurrent of emotionality, the author employs a strong, positive, matter-of-fact approach that avoids sentimentality. We see Buddy develop, a very real little boy, a very real young man; trying hard to please; trying hard to learn; a solid, dependable family member who takes his responsibilities, his training, and his bowling very seriously. (He was the proud possessor of numerous bowling trophies.) His long illness, nearly overcome despite medical advice and treatment that sometimes worsened his condition, was the ultimate test for both Buddy and his family, which eventually included a loving stepfather. The end of Buddy's life is a gripping, sad story that shows how much he meant to those around him, and how much they meant to him.

Curtiss, Susan. *Genie: A Psycholinguistic Study of a Modern-Day "Wild Child."* New York: Academic, 1977. 288 pp. Reading Level: Grades 10–12.
Disability: Mental retardation

The author is a linguist who worked with the severely abused and neglected girl Genie after she was brought to the attention of authorities at the age of 13. A child of obviously disturbed parents, she lived from the time she was 20 months until the age of 13 isolated in a small remote room, tied to a potty chair or lying in a straitjacket. Her mother made a brief visit once a day to feed her baby food. In the first six months in the hospital, she learned language, an accomplishment scientists had not thought possible so late in development. The book chronicles Genie's laborious movement toward normalcy. Genie was taught some American Sign Language, which helped her improve her spoken language and communication.

Analysis. This story deals with the restitution of a child who probably would have been normal were it not for intense abuse and deprivation. Genie's terrible story is, unfortunately, not as exceptional as one would like to think. This extreme case of child abuse might provide points of identification for readers who have suffered family violence and abuse. The account of Genie's rehabilitation in the hospital in some measure provides redemption for the earlier horrors, and it concludes on a hopeful note.

deVries-Kruyt, Truus. *A Special Gift: The Story of Jan.* Foreword by
Mary Coleman. New York: Wyden, 1971. 115 pp. Reading Level:
Grades 7–12.
Disability: Down's syndrome

Jan deVries was born in 1940. His parents, especially his father,
recognized early that there was something different about their son,
and their uneasiness was confirmed by a diagnosis of what was popu-
larly termed mongolism, or Down's syndrome, when the baby was
eight months old. The doctor expected that he would not live into his
ninth year. The parents then made two promises: one, "If it is not
granted to us to keep this child for long, let us consciously each day
enjoy every lovely thing he brings us, and let us not plan too far
ahead," and two, despite advice to find a good institution for the
infant, they decided to keep Jan at home until such time as his condition affected the family (particularly other siblings) adversely.

That time never came. Growing up in a home where love and
praise offered encouragement, where discipline was firm and consistent, where he was challenged and yet permitted to develop at his own
pace, Jan stretched beyond the usual expectations for such a child. He
spent nine years as a day student in a special school run by nuns,
where he learned to read and write and count to ten and to do hand-
work. He had religious instructions and was confirmed. At ease in
social situations, he was a fully participating member of his family. He
traveled with them, took photographs, learned to swim, and played
the drums. Always frail in health, Jan developed diabetes at 15, and his
parents took him from school. He stayed at home, "a working, active,
irreplaceable member of the family," until his death as a young man.

deVries-Kruyt wrote this book at least partly to answer the question they were frequently asked: "Why is your son so normal?" The
family was fortunate in their material circumstances (which permitted,
for example, the hiring of a nurse for Jan); the parents were intelligent
and read widely about their son's condition; they had access to excellent medical advice. But even more important was their attitude toward
their child, the loving attention, acceptance, and appropriate stimulation with which they brought him up.

Analysis. As she describes Jan's life, deVries-Kruyt generally uses
the third person singular, even when referring to herself. She has done
the translation from the original Dutch text, and the style is straightforward, although sometimes leaning heavily on repeated images (such as
often speaking of Jan as "a frail craft"). The general context of the
attitude of family and teachers toward Jan is clear, but readers wanting
specific details and guidelines may have questions—for example, about

the books and teaching aids used in the boy's school and at home. She gives a much more precise picture of how she handled the natural curiosity of other children toward Jan's differences.

Dougan, Terrell, Lynn Isbell, and Patricia Vyas, comps. *We Have Been There: A Guidebook for Families of People with Mental Retardation.* Nashville: Abingdon, 1983. 206 pp. Reading Level: Grades 7–12. *Disability:* Mental retardation

Thirty-five authors—parents and siblings of retarded people and some retarded people themselves—share their feelings, reactions, and experiences in one or more essays in the book. It is divided into nine sections: "How to Survive What the Doctor Just Told You," "What to Do with a Preschooler," "Your Child, School, the Law, and How to Stand Up to It All," "Growing, Changing, Moving Out," "What of the Brothers and Sisters?," "What's an ARC?," "Services: How to Get Them, How to Improve Them," "Anger," and "Who Are They?" The compilers, all with family members who are retarded and all active in work with the Association for Retarded Citizens, have written a number of the pieces.

Analysis. Each voice in this collection is sharply individualized. Rueful, angry, humorous, grateful, accepting, or determined, the writers take their audience with them. Their presentations show how much has changed in the treatment of mental retardation in the past 25 or 30 years, but the authors never forget how much is still to be done, or how many obstacles face the advocates of retarded people. Without sentimentality or self-pity, they describe painful moments and joyous ones, emphasizing growth and development, however slow, and urging the need for more work, more meetings, more facing up to misunderstanding, fear, ignorance, and the slow wheels of bureaucracy. This is a book for families in similar situations, for professionals, for volunteers, and a vehicle to convince young readers that mentally retarded people deserve as many opportunities to grow as do their fellow citizens.

Edwards, Jean Parker. *We Are People First.* Foreword by Robert Perske. Photog. by John Stewart. Portland, Oreg.: Ednick, 1982. 92 pp. Reading Level: Grades 7–12. *Disability:* Mental retardation, Cerebral palsy

The spark for the organization People First came from a Canadian meeting, the "first Convention for the Mentally Handicapped in North America," held in 1973. Two staff members and three residents from Oregon's Fairview Hospital and Training Center, a facility for people with retardation, attended and came home to start the work of developing a self-advocacy group. After People First was founded, conventions were held in Oregon beginning in 1974; the last listed here was an international meeting in 1981, attended by 1,500 people. This book discusses the conventions, their membership, goals, and accomplishments. There are profiles of members, including the first president, and of helpers. Members of the organization are quoted extensively, giving their experience and ideas. One past president of a statewide People First organization has cerebral palsy and although she is not retarded, spent seven years in an institution for people who were. The author gives historical background for current attitudes toward and facilities for people with mental retardation. One section gives goals written to offer guidance to People First chapters. There is a resource material list for people who want to know more about self-advocacy and about starting a chapter.

The book is illustrated with many black-and-white photographs of People First members.

Analysis. The self-advocacy movement is an important one, and the author succeeds in giving the movement, the People First organization, and its members, the dignity and respect they deserve. There is much material here for those interested in similar activity and for readers seeking general information. The pictures graphically illustrate the text. It is too bad, especially given the constituency the author represents, that the book was printed with many misspellings and typographical errors. Organization of the material is sometimes confusing. Nevertheless this book's valuable message can give young readers a sense of the importance of advocacy and self-advocacy and of the dignity of all human beings.

Grollman, Sharon Hya. *More Time to Grow—Explaining Mental Retardation to Children: A Story.* With a Parents' and Teachers' Guide by Robert Perske. Illus. by Arthur Polonsky. Boston: Beacon, 1977. 98 pp. Reading Level: Grades 4–6.
Disability: Mental retardation

The first 39 pages of this book are a fictional story about a nine-year-old girl who learns that her five-year-old brother is mentally retarded. The parents' grief and the girl's dismayed reaction and her initial avoidance of her brother are described. Eventually, with the help of a druggist who also has a retarded child, Carla is able to approach her brother again; he teaches her a song he has made up, they sing and laugh together, and the parents join in their happiness.

The story is followed by questions to think about and by activities for young readers—for example, role playing the disabled child who is left out of games and simulating disabling conditions. This section is illustrated with line drawings and printed in large type. Robert Perske's guide for parents and teachers, in small type, follows. Perske suggests ways in which the story can be used and thought about; he also discusses the implications of Public Law 94-142 (the Education of All Handicapped Children Act, passed by Congress in 1975) as well as other changes in the treatment of children with disabilities. The book ends with "Recommended Resources on Retardation," including a list of organizations, suggested further reading for children preschool through high school, a list of available publications, and recommended films for children.

Analysis. This book is an important resource in meeting the need to educate and sensitize all children, whether they are disabled or not. While both story and illustrations have a stilted, artificial quality, they could provide a useful context for discussions in family groups and in the classroom; Perske's contribution reinforces this approach and is skillfully done.

Hirsch, Karen. *My Sister.* Photog. by Nancy Inderieden. Minneapolis: Carolrhoda Books, 1977. 32 pp. Reading Level: Grades K–3.
Disability: Mental retardation

A young boy talks about his older sister, who is mentally retarded. He describes her behavior and her childlike speech. She is a gentle child, and he loves her. This love, however, is tempered by the anger he sometimes feels because his parents must devote so much attention to her and because she often seems to get the best of everything, such as the largest bedroom. He also expresses anger and sadness over the fact that his sister makes their family different in a way that is publicly visible. He gives a graphic account of a day at the beach where various people stare at his sister and make audible comments about her.

Analysis. This book deals frankly and simply with the variety of negative emotions that the sibling of a mentally retarded child will of necessity experience. The story, told in the first person as a direct narrative, contains simple, expressive language and short sentences appropriate to the speech of a young child. The emphasis is on the feelings generated by various everyday events, feelings that often conflict directly with the boy's expressed love for his sister. He resolves the conflict by his acceptance of his sister as she is. The resolution is not simplistic, however, because the negative emotions are also part of his acceptance. The large black-and-white photographs are clear and simple and an appropriate accompaniment to the text.

Hunt, Nigel. *The World of Nigel Hunt: The Diary of a Mongoloid Youth.* Illus. New York: Garrett, 1967. 126 pp. Reading Level: Grades 7–12.

Disability: Down's syndrome

Hunt was born in 1947 in England with Down's syndrome. His parents were soon told "that no matter how much trouble we went to, and no matter how much love and care we gave Nigel, he would be an idiot and that nothing we could do would alter the fact" (p. 22). They refused to accept this verdict. His mother taught him to read, and he learned to type on his own. His education was in a special school for retarded children (a mistake, his father feels, because the other children had more severe disabilities and Nigel was discouraged from making an effort), then in a small private school, and last in the school in which his father was a teacher and later headmaster.

L. S. Penrose, from the Kennedy-Galton Centre for Mental Retardation Research and Diagnosis, has contributed a foreword analyzing Nigel's diary, which is the centerpiece of the book, and attesting to its authenticity, and Douglas Hunt, Nigel's father, provides a biographical framework. Nigel wrote the essay when he was in his late teens. Before it was finished, his mother died; at the end of his introduction, Douglas Hunt tells the reader that he and his son have moved to one of the Camphill Villages set up for adults with disabilities.

Nigel Hunt's essay itself is a series of short chapters about subjects such as visiting Royal Windsor, holidays abroad, his parents, his school, pop music, and the United States. There are black-and-white family photographs.

Analysis. Douglas Hunt tells us that his son is a "high-grade mongoloid type," a fact clearly indicated by Nigel's ability to learn to read, write, type, and get around independently. Nonetheless, this extraordinary document is interesting not so much for its content (which reads rather like the effort of a young grade school child) as for its significance. Douglas Hunt offers it as evidence that people like Nigel can accomplish much more than they are often given credit for or expected to. It could be read by the siblings, friends, and parents of people with mental retardation, as well as by young people contemplating a career in special education.

Jablow, Martha Moranghan. *Cara: Growing with a Retarded Child.* Philadelphia: Temple Univ. Pr., 1982. 210 pp. Reading Level: Grades 10–12.

Disability: Down's syndrome

Cara is a child with Down's syndrome, born in Philadelphia in 1975 to two reporters, Paul and Martha Jablow. Two years later they had a second child, David. This book is the mother's story of her daughter's first eight years of life.

After the initial shock of the diagnosis came the inevitable rounds of medical examinations, some of them handled coldly, rudely, and without feeling. The Jablows received a firm diagnosis from an understanding physician-geneticist at Jefferson Medical Center. A social worker in his unit referred the family to an early intervention (or infant stimulation) program, Ken-Crest, near their home. Cara made amazing progress; although she was slower than the usual age for accomplishing many developmental tasks, she eventually learned motor and social skills that put her not too far behind her nonretarded peers.

After leaving Ken-Crest at two and a half when her parents went to California on a one-year fellowship, Cara attended other schools and received different types of tutoring, with varying degrees of success. Ironically, Cara was refused for the Philadelphia school district's program PEACH (Prescriptive Educational Approach for Children with Handicaps) because at the age of 3.7 years she tested at normal or near-normal on the battery of tests that were administered. At the age of four, she began sounding out words. She began an all-day Montessori program at five and a half, and her development has been slow but steady. Once again Cara was ineligible for public school special education programs because, although she was clearly retarded and delayed in certain areas like fine motor skills, she did not test in the retarded range. As a result, Cara and her brother David began first grade together at the Montessori school Cara had been attending. She continues to progress; her verbal skills are her strongest area; her social skills, the weakest.

Interspersed throughout the text is factual information about the genetic cause of Down's syndrome, training activities for developmentally delayed children, diagnostic tests, and similar material. The book concludes with a "Letter to Parents and Professionals." It also has a resource list of books, periodicals, films, and organizations that deal with children who are developmentally delayed and those with mental retardation. A name-subject index gives access to the parts of the text that deal with facts and information about Down's syndrome, mental retardation, and work with developmentally delayed children.

Analysis. This is a factual book about Down's syndrome as well as an inspiring story about the progress made by one child as the result of her mother's concentrated efforts and determination, and the guidance and tutoring offered by skilled professionals. Although directed mostly to professionals who work with children and parents of children who are disabled, the combination of fact and true story holds potential appeal for young adult readers.

The subject of prenatal diagnosis by amniocentesis (which Martha Jablow had during the course of her second pregnancy), and of the decision concerning abortion versus carrying a fetus with Down's syndrome to term, is handled in an objective fashion, with each parent leaning in a different direction about whether to abort.

Larsen, Hanne. *Don't Forget Tom*. Trans. from the Danish by Peggy Blakely. Illus. New York: Crowell, 1978. unp. Reading Level: Grades K–3.
Disability: Mental retardation

Six-year-old Tom lives with his parents, his older sister, and his younger brother. Stating that Tom is handicapped, Larsen goes on to explain what this means; in Tom's case, "It is a part of his brain which won't work properly; Tom is *mentally* handicapped [italics in original]. This means he can't understand as quickly as you or I. He needs more time to learn and to do things." The writer takes us through Tom's day: attempts to feed and dress himself, outdoor play, lessons with the visiting teacher, family dinner, bath with his little brother, a picture book at bedtime. Large color photographs illustrate every spread.

Analysis. It is difficult to show mental retardation in pictures, and in most of the illustrations Tom looks like a very ordinary little boy. We are told that he is sometimes sulky or jealous or frustrated, but the photographs and most of the text show Tom and his family as happy and productive. Although Tom is Danish, and we see his mother holding a huge goose and Tom wearing a Scandinavian hat and sweater, national differences are minimized; they would have added to the interest of the book.

Lynch, Maureen. *Mary Fran and Mo*. New York: St. Martin's, 1979. 169 pp. Reading Level: Grades 7–12.
Disability: Mental retardation

Teenagers Maureen Lynch and her sister Mary Fran, who is retarded, spent a year living in a Seattle suburb while Maureen (Mo) taught Mary Fran the basic skills that she would need to live independently—handling money, cooking, shopping, riding on buses. This book is Mo's account of that exciting, frustrating, but ultimately rewarding year. It is a detailed narrative of their daily life, accompanied by descriptions of their childhood, spent in a small town in Michigan with parents and a brother and another sister who was often less than sympathetic to her retarded sibling.

Mary Fran had been working in Michigan in a sheltered workshop and living at home with her mother. Always an agreeable, cooperative family member, although given to spells of hyperactivity and sometimes to dawdling, Mary Fran had suddenly become rebellious, uncooperative, and temperamental. She was bored, resentful, and acutely aware of her "difference." She had become tired of a long schoolbus ride, accompanied primarily by youngsters, to a sheltered workshop where she spent the day sanding wood, and she was tired of weekends spent at home alone with her mother since the other family members were now away. Her father had died years earlier.

Seattle, chosen partly because their brother lived there, was Maureen's effort to find a solution to Mary Fran's problems, and she took a year off from college to devote full time to this endeavor. Although both of their efforts at job hunting were only marginally successful, and although the institutional and societal barriers raised to people who are retarded were just as evident in Seattle as in a small town in Michigan, the year was productive. Mary Fran's social skills improved remarkably along with her ability to handle the details of everyday living. At the end of the year, Mary Fran returned to Michigan to live in a group home and to attend a vocational training program that was more suitable for her than the sheltered workshop had been. Maureen transferred from a midwestern college to a university in New York City, worked in a group home after she graduated, and later took graduate work in special education at Columbia University.

Analysis. This is a warm, relaxed, funny narrative. It is also courageous, revealing, and touching. Above all, it is real. It is living in Seattle with Mary Fran and Mo for a year. It is living with the agony of the family every Sunday when they take Mary Fran back to the residential school that she attended for some years. It is being frightened when Mary Fran disappears and being relieved when she reappears. It is being furious with the callousness of bureaucracies that deal with people who are disabled, and furious with the attitudes of people toward those who are mentally retarded.

In the course of this story, Mary Fran becomes a vividly real person who is both different because of her mental retardation and also very like any young woman who wants to have a life of her own. One of Maureen's Seattle friends jokes with her about her tendency to give frequent "The Mentally Retarded Are People, Too" lectures. The book is not didactic, but it is a living illustration of that fact.

Mary Fran and Mo might be particularly recommended for siblings of disabled youth. It addresses many family issues honestly and thoroughly.

Meyers, Robert. *Like Normal People.* New York: McGraw-Hill, 1978. Illus. 203 pp. Reading Level: Grades 10–12.
Disability: Mental retardation

Robert Meyers is a reporter for the *Washington Post,* which in August of 1977 printed his three articles about the wedding of his retarded brother and sister-in-law and the journey that had brought them to that point. *Like Normal People* grew out of these articles. It describes and analyzes the experiences of Roger Meyers and Virginia Hensler and their families, interweaving the personal stories with a history of the treatment of mentally retarded people. Both Roger and Virginia are mildly retarded and both received an education, although in very different settings. Neither Roger's parents nor Virginia's mother listened to medical opinions, which advised them to put their children in institutions, and both families struggled to help their children develop as fully as possible and to find appropriate living arrangements for them as they grew up. They met in the residential facility in California where both had gone to live. At the time of the writing of this book, they had been married for a few months and were living in their own apartment with assistance when necessary from a counselor; Roger was working as a busboy, a job he found for himself and had held for some time, and Virginia was preparing herself for hotel work.

Each chapter is headed by one of Roger's poems. Meyers includes in an appendix a list of state associations for retarded children.

Analysis. Meyers has written an engrossing, moving, and informative book. He is able to look at his subject with both an engaged heart and an objective mind; he describes himself and his family honestly, acknowledging both frailty and strength, conveying love and admiration.

Roger was born in 1948, Virginia in 1951. Their lifetimes have seen enormous changes in the treatment of mental retardation; Meyers documents these changes with full but never overwhelming detail, as, for example, in the section on "normalization" and on the work of Niels Erik Bank-Mikkersen, Bengt Nirje, and Wolf Wolfensberger.

This book explores a relatively new living arrangement for disabled young people who until recently were discouraged from marriage and independent living. Not only is it highly recommended for unimpaired young readers, but it could be used judiciously with disabled young people contemplating a similar move.

The attractive photographs add to the text.

Murray, Dorothy Garst. *This Is Stevie's Story*. Nashville: Abingdon, 1967. 192 pp. Reading Level: Grades 10–12.
Disability: Mental retardation

The author's son Stevie was born in 1945. For two years, his parents noticed nothing particularly amiss; Stevie's development seemed slow, but they ascribed this to normal differences. Gradually, they became aware that all was not well, and when their son was four they were told that he was mentally retarded. At that time, there was very little information available for parents to read, and there were no training facilities within commuting distance of their home in Roanoke, Virginia.

When Stevie was seven, his parents brought him to the Lynchburg State Training School and Hospital, about 50 miles from their home. This decision, painfully arrived at, was reached because they realized that they could not meet Stevie's needs at home and that his sometimes difficult behavior put unbearable burdens on their three other children. Stevie lived at the school for the next 14 years, except for holidays and vacations. When he was 21, he had developed so much that his parents brought him home, where he was able to do simple jobs on their apple farm.

Because of the experience of having Stevie, the Murrays became active in national and local associations for retarded children. The author includes advice and suggestions for other parents who face similar situations. She concludes with a list of state associations for retarded children.

Analysis. Murray writes movingly and honestly about the heartache of recognizing that a beloved child is retarded. She is specific in the material addressed to parents. This book is also interesting in what it shows about the changes that have occurred since 1945. Some of Murray's language—her use of words like *retardates* and *defectives*—is not considered acceptable today.

This book takes a positive view of institutionalization, and might therefore be particularly useful for a family faced with this circumstance.

Ominsky, Elaine. *Jon O.: A Special Boy*. Photog. by Dennis Simonetti. Englewood Cliffs, N.J.: Prentice-Hall, 1977. unp. Reading Level: Grades K–3.
Disability: Down's syndrome

Jon O.'s parents were told at the time of his birth that their baby would always be different from other children. The book describes the ways in which Jon differs and also the ways in which he is the same as his brothers and his classmates. The simple text is illustrated with photographs on every page: Jon is shown at school, building a fort with his brothers, eating birthday cake, sharing a picture book, embracing his teacher. The last picture shows Jon smiling in evident self-satisfaction, with the words "Jon O. is a very special boy."

Analysis. This is a good introduction to Down's syndrome for very young children. The author does not flinch from using words like *retarded* or indicating that other children sometimes find Jon's speech and behavior bizarre. The text seems to imply that Jon attends an ordinary school; if this is so, it would be helpful to have it made clear. This is a book to be shared by adult and child, for the young reader may very well have questions and anxieties that go beyond the text. For example, although the author states that Jon's body and brain will not grow normally, she is not explicit about the ways in which his physical development differs from that of normal children.

Roberts, Nancy. *David.* Photog. by Bruce Roberts. Richmond, Va.: Knox, 1968. 72 pp. Reading Level: Grades 7–12.
Disability: Down's syndrome

Within a few days of his birth, David Roberts was diagnosed as having Down's syndrome. He was a healthy infant, without the cardiac complications that sometimes accompany the syndrome. His parents went through stages of shock and questioning, but were able before too long to accept David as he was and to rejoice in his progress, at whatever pace it occurred. Roberts credits the Association for Retarded Children in Charlotte, North Carolina, with giving them support and help, including reading material.

Her book takes David up to the age of four. His IQ is somewhere above 50 and he functions on a level of from two and a half to three and a half years. He is going to a nursery program for retarded children and will attend special education classes provided by the public school system.

Bruce Roberts, David's father, is a professional photographer, and the book is liberally illustrated with black-and-white pictures. The appendix has a bibliography and a list of associations that can provide resource material.

Analysis. Roberts's text is clear and competent, although tenses could be more consistent. Her love for and acceptance of David are obvious, as is her strong religious faith. The most outstanding feature of the book is the photographs.

David is an attractive, responsive, lively little boy, and the pictures show him in a variety of activities. The book could be enjoyed by siblings and classmates of retarded youngsters as well as by young readers interested in exploring careers in work with mentally disabled people.

Rogers, Dale Evans. *Angel Unaware*. Westwood, N.J.: Revell, 1953. 63 pp. Reading Level: Grades 7–12.
Disability: Down's syndrome

Actress-singer Dale Evans Rogers and her husband, western star Roy Rogers, were the parents of Robin, born with Down's syndrome and a number of health problems associated with it, which at that time were difficult to treat. Rogers recounts her daughter's brief years of life, very much a part of her loving family; the Rogerses also had older children, who quickly became attached to gentle, placid, smiling Robin. After two short years, Robin's heart and respiratory abnormalities proved too much for her body to handle, and she died.

Analysis. This is a sentimental and personal story. Rogers, who is deeply religious, felt that Robin brought a spiritual, heavenly quality into the family and that this had been the purpose of her short life. The dual themes are coping with disability and coping with death. This early book has become something of a classic in the genre.

Sobol, Harriet Langsam. *My Brother Steven Is Retarded*. Photog. by Patricia Agre. New York: Macmillan, 1977. 26 pp. Reading Level: Grades 4–6.
Disability: Brain injury

Eleven-year-old Beth talks about her older brother, Steven, who is severely retarded as the result of brain injury at birth. The focus of the book is on Beth's feelings, good and bad. She describes his appearance and behavior and her own reactions and worries, as well as those of others. She talks about her embarrassment, sadness, and anger in response to Steven, and her fear that retardation is catching. She acknowledges that she is glad not to be the one who is retarded. One resolution worked out in the book is the children's mutual pride when Steven learned to spell his name out loud. Another resolution is acceptance: "They [the children's parents] say we will always be sad about it, but there really is nothing anyone can do to change it." The final resolution is Beth's understanding about her brother's probable future and a wish for his happiness.

Large black-and-white photographs of the children in candid shots illustrate every spread.

Analysis. The sensitive and honest text, written by a woman whose eldest child is retarded, captures Beth's voice and her ambivalence toward her brother. It is unusual in that its focus is almost completely on feelings, a welcome change from the objective, cognitive approach of so many books for young children. Beth's narrative addresses some profound truths that are frequently glossed over in more upbeat, optimistic books. Although the book is short, it manages to touch on many points; the language is appropriate for primary school children, but the information and attitudes conveyed make it a good introduction to the subject for older readers, particularly since Beth herself is 11 years old. The family's caring, gentleness, and honesty as portrayed in both text and pictures foster a positive as well as realistic attitude toward the subject of severe retardation.

Speech and Language Impairments

Berger, Gilda. *Speech and Language Disorders.* Illus. New York: Franklin Watts, 1981. 87 pp. Reading Level: Grades 7–12.
Disability: Stuttering and other language disorders

Berger begins by discussing prehistoric origins of speech. She gives examples of speech and language disorders and explains how speech is produced. Chapters discuss specific conditions such as stuttering, unpleasant voices, speech and language difficulties, and multiple difficulties.

The text is illustrated with black-and-white photographs showing how people speak, hear, and interpret sounds. The book ends with a glossary, a list of speech organizations, a short bibliography, titles for suggested reading, and an index.

Analysis. The author, a professional writer, presents her material in clear prose and short chapters, illustrating concepts with specific cases. Several chapters end with brief summaries of the material. The attractive photographs show children being tested and working with speech and language therapists. The book could be easily understood by middle-school readers and might also be a useful introduction to the subject for high school students.

Browning, Elizabeth. *I Can't See What You're Saying.* New York: Coward, 1973. 198 pp. Reading Level: Grades 10–12.
Disability: Aphasia

Elizabeth Browning is an Englishwoman. Her son Freddy was born 10 weeks prematurely and delivered by Caesarean section; he had to stay in the hospital for the first 13 weeks of his life. A fat, cheerful baby, he was slow to sit up, walk, and talk; even his two older sisters noticed that he did not answer their calls. After his parents recognized that his development was not progressing normally, they began a search for diagnosis and treatment. The first expert said he must be deaf, another said, "highly intelligent but not deaf," still another that if he did not speak by the age of three and a half, it was unlikely that he ever would. His family, particularly his mother, had developed non-verbal means of communication with him, but Freddy was increasingly frustrated by his inability to make his wants known. Finally, when he was three, he was interviewed at a residential special school where the parents were told, "This is a straightforward case of aphasia and he must come to us when he is five" (p. 27). (Aphasia is described as the inability to use words as symbols.)

Finding the appropriate education for Freddy was as difficult as getting a diagnosis. First he went to a nursery school for normal children, then to the residential special school for three and a half years; it was an excellent school, and Freddy did learn to talk and made some academic progress. Subsequent school placements, usually dictated by edicts of the school system and by the fact that often there was no facility equipped to meet his needs, were very uneven in quality. His father, a schoolteacher, and his mother were indefatigable in their efforts to find the programs that would be best for him, that would help him make the most of his intelligence and give him the greatest chance to become independent. His parents frequently met with frustration. They tried education in public and private schools, special and regular, in a residential tutorial arrangement, and at home by private tutors and by his parents. Over and over, the Brownings found that neither medical nor education professionals really listened to what they said about their son or looked at Freddy realistically, although there were, of course, exceptions. The combination of partial hearing loss and aphasia made verbal communication erratic and idiosyncratic, as demonstrated by a sample of Freddy's letters.

In addition to seeking the most appropriate education, the Brownings also tried to give Freddy other experiences, for example, skiing, sailing, and horseback riding. He comes across as a thoroughly engaging youngster. As he grew into his teens, his parents became increasingly anxious about his future. Eventually, Freddy decided that he would like to try blacksmithing, and after a seemingly endless effort to find the right place, and one abortive job, his father located a young smith in a village 25 miles from home who was willing to take Freddy on. At the end of the book, Freddy is happy in his new life, learning the farrier's trade, and living independently in lodgings during the work week.

In the course of their long search for support in raising Freddy, the

Brownings came into contact with many people, including a writer who described their experience in an article in the *New Statesman*, which in turn brought contacts with other parents. The foreword is written by O. L. Zangwill, professor of experimental psychology at the University of Cambridge; a note on aphasia at the end is contributed by Pauline Griffiths, formerly Senior Speech Therapist, Invalid Children's Aid Association.

Analysis. Browning writes with insight, a kind of rueful humor, and controlled passion. Granted that Freddy's condition—possibly the result of brain damage—was baffling and difficult, still the Brownings often met unnecessary obstacles in the form of rigid authorities and cold professionals. On the other hand, some of the people whom they consulted were helpful, as were their families and friends.

Cameron, Constance Carpenter. *A Different Drum.* Englewood Cliffs, N.J.: Prentice-Hall, 1973. 241 pp. Reading Level: Grades 10–12.
Disability: Aphasia

Evan was the Cameron's third child, born after a normal pregnancy and delivery, a beautiful and healthy baby; there are two daughters, six and seven years older than Evan. As a toddler, he had increasingly frequent tantrums; his speech development was slow and he sometimes echoed what was said to him. The pediatrician who saw him at two and a half said he was hanging onto immaturity because his family spoiled him and gave him no incentive to become independent; the doctor recommended nursery school, and after initial tears and tantrums, Evan seemed to enjoy this. His mother noticed other unconventional behaviors besides limited speech, such as insistence on ritual and an odd interest in smelling everything he met for the first time. He was also unable to sit still and concentrate long enough to have a story read to him.

When the doctor saw him at three, he thought the child might be retarded. Shocked and appalled, the Camerons took Evan to be tested by Thomas Ward, psychologist at the Orange County (California) Children's Hospital; Ward diagnosed severe developmental aphasia, certainly receptive and possibly expressive, and probable visual-motor impairment. Later the Camerons took Evan to Merl Carson, a pediatric neurologist, who confirmed Ward's diagnosis and advised structure and orderliness at home, an electroencephalogram, a hearing test, a speech evaluation, medication, a play group, and therapy to be followed by special schooling. The Camerons were convinced that Evan was not mentally retarded, whatever his other impairments, and although the doctor pointed out that there was as yet no way to measure his intelligence, he agreed that the parents might be right.

Armed with all the information she could gather in her own research plus the determination that Evan would make it, Constance Cameron began an intensive program of home education for her son. She worked with him every day, devising lessons and materials as she went along. While she took care to make their sessions enjoyable, she was firm in her insistence that Evan join her in whatever she had planned. She had to teach him by conscious effort nearly everything that children without impairments learn effortlessly, even how to ask a question. "It was like programming a computer," she writes. "Evan's brain, or at least the part of it I was working with, seemed completely separate from Evan himself. I had to program this portion of his mind, feed into it all necessary information and set up certain connections in order to make the system operational. Evan's personality was in no way integrated with this system any more than it was with his hand or foot" (p. 104).

The epilogue tells the reader that Cameron's program plus outside therapy have carried Evan to the point where, at eight, he is enrolled in the aphasia program in the neighborhood school district, working in a class with children 18 months older than he; he is at the normal academic level.

Analysis. Cameron's book is an extremely detailed description of the program she developed. Clearly and authoritatively, she tells Evan's story. She knows that some of the professionals who saw Evan thought that she was self-deceived in her insistence that he could perform certain tasks and that he was not mentally impaired; ultimately, as Evan gave up the disguises he had adopted as self-protection, these people came to see what she saw. In telling this she is neither hostile to professionals nor self-congratulatory. The reader, and indeed everyone who worked with Evan, comes to share her sense of triumph. The book would be of interest to young people contemplating work with neurologically impaired children as well as to those with personal experience in this area.

Evans, James S. *An Uncommon Gift.* Philadelphia: Westminster, 1983. 180 pp. Reading Level: Grades 7–12.
Disability: Hyperkinesia, Stuttering

The author was born in 1959, the youngest of four children. As a baby and small child, he was extremely active and restless, unable to sit still, and experienced difficulty in relaxing and falling asleep. Large for his age, he was clumsy and poorly coordinated. From about the ages of eight to ten, he stole money from his parents and did a little shoplifting, activities that he himself later recognized as a call for help. In third grade his parents took him for extensive testing that revealed his problems: perceptual difficulties and hyperkinesia, learning disabilities compounded by moderate stuttering. Supported by his loving and understanding parents and helped by the advice and training of professionals, such as the doctor who made the diagnosis and the woman who tutored him, Evans was able to develop discipline and learning strategies to meet his academic challenges. He attended both public and private schools in his native California and in Washington, D.C., where his parents moved when he was in junior high. Once he understood the source of his difficulties and was able to manage them, Evans not only handled his academic schedule but began to participate in sports and dramatics. After high school, he attended Wooster College in Ohio and at the time of the writing of this book he was a seminary student.

Evans describes not only his academic struggles but also his psychological difficulties; these he understood and began to resolve much later than his learning disabilities. By the end of the book, he has come a long way in understanding and dealing with his anger, as well as with his need to dominate, which has spoiled some of his relationships, particularly with women. He has also begun to establish newly close ties with his siblings. Evans is a devout Christian and has found comfort and strength in his faith.

The book ends with an epilogue of short contributions by the author's parents, brothers, and sister.

Analysis. Like other first-person accounts of learning disabilities such as Susan Hampshire's story (see this chapter under Learning Disabilities), *An Uncommon Gift* offers valuable insights into the frustrations and confusion experienced by a child growing up with these problems. Evans describes the techniques used by the teachers who were most successful in helping him, as well as strategies he developed himself, such as gathering information through the spoken word rather than through print. With honesty and without self-pity, he writes about the effect of his disability on his personality and his relationships. While he asserts his Christian faith early in the book and refers to his religious experiences at intervals throughout, he does not assume the voice of the proselytizer.

This account will be of most interest to the young person who has similar problems and also to his or her parents and siblings. A recurrent theme in such books is the child's feelings of isolation and confusion, a sense of being set apart by something mysteriously askew, and then the relief of learning that he or she is not to blame for the condition nor the only one to experience it.

Helfman, Elizabeth. *Blissymbolics*. Illus. New York: Elsevier/Nelson, 1982. 152 pp. Reading Level: Grades 7–12.
Disability: Inability to speak

Blissymbolics is a system of graphic symbols logically designed for communication among nonverbal people. Not based on any special language, it can be used across language groups. It was developed by Charles Bliss, an Austrian who eventually emigrated to Australia, after release from Hitler's death camps.

After years of studying languages, Bliss conceived of his pictographs as a way of bringing peace to the world. Actually, however, the main use has been for disabled people who are nonspeaking and those around them. Many examples are given of young people and their friends who have easily mastered the system, and many are pictured in black-and-white photographs. In a chapter called "Other Ways," computer-assisted language production, even that used with the chimpanzee Lana, is explained.

Analysis. This is the second book that Helfman has written about language. Her first, *Signs and Symbols around the World* (Lothrop, Lee & Shepard, 1967), devoted some pages to the work of Charles Bliss as well. Her prose is direct and her illustrations and photographs are helpful, both for learning the graphic system and for understanding its utility for nonverbal people.

There is disagreement among professionals on the advisability of teaching a language system that differs from one's native language, as is obvious in the controversy over American Sign Language. Helfman offers a strong case for Blissymbolics, and her presentation makes the system seem interesting enough to intrigue speaking children to master it for conversation with disabled peers.

Pizer, Vernon. *You Don't Say: How People Communicate without Speech*. Illus. by Janet McCaffery. New York: Putnam, 1978. 95 pp. Reading Level: Grades 7–12.
Disability: Mutism, Hearing and visual impairments

Early in the book, Pizer discusses pasimology, the science of communication by gesture. He describes Amer-Ind, the system of communication based on universal American Indian hand talk developed by part Iroquois Madge Skelly, who is a professor of communication disorders and of community medicine. Amer-Ind is a speech system for people who, although they can hear, have lost the power to speak. Pizer then moves on to communication systems used by people with hearing impairment and the work done at Gallaudet College. In the last chapter he describes Braille's invention of an alphabet for the blind.

Black-and-white prints head every chapter. There is an index.

Analysis. Although this book is about nonspeaking communication in general, Chapters 3 and 7 are of particular interest to those wanting information about communication available to people with hearing, speech, and visual impairments. The text is clear and readable and the illustrations attractive.

8

Books Dealing with Multiple/Severe and Various Disabilities

This chapter contains titles classified in two sections: Multiple/Severe Disabilities, dealing with people each of whom has several significant disabilities, and Various Disabilities, containing collective biographies of people who have different disabilities.

■ Citations are alphabetical by author in each section.

Multiple/Severe Disabilities

Browne, Helene. *Yesterday's Child*. Philadelphia: Lippincott, 1977. 209 pp. Reading Level: Grades: 10–12.
Disability: Cerebral palsy, Deafness, Mental retardation

This story chronicles the interlocking lives of the author and her daughter. The mother's life is detailed from the time she is a young and impossibly romantic teenager through maturity in middle age as a contented and fulfilled parent and career woman. Her catalyst to change and growth was always her daughter Karen, her first child, born to her at age 20. Her love, anxiety, and agony over her deaf, cerebral palsied, and mentally retarded child form the fulcrum of her life. The reader gains a few insights regarding the author's highly successful career as an interior designer and editor. She was constantly striving in order to pay for the right, always elusive, treatment and education she sought for her daughter. The book ends when Karen is an adult living in a special facility. Her brother has graduated from college and their mother has found peace and fulfillment.

Analysis. The author writes in a simple, honest, and compelling style. Most of the events in the book relate to the needs of her daughter. They illustrate the frustration the family of a severely disabled child must bear—the strain (here fatal) on the marriage, the

291

constant and often unrewarding care, the countless efforts of professionals and friends, the unfeeling bureaucracy of social agencies, and the unending financial burden. The book also explores the particular problems of a woman coming from a traditional family outlook trying to reconcile the demands of motherhood (including a normal son), divorce, and a challenging career. The book ends on an optimistic but realistic note.

Carson, Mary. *Ginny: A True Story.* New York: Doubleday, 1972. 215 pp. Reading Level: Grades 7–12.
Disability: Blindness, Orthopedic/neurological impairment

Carson, Ginny's mother, writes of her daughter's rehabilitation after a truck hit her, causing fractures on both sides of the skull that left her paralyzed and blind. Physicians performed surgery immediately, but afterward told Carson that Ginny would not survive the night. Despite this gloomy prognosis, the child did live. Carson recounts her daughter's slow recovery, aided by deep religious faith and excellent medical care. The large family of seven children was close and loving, and good neighbors helped with the home and child care tasks during this difficult and extended period.

Analysis. This account of a child's struggle to live and reenter the mainstream of life should hold appeal for teenagers who like inspiring stories. Both the mother's faith and determination and the daughter's will to live a full life are pivotal features of this book.

Haggai, John Edmund. *My Son Johnny.* Illus. Wheaton, Ill.: Tyndale, 1978. 238 pp. Reading Level: Grades 7–12.
Disability: Congenital neurological impairment

John Haggai, Jr., was born after a protracted and difficult labor. The doctor, apparently drunk by the time he appeared at the hospital, bungled the delivery, which should probably have been accomplished hours earlier by Caesarian section. As a result of the delay and/or "inept procedure during delivery," the baby was born with extensive injuries and was not expected to live. Once he did, his mother devoted almost her entire attention to him for the 24 years of his life. Haggai writes repeatedly about the extent of his wife's devotion to their son. He could neither walk nor talk, except for two sounds indicating yes and no; he had no control of bodily functions, could swallow only soft food, and had continual digestive and respiratory problems. Yet he could laugh and had a well-developed sense of humor; he had acute hearing and expressive eyes, and used them to communicate. The book describes Johnny's life and its relation to his parents' Christian belief and his father's evangelical mission.

Analysis: John Haggai is an evangelical Baptist preacher. Although he describes the human errors that caused his son's extensive impairment, he believes that Johnny's condition was part of God's plan. The child's disability, together with the force of his personality and spirit, affected his parents profoundly and, Haggai feels, increased the power of his own evangelical work. He has preached both in the United States and abroad, with particular emphasis on missions to the third world, and Johnny often accompanied his parents to religious meetings. The book is testimony to the effect of loving, devoted care in giving value to a life that many would have deemed valueless. Readers who do not share the author's religious orientation may find this aspect of the book out of balance.

Jones, Ron. *The Acorn People.* Illus. Nashville: Abingdon, 1978. 77 pp. Reading Level: Grades 10–12.
Disability: Complex physical and medical problems

This is the first of several books Jones was to write about his adventures as a maverick teacher. Here, he has taken an assignment to be a counselor in a camp with a group of children with complex physical and medical problems. (The title of the book is taken from the name of the club they formed, which had as its badge necklaces made of acorns.)

At first Jones could not see beyond the twisted, contorted bodies of his young charges, but as they began to live together in the outdoors, sharing simple pleasures such as the campfire, Jones came to see the inner loveliness of the children. The culmination of the book is an adventure that serves as a metaphor. The little troop had decided to climb a mountain. Even the most disabled child struggled and finally reached the top.

An epilogue tells us that all of these children died within the next several years. However, their joy and triumph in the summer they spent together would always stay in Jones's heart.

Analysis. Jones is an especially graphic author who writes in a deeply affecting manner. The lesson he learned and communicates is that it is not disability or length of days that is important, but the quality of life and the ability to love and share.

The camp situation should be of interest to schoolchildren, and a good reader in middle school might enjoy the book as well as older youth.

Kupfer, Fern. *Before & After Zachariah: A Family Story about a Different Kind of Courage.* New York: Delacorte, 1982. 241 pp. Reading Level: Grades 10–12.
Disability: Degenerative brain disorder

Fern and Joe Kupfer's son Zachariah was born in April 1976, after a pregnancy uneventful except for some unexplained bleeding in the early months. Like their daughter, then four, he was born by Caesarean section. He was a fussy baby who cried a lot, needed to be carried constantly, and had trouble eating; he was beautiful but slow to develop. His worried parents took him for tests, which confirmed what they had suspected: "delayed development, etiology unknown."

The summer after Zach's first birthday, his parents took him from their home in Iowa to the Neuro Developmental Therapy Program in Virginia; they divided the weeks of the program between them. It was there, Fern Kupfer writes, that she understood that she "could not take care of Zach for the next fifteen, ten, even five years. I realized it because of what my body was telling me" (p. 79).

Joe Kupfer is a philosophy professor; Fern Kupfer teaches English part-time at a community college. They did everything they could to stimulate Zach at home and to arrange therapy programs. They were able to hire a woman to help with Zach, and they took turns in caring for him so that each would have time for professional demands and for their other child, a bright, charming little girl. They also were occasionally able to arrange respite care.

Zach was an attractive child who responded minimally with smiles and sounds, and both parents clearly loved him. Nevertheless, they came to realize that the strains imposed by Zach's needs on their marriage, their family life, and their personalities were unbearable, and that things could only get worse. Eventually, they were able to find a good residential facility in Dubuque, four hours' drive from their home, and they placed Zach there when he was two years and four months old. The care he received was excellent; the Kupfers could visit him and bring him home for weekends. However, after a while his condition began to deteriorate, and tests and examination revealed that he had a degenerative brain disorder found in children whose parents are Jewish with families who came from Vilna, in Lithuania.

Fern Kupfer first wrote her story for the *Redbook* "Young Mother" series. When this book was published, Zach was five years old, blind, even more severely disabled, but still able to smile whenever he heard his father's voice.

Analysis. Fern Kupfer has written a searing, passionate book. With the trend toward deinstitutionalization, new pressures and new burdens of guilt have been placed on parents who, for whatever reasons, have to make the bitter decision to have their disabled children live apart from them. She weaves into her book the stories of some of the other women and children she met at the therapy program in Virginia, and each chapter is headed with a quotation from another parent. She speaks not only for her family but for all who face the challenge and burden of a Zachariah, who have to search to find humane facilities for their children and then fight to get them in.

This book could be read by young people interested in social attitudes toward and provisions for disabled children, as well as by the siblings of such children, particularly if the family has chosen institutional placement. Families who have genetic disorders might particularly appreciate Kupfer's honesty about the causes of Zach's condition and her ability to accept without guilt the vagaries of heredity.

Kupfer calls her book *Before & After Zachariah;* actually, much of the emphasis is on the two years and four months that Zach lived at home. Whatever the title, she has been able to share her family's experience in a beautifully written book that has moments of humor and joy as well as pain and grief.

Linedecker, Clifford, with Michael Ryan and Maureen Ryan. *Kerry: Agent Orange and an American Family.* Illus. New York: St. Martin's, 1982. 240 pp. Reading Level: Grades 10–12.
Disability: Multiple abnormalities

Maureen and Michael Ryan's daughter Kerry was born in January 1971. Maureen's pregnancy had been normal, and the first sign of abnormality was the excess loss of fluid that immediately preceded delivery. Michael Ryan's mother was an experienced obstetrical nurse who was on duty when Maureen came to the hospital; she was the first to suspect difficulty. After hours of labor, Kerry was born, weighing barely five pounds. Her right arm was missing a bone, she had no rectum, she had a heart problem, and she was critically ill. Later, more disabilities would be revealed. The baby had an improperly formed ureter, and one hand, attached to what should have been her elbow, was missing the thumb and had contracted fingers. The heart problem was a tear in the septum. Her sacrum—the lower portion of the spine—was underdeveloped. She also had digestive difficulties. When she was 18 months old, an embolism followed surgery and did neurological damage; she was in a coma and appeared to be blind, but contrary to the doctors' expectations, she regained consciousness and eventually her sight returned, as did some bodily control. After the next surgery, there were more complications, and then still more abnormalities were discovered—a neurogenic bladder, two vaginas, two cervixes, two uteruses, four ovaries. Still more operations followed.

Through all this, the Ryans refused to give up. Supported by their large family, encouraged by Kerry's own tenacity, they persisted in their struggle. At three, Kerry went to a rehabilitation center, at six to a local school.

In addition to being Kerry's story, this is an account of Michael Ryan's military service in Vietnam, where he was exposed to Agent Orange (which contains dioxin), and his subsequent health problems. He had a chronic skin disorder, intolerance of alcohol, migraine headaches, hearing loss, and what was called a nervous condition. He also discovered that exposure to the sun caused dots to appear on his skin, a further sign of dioxin poisoning and a warning that too much sun could cause skin cancer.

In 1976, Maureen Ryan began to suspect that both Kerry's abnormalities and her husband's health problems were connected to Agent Orange. She read widely on the subject and became convinced that she was right; eventually, she persuaded her husband of this. The Ryans will never take the chance of having another child. When they realized that the government had known about the danger, they were shattered. They became active in Agent Orange Victims International, and in 1979 joined 19 other couples as plaintiffs in a class-action product-liability suit against Dow Chemical Company and five other companies that had manufactured defoliants and herbicides used in Vietnam. In 1980, the chemical companies filed motions to implicate the government as a third party. If the veterans won, the suit said, the government should reimburse the companies. The huge and complex suit had still not been resolved at the time of the writing of this book. [Authors' note: The suit was decided in favor of the plaintiffs in 1984, although not for the amount sought.]

Kerry ends in 1981. Orthopedic specialists examining her discovered still more abnormalities—scoliosis, an internal form of spinal bifida, and missing sacrum and coccyx bones. The Ryans planned, at the settlement of the suit, to buy or build a specially designed house and van to give Kerry more mobility and control.

There is a selected bibliography of books, magazines, pamphlets, and papers. Appendix A gives the testimony of Christopher H. Johnson to the Congressional Subcommittee on Medical Facilities and Benefits, July 22, 1980. Johnson was speaking for himself and for other Vietnam veterans and their families injured by exposure to Agent

Orange. Appendix B gives the testimony of Maureen Ryan and of Frank McCarthy, national chairman of Agent Orange Victims International, before the U.S. Senate Committee on Veterans Affairs. Appendix C is a directory of the Veterans Leadership Conference, its members and supporters, and the membership list of the National Veterans Task Force on Agent Orange. There is also an index.

Analysis. The Ryans are people of dogged courage and persistence. Linedecker tells their story, and through them the extended story of the medical, legal, political, and social results of Agent Orange, in a book that is at once informal in tone and formidable in its clear presentation of the facts supporting the central argument. The Ryans, hardworking, patriotic young people, feel betrayed by their government, and readers may share their fierce anger. Kerry as a patient is more central to the book than is Kerry as a person.

Rosenberg, Maxine B. *My Friend Leslie: The Story of a Handicapped Child.* Photog. by George Ancona. New York: Lothrop, 1983. Unp. Reading Level: Grades K–3.
Disability: Hearing, muscular, visual impairments

Leslie Parson is a multiply handicapped child with visual and hearing impairments, cleft palate, muscular problems, and ptosis (drooping) of the eyelids. The narrator, Karin, is Leslie's fellow-student in a kindergarten where Leslie is the only disabled child. Karin explains Leslie's physical problems and describes the way in which she copes with them, but she also tells about the ordinary pleasures and experiences the girls share. The photographs fill a large portion of every spread; text is printed in big letters. A postscript gives details about Leslie's impairments, their causes (unknown) and treatment, and her present condition. At the time of writing she was in third grade.

Analysis. Karin's matter-of-fact voice sets the tone for this informative, perceptive book, and the outstanding black-and-white photographs vividly enhance the text. One picture shows Leslie leaning so close to Karin in an effort to see her that the two giggle as they clunk heads. Another shows them telling secrets behind the bookshelves, because if they whisper out in the classroom, Leslie cannot hear. Leslie's sturdy independence and her comic flair come through. So does her angry frustration when she cannot hear the piano at music time and her unhappy isolation when she cannot see the animals on a class trip to a nature center. This book is highly recommended for all children, and especially for primary classes that include both disabled and nondisabled students.

Schaefer, Nicola. *Does She Know She's There?* New York: Double-day, 1978. 235 pp. Reading Level: Grades 10–12.
Disability: Cerebral palsy, Mental retardation

Nicola Schaefer's first child, Catherine, was born in 1961. In her early months, the baby screamed almost incessantly. She seemed to be developing very slowly, and Schaefer, no longer able to accept her pediatrician's reassurances, took her to a child development specialist, who said bluntly, "I suggest you go home, put this baby in an institu-tion and have another" (p. 10). Catherine, he said, was grossly abnor-mal, had cerebral palsy, a neuromuscular disorder, and extensive brain damage, and would never walk or talk.

Schaefer was a young Englishwoman living in Winnipeg, Canada, with her Canadian husband, a scientist. They refused to institutional-ize their daughter. Once she had gotten over the initial shock, Schaefer decided that she would accept and enjoy Catherine for what she was, take life a step at a time, and make it impossible for anyone to pity the family. On a visit to her family in England, she took the baby to a clinic in Edinburgh where a doctor, more sympathetic than the Canadian specialist, explained the child's condition more fully and told her that physiotherapy and as much stimulation as possible were the only things that might be done for Catherine. Winnipeg offered almost nothing in the way of services for such children. Over the next years Schaefer managed the care of her daughter plus two able-bodied younger sons, using ingenuity, strength, and love, and support by family and friends. Although severely and multiply handicapped, Catherine learned to sit up and to feed herself with a spoon. She showed a sense of humor and was a happy child; her limited mental capacity prevented her from understanding her own situation.

Sometimes the parents were able to leave Catherine in the special ward of a Catholic hospital while they traveled. Eventually, they were able to locate a special class for her and to get specially designed equipment for her. Schaefer and other parents became involved in a group fighting to build a center for their disabled children so that they could remain in the community, but as the book ends they have met with a discouraging lack of receptiveness and understanding at high government levels.

Analysis. Schaefer writes very well, in a fast-moving, breezy style and with keen powers of observation and description. She wastes no time in self-pity, although she is honest about the difficulties of caring for Catherine, her fears about the future, her own occasional emotional outbursts, and the hypochondria that developed once she began to worry about what would happen to Catherine if she were to die. Cath-

erine herself comes across as charming and lovable. Avoiding sentimentality, Schaefer can make the child's hoots of laughter and smiles
of recognition and pleasure as meaningful as the higher level communication of a youngster with language and physical movement at her
command. The book not only pictures a severely disabled child and her
family, but, in the last section, narrates a community effort.

Various Disabilities

Adams, Barbara. *Like It Is: Facts and Feelings about Handicaps from
Kids Who Know.* Photog. by James Stanfield. New York: Walker,
1979. 96 pp. Reading Level: Grades 7–9.
Disability: Various

In six chapters, Adams and Stanfield look at hearing and speech,
visual and orthopedic impairments (they use the word *handicaps* here),
developmental disabilities and mental retardation, learning disabilities,
and behavior disorders. An introduction discusses the words *handicap*
and *disability* and common misconceptions about both. Each chapter
opens with expository material about the particular condition, printed
in italic type. A first-person narrative by an individual youngster follows. A 13-year-old boy has been deaf from birth, and Toni, an eighth-
grader, was born without sight. Jed has Legg-Perthes Disease, a condition he will grow out of; his section also includes descriptions of a boy
with peroneal muscular atrophy, a girl with cerebral palsy, and a boy
who wears a prosthesis to substitute for his amputated lower leg. One
narrator who is mildly retarded discusses a young woman with
Down's syndrome and a boy with cerebral palsy. A boy with a learning
disability talks of his perceptual handicap as well as other types of
learning impairment. In the last chapter, on behavior disorders, three
youngsters are described in the third person by the author: One lives
in a frightening, distorted world, one feels left out and depressed, and
one is very angry. Following these sketches, their school principal discusses their situations and some of the measures being taken to help
them.

Each two-page spread is illustrated with black-and-white photographs; a glossary of terms concludes the book.

Analysis. Text and pictures go a long way toward explaining the
impairments discussed. In some places, the reader may want more information than is given: for example, what is the cause of Toni's visual
impairment and is her world totally dark? (The latter question is raised
in the introduction and never answered.) One might question whether

the words of the young narrators are in fact completely authentic; more likely, they have been edited. However, this does not detract from the essential worth of the book as a valid presentation of impairing conditions and of individuals who are shown as active and, with the exception of those with behavior disorders, happy youngsters.

Allen, Anne. *Sports for the Handicapped.* Illus. New York: Walker, 1981. 80 pp. Reading Level: Grades 7–9.
Disability: Various

The author surveys six sports in which people with disabilities engage: skiing, wheelchair basketball, swimming, track and field, football, and horseback riding. In pictures and text, she shows people with a variety of disabling conditions, engaging actively in vigorous exercise and in competitive athletics. The athletes themselves are quoted extensively. A young woman with one leg describes skiing; a 43-year-old man who is blind talks about his inactive, overprotected childhood and contrasts it with his present life that includes water and snow skiing, wind surfing, hang-gliding, skating, and swimming; a young woman whose head injury at 22 resulted in cerebral palsy talks about the therapeutic effects, physical and emotional, of horseback riding.

There are many black-and-white photographs. The book ends with a list of resource and sports organizations serving those with disabilities.

Analysis. Allen has been a newspaper reporter and now works with a philanthropic foundation. Her text is clear and well focused, and by using the voices of the people she describes, she emphasizes the importance to their lives of their activities. Diana Golden, a one-legged skier, is quoted as saying, "For every physical disability there is a solution" (p. 20); a riding instructor says that "there was almost no physical handicap she could think of that would prevent a person from learning to ride to at least some degree" (p. 74). Sports, once considered beyond the reach of most disabled people, are here shown to be accessible in some measure to participants of all descriptions. It is unfortunate that the word *handicapped* appears in the title and rather frequently in the text.

Antonacci, Robert J., and Jene Barr. *Physical Fitness for Young Champions.* Illus. by Frank Mullins. New York: McGraw-Hill, 1975. 144 pp. Reading Level: Grades 7–9.
Disability: Various

Although most of this book is addressed to those without disabilities, Chapter 11, "Everyone Can Try to Be Fit," is subtitled: "Imaginative Drills for Those Who Can't Join in Sports and Games, and for the

Physically Disabled and Mentally Slow." The writers urge youngsters in these categories to work at developing as far as possible their ability to take care of themselves and to make movements under their own power in order to use their limbs and muscles effectively. They discuss associations, programs, and competitions available to youngsters with physical and mental disabilities, for example, the National Wheelchair Athletic Association and the Special Olympics sponsored by the Joseph P. Kennedy Jr. Foundation. There are descriptions of exercises designed to improve the use of specific body areas, such as elbows and shoulders. The chapter closes with a list of suggested ways to enjoy sports without full physical participation.

The text is illustrated with small black-and-white figures showing the exercises.

Analysis. Antonacci and Barr believe that everyone should and can be fit, and they direct this message without condescension or pity to youngsters with disabilities, as well as to able-bodied individuals. Although they have adopted a style that makes liberal use of exclamation points, the breezy informality of the text makes the information easily accessible to young readers. Lively sketches reflect this tone.

Ayrault, Evelyn West. *Sex, Love, and the Physically Handicapped.* New York: Continuum, 1981. 150 pp. Reading Level: Grades 10–12.
Disability: Various

Ayrault is a clinical psychologist who has written a number of books about disabled people. Here she discusses such subjects as the essential part love plays in human development, the importance of sexuality, development in childhood and adolescence, adjustment to sudden disabling conditions, experiences that enhance sexual and emotional growth, and the process of falling in love. Appendices give a selected bibliography, a glossary of terms associated with disability, a list of doctors doing research related to sex and disability, and lists of federal and national headquarters of service agencies, state service agencies, and other, nongovernmental agencies.

Analysis: As a person who has worked actively to promote the rights of disabled people, Ayrault emphasizes throughout that such individuals must be recognized as having the same needs for love, acceptance, and fulfillment as everyone else. Parents and health professionals have an obligation to encourage feelings of self-worth, dignity, and as much independence as is realistically possible; for those with impairments, as for everyone, self-love and acceptance are essential to mature development. Certainly Ayrault presents her views persuasively. She does, however, use the term *handicapped* extensively, where *impaired* or *disabled* would be more accurate and preferable, and often does not include details indicating the nature of the impairment, an omission that can be frustrating to the reader. In at least one section, she falls into a sexist pattern, assigning the young woman to indoor housekeeping tasks and the young man to outdoor activities. These criticisms notwithstanding, this is a valuable book.

Berger, Gilda. *Learning Disabilities and Handicaps.* Illus. New York: Franklin Watts, 1978. 83 pp. Reading Level: Grades 7–9.
Disability: Various

Chapters in this book cover various disabilities that make learning a problem in some way: mental retardation; emotional disturbance; speech and language, hearing, and visual impairments; orthopedic and neurological impairments; and learning disabilities. Each chapter is introduced by a case study that describes a specific child with the disability and his or her characteristics, difficulties, and progress. Then the disability is described in detail—its symptoms, causes, and medical, psychological, and educational treatment.

Black-and-white photographs illustrate the text, along with a few children's drawings. A three-page glossary defines the basic technical terms that have been used. At the conclusion of the text and glossary, there is a bibliography of fiction and nonfiction books for further reading.

Analysis. The biggest problem with this book is its title. Only one chapter deals with learning disabilities; the rest discuss disabilities that make learning difficult. These disabilities are grouped under the now-questionable term *handicap.* Otherwise, the writing is excellent. Explanations are clear, and examples that illustrate the explanations are plentiful and interesting. The children's drawings exemplify the use of art and art therapy in treating emotionally disturbed persons. The appendices are appropriately succinct and give additional useful information. The author is a professional writer who has been a special education teacher.

Berger, Gilda. *Physical Disabilities.* Illus. New York: Franklin Watts, 1979. 119 pp. Reading Level: Grades 7–9.
Disability: Various

Berger discusses the causes and characteristics of a broad range of physical disabilities—orthopedic, neurological, chronic health, and sensory impairments. In addition to describing the history and treatment of the various disabilities, she explains past and present attitudes toward them, emphasizing negative societal attitudes and newer, more enlightened ones as well. She also discusses the rights of disabled persons and federal legislation designed to protect those rights.

Analysis. This is a scientific, accurate, and simple explanation that covers the subject comprehensively if not in great depth. Both the factual information and the sociocultural factors discussed might be especially useful for a mainstreamed classroom situation, and for social science and science lessons.

Berger, Melvin. *Bionics.* Illus. New York: Franklin Watts, 1978. 82 pp. Reading Level: Grades 7–12.
Disability: Various

Bionics is "the study of the systems and structures of living animals and plants, and the application of these principles to devising machines and artificial systems for the benefit of humans" (p. 5). Because of modern research in bionics, people who are disabled now have more access to a variety of mobility aids, sensory aids, and synthetic limbs and organs than ever before. In addition, these devices, or substitute body parts, are of a quality and level of sophistication undreamed of only a short time ago. Approximately two-thirds of this book recounts these advances, including chapters on artificial limbs, artificial organs, and artificial senses. These chapters are preceded by an introduction detailing historical background, giving definitions, and setting bionics within its present scientific context. The application of each type of device is illustrated by giving a case history of a person who uses it.

The book is illustrated with black-and-white photographs and contains a name-subject index.

Analysis. Although scientific and factual, the text is a readable and interesting introduction to the subject. Plentiful examples and case histories make the explanations come alive. Pertinent illustrations and the format of the text (dark, clear type, appropriate spacing, use of many headings and subheadings) also heighten interest and appeal. Inasmuch as this field is advancing rapidly, new developments really call for an update to this information.

Blank, Joseph P. *19 Steps Up the Mountain.* New York: Lippincott, 1976. 90 pp. Reading Level: Grades 7–12.
Disability: Various

This book recounts incidents in the lives of the Debolt family, which includes 15 adopted children, nine with severe physical handicaps. The Debolts, who married as widower and widow, took on multiply disabled children, one by one. Some were from interracial families; some had been deserted and had lived in orphanages. Chapters focus on the individual children and recount the miraculous way in which each discovers his or her own integrity, fortitude, and self-reliance through contact with the Debolts and the others.

The Debolts' philosophy is to be very honest with the youngsters about their disabilities and to give no special assistance unless the child cannot do something him- or herself. It is always assumed that the children can handle almost anything. Mrs. Debolt says at one point to a child who is feeling sorry for herself, "So you have a couple of legs that don't work!" Vignettes such as the following illustrate the tone of the book: Adopted daughter Karen, who is without limbs, wet the bed at night constantly when she first moved into the family. Mr. Debolt tucked her in one night saying, "I love you," and kissing her on each of her stumps. She responded with a gentle tapping of her stumps on his wrists. She had a completely dry bed the next morning.

Analysis. Blank's prose is rather awkward and the writing might seem oversentimental and somewhat preachy to a sophisticated reader. However, the power of this family's undertaking comes through to make this an inspiring and worthwhile book for young people who will soon be considering parenthood themselves. The message of hope and respect for all people is clearly heard.

Bosworth, Patricia. *Diane Arbus: A Biography.* Illus. New York: Knopf, 1984. 366 pp. Reading Level: Grades 10–12.
Disability: Various

Bosworth is a scholarly biographer who has carefully documented notes and sources for her detailed account of this famous pioneer of the new photo-journalism. Her subject, Arbus, was herself an eccentric, enigmatic person whose chronic depressions finally led to her suicide in 1971 at the age of 48.

Arbus was one of three children born to the Nemerov family, which owned Russek's department store on Fifth Avenue in New York City. The children were well educated and pampered; all showed artistic talent, and had a close although ambivalent family attachment.

Diane Arbus finally achieved her goal of becoming a photographer of people "without masks." She photographed dwarfs and giants at Hubert's Freak Museum, nudists, eccentrics, always searching for the secret reality behind the permanent mask. She went to places no photographer had gone before, and would wait in all kinds of weather for hours to take the right picture. "The term 'freak' or 'normal' in her context became meaningless. Because Diane had made no distinctions—no concessions either" (p. 199).

Bosworth hoped in her book to understand the personality of Arbus, a devoted mother to her two daughters. Arbus was a supportive and submissive wife to her photographer husband for many years and was deeply disappointed when her marriage broke up. She was physically intimate with men of all ages, races, and stations in life, and with women as well. A gifted teacher of her craft, she had many friends in her professional life. She loved her family although she could not ever achieve a satisfying relationship with her sister, or a closeness with her mother. After her death, her poet brother, Howard Nemerov, wrote a poem for his famous sister:

To D—Dead by Her Own Hand

My dear, I wonder if before the end
You ever thought about a children's game—
I'm sure you must have played it too—in which
You ran along a narrow garden wall
Pretending it to be a mountain ledge
So steep a snowy darkness fell away
On either side to deeps invisible;
And when you felt your balance being lost
You jumped because you feared to fall, and thought
For only an instant: That was when I died.

That was a life ago. And now you've gone,
Who would no longer play the grown-ups' game
Where, balanced on the ledge above the dark,
You go on running and you don't look down,
Nor ever jump because you fear to fall.

The book does contain some black-and-white photographs, but not those for which Arbus is famous.

Analysis. This long and detailed book opens up the world of photography for the reader, and exposes the almost voyeuristic fascination with odd and different human images of a great photographer. Bosworth never does present the "real" Diane Arbus because she was so many things to so many people, and so volatile. What does come across is Arbus's single-minded obsession with her art.

Bowe, Frank. *Comeback: Six Remarkable People Who Triumphed Over Disability.* Foreword by William Glasser. New York: Harper & Row, 1981. 172 pp. Reading Level: Grades 10–12.
Disability: Various

The author is himself hearing-impaired; he has written a number of books on disabilities and rehabilitation and has been a director of the

American Coalition of Citizens with Disabilities (ACCD). Here he writes about six people who have not only triumphed over disabling conditions, but have achieved more than many able-bodied people, making contributions that have effected positive social change.

Eunice Fiorito describes herself as "a human being who happens to be blind, not a blind being who happens to be human." A bright, energetic, assertive woman, she helped to found ACCD and served as its first president, working to unite the 36 million disabled Americans and to win long-delayed assistance and improvements.

Susan Daniels, who had a congenital hip malformation and then contracted polio as an infant, was refused admission to medical school because of her disability; she went on to pioneer work in sexuality counseling for people with disabilities.

Robert Smithdas lost both hearing and sight in 1930 as a result of meningitis at the age of five. He was the first deaf-blind man to earn a B.A. degree and the first deaf-blind person to get an M.A. He is a poet, director of community relations of the Helen Keller National Center for Deaf-Blind Youths and Adults on Long Island, New York, speaks widely on deafness and blindness, and has won many honors. He is married, owns his home where he does many of the repairs, and is a fisherman.

Roger Meyers, whose story was told by his brother in the book *Like Normal People* (see Meyers, Ch. 7, p. 279), is mildly retarded. His parents resisted all advice to institutionalize him and, not without significant effort and cost, brought him up at home. Meyers is now married and lives independently with his wife, supporting them with a combination of his earnings as a busboy and their government benefits. His life is an example of the extent to which mildly retarded persons can become productive members of society if they are aided by familial and societal support.

Stephen Hawking is a world-renowned theoretical physicist working at Cambridge University, England. He has had amyotrophic lateral sclerosis (Lou Gehrig's disease) for more than 20 years and has significant and progressive disabilities. Before the onset of the disease, he was not outstanding as a student or scientist; after he recovered from the initial depression, he began to work and live with new intensity. He married after the diagnosis and has children.

Nansie Sharpless became deaf as the result of meningitis when she was a high school freshman. She went on to finish her schooling in regular classes, attended Oberlin College, and received graduate degrees from Wayne State University in Detroit. She is now a biochemist working at Albert Einstein College of Medicine in New York to explore the way the brain functions.

Bowe's last chapter, "Reflections," discusses characteristics and experiences common to successful disabled people. At the end of the book he lists sources of additional information and gives a bibliography.

Analysis. Dedicated to helping people with disabilities get equal opportunities to "live, grow, and support themselves" (p. xvi), Bowe has focused his book on people who have achieved these goals—often in the face of discouragement and without the support of society and government. He writes clearly and without sentimentality; the passion and force of his convictions and message come from the subjects he has chosen for his profiles and the details he uses in presenting them. His book should be of interest to a wide audience of young people, whether they have disabilities or not, as they grow toward independence and seek fulfillment.

Boy Scouts of America. *Handicapped Awareness.* Irving, Tex.: 1982. 48 pp. Reading Level: Grades 4–12.
Disability: Various

This merit-badge pamphlet is intended to guide scouts through the requirements for a badge indicating that the scout has learned about disabilities and done service to disabled people. The requirements for earning the badge include visiting an agency that works with people with disabilities; simulating a disabling condition; spending 15 hours with a sheltered workshop for adults or a special Cub Scout pack or Boy Scout troop; locating and studying literature about accessibility or nonaccessibility of public and private places and making personal observations of places in the scout's environment; displaying publicly a collection of informational material about disabilities; and making a commitment for future service to people with disabilities.

The first chapter asks who disabled people are and answers that they are our brothers and sisters before going on to more specific information. Other sections cover agencies that help people with disabilities, discuss what it is like to be disabled, make suggestions about helping, discuss environmental barriers, and suggest ways in which the scout can make a commitment. One section lists and describes common disabilities. Another gives information on degrees and characteristics of mental retardation.

Some organizations serving people with disabilities are listed. The section titled "Resources for Handicapped Awareness Merit Badge" gives a bibliography of books, pamphlets, scouting literature, and films and filmstrips. The pamphlet is illustrated with line drawings.

Analysis. This booklet does a good job of heightening awareness of disabilities. While it points out that no simulation can duplicate the experience of a disabled person, the suggested exercises should be useful to increase understanding among young people. Emphasis is on both acquiring information and giving service. Boys who earn this merit badge may feel less separation between themselves and people with disabling conditions. It could be an activity that would help to integrate a disabled member into a scout group. Perhaps a future edition will find a substitute phrase for the distancing words *the handicapped*.

Boynick, David K. *Champions by Setback: Athletes Who Overcame Physical Handicaps.* New York: Crowell, 1954. 203 pp. Reading Level: Grades 7–12.
Disability: Various

In separate chapters, the author tells the stories of ten athletes who overcame physical disabilities caused by accidents, illness, and congenital conditions. For example, Glenn Cunningham suffered severe injuries to his legs when he was burned in a schoolhouse fire, but he went on to become a champion runner (see Cunningham, *Never Quit*, Ch. 5. p. 52). Hamilton Richardson was already a successful young tennis player when he developed diabetes at the age of 15, but he was able to manage his condition and compete in tennis tournaments. After losing his eyesight in World War II, Charles Boswell became a championship golfer. The book ends with an index.

Analysis. Keeping close to his stated focus of triumph over physical adversity, the author gives detailed descriptions of both disabilities and athletic events. The book should appeal particularly to young readers interested in sports, including those who themselves have a disability. There are no young women among the subjects; one cannot tell whether this is because no female athletes fit the book's design or because they have simply been overlooked.

Brightman, Alan J., ed. *Ordinary Moments: The Disabled Experience.* Photog. by Alan Brightman. Baltimore: Univ. Park Pr., 1984. 192 pp. Reading Level: Grades 7–12.
Disability: Various

The eight chapters of this book are written in the first person by young people with disabilities such as spina bifida, paralysis, amputation, blindness, muscular dystrophy. They talk about their feelings, their childhood experiences, and also of intimate subjects. One paralyzed young man shares his many unsuccessful attempts to have sex, for example.

Black-and-white pictures of the various writers accompany the vignettes. A brief annotated bibliography is included.

Analysis. The ideas and events portrayed are absorbing and thought-provoking. Some accounts are optimistic, others are sad or wistful, and sometimes poetic. Brightman's black-and-white photographs enhance the text beautifully.

Brown, Tricia. *Someone Special, Just Like You.* Photog. by Fran Ortiz. New York: Holt, 1984. 64 pp. Reading Level: Grades K–3.
Disability: Various

The impetus for this book came when Tricia Brown looked for a book for her nursery school child, one of whose classmates had a disability. She wanted "to find a book for my own child to help him understand that we should accept one another for the love we have to share with the world, and not judge on the basis of physical appearances or limitations" (p. 5). There was no such book, so Brown and Ortiz collaborated to produce this one. Each double-page spread has a few words of simple text printed in large type and at least one black-and-white photograph. Children, some with obvious disabilities, are shown engaged in activities that all youngsters love: blowing bubbles, eating ice cream, painting pictures. They follow familiar daily routines such as going to school, eating lunch, washing, and resting. Disabled children are shown reading braille with fingers and learning to talk with their hands. The book ends with an annotated bibliography of titles for adults and children prepared by Effie Lee Morris.

Analysis. Brown and Ortiz successfully use text and illustrations to present their message that this is "not only a book about children with disabilities, but about all of us. Young and old alike, we all have our own disabilities, and each of us is someone special" (p. 5). They do not attempt to explain the conditions that are pictured except in general terms ("Someone who may not walk the same way you do," p. 9), but as this is a book for preschool children, it is appropriate that the adult who is reading would answer questions. Throughout, they emphasize what children have in common ("For even without seeing the same things you do, he can brush his teeth, pet a rabbit, and walk a balance beam," pp. 38–39). The words of the text move in a pleasant cadence and use both feminine and masculine pronouns. The photographs show active, joyous, appealing children. This is a highly recommended book.

Carrillo, Ann Cupolo, Katherine Corbett, and Victoria Lewis. *No More Stares*. Illus. Berkeley, Calif.: The Disability Rights Education and Defense Fund, Inc., 1982. 128 pp. Reading Level: Grades 7–12. *Disability:* Various

This book provides a frank discussion of growing up female and disabled. Persons with many disabilities recount their experiences as children and their hopes, aspirations, and philosophy of life. Their stories are also shown in black-and-white photographs, which comprise half of the book. The pictures depict action shots of children, youth, and adults interacting in many situations.

Analysis. These insightful vignettes are provocative and conducive to group discussion among disabled and nondisabled people. One young woman begins, "I never saw an inchworm until I was 19." The pictures "show it like it is"; that is, some of the characters are obviously disabled, but they are shown in a positive fashion, working, playing, and loving—integrated in the community.

Cohen, Shirley. *Special People: A Brighter Future for Everyone with Physical, Mental, and Emotional Disabilities*. Englewood Cliffs, N.J.: Prentice-Hall, 1977. 177 pp. Reading Level: Grades 10–12. *Disability:* Various

The author, a professor of education at Hunter College and director of the Special Education Development Center at the City University of New York, writes about being the parent of a disabled child and about the process of growing through adolescence and to adulthood as experienced by disabled persons. She devotes chapters to the rights of disabled people to live as well as possible, enjoying the benefits of education and of full access to facilities available to the nondisabled. She discusses the images of disabled people promoted by the media and the impact of medical and technological advances on those with disabilities. In a short final chapter she asks the reader pointed questions about her or his attitude toward disabled people.

A coda reprints the bicentennial declaration of human rights for handicapped persons. There is also an index, as well as references at the end of each chapter.

Analysis. Cohen has previously written training materials for teachers and parents and a curriculum designed to help children accept disabled people. Here she addresses her subject with honesty and without sentimentality. While she recognizes the changes in the social and medical treatment of people with disabilities, she sees clearly the areas in which progress lags. The text includes vignettes about individual people, heightening interest for the general reader.

Coombs, Jan. *Living with the Disabled: You Can Help—A Family Guide*. New York: Sterling, 1984. 192 pp. Reading Level: Grades 10–12.
Disability: Various

In 1977, Lisa Coombs, then 18 years old, was severely injured in an automobile accident. Although Jan Coombs and her husband are both medical professionals, they found there was much that they did not know about the experience of dealing with disability in a family member and about finding appropriate services. Lisa survived, came through years of rehabilitation, and grew into "a self-assured woman who knows she can take on the world despite her residual handicaps" (p. 11). The book her mother has written has its origins in the family's experience, but that is not the primary focus. Instead, she sets out to provide detailed information about resources, attitudes, and management for people dealing with unexpected, often sudden, disability. She covers such topics as adjustment to disability for the affected person, family, and friends; selecting hospitals and medical professionals; making choices about rehabilitation; handling convalescence creatively; returning to active life; and finding financial resources.

The text includes brief descriptions of the experiences of specific disabled people; pseudonyms are used for everyone except Lisa Coombs. A postscript, "Turkeys and Eagles," is based on an interview with Charles Sabatier, Jr., a paraplegic veteran of the Vietnam War and, at the time of writing, assistant director of the Massachusetts Office of Handicapped Affairs. Appendices list organizations for various disabilities and names of organizations providing specific types of services, such as those connected with recreation and travel, with a brief description of the services offered. There are reference notes for each chapter, a recommended reading list, and an index.

Analysis. Coombs writes soberly and realistically. While never underestimating the tasks facing the disabled person and her or his family, she promotes an optimistic and positive attitude, emphasizing the need for disabled people to make the most of their remaining abilities rather than focusing on what may have been lost. She has written a book that is full of practical, commonsense suggestions and that supports the goal of the individual's right to personal dignity and to the best, most appropriate treatment. Early in the text, Coombs makes the important distinction between disability and handicap: "Anyone with an injury or disease is disabled; however, not everyone with a disability is handicapped. The handicapping comes from the attitude of the patient and those around him who think he is no longer capable of leading a useful life" (p. 26).

Although written for adults, *Living with the Disabled* could be read by young people planning careers in the medical and social service professions, by a young person with a disability, and by one with a disabled family member or friend.

Craig, Eleanor. *If We Could Hear the Grass Grow*. New York: Simon & Schuster, 1983. 220 pp. Reading Level: Grades 10–12.
Disability: Various

Eleanor Craig has worked as a counselor, teacher, and therapist. She is the author of other books on disturbed children—*P.S. You're Not Listening* and *One, Two, Three: The Story of Matt, a Feral Child* (see Ch. 7, p. 238 and p. 237). In this book, she describes a summer camp that she ran in her home for a small group of variously disturbed and disabled children. The summer followed a period of upheaval and change in her own life: She had recently been divorced; both she and her young-adult children were struggling with this breakup of the family structure and also with her children's own growing independence; she had had to put the family home on the market. The children who came to Craig's program presented a variety of challenges. Three siblings were not themselves disturbed but came from an abusive home; a 13-year-old boy was locked with his mother into a terrifying pattern of mutual fear and interdependence; an 11-year-old girl who was placed with a foster family had to deal with abandonment by her mother and the finality of adoption by the foster parents; one child had a severe, debilitating, and potentially fatal illness.

Three of Craig's four children agreed to work as counselors; a friend and fellow clinician shared direction with her. By the end of the summer, everyone, both staff and campers, had grown and changed. For example, the boy who refused to let his mother out of his sight had gone on an overnight camping trip without her; another boy who hid his fears under jive-talking bravado had learned to swim; the 11-year-old was able to turn to her foster mother and say she wanted to be adopted. The Craigs had also developed a new closeness. An epilogue brings each of Camp Hopewell's participants up-to-date six months later. The title comes from a comment by one child about his pet snake and why he is not lonesome: "And nobody wouldn't never be sad if we could hear what my snake hears. If we could hear the grass grow" (p. 88). Their lives had taken new directions, which were for the most part more satisfying.

Analysis. One of Craig's sons suggested that she write this account of Camp Hopewell—"But really tell it. Don't try to present us ideally"

(p. 175). The author is successful in presenting a graphic, detailed picture of the camp and its participants, and honest in her description of her own feelings, including anger and ambivalence. She uses artistic license to reproduce conversations that she probably could not remember so fully, but the dialogue adds interest. Craig seems a perceptive observer and therapist. Most of the children show considerable growth and development over the course of the summer. The extent to which they are able to put aside hostilities and suspicions and join in a cooperative effort sometimes seems too good to be true, but not every individual story is a success nor are bitter, angry feelings entirely supplanted. What comes across is a picture of people in process, developing and growing and on the way from a bad situation to a better one.

Drimmer, Frederick. *Very Special People: The Struggles, Love, and Triumphs of Human Oddities*. Illus. New York: Amjon, 1973. 413 pp. Reading Level: Grades 7–12.
Disability: Various

Drimmer has arranged his profiles of many special people into categories: for example, Siamese twins and those with extra limbs, armless and legless persons, little people, giants, and so on. He gives information about the incidence, causes, and results of the condition as well as many personal histories. He includes Sir Frederick Treves's essay, "The Elephant Man" about John Merrick (see Howell and Ford's book in Ch. 5, p. 115). There are many illustrations and a bibliography.
    Analysis. Drimmer dedicates his book to "The Very Special People—Outwardly different from you and me, Inwardly the same," and it is in this spirit that he has written it. Although in some ways it is like a visit to an endless sideshow at an old-fashioned circus, Drimmer succeeds in presenting his subjects as people of dignity. Unfortunately, most of the photographs are poorly reproduced and have a dull, grainy appearance.

Exley, Helen, ed. *What It's Like to Be Me*. Illus. New York: Friendship, 1984. 127 pp. Reading Level: Grades 4–9.
Disability: Various

This book, written and illustrated by children with disabilities, was prepared during the International Year of Disabled People. The contributors come from all over the world, represent a variety of disabilities, and range in age from 6 to 18. The writings and illustrations (both black-and-white and color) are grouped by topics—for example,

"Please don't tease me," "Why do they scorn me?," "Triumph," "We have certain rights," and "Facing death." Occasionally the editor adds a comment or explanation. The book ends with a list of schools and organizations that helped in the preparation.

Analysis. This is a moving, revealing, sometimes funny book. (A nine-year-old boy writes, "What I like about being disabled is that I never do any housework"; a ten-year-old says, "It's not nice being handicapped, but I'm not unhappy with my situation as I could have been born a chicken or a duck.") The contributions give compelling glimpses into the lives and thoughts of these young writers and artists. The repeated, insistent message is that youngsters with disabilities want to live as fully as possible, to have friends, to be accepted, to assert themselves against pity and ridicule.

This would be an excellent book to use in a classroom situation, as a springboard for discussion and projects.

Feingold, S. Norman, and Norma R. Miller. *Your Future: A Guide for the Handicapped Teenager.* Illus. New York: Rosen, 1981. 177 pp. Reading Level: Grades 7–12.
Disability: Various

Feingold is a vocational consultant and Miller writes for health, trade, education, and professional associations. Addressing the young reader directly, they have written on such topics as planning for a career, finding the right school and financing education, getting an appropriate job, legal rights of people with disabilities, travel, and leisure activities. Each chapter has brief profiles and photographs of people with disabilities that are primarily physical and sensory, and each ends with specific information. The last chapter, "Words to Live By," quotes people with disabilities on a variety of subjects. The appendix repeats facts given in some of the preceding chapters and adds information on resources to help readers find the right career and the right life-style.

Analysis. Feingold and Miller have written a direct, practical book full of useful information. Without being unrealistic, they encourage their readers to make the most of all their abilities and, when necessary, to fight for acceptance and services. The personal vignettes are well chosen to illustrate points. Although some of the information may rapidly become dated, much of it is of more general application and will remain timely. Many of the problems faced by disabled youth in choosing a career are magnifications of those faced by all young people; the suggestions offered in this book could be used for all teenagers.

Forrai, Maria S. *A Look at Physical Handicaps*. Illus. Text by Margaret
Sanford Pursell. Minneapolis: Lerner, 1976. 32 pp. Reading Level:
Grades 4–6.
Disability: Various

Black-and-white photographs show disabled children and adults in
various activities of everyday life. On the page opposite each photograph
is a brief description and/or comment pertinent to the photograph.

Analysis. The large, clear, and well-composed photographs are an
excellent introduction to the subject of people with disabilities. The
reading level refers only to the text; the book could be used at almost
any level, including preschool, to introduce the subject of disabilities.
Since the text is so brief, it could easily be paraphrased.

A discordant note is the constant use of the word *handicapped* and the
reference to persons with disabilities as *the handicapped*. Given the 1976
publication date, this fault is understandable. The text also contains some
condescending stereotypical sentences. The book is, nevertheless, useful. Its intent is positive, and the photographs are truly excellent.

Gifford, Frank, with Charles Mangel. *Gifford on Courage*. New
York: Evans, 1976. 253 pp. Reading Level: Grades 7–12.
Disability: Various

A professional writer and sportscaster and former professional football player, Gifford writes about ten athletes who had to face great demands on their courage. Rocky Bleier played football after devastating
wounds received in the Vietnam War (see his story in Ch. 5, p. 91). Herb
Score, rated a pitcher the caliber of Bob Feller, eventually had to give up
the game after injuries to his eye and arm, and his acceptance of this
situation was as courageous as Bleier's comeback. Other subjects include
a blind golfer, a young basketball player, and a wrestler.

Analysis. Gifford writes for both active and armchair athletes, giving detailed descriptions of training, injuries, and games. His tone
throughout is optimistic and admiring. There are no women in this
collection of profiles.

Glazzard, Margaret H. *Meet Camille and Danille: They're Special Persons* (53 pp.), *Meet Danny: He's a Special Person* (47 pp.), *Meet Lance:
He's a Special Person* (43 pp.), *Meet Scott: He's a Special Person*
(46 pp.). Photog. by Hank Young. Lawrence, Kans.: H & H Enterprises, 1978. Reading Level: Grades K–3.
Disability: Various

Camille and Danille are twins with hearing impairments, Danny is
multiply handicapped, Lance is a trainable mentally retarded child,

and Scott has a learning disability. Each youngster is introduced with the phrase "special person." They are shown exclusively in their school situations, in both special classes and integrated classrooms and activities. For example, Scott spends part of his day in a mainstreamed group, but he also works individually with a special education teacher who has techniques and equipment to help him overcome his disability. The educational activities include not only academic work but lessons in self-care and manipulative skills. The texts have been prepared according to readability formulas and very large type is used. Vocabulary lists appear at the end of each book. Story records packed in pockets on the inside back covers make the books accessible to preschool children and beginning readers. Each spread has a page of text and a full-page black-and-white photograph.

Analysis. In the foreword, Glazzard, an educator, says that the purpose of the series is to explain children with disabilities to able-bodied youngsters who may be in the same class or the same school. She has made very clear the differences that mark the children as "special," but she also emphasizes in each book the things that all children share. In preparing the material, Glazzard worked with a number of educational consultants. The result is an excellent series that presents disabled children and their accomplishments without condescension or pity and that should encourage all children, whatever their abilities, to ask questions, to understand and respect each other, and to cooperate with each other. These are good books that teachers and children can use together, so that discussion can take place during the reading. The black-and-white photographs ably illustrate and extend the text.

Gollay, Elinor, and Alwina Bennett. *The College Guide for Students with Disabilities.* Cambridge, Mass.: Abt Publications, and Boulder, Colo.: Westview Press, 1976. 545 pp. Reading Level: Grades 10–12. *Disability:* Various

This directory, while not intended as the sole source of information about colleges, covers a number of topics. There is a section on legal rights in higher education, information about sources of financial aid, both public and private, and suggestions to help disabled students in the application process. General handbooks and directories are included as well as publications written specifically for disabled students, with information on federal and state agencies offering assistance to those with disabilities. The book includes a summary of information about the services and policies of colleges listed in the guide, detailed data for each college, and an alphabetical index of colleges.

Analysis. While this can be a helpful source of information for the college-bound student who is disabled, much of the material would probably have to be updated by further investigation on the part of the student.

Harries, Jean. *They Triumphed Over Their Handicaps.* New York: Franklin Watts, 1981. 88 pp. Reading Level: Grades 4–9.
Disability: Various

Harries has written short biographies of six contemporary people who have won out over their disabilities—lack of legs, blindness, amputation of the hands, brain and leg injuries, amputation of the leg due to cancer, and deafness. Some of her subjects are well known: Ted Kennedy, Jr., Ray Charles, and Kitty O'Neal. There are black-and-white photographs and an index.

Analysis. Harries writes in a clear style, with many short sentences. She usually gives good details—for example, in her description of young Ted Kennedy's operation and prosthesis, but there are places where the reader might want more information, as when she says that John Fryn, born without legs, walks on his hands. The title reflects the constantly repeated theme of perseverance, courage, and triumph. The author does not omit difficulties or unpleasant details, such as Ray Charles's drug problems and divorces or Joan Kennedy's alcoholism, but her tone is optimistic.

Haskins, James. *Who Are the Handicapped?* Illus. New York: Doubleday, 1978. 110 pp. Reading Level: Grades 10–12.
Disability: Various

The author, a teacher, educational consultant, and book reviewer, has written a number of books dealing in some way with disabled people. This book begins with the definition of "normal" and attitudes toward those with disabilities. In the middle section, Haskins examines a number of specific conditions: blindness; deafness; neurological dysfunctions such as epilepsy, cerebral palsy, and multiple sclerosis; muscular dystrophy; mental retardation; and orthopedic and musculoskeletal defects. The last section discusses changes in societal attitudes toward people with disabilities and asks "What next for the disabled?"

The text includes a glossary of terms; a bibliography of books, pamphlets, and articles; and an index.

Photographs and prints showing both famous and ordinary people with impairments enhance the text.

Analysis. Haskins writes from a firm, realistic, yet impassioned advocacy of the rights of disabled persons to attain the fullest possible development of their gifts and abilities. The text is honest and detailed, with emphasis on what people with disabilities have and can accomplish; the author refers repeatedly to the obligation of the so-called normal members of society to meet and accept those who deviate from the norm.

Haskins, James, with J. M. Stifle. *The Quiet Revolution: The Struggle of Disabled Americans.* Illus. New York: Crowell, 1979. 147 pp. Reading Level: Grades 7–12.
Disability: Various

The writers survey the background of the Disabled Rights Movement, discussing the rights of disabled people and the efforts made to secure them. Subsequent chapters treat the rights to prevention of disability, to treatment, education, employment and compensation, to a barrier-free environment, and the right to choose. The writers respond to prevalent myths and inaccuracies about people with disabilities and show how all of society can benefit if such people can develop their maximum potential.

The book concludes with a selected bibliography and an index. It is illustrated with black-and-white photographs.

Analysis. The authors write from a clearly expressed philosophy, the belief that disabled citizens are entitled to lead lives that are as full and active as possible. Descriptions and analyses are clear and informative; laws aiding people with disabilities are discussed in detail. The text provides valuable reading for young people and adults alike. There is one discordant note: A photograph of a boy wearing leg braces is labeled "This crippled child . . ." (p. 55).

Hayman, LeRoy. *Triumph! Conquering Your Physical Disabilities.* New York: Messner, 1982. 159 pp. Reading Level: Grades 10–12.
Disability: Various

In 1953, when he was still a young man, the author was injured by an object that fell from a window onto his head, leaving him with a foot drop and a limp and with impaired control over his handwriting, his speaking voice, and his emotions. Eventually he was able to return to his work as an editor. This book and its philosophy grew from his experiences and observations over 30 years. Hayman discusses the attitudes and aims that disabled people should cultivate, makes suggestions for dealing with daily living, and emphasizes the rights of and opportunities open to people with disabilities as well as the barriers that can impede them; he devotes one chapter to people with visual or hearing impairments and another to family and friends of disabled people. Interspersed throughout the text are interviews with disabled people, and there is also a chapter called "Great Lives" about famous people with disabilities.

There is a bibliography and an index.

Analysis. Optimistic and insistent, Hayman addresses disabled readers directly, calling on them to recognize the value of their lives, to love themselves, and to attack their challenges with pride, determination, and intelligence. The specific information he gives could be helpful to disabled people and could help to broaden the understanding of nondisabled individuals. The tone is occasionally cloying (one section is called "Count Those Blessings," another is "Love, Sweet Love"), but Hayman speaks with an authentic voice born out of his struggle.

Henriod, Lorraine. *Special Olympics and Paralympics.* Illus. New York: Franklin Watts, 1979. 66 pp. Reading Level: Grades 4–6.
Disability: Various

Henriod gives the history of Special Olympics and Paralympics for disabled persons. She discusses the importance of athletics for people with mental and physical disabilities, describes the relatively recent emphasis on physical activity for disabled persons, and gives information on individuals who have contributed to the enormous success and growth of the Special Olympic movement. She singles out physicians like Sir Ludwig Guttman of England; organizers like Benjamin H. Lipton; well-known public figures like Senator Edward J. Kennedy; and many participants in the games. In addition, she discusses the thousands of volunteers who support the Special Olympic movement.

There is a short bibliography and an index. Many black-and-white photographs add to the text.

Analysis. Henriod's message is unmistakable and her commitment to the cause of athletics and olympics for those with disabilities is clear. Unfortunately, the text is marred by repetition and poor organization of material.

Herman, William. *Hearts Courageous: Twelve Who Achieved.* Illus. by James MacDonald. New York: Dutton, 1949. 254 pp. Reading Level: Grades 4–9.
Disability: Various

In these twelve profiles, the author presents people who overcame physical challenges and made significant contributions to the world. For example, Robert Louis Stevenson was in frail health all his life;

Josiah Wedgwood, the great English potter, survived smallpox and later had a leg amputated without anesthesia; Edward Trudeau, the doctor who developed a tuberculosis sanitarium at Saranac Lake, New York, was himself a tuberculosis patient. Among other figures profiled are Franklin Roosevelt, Beethoven, Helen Keller, Charles Steinmetz, and Glenn Cunningham. Each chapter is headed with a black-and-white drawing of the subject.

Analysis. Using a fictionalized biography, with imagined dialogue, the author stresses the strength and achievement of his subjects. He does not so much skim over difficulties as use them to point up courage and heroism. Although the people described here may seem almost too good to be true, and although the book was published many years ago, the collection may offer interesting reading to middle-school students.

Hobby, Janice Hale, with Gabrielle Rubin and Daniel Rubin. *Staying Back.* Illus. by Carol Richardson. Gainesville, Fla.: Triad, 1982. 93 pp. Reading Level: Grades K–6.
Disability: Various

The idea for this book came from a story written and illustrated by a nine-year-old boy after he repeated third grade. His story is included. Using the first person, the authors tell the stories of seven other children who, for a variety of reasons, repeated a grade between one and six. The first-grader is just small, young, and immature; the second-grader, who has sickle-cell anemia, misses a lot of school because of illness. One girl is hearing-impaired, another is emotionally troubled by parental discord. One fifth-grade boy has a learning disability, the other is unhappy because he has had to move in the middle of the school year. The sixth-grader has been pressured by parental expectations. Each child is helped to find solutions to problems and each benefits by repeating the school year. Following the original story, the authors invite readers to send in stories and pictures about their experiences with disappointments and problems, and promise to make of them another book.

Dr. Barry M. Dym, a family therapist, has contributed a message to parents with suggested steps for dealing positively with school failure. The concluding section, also addressed to adults, comments on each story and gives questions that might spark discussion between parents and children.

Attractive and animated pencil drawings appear on each page, and serve to heighten each child's different personality and situation.

Analysis. The authors are all professionals: Hobby teaches exceptional students, Gabrielle Rubin is a teacher of deaf children and a communications therapist, and Daniel Rubin is a writer. They have captured the child's point of view and the voices of both adults and children without artificiality. The youngsters experience anger, bewilderment, chagrin, and relief as they face the challenge of repeating a grade; both their initial reactions and ultimate improvement are presented convincingly. The book could be read by all grade-school children, whether or not they have similar problems. Young nonreaders might enjoy hearing the story read aloud.

Jones, Reginald L., ed. *Reflections on Growing Up Disabled*. Reston, Va.: Council for Exceptional Children, ERIC Clearinghouse on Handicapped and Gifted Children, 1983. 103 pp. Reading Level: Grades 10–12.
Disability: Various

The book opens with a preface introducing the subject matter. Chapters 2 through 8 are firsthand accounts of the childhood feelings, insights, and self-perceptions of disabled people. A learning-disabled woman describes her frustrations with "the handicap that has no name" as a hyperactive, clumsy, inept child. Others tell about coping with spinal cord injury, cerebral palsy, blindness, and progressive deafness. Two closing chapters of a professional nature are followed by a bibliography.
Analysis. This book seems to have as its purpose the overcoming of barriers to mainstreaming disabled students, even those far less articulate than its contributors, but it suffers from unevenness in the writing. Some chapters are addressed to parents and professionals in erudite language. The majority of chapters, however, are reminiscences of the childhoods of disabled persons with interesting and very personal observations. The various stories are rather truncated.

Kamien, Janet. *What If You Couldn't . . .? A Book about Special Needs*. Illus. by Signe Hanson. New York: Scribner's, 1979. 83 pp. Reading Level: Grades 4–6.
Disability: Various

This book grew out of a museum exhibit on special needs. The author is associate director of the Visitor Center of the Children's Museum of Boston, where she has worked with children with special needs and has trained interns to lead children and adults with special needs through the museum. Using the "What if . . ." motif (What if you couldn't see as well as everyone else? What if you had trouble with your feelings?), Kamien describes a number of impairments and disorders, such as physical, sensory, and learning problems, and the methods and devices available to treat them.

Signe Hanson's black-and-white drawings bring additional energy and information to the text and include a variety of racial types.

Analysis. Kamien makes effective use of a natural, informal style that addresses the reader directly. Her descriptions and analogies have force and clarity, and her anecdotal comments heighten the sense of the personal. She is honest about the reactions that so-called normal people sometimes have in the presence of abnormality, but she is able to help the reader share the experience of those she describes. Without minimizing the challenges and limitations faced by those with impairments, she emphasizes their ability to lead full lives and to be part of society.

Kleinfield, Sonny. *The Hidden Minority: A Profile of Handicapped Americans.* Boston: Little, 1979. Reading Level: Grades 7–12. *Disability:* Various

Kleinfield, a professional writer, has traveled coast to coast to interview disabled persons, their families, and their advocates. He tells the stories of his interviewees and presents historical material, providing factual information about the present situations of Americans who are disabled. Portions of this book have appeared in the *Atlantic* and *Psychology Today.*

Noted child psychiatrist and author Robert Coles has written an introduction in which he describes himself as a young psychiatrist, speaking to a ten-year-old girl who had had polio. He attempted to get her to be "realistic" about her possibilities in life. Later Cole realized that his behavior had been "more arrogant, blind, condescending than I apparently had any way of knowing." In response to his "not so innocent inquiry" about her plans for the future, she screamed at him, "I want to live my life. And I will." Coles describes this "leading a life" as what the people portrayed in this book are doing; he calls this "the essence of personal affirmation" (pp. ix–x).

Analysis. This is a fast-paced narrative, detailed and descriptive, that provides a broad picture of the lives of disabled people in the United States today. It is also an interesting account of the movement for the rights of disabled people that has resulted in laws such as the Education of All Handicapped Children Act and in more public concern for matters such as accessibility to public buildings. The combination of biography, factual narration, and description is good and will appeal to many teenagers.

Krauss, Bob, ed. *An Exceptional View of Life: The Easter Seal Story.*
Written and illus. by handicapped children. Norfolk Island, Aus-
tralia: Island Heritage Ltd., 1977. 64 pp. Reading Level: Grades 4–12.
Disability: Various

More than 80 Hawaiian children with various disabilities have
written stories, vignettes, and poems or have painted colored pictures
in which they depict their lives, thoughts, dreams, and sometimes
their disabilities. This project, one of a series of publications issued by
Island Heritage, was carried out by the Child's Point of View Library in
cooperation with the Easter Seal Society.

Photographs and brief biographies of some of the children are
included at the end of the book.

Analysis. This is a beautiful book—excellent layout, paper, and
type and clear, strong reproduction of the vivid paintings. Some of the
writings and art show genuine talent; all of it is good, honest, and
touching. This fine work might appeal to a broad range of age groups.

LaMore, Gregory S. *Handicapped: How Does It Feel.* Illus. Rolling
Hills Estates, Calif.: Winch, 1981. Reading Level: Grades 4–6.
Disability: Various

This book was written to aid the classroom teacher or parent in
helping normal children understand physical, learning, and speech
problems that mainstreamed children might have. It provides a low
language level and text with plentiful black-and-white photographs.
Some of the photos depict children with braces, wheelchairs, hearing
aids, and the like. Others show normal children simulating a disability,
with blindfold, arm tied to the body, and so on.

Causes of conditions are simply described. In the section for each
disability, straightforward, practical ways a disabled child might be
helped in school are described: carrying books, opening doors, indicating when the bell rings, telling your name if you can't be seen. Resource rooms are explained in the context of learning disabilities.

Analysis. The bulk of the book is clear, compassionate, and practical. A problem with the first 60 pages is the assumption that the reader
is normal. It is doubtful that the teacher would want to include a
disabled child in a lesson and discussion using this book. It is too much
a "how-we-will-help-them" approach. This problem is greatly compounded in the last chapter, "How We Help These Kids," which com-
prises the last six pages of narrative. The chapter begins, "There are
many ways that we can help handicapped people. We have special
places for them to park their cars. Then they don't have to walk or
wheel too far" (p. 61).

It has apparently not occurred to the author that a major reason there are special parking places, phones, ramps, and other devices for those who need them is because disabled persons fought for them and help pay for them. These are *not* charitable enterprises.

The author gratuitously continues, saying, "Handicapped people are just like you and me. They want to go to parks. They want to go to the movies, they want to go to ballgames, and they want to do everything else that we do" (p. 65).

Although this book is flawed, it is a good resource for an elementary classroom teacher, if used with care, and the black-and-white photos are excellent.

McConnell, Nancy P. *Different & Alike.* Illus. by Nancy Duell. Colorado Springs: Current, 1982. 28 pp. Reading Level: Grades K–3. *Disability:* Various

McConnell begins with a discussion about how widespread differences among people are and how important they are in making each person an individual. She defines a "handicap" as "a difference which makes it harder for the person to do something that is easy for you to do—something like walking, seeing, speaking, or hearing" (p. 4). Relating specific disabilities to a child's experience of temporary change (such as being blindfolded in a game, breaking a leg), she talks about deafness, blindness, deafness and blindness together, learning disabilities, speech disorders, and physical and mental disabilities. The book closes with a section on helping a disabled person.

Cartoonlike illustrations, most in color, appear on every spread; the manual alphabet is illustrated and there is a page of braille.

Analysis. Addressing the reader directly, McConnell couches her descriptions and explanations in simple, informal language. Her optimistic tone is echoed by the cheerful, exaggerated style of the illustrations. In the effort to emphasize that people with disabilities "are like you in more ways than they are different" and that "we are all alike on the inside" (p. 28), McConnell and Duell make little of the challenges and handicaps presented by impairments. "After a while," McConnell writes, "most handicapped people realize there is still so much for them to learn, experience and feel that having the handicap doesn't really matter so much after all." Such an attitude could be seen as an unintended minimizing of the enormous and courageous efforts made daily by most persons with disabilities. The book uses the phrase "partially blind" where "partially sighted" is preferred. In an illustration, a youngster is shown with a dog guide, although such dogs are not advocated until a blind person is in the teenage years. Despite such flaws, this would be a helpful first book for parents, teachers, and librarians to initiate discussion of differences with children and to answer some of their questions.

Matson, Virginia F. *A School for Peter*. Carol Stream, Ill.: Creation House, 1974. 299 pp. Reading Level: Grades 10–12.
Disability: Various

Virginia Matson, an Illinois schoolteacher and mother of five children, agreed to teach Peter, the younger brother of one of her students, for one hour on Saturday mornings. Peter was not socialized and could not speak; his psychiatrist had recommended institutionalization unless someone could work with him.

From this beginning in 1958, Matson evolved into a full-time teacher of disabled children, holding classes at first in her own home. Surrounding school districts paid for the education of students from their respective areas, despite the fact that state education law forbade this kind of arrangement at that time. Eventually, Matson returned to school to take special education courses, working with Helmer Myklebust, among others. She also read extensively, visited specialists in the field, and observed programs both in the United States and in other countries.

The school in her home expanded and moved to a church building, where it became known as Grove School. One of the students was Michael Agress, whose father tells his son's story in *"Why Me?"* (see Ch. 7, p. 267). Problems with the state's special education coordinator and resulting loss of support from some school districts had just been resolved when a negative attitude developed on the part of the minister in whose church the school was being held. Because of this situation, Matson began looking for property to buy, and although she had little capital to invest, sufficient funds appeared from various sources. She was finally able to purchase a large piece of property called Ridge Farm, complete with excellent brick buildings, formerly used as a school and "fresh-air camp" for poor city children. The new site was just ready to be occupied at the end of the book.

Matson is a practicing Quaker, a Sunday school teacher, and a deeply religious woman who credits her career and its achievements for disabled children to the guidance of God in her daily life. She has written two other books, including an award-winning novel, and more than 500 articles published in educational and religious periodicals.

Analysis. Matson is a good storyteller and an experienced writer, and she has produced a well-written and useful publication. Although the subject matter is special education programming, she explains what she has done by describing the lives and progress of a number of the children she has taught. These biographical vignettes should appeal to teenage readers. In addition, her description of teaching problems and methods would be of interest to anyone contemplating a career in special education.

Mitchell, Joyce Slayton. *See Me More Clearly: Career and Life Planning for Teens with Physical Disabilities.* New York: Harcourt, 1980. 284 pp. Reading Level: Grades 7–12.
Disability: Various

The author, an education consultant and former school counselor, has written a number of books on career planning. Here she addresses the disabled teenager directly. The book is divided into sections: "Teens with Physical Disabilities," "Beyond Your Disabilities" (with material on the Disabled Rights Movement, making friends, participating in sports, and life survival skills), "Independence" (including information on legislation affecting people with disabilities), and the last section, "Charting Your Course: Life Career Skills," which includes exercises designed to help all young people identify skills and strengths, collect information, and make decisions.

The appendix lists national organizations dedicated to disabilities, gives sources for access guides published in various cities as well as information guides for air and rail travel and more general access guides, lists tours for people with disabilities, gives information on sports, and offers bibliographies. There is also an index.

Analysis. Mitchell addresses her readers in an informal, no-nonsense voice, without condescension. Her purpose is to provide information that will help people with disabilities see themselves more clearly, emerge from stereotyped expectations held by others and perhaps by themselves, and in the process join the mainstream of life as fully as possible. She reinforces her material with quotations from disabled people and from professionals in the field (some of them persons with disabilities). This is a thorough and valuable source book for young people with physical disabilities, as well as for the adults in their lives.

Myers, Caroline Clark, and Walter B. Barbe, comps. *Challenge of a Handicap: Understanding Differences, Accepting Limitations.* Illus. Columbus, Ohio: Highlights for Children, 1977. 33 pp. Reading Level: Grades 4–6.
Disability: Various

This handbook contains stories and articles, fiction and nonfiction, about people with disabilities. One writer describes the work of Ed

Lucks, a ski instructor in Aspen, Colorado, who has devised equipment and methods to help disabled people ski. A letter from a young reader asks how a blind person can see in his dreams; Barbara Collins of the Braille Institute of America gives the answer. Another letter from a ten-year-old reader describes her older retarded brother and their relationship, ending, "I think he will still improve greatly. I think of him as my big little brother." There is a description of the special garden for blind people at the Brooklyn Botanic Garden. Another article describes the training and work of dog guides. In addition to brief biographies of Thomas Gallaudet and Helen Keller, there is an account by a 12-year-old girl whose hearing and vision are impaired as the result of the rubella contracted by her mother during pregnancy. There is also an article about Dr. Thomas E. Strax, who has cerebral palsy and works with patients with the same disability.

The braille alphabet is punched out on the inside of the back cover. The text is illustrated with black-and-white photographs and colored drawings.

Analysis. This handbook has excellent material, attractively presented. All of it is in keeping with the quotation from Dr. Strax, who stresses the importance of knowing the difference between a handicap and a disability: "A disability is something that a person lacks physically, mentally, or emotionally. A handicap is something that the person cannot do because of his disability" (p. 27). Teachers and parents could use the handbook to spark discussions. Young readers, both those with disabilities and those who are able-bodied, could find enjoyment and inspiration here.

Orlansky, Michael S., and William L. Steward. *Voices: Interviews with Handicapped People.* Illus. Columbus, Ohio: Merrill, 1981. 263 pp. Reading Level: Grades 7–12.
Disability: Various

The authors are professional educators who set out to meet and talk with a representative cross-section of disabled children and adults to discover their points of view on such issues as acceptance, coping with school, disinstitutionalization, and employment opportunities. They conducted open-ended discussions and conversations, which resulted in vignettes about young persons as diverse as a man in university work who stutters and a disinstitutionalized retarded young woman in a group home. A brief paragraph summarizing the person's situation precedes each testimonial. Each section has a black-and-white shot of the interviewee.

Analysis. The diversity of the people interviewed, in terms of walks of life, age, disability, and circumstances, adds to the appeal of this interesting book. Each person comes across as a personable and admirable human being, whether highly gifted or retarded, and without relation to the extent of disability, which in some cases is immense. The pictures are truly candid, and make the reader appreciate the willingness of the interviewees to be shown just as they are.

Pizer, Vernon. *Glorious Triumphs*. Illus. New York: Dodd, 1980. 189 pp. Reading Level: Grades 7–12.
Disability: Various

Subtitled "Athletes Who Conquered Adversity," Pizer's book is a collection of brief biographies. Many of the challenges involve physical disability. The subjects include Glenn Cunningham, a champion runner who was critically burned as a child (see Cunningham, *Never Quit*, Ch. 5, p. 52); Jerry Kramer, the football player who survived numerous accidents and operations; Pete Gray, who lost an arm in an accident when he was five but taught himself to play baseball and played in the major leagues (see Nicholson, *Pete Gray*, Ch. 5, p. 128); Tenley Albright and Carol Heiss, both of whom survived devastating childhood illness to become world-class skating stars; Sammy Lee, Korean-American diver and doctor who beat the odds imposed both by his small stature and by racial bigotry to become an Olympic gold medal winner; and Alonzo Wilkins, a superb black athlete who became a paraplegic after two injuries related to his military service and went on to become a successful wheelchair athlete.

There are black-and-white photographs of some of the subjects, and an index.

Analysis. Pizer, a professional writer, is skilled at writing brief, fast-moving profiles that focus on the central theme linking his heroes. While not minimizing the pain and difficulties faced by each of his subjects, he nevertheless takes the tone indicated by his title, upbeat and optimistic. Although the book may be of particular interest to readers who enjoy sports and/or who face a challenge, it can be recommended to a general audience.

Richter, Elizabeth. *The Teenage Hospital Experience: You Can Handle It!* Photog. by the author. New York: Coward, 1982. 128 pp. Reading Level: Grades 7–12.
Disability: Various

Richter devotes most of her book to interviews with teenaged patients in children's hospitals in Washington, D.C., Philadelphia, and New York. These adolescents have conditions that include diabetes, broken thigh bone, paralysis due to spinal damage, anorexia nervosa, and cancer. The author uses her own words and those of the young people to describe their illnesses and injuries, the treatment they are receiving, and their thoughts and fears. Interviews with professionals follow; physicians, a nurse, a surgeon, and an anesthesiologist talk about their work and about what patients can expect. The section called "Useful Information" includes the "Position Statement on the Care of Adolescents and Families in Health Care Settings" issued by the Association for the Care of Children's Health, a checklist of questions, glossary of medical words and abbreviations, and an index.

Analysis. Richter writes clearly and directly. The young people she interviewed discuss their experiences and feelings freely and honestly. This material, as well as the interviews with professionals and Richter's own exposition, emphasizes the right of patients to be fully informed and the need for all patients, of whatever age, to express their feelings to their families and those who treat them. The book could be helpful to young people from the age of about 10 up to 18 facing medical procedures, as well as to their friends, families, and teachers.

Rivera, Geraldo. *A Special Kind of Courage: Profiles of Young Americans.* Illus. by Edith Vonnegut. New York: Simon & Schuster, 1976. 319 pp. Reading Level: Grades 7–12.
Disability: Various

This is a book about courage. It presents the stories of 12 young people in difficult situations, which they face with courage, determination, and perseverance. Four of the stories deal with disabilities. Bernard Carabello was diagnosed as retarded and committed to the now infamous Willowbrook Hospital in Staten Island, New York. Despite spending most of his youth in this institution, he is an intelligent young man with cerebral palsy, living independently, who managed to survive and to learn in spite of his surroundings.

Ted Kennedy, Jr., had a leg amputated because of bone cancer when a youngster. Now grown to maturity, he lives an active life and wears a prosthesis, except when he skis. The story of his surgery and rehabilitation is told.

Tia Grant, born Thu Van in a small Vietnamese village, had polio at the age of five or six during the Vietnam War. With only a severely ill mother and an elderly grandfather left in her family, she was taken to an orphanage where she was adopted by an American family during Operation Babylift at the close of the war. Her integration into her new family is chronicled here.

Joey Cappeletti, the younger brother of Penn State quarterback

John Cappeletti, was ill with leukemia at the time his brother received the Heisman Trophy as the best college football player in the country. The older brother dedicated the trophy to Joey, whose story of a long bout with illness is recounted.

Attractive black-and-white drawings of the individuals precede the biographies.

Analysis. Rivera, a popular television personality, is a good story-teller. He includes plenty of detail and description, and has a flair for presenting dramatic narrative. All the stories are interesting reading and should appeal to teenagers.

Rosenberg, Nancy, and Reuben K. Snyderman. *New Parts for People: The Story of Medical Transplants.* Illus. New York: Norton, 1969. 126 pp. Reading Level: Grades 4–9.
Disability: Various

This book is written specifically for young people by a teacher and author of children's books in collaboration with a plastic surgeon. In simple language, medical procedures such as grafting and kidney, heart, and corneal transplants are explained and illustrated with black-and-white photographs and line drawings. One chapter is devoted to useful prostheses for paralyzed limbs. The last chapter discusses some legal and ethical issues.

An appendix describes procedures for eye bank donors, and an index follows.

Analysis. The authors had foresight when they wrote this book in 1969. Because events have occurred so rapidly in medicine and biotechnology, the book is now dated. However, since more and more young children are being subjected to these procedures, it may still be useful. It is clearly written and presents material in a matter-of-fact, nonthreatening manner.

Siegel, Dorothy Schainman. *Winners: Eight Special Young People.* New York: Messner, 1978. 188 pp. Reading Level: Grades 7–12.
Disability: Various

Siegel has drawn portraits of eight young people who are different, have accepted their differences, and have moved beyond them, refusing to allow them to be the governing force in their lives. Her subjects are a 26-year-old man who developed leukemia at 13; a student at Gallaudet College who was born profoundly deaf; a high school senior who has had chronic juvenile rheumatoid arthritis since she was 11; a college student who became a paraplegic as the result of a high school football accident; a young woman who has licked drug addiction; a 19-year-old college student who lost his sight at 13; a 17-year-old sportswoman who was born with a right leg that ends in a small foot at about the place where her knee should be; and a 30-year-old successful executive with hemophilia.

Analysis. Siegel has her subjects tell their own stories; although she does not say so, she probably taped interviews with them, and occasionally with other family members. These voices, informal and direct, give authenticity. She supplies additional background and descriptive material. She uses initials or blanks in place of proper names of people, hospitals, and schools, although she does occasionally name one of the latter institutions. All of the accounts are valuable for the insight they give into the experience of disability, both for the individuals described and for their families. The fact that all the subjects are quite young heightens the appeal to a youthful audience.

Splaver, Sarah. *Your Handicap: Don't Let It Handicap You.* Illus. New York: Messner, 1967. 224 pp. Reading Level: Grades 7–12.
Disability: Various

The author addresses herself to the young person with physical limitations. Her thesis is that whatever the disability, it is exceeded by ability and that a positive, constructive attitude can overcome many difficulties. She discusses such topics as education, including descriptions of colleges with funds and facilities to help students with physical limitations; career choices; visual and hearing impairments; orthopedic disabilities; cardiac and respiratory disorders; diabetes; and epilepsy.

Sources for further information are given in the text as well as in lists at the end of the book. Splaver includes a bibliography of biographies as well as an extensive list of pamphlets on various disabilities and services. There is an index. Black-and-white photographs show people with disabilities using appliances and participating in activities.

Analysis. Splaver's philosophy is clear and optimistic. Without minimizing disabilities or the effort necessary to compensate for them, she consistently emphasizes the ways in which success and self-fulfillment can be attained. In the opening chapter she discusses some of the terms that have been used to describe disabilities and stresses "that the person who possesses a handicap need not necessarily be handicapped" (p. 19); her preferred phrase is *physically limited.* With this sensitivity to language, it is unfortunate that she herself uses the word *suffer* so frequently; *victim* also appears. Both these words carry the connotation of passivity, which runs counter to the author's expressed beliefs. There is a great deal of practical information and advice in the book, but much of it is somewhat dated.

Stockton, William. *Altered Destinies: Lives Changed by Genetic Flaws.* New York: Doubleday, 1979. 237 pp. Reading Level: Grades 10–12. *Disability:* Various

This book is credited to a press writer and reporter who has collaborated with a physician, Ian Porter, chairman of the Department of Pediatrics at Albany Medical College and director of the Birth Defects Institute of the New York State Department of Health. In Porter's introduction, he explores attitudes that may have contributed to the public's lack of awareness concerning heredity and the transmission of genetically related disorders. The thesis of the book is that a knowledge of genetics can serve young people by increasing their control over their lives with respect to reproduction options and by allowing them to utilize helpful professionals.

Each chapter focuses on a family confronted with a disorder associated with their genetic identity. Such problems as muscular dystrophy, diabetes, leukemia, and RH incompatibility are described as they have affected actual patients. The misunderstandings, ethical dimensions, and anguish are described from the standpoint of the children and adults who have faced altered destinies. The reader is introduced to the basic principles of human heredity and to some rather recent advances in this fast-developing field.

Analysis. This book emphasizes the human aspects of genetic realities. It is appropriate for young people, disabled or not, who are contemplating parenthood. The illustrative stories are told in an interesting and compassionate manner. The explanations of genetic mechanisms, although couched in layman's terms, still might be complex for those unfamiliar with the subject. The book is nonjudgmental in discussing options that people have chosen—whether therapeutic abortions or a decision to produce an offspring with a genetic flaw. One ethical point uniformly stressed is that people have a right to knowledge about heredity. This book fulfills its purpose in adding to that knowledge.

Sullivan, Mary Beth, et al. *Feeling Free.* Illus. by Marci Davis and Linda Bourke. Photog. by Alan J. Brightman. Reading, Mass.: Addison-Wesley, 1979. 186 pp. Reading Level: Grades 4–9. *Disability:* Various

This book is based on the television series of the same name and shares the same goal of helping young people and adults feel more comfortable with disabled people by providing insight and information. The focus is on five youngsters with five different conditions: visual impairment, cerebral palsy, learning disability, hearing impairment, and dwarfism. In their own voices, the children describe aspects of their lives and talk about their thoughts and feelings. In addition, there are contributions from "guests," as well as activities, little dramas, cartoon strips, mysteries, and a serial story about a blind boy at a camp where he is the only nonsighted person.

Every spread is illustrated with photographs or drawings. The music for the song "Feeling Free" appears at the end.

Analysis. Although the tone is informal and often humorous, there is no mistaking the essential seriousness and thoughtfulness of this book. As the children discuss their lives and their conditions, they emphasize repeatedly their determination to be independent, their dislike of pity and condescension, their demand to be seen for what they are—individuals who may have a disability but who want to be known as people. This is a book with a message, but the points are made without didacticism or preaching. The engaging photographs and amusing, lively drawings enhance the text.

Turnbull, H. R., III, and Ann P. Turnbull. *Parents Speak Out: Then and Now.* Illus. Columbus, Ohio: Merrill, 1985. 287 pp. Reading Level: Grades 7-12.
Disability: Various

The authors are prestigious contributors to the field of special education, as well as parents of a disabled youth. This book, a second edition, is a collection of stories that describe "how those who sought help for persons with disabilities and their families, and those who tried to provide it, met with a mixture of success and failure" (p. 9). The contributors are diverse with respect to the regions, ages, and disabilities about which they speak. Most are professional advocates of disabled citizens.

Each of the accounts is accompanied by a black-and-white photograph of the family. Following each are a few questions designed to help the reader analyze the writer's point of view and respond to it.

Analysis. Although this book is written by parents, siblings' accounts and letters are frequently included. The writing is personal and often emotional. Some writers are vitriolic or sarcastic; others, like Senator Weicker, are impassioned in the plea for a new enlightenment about treatment of disabled persons. A spirit of compassion and optimism pervades the book.

The various stories, of compelling interest, bring up many issues surrounding disability, such as the advisability of saving the life of a severely impaired infant. The provocative questions at the end of each chapter would be helpful for discussion with high school classes covering parenting or family living.

Viscardi, Henry, Jr. *A Laughter in the Lonely Night*. Drawings by Charles Rowe. New York: Eriksson, 1961. 338 pp. Reading Level: Grades 10–12.
Disability: Various

Henry Viscardi is director of a multimillion dollar manufacturing concern on Long Island called Abilities, Inc. Started in 1952, the plant employs people with a variety of physical impairments; Viscardi himself was born with malformed stumps instead of legs. In *A Man's Stature* (see Ch. 5, p. 144), he told his own story; here, he records the histories of more than a dozen people who came to Abilities, Inc. Some were polio victims, some injured by war; some suffered congenital defects; one had a neurological disorder called dystonia. Viscardi alternates the histories with his own comments and experiences.

Each personal history is illustrated with a black-and-white drawing of the subject.

Analysis. Each of these stories records courage and determination; each has a happy ending as the speaker finds her or his niche at Abilities, Inc.; each illustrates Viscardi's philosophy of energetic, realistic optimism. The writer says that he is telling these stories simply, just as they were told to him; there is a certain similarity among the voices, indicating that perhaps Viscardi shaped the material more than he realized, and also a kind of fairy-tale quality to the happy endings, but this does not diminish the validity of the experiences or the strength of the people described.

Viscardi, Henry, Jr. . . . *a Letter to Jimmy*. New York: Eriksson, 1962. 165 pp. Reading Level: Grades 7–12.
Disability: Various

Viscardi addresses his letter to Jimmy, who is meant to symbolize the young people who have written to him for advice over the years. He discusses such topics as meeting the challenge of discrimination, definitions and perceptions of disabilities, preparing for employment, and achieving independence and personal satisfaction. As examples, he refers frequently to his own experience as a disabled person and to the stories of those he has met, particularly people working at Abilities, Inc., the company Viscardi founded (see preceding annotation).

Analysis. Viscardi's books are somewhat repetitive, but this may appeal particularly to the young disabled person to whom it is addressed.

Viscardi, Henry, Jr. *The Phoenix Child: A Story of Love.* New York: Eriksson, 1975. 208 pp. Reading Level: Grades 7–12.
Disability: Various

The prolific Viscardi has again turned his attention to events pertaining to the Human Resources School he and his colleagues formed to enable "crippled" children, previously on home-bound instruction, to attend day classes like "normal" children. In the course of this successful and growing project, the staff opened a house to seven institutionalized and foster children with severe physical problems.

Darren, a four-year-old black child who had been abandoned at birth and shuffled among foster homes, was the youngest and the least disabled. He had a cleft lip and palate, and one side of his face was undeveloped. He was shy but in some ways had a magnetic personality. A Jewish family sent their daughter Alisa, with dysautonomia (a neurological disorder), to the Human Resources School. Their older daughter, Stephanie, developed a very special relationship with Darren. When the burning of the children's residence necessitated Darren's placement with Stephanie's family, he so won their hearts that they fought in court and were given the right to care for him permanently. The story takes him through several restorative operations and transfer into regular school. He seemed to be truly a "phoenix child," rising from the ashes to a new life.

Analysis. Viscardi writes in a sentimental but sincere style. His book is fast moving and full of suspense, as he pits the needs of his lovely disabled children against an often rejecting society and the vagaries of fortune. He frames his story as a morality piece—as a demonstration of how the world could be if love were to break down the barriers that divide people.

Viscardi seems more conscious of Darren's racial differences than of his physical problems. He is constantly reminding the reader of the boy's color and of Stephanie's Jewishness. However, he presents the issues of racial, ethnic, physical, and religious differences simply and clearly in a way that could be well understood by a young reader.

Professional Bibliography

Arbuthnot, May Hill, and Zena Sutherland. *Children and Books.* 4th ed. Glenview, Ill.: Scott, Foresman, 1972.

Azarnoff, Pat. *Health, Illness and Disability: A Guide to Books for Children and Young Adults.* New York: Bowker, 1983.

Baskin, Barbara H., and Karen H. Harris. *More Notes from a Different Drummer: A Guide to Juvenile Fiction Portraying the Disabled.* New York: Bowker, 1984.

———. *Notes from a Different Drummer: A Guide to Juvenile Fiction Portraying the Handicapped.* New York: Bowker, 1977.

Bernstein, Joanne E. *Books to Help Children Cope with Separation and Loss.* 2nd ed. New York: Bowker, 1983.

Bettelheim, Bruno. *The Uses of Enchantment: The Meaning and Importance of Fairy Tales.* New York: Random House, 1976.

Biklen, Douglas, and Robert Bogdan. "Media Portrayals of Disabled People: A Study in Stereotypes." *The Bulletin: Interracial Books for Children* 8 (1977): 4–9.

British Education Index. Vol. 17. London: British Library, Bibliographic Services Division, 1981.

Children's Books in Print. New York: Bowker, annual.

Dreyer, Sharon S. *The Bookfinder: A Guide to Children's Literature about the Needs and Problems of Youth Aged 2–15.* Circle Pines, Minn.: American Guidance Service, 1980.

Fassler, Joan. *Helping Children Cope: Mastering Stress through Books and Stories.* New York: Free Press, 1978.

Fiedler, Leslie. *Freaks: Myths and Images of the Secret Self.* New York: Simon & Schuster, 1978.

Gallagher, James J. "The Sacred and Profane Uses of Labeling." *Mental Retardation* 14 (December 1976): 3–7.

Guidelines for the Representation of Exceptional Persons in Educational Material. Reston, Va.: National Center on Educational Media and Materials, n.d.

Hobbs, Nicholas C., ed. *Issues in the Classification of Children.* 2 vols. San Francisco: Jossey-Bass, 1976.

Hooge, Norman C. "Labeling in the Counseling Process." *Journal of Applied Rehabilitation Counseling* 8 (Summer 1977): 84–88.

Huck, Charlotte. *Children's Literature in the Elementary School.* 3rd ed. New York: Holt, 1976.

Lane, Elizabeth, and James Lane. "Reference Materials for the Disabled." *Reference Services Review* 10 (Fall 1982): 73–76.

Lass, Bonnie, and Marcia Bromfield. "Books about Children with Special Needs: An Annotated Bibliography." *Reading Teacher* 34 (February 1981): 530–533.

Lonsdale, Bernard J., and Helen K. Mackintosh. *Children Experience Literature.* New York: Random House, 1973.

The Mainstreamed Library: Issues, Ideas, Innovations. Ed. by Barbara H. Baskin and Karen H. Harris. Chicago: American Library Assn., 1982.

Manus, Gerald I. "Is Your Language Disabling?" *Journal of Rehabilitation* 41 (September–October 1975): 35.

Mercer, J. R. "Institutionalized Anglocentrism: Labeling Mental Retardates in the Public Schools," in *Race, Change, and Urban Society,* ed. by P. Orleans and W. R. Eliss. Los Angeles: Sage, 1971.

Meyers, Robert. *Like Normal People.* New York: McGraw-Hill, 1978.

Mullins, June B. "Making Language Work to Eliminate Handicapism." *Education Unlimited* 1 (June 1979): 20–24.

———, and Suzanne Wolfe. *Special People behind the Eight Ball: An Annotated Bibliography of Literature Classified by Handicapping Conditions.* Johnstown, Pa.: Mafex Associates, 1975.

Physically Disabled People. "Personal Narratives: A Review of Recent Works" by Richard E. Bopp, and "A Bibliography of Media Resources" by Judith Lessee. *Reference Services Review* 10 (Spring 1982): 45–57.

Reading Ladders for Human Relations. 6th ed. Ed. by Eileen Tway. Washington, D.C.: American Council on Education, and Urbana, Ill.: National Council of Teachers of English, 1981.

Rudman, Marsha Kabakow. *Children's Literature: An Issues Approach.* Lexington, Mass.: Heath, 1976.

———. *Children's Literature: An Issues Approach.* 2nd ed. New York: Longman, 1984.

Sapon-Shevin, Mara. "Teaching Children about Differences: Resources for Teaching." *Young Children* 38 (January 1983): 24–31.

Schwartz, Albert V. "Disability in Children's Books: Is Visibility Enough?" *The Bulletin: Interracial Books for Children* 8 (1977): 10–15.

Severence, Laurence, and L. L. Gasstrom. "Effects of the Label 'Mentally Retarded' on Causal Explanations for Success and Failure Outcomes." *American Journal of Mental Deficiency* 81 (May 1977): 547–555.

Sutherland, Zena, Dianne L. Monson, and May Hill Arbuthnot. *Children and Books.* 6th ed. Glenview, Ill.: Scott, Foresman, 1981.

Thesaurus of ERIC Descriptors. 10th ed. Phoenix, Ariz.: Oryx, 1984.

Thesaurus of Psychological Indexing Terms. 3rd ed. Washington, D.C.: American Psychological Assn., 1982.

U.S. Library of Congress, Subject Cataloging Division. *Library of Congress Subject Headings.* 9th ed. Washington, D.C.: Library of Congress, 1980.

Velleman, Ruth A. *Serving Physically Disabled People: An Information Handbook for All Libraries.* New York: Bowker, 1979.

Weinberg, Nancy, and Santana Rossini. "Comic Books: Champions of the Disabled Stereotype." *Rehabilitation Literature* 39 (November–December 1978): 327–331.

Author Index

Title Index

Subject Index

Persons who are notable because of special accomplishment or distinction are listed in this index. Names of those individuals who are themselves disabled appear in boldface.

Mental hospitals, 41, 247. *See also* Institutionalization

Mental illness, 250. *See also* Emotional disturbances

Mental retardation, 4, 9, 15, 25, 27, 36, 38, 41, 99, 166–167, 245, 250, 257, 258, 267–283, 291, 298–299, 306, 315, 317, 327. *See also* Down's syndrome

Merrick, John, 115, 313

Metabolic disorders, 133

Miers, Earl Schenck, 125–126

Minimal brain dysfunction (MBD), 262

Missing limbs, 99–100, 123–124, 144–145, 151, 317. *See also* Amputation

Multiple impairments. *See* Deaf-blind disability; Multiple/severe disabilities

Multiple sclerosis, 129–130, 317

Multiple/severe disabilities, 15, 176–177, 291–335. *See also* Deaf-blind disability; names of specific illnesses or disabilities

Muscular dystrophy, 104–105, 308, 317, 332

Muscular impairments, 297, 299

Music therapy. *See* Therapy

Muteness, 27, 153, 241–242, 288–289. *See also* Autism

National Association for Anorexia Nervosa and Associated Disorders (ANAD), 66

National Association of the Deaf, 175

National Foundation for Ileitis and Colitis, 88

National Foundation for Infantile Paralysis, 107, 114

National Fraternal Society of the Deaf, 169

National Royal Institution for the Deaf (Paris), 174

National Theatre of the Deaf, 168, 183, 186

National Wheelchair Athletic Association, 301

Neurofibromatosis, 115

Neurological impairments, 12, 36, 90–151, 292–293, 302, 317

Neurosis, 27, 235–236, 250

New England Education Center, 171

New York Hospital for Deformities and Joint Diseases, 144

New York League for the Hard of Hearing, 194

New York School for the Deaf, 186

Nitchie School of Lip-Reading (N.Y.), 194

O'Neil, Kitty, 179

O'Neill, Cherry Boone, 74–75

Optacon, 204

Oral communication. *See* Communication for hearing impaired

Oralism. *See* Communication for hearing impaired

Orthopedic disability and injury, 12, 36, 90–151, 292, 302, 306, 317, 331, 334. *See also* names of specific conditions, e.g., Muscular dystrophy; Paraplegia

Osteogenesis imperfecta (OI), 41, 133

Osteosarcoma. *See* Cancer, bone

Otosclerosis, 193

Overbrook School for the Blind (Pa.), 206

Oxygen deprivation at birth. *See* Little's disease

Panzarella, Joseph J., Jr., 131

Paralysis, 308. *See also* Polio

Paraplegia, 45, 119–120, 127–130, 137–138, 149–151, 330. *See also* Quadriplegia

Partially sighted, 205–206, 215, 218, 219–220

People First groups, 273

Perkins Institution for the Blind (Mass.), 9, 157, 158, 159, 160, 161, 163, 197, 215

Phocomelia. *See* Missing limbs

aids for, 196, 203, 204, 206, 331, 332

clock system for eating, 197

Volta Bureau. *See* Alexander Graham Bell Association for the Deaf

Water on the brain. *See* Hydro-cephalus

Wedgwood, Josiah, 320

Western Pennsylvania School for the Deaf, 171

Wheelchairs. *See* Prostheses, and other aids

Wilkins, Alonzo, 328

Wonder, Stevie, 202, 207–208, 230

Wright-Humanson Oral School for the Deaf, 162

Yang, Chung Syn, 201–202